The Power of Communication

D0161005

The Power of Communication

Managing Information in Public Organizations

Doris A. Graber
University of Illinois at Chicago

CQ PRESS

A Division of Congressional Quarterly Inc.
Washington, D.C.

CQ Press
1255 22nd Street, N.W., Suite 400
Washington, D.C. 20037

(202) 729-1900; toll-free, 1-866-4CQ-PRESS (1-866-427-7737)

www.cqpress.com

∞ The paper used in this publication meets the minimum requirements of the American
National Standard for Information Sciences—Permanence of Paper for Printed Library
Materials, ANSI Z39.48-1992.

Printed and bound in the United States of America

06   05   04   03   02   5   4   3   2   1

Typeset by Picas Rule, Baltimore, Maryland
Cover design by Naylor Design, Inc.

Library of Congress Cataloging-in-Publication Data
Graber, Doris A. (Doris Appel)
   The power of communication : managing information in public
organizations / Doris A. Graber.
          p.   cm.
Includes bibliographical references and index.
   ISBN 1-56802-211-5 (alk. paper)
   1. Communication in public administration.
2. Communication—Political aspects.   3. Communication in organizations.
4. Government information.   5. Administrative agencies—Information
services.   I. Title.
   JF1525.C59 G728 2002
   352.3'84—dc21

                                                                    2002012871

To my intellectual godfather and role model,

Arnold J. Lien

Contents

Tables, Figures, and Boxes

Preface

Certain classic communication questions burst into the news again and again when major shortcomings in government performance surface: What did the president, the governor, the FBI director, and others know about a major civilian or military disaster? When did they know it, and what preventive or remedial action did they take? Such questions become especially poignant in the wake of catastrophes like the terrorist assaults on the United States on September 11, 2001, that killed thousands and laid waste to the World Trade Towers and parts of the Pentagon.

When disaster strikes, investigators and the public focus on how well or how poorly information has been managed. They examine the structure of message systems and the content of the messages transmitted before the disaster. But when the crisis has passed, officials and the public soon abandon their vigilance. That lapse in attention is a serious mistake: Information management is a perennial challenge that requires constant attention.

Communication has become a tougher challenge than ever before in all types of organizations—private and public—for many reasons. Government agencies now administer more controversial programs that affect ever-larger numbers of people. The messages that need to be disseminated are increasingly complex at a time when audiences speak different languages and are less in tune with the dominant American culture than they were when rapid acculturation was prized.

Sound information management is more crucial than ever to politics—and more challenging. The flood of data that the government must process is overwhelming. For example, the National Security Agency, which is responsible for intercepting and analyzing electronic messages that might spell danger to the United States, collects more than two million messages every hour from satellites and listening posts around the world. Many of these messages are in code or in any number of foreign languages. How can such a flow be monitored? It is critical that we find answers to such questions because the government's handling of such information affects the security and welfare of every American.

Most studies of information management focus on communication within business organizations. Organizational communication in the public sector has largely been ignored, even though it poses unique problems and the number of public organizations that provide essential services is huge. In fact, few private organizations match the largest government organizations in size, volume, and overall significance of activities. If public organizations are to benefit from research findings about information management, these findings must be adapted to public sector conditions and needs. The mission of this book is to explain how communication works in the public sector and how research findings can help government officials meet their unique challenges.

The Power of Communication has a dual focus. Using scholarly perspectives, it presents current theories and analyses of organizational communication and information management. It also emphasizes practical aspects of communicating in public agencies. It shows how an understanding of organizational communication can contribute to designing institutions in which well-formulated messages circulate in a communications-friendly environment that enhances the organization's performance. Because the subject matter is interdisciplinary, the book blends findings from the literature of organizational behavior and decision making in sociology, communication, and, above all, political science.

Chapter 1 presents a brief overview of the importance and distinctiveness of organizational communication and the theories that have guided investigations in the field. It explains why the complexity of communication in the public sector will always create major problems of information management. It also shows that careful attention to such problems can ease or even resolve many difficulties.

Chapter 2 begins the dissection of common information management problems. It analyzes the typical challenges officials face when they select information. How do they judge the quality of information? How do they know what is important and requires immediate attention and what can wait or be ignored? How can they collect the information they need to make informed decisions when the people who control the data guard them tightly?

Securing good information is only the first step in information management. The second step requires the structuring of organizations so that information flows smoothly to the places that need it. Chapters 3 and 4 address these issues. The main message of Chapter 3 is that the structural arrangements that shape the direction, speed, and accuracy of information streams within an organization influence how well the organization functions. Structures must be regularly reexamined because situations and technologies change constantly. Chapter 4 focuses on networking, one aspect of the quest for effective structures. How should people and structures be connected so that they can share essential information? What leads to the development of complex communication networks and what configurations are most useful?

Effective communication also requires knowing the cultural environments that affect senders and receivers of messages as well as the climates of opinion prevailing at the time. Chapter 5 explains the impact of these crucial contextual factors that shape the meanings of messages and affect the reactions they produce. It also analyzes the changes in culture and climate that can be expected when established message transmission technologies are melded with new ones.

Among the perennial communication challenges facing government, none is more pervasive and important than managing information to produce sound decisions. Chapter 6 shows what bearing the issues in the first five chapters have on the ability of government to make decisions that cope with problems fairly and efficiently. The chapter presents decision-making models and their underlying theories. It points out common decision-making errors that lead to costly mistakes and suggests remedies to prevent them.

The emphasis of the book then switches from intraorganizational communication to external communication. Chapter 7 covers public information, lobbying, and public relations campaigns, among other issues. It explains the many misunderstandings surrounding these important activities and the costly consequences. Many public agencies, such as the Internal Revenue Service and the Social Security Administration, deal directly with millions of individual citizens. These interpersonal relationships differ vastly from those of their counterparts in private business because public agency clients have no choice in determining who will provide them with essential, often vital, services; they are forced to work with government bureaucrats. Chapter 8 deals with the unique problems created by clients' dependency on government. It also discusses the challenges facing administrators who must reach out to groups that are unaware of the valuable services available to them.

The last chapter reflects on the political significance of the issues discussed in the book and sketches possible scenarios for the future in light of past and present trends. The chapter maps out areas where improvements seem politically and technically feasible, but it also acknowledges that some barriers to progress currently are insurmountable.

Like most social science studies, this book is a product of extensive collaboration. My many collaborators are listed in the references throughout the chapters. Without their published work, mine would have been far more arduous and less complete. I thank them all.

Special thanks are due to the three reviewers who read the draft manuscript: Stuart Bretschneider at Syracuse University, Louis Cusella at the University of Dayton, and Eugene McGregor Jr. at Indiana University. Their insights and suggestions helped me sharpen my own perceptions of the subject. The book has benefited from the careful work of my research assistants: Adam Stretz, Shikha Jain, and Leta Dally. As usual the staff of CQ Press provided outstanding support; I am very grateful to these talented professionals. Freelance editor Debbie Hardin polished the finished manuscript with an eagle eye for finding flaws and a talent for clarifying murky points. Finally, I want to thank Tom and the rest of my family for their never-ending support for all my time-consuming ventures and, above all, for their love.

Doris A. Graber
University of Illinois at Chicago

The Power of Communication

Chapter 1 **The Past As Prologue for the Future:**
Theories and Applications

In October 1999, scientists from the National Aeronautics and Space Administration (NASA) lost track of a $125 million spacecraft—the *Mars Climate Orbiter*—as it approached the red planet for a landing. The reason: faulty communication. Engineers at Lockheed Martin Corporation, which had built the spacecraft to monitor the Martian climate, had calculated the thrust of the spacecraft in the nonmetric units commonly used in the United States. This important information had failed to reach the NASA scientists who had based their spacecraft steering on metric units. The result was that the spacecraft never reached its target because it was off-course by about 60 miles in its roughly 416 million mile journey. *Orbiter's* precise fate has remained a mystery.

In the wake of the costly disaster, government authorities created several review committees to investigate how the error happened and to recommend procedural changes to prevent repetitions. The initial investigations identified eight factors that contributed to the loss of the craft. They include multiple communication problems such as (1) failure to provide the NASA scientists with detailed information about the positioning of the spacecraft, (2) inconsistent communication and training for project members, (3) unduly informal communication channels among project engineering groups, and (4) failure to check computer models sufficiently to detect quite obvious calculation errors.[1]

The calamity resulted from a series of errors that are quite common in large organizations in which multiple units must coordinate their activities. The system used to make automatic flight calculations was unavailable during the first four months of the project because of computer file format and other glitches. This forced the navigation team to make their own calculations based on e-mail messages from the contractor. When the files became accessible, the non–metric-based data seemed anomalous, discouraging the NASA navigation team from relying on them. The team also lacked adequate information about the characteristics of the spacecraft that affected flight direction and velocity. Other teams had developed and tested the craft, but their communication with the NASA navigation team was inadequate. The failures of various teams to communicate with each other were endemic in the system. They occurred between the development and operations teams, the operations navigation and operations teams, the project management and technical teams, and the project and technical line management.

The spacecraft disaster is a graphic example of the difficulty of establishing good communication patterns in complex organizations and the serious consequences that may ensue when communication is mishandled. In the *Orbiter* case, the channels connecting the various teams working on the *Orbiter* project were not programmed to function properly. Important information available within the network did not reach people who needed it, and a number of misunderstandings among the teams involved in the *Orbiter* project were not detected until it was too late.

The *Orbiter* case also illustrates that it is possible to learn from mistakes and to take precautions to reduce the incidence of such problems. The officials who investigated the space shuttle mishap recommended that the teams involved in the project "should increase the amount of formal and informal face-to-face communications with all team elements. . . . should establish a routine forum for informal communication between all team members at the same time so everyone can hear what is happening. . . ."[2] In addition, the investigators stressed the importance of informing all teams fully about various deadlines that had to be met to conduct the mission successfully, with an opportunity to suggest needed revisions of the specified schedules.

Communicating in Organizations: Basic Concepts

Before we can embark on a wide-ranging study of information-management problems in complex organizations, we need to define the vocabulary that we shall be using.

All organizations generate, receive, and use *data*—accounts about happenings—that become *information* only when they are arranged in meaningful patterns.[3] All transmit information internally as well as to people outside the organization through various forms of *communication*—the use of symbols to share information. The carefully planned and controlled steps taken to collect information and to communicate successfully constitute *information management*. As used in this book, the term includes both information collection and communication of information. When information becomes an organized body of thought, through management or other happenings, it constitutes *knowledge,* which gives those who possess it a clear perception of a particular situation.

Members of organizations communicate because they must receive and transmit information to coordinate their activities and perform their jobs. Messages are intended to change the receiver's knowledge, attitude, or overt behavior in some predetermined manner. This is why communication has been defined as "a process in which there is some predictable relation between the message transmitted and the message received."[4] Communication can take many different forms, such as words, gestures, or symbols, and senders and receivers can be individuals or groups.

The renowned social scientist Harold Lasswell, in a now classic conceptualization of the communication process (grounded in the work of mathematician Claude Shannon and electrical engineer Warren Weaver) identified five major elements that deserve attention: *sources, messages, channels, receivers,* and *effects.* Scholars have subsequently added *feedback* as a sixth element.[5] Communications are originated by *sources,* or senders. Message content, meanings, and authoritativeness vary, depending on the source. When the country's president, based on economic data, declares that the U.S. economy is in trouble, the message carries far more weight than if the same message had come from a sports hero or movie star. Sources transmit information through *messages* that are designed to communicate the meanings that the sources wish to convey. The messages are sent through *channels,* such as telephone calls, faxes, electronic mail, letters, or stories publicized in the mass media. We shall examine this message-transmission process to pinpoint problems in obtaining sound information for transmission, formulating it into effective messages, and choosing appropriate channels for sending the message to properly selected *receivers.*

We shall also examine why messages often fail to produce the *effects* desired by the sender or have unexpected effects on behaviors, knowledge, or attitudes of the intended receivers or even on others who may encounter them. A warning by the U.S. Treasury secretary that the economy is in trouble, intended to enlighten the public about the nation's economic status, instead may generate feelings of pessimism and despair. Investors may then sell off assets, producing unexpected stock market declines. To discover the actual consequences produced by messages, organizations need *feedback.* Feedback—information about the impact produced by the message and the consequences attributable to the impact—permits people to learn from their past actions and to incorporate this new knowledge into future actions. Communication systems, therefore, should be structured to elicit good feedback. Mandating acknowledgment of messages, or reports about activities, or formal impact evaluations of existing programs are examples.

Effective communication requires framing messages—*encoding* is the technical term—so that they are comprehensible to the receivers who *decode* them. Message senders must therefore know the culture and comprehension levels of receivers. It seems ill-advised, for instance, to couch welfare application forms in legal jargon that is incomprehensible to most of the people who must complete these forms. Yet this happens frequently. Throughout this book we will discuss a number of aspects of message production that enhance or detract from its effectiveness. For example, in many cases, *homophily*—cultural uniformity between source and receiver—makes it easier to formulate effective messages; *heterophily*—cultural diversity of sender and receiver—makes it harder. A Hispanic public health nurse, for example, may find it easier to advise Hispanic women about maternal health issues than a nurse drawn from a different ethnic group. Effectiveness also suffers if there are distortions in messages, delays in transmission, or various transmission channels are obstructed or unavailable.

Conflicting or unrelated messages in the transmission channels may interfere with the transmission and effects of desired messages. For example, non-emergency calls to emergency police telephone lines may block urgent messages. Extraneous messages are often called *noise*. Repetition of essential messages—*redundancy*—is commonly used as a means to compensate for noise. A simple example would be an air force pilot's repetition of control tower landing instructions. Redundancy is time-consuming and may seem wasteful, but it may be essential for accuracy of transmission and comprehension. In normal conversations, half of the messages usually are redundant.

What do we mean by *organizations?* The term refers to stable groups of individuals who communicate to coordinate their work to achieve collective goals. When working collaboratively involves many people, it usually entails a division of labor and an organizational hierarchy. Division of labor within organizations may also require establishing subunits. Communication is needed to keep these subunits integrated with the larger whole.

Within hierarchies, some individuals are designated as superiors and others as subordinates. These ranking systems institutionalize inequality in organizations, even between people who may be social equals otherwise. Organizational roles strongly affect communication behavior. People designated as superiors are generally authorized to transmit messages that their subordinates are expected to heed. At the top levels, superiors are often the information managers par excellence within the organization. Control over the selection and transmission of information makes them powerful. When companies allow all members of their organization to access its information streams, as happens increasingly in the Internet age, these inequities diminish.

Because good information is crucial to the sound functioning of organizations, the organizations must devise ways to obtain it, process it, and distribute it to the appropriate people within the organization. This raises a number of information-management issues. What must be done to ensure that essential information will be available at the appropriate time? How can administrators ascertain that the information received is accurate and complete enough to manage the organization effectively? What will guarantee adequate feedback? Given the surfeit of information in an age when overabundance rather than scarcity of information is the main problem, administrators must be selective about what information they produce or gather from their environment and what information they disseminate. Information must be affordable in terms of money and effort and collection must respect the rights of people to whom the information relates. Administrators also must decide what information should be stored in organizational memories and what should be discarded after it has been used. They must develop effective internal information retrieval mechanisms for stored information.

Large organizations develop elaborate, interconnected communication channels for receiving information from their environment, for processing it to serve their purposes, and for sending internal and external messages. These channels constitute the organizational communication structure, or *network,* through which information flows are managed. Collecting adequate information permits organizations to make informed decisions and to get feedback about their wisdom so that corrections become possible. Exchanging information with the external environment embeds the organization in that environment.[6]

Why Information and Communication Management Is Crucial

Thanks to new technologies, the stream of data that most complex organizations collect, store, process, and use is growing steadily. Every person's life, in good times and bad, in peace and war, is affected by the ways in which government organizations, including thousands of administrative agencies, handle these information flows. That is why the study of communication in public organizations is so vital. It is also uniquely rewarding because communication flows that are essential to the life of organizations are amenable to human control. This is the province of information and communication management. It is also the substance of this book.

Three major aspects of information and communication management will be the central focus of discussion. Following the overview in this chapter, Chapter 2 covers problems faced in the selection and collection of essential data to provide the information that government agencies need to perform their missions. This information needs to be shared widely, requiring the creation of communication channels and policies for selecting network patterns of channels. Chapters 3 and 4 therefore deal with issues involved in constructing channels for the flow of information and arranging them in networks that ensure that stakeholders in public policies are appropriately connected.

Channeling information flows can never be a purely mechanical process. The psychological and cultural context in which the flow occurs must be considered in message framing and channeling. Chapter 5 deals with these contextual aspects that reflect the fact that human nature is always a major component in public sector communications. The remaining chapters deal with issues that arise when information must be created for particular uses and transmitted to specific audiences. Chapter 6 covers the information and communication needs of government officials charged with making policy decisions. What happens between the initial selection of data and the final decision and what are the explanations? Chapter 7 concentrates on the communication that needs to take place between government officials and citizens as each constituency serves the needs of the other. Officials need to transmit information to citizens, but the reverse flow is equally important.

Chapter 8 focuses both more narrowly and more broadly than the previous chapter on how government communicates with citizens to shape their opinions and win their support. To top off the discussion, Chapter 9 sketches glimpses of the future based on current trends.

Knowledge about managing organizational information and communication needs in the public sector is increasingly vital in an age where knowledge is, indeed, power. At the same time, communication is becoming more difficult for numerous reasons: It is harder to formulate clear messages when the subject matter to be communicated to nonspecialists becomes highly technical. Public agency messages must deal with such complex matters as chemical and radiation hazards in industries, eligibility for various types of individual retirement accounts, or the control of sexually transmitted diseases. Besides messages that are required to carry out the tasks assigned to various agencies, they must also determine what information they need to craft messages designed to maintain their social fabric, to integrate their diverse parts, to motivate good job performance, and to stimulate innovation.[7]

Another problem is the growing diversity of the audiences to whom information must be transmitted. The personnel of public agencies, as well as public agency clienteles, are more ethnically and culturally diverse than ever before. This is especially true for the largest public agencies, such as the Social Security Administration and the Internal Revenue Service. Governments at all levels are also performing many new, often controversial, functions that intrude on citizens' lives. More citizens, using more sophisticated methods, are ready to challenge government actions. Obviously, these complex tasks that face governments at all levels require skilled information and communication management. Information needs to be selected, assessed, and framed wisely so that it can be communicated effectively and information flows can be guided properly to reach targeted audiences. Without effective and responsible information and communication management, the flood tide of information can become a menace rather than an asset to good government.

The Uniqueness of the Public Sphere

The special focus of this book is on information management in *public* organizations—institutions established by governments at various levels to do its work. This means primarily, but not exclusively, administrative departments and agencies, such as the Department of Defense and the Environmental Protection Agency at the federal level, the insurance department or the auto license division at the state level, or the police department or city clerk's office at the local level. Although legislative bodies or top-level executive staffs are not the main focus of this book, examples relating to the presidency and Congress are included to make use of several interesting studies for which, unfortunately, no counterparts exist in the literature covering administrative agencies.

Communication in public sector agencies has been largely ignored by researchers despite the fact that public organizations have a tremendous impact on the life of every American. This oversight is puzzling, as well as unfortunate, because the communication problems of public bodies differ from those in the private sector in many important ways.[8] This book focuses on these marked differences and their implications.[9] There are, of course, many similarities among the public and private sector organizations. Both live in the same political universe and share the problems inherent in large organizations, but the magnitude of many shared problems varies so dramatically that resemblances fade. After all, a toy poodle and a St. Bernard are both dogs, but feeding and grooming them are hardly comparable chores.

Some scholars, like the authors of the *Handbook of Administrative Communication* (1997) distinguish between *administrative communication* and *political communication* in public sector organizations.[10] This distinction seems artificial because the political aspects and administrative performance aspects of communication are so intertwined that clear separations are impossible. For instance, when the Central Intelligence Agency (CIA) failed to warn the Federal Aviation Administration in September 2001 about an impending hijacking of American airliners by foreign terrorists, this was both a political issue concerning the adequacy of antiterrorist policies and an administrative issue concerning CIA warning procedures. Even biblical King Solomon who could resolve the trickiest disputes might have had trouble deciding how to classify it.

Box 1–1 summarizes major differences between public and private organizations in terms of environments, interaction with their environments, and internal structures and processes. It constitutes a resume of the major differences reported in the scholarly literature.

Political Pressures

Above all, as Box 1-1 indicates under the "environmental factors" heading, public agencies are part of the political system. Their structure, resources, personnel, goals, and even day-to-day decisions are shaped by the country's political culture and by political events. This forces public agencies to structure their activities and communications to stay afloat in the sea of politics. Administrative efficiency cannot be the lode star in a country that values structural brakes on governmental power and control, unrestrained communication, and pragmatism over principle. For example, an agency like the Equal Employment Opportunity Commission may limit its investigation of discrimination cases when the cases are apt to annoy or embarrass powerful political interests. Professional and technical goals that clash with political requirements are likely to be adjusted through compromises that may be quite uncomfortable for the agency. If possible, public agencies try to channel the political currents so that they are favorable to the course that the agency's captains would like to steer. More often, the political currents dominate.

Box 1-1 **Attributes of Public Organizations Compared with Those of Private Organizations**

Environmental Factors—Consequences

Less-open market competition:
- Less incentive to reduce costs, operate efficiently, and perform effectively
- Less concern with consumer preferences and proportioning supply to demand
- Less information and fewer market indicators to judge performance

More legal and more formal constraints (courts, legislature, hierarchy):
- More constraints on managers' choice of procedures and spheres of operations
- More proliferation of formal specifications and controls
- More external sources of formal influence
- Greater fragmentation of external sources of formal influence

Political influences:
- Greater diversity and intensity of external information influences on decisions
- Greater need for support by "constituencies"

Organization–Environment Transactions

Coerciveness:
- Greater coercion because of government's unique sanctions and coercive powers, including financial controls

Breadth of impact:
- Greater symbolic significance of actions of public sector personnel

Public scrutiny:
- Greater public scrutiny of public officials and their actions; concern about "public interest"

Unique public expectations:
- Greater expectations of fairness, responsiveness, accountability, and honesty

Internal Structures and Processes

Complexity:
- Greater multiplicity and diversity of objectives and decision criteria
- Greater vagueness and obscurity of objectives and decision criteria
- Greater chance of conflicting goals; more trade-offs

Top-level control:
- Less decision-making autonomy and flexibility
- Weaker, more fragmented authority over subordinates and lower levels
- Greater constraint in devising incentives for effective and efficient performance
- Greater reluctance to delegate, more levels of review, and greater use of formal regulations
- More political and promotional roles for top managers

Organizational performance:
- Greater cautiousness and rigidity; less innovativeness
- More frequent turnover of top leaders disrupting plans

Employees:
- Variations in personality traits and needs, such as higher dominance and flexibility, and a higher need for achievement on the part of government managers
- Lower work satisfaction and lower organizational commitment

SOURCE: Adapted from Hal G. Rainey, Robert W. Backoff, and Charles H. Levine, "Comparing Public and Private Organizations," *Public Administration Review* 36 (March/April) 1976): 236–237.

When agencies manage to ingratiate themselves with political leaders and influential publics, they are more likely to be well-financed, regardless of their past efficiency or effectiveness. Agencies are therefore greatly concerned about the images they present to important leaders. Agency heads strive to show off activities likely to attract favorable publicity. Focusing on readily demonstrable successes may lead to neglect of long-range problems. In the *Challenger* disaster in 1986, for example, when a space shuttle exploded ninety seconds after take-off, the desire to demonstrate success to critics of the program in and out of government and thereby ensure continued support was cited as one reason for making light of safety concerns. The fact that the mass media had repeatedly publicized delays in the program also created pressures to proceed under questionable conditions.[11] The investigating committee that tried to pinpoint the causes of the tragedy concluded that there was evidence of "chronic failure in the space agency and its contractors to communicate life and death problems up the chain of command." Other comments pointed out the "general ignoring of urgent memos seeking redesigning of critical booster-rocket joints" and the fact that "red flags were simply obscured in paper work."[12]

Subordination to political concerns makes public agencies also far more vulnerable than private organizations to having unwanted communication tasks thrust on them, commonly without the additional required resources. Legislators or the executive branch often prescribe major policy directions for them and control personnel and budget decisions. For instance, when Congress passed the Freedom of Information Act in 1966 to ease public access to government records, many agencies were flooded with requests for time-consuming searches of their records. But Congress provided no additional funds for handling these tasks, forcing agencies to reassign personnel. Reassignments often proved difficult because laws governing public sector personnel decisions sharply reduce options that would be available in the private sector.

Another major difference between private and public agencies that has a bearing on communications is the absence of widely accepted yardsticks—such as earning good monetary profits—for gauging and publicizing a public agency's success. For instance, if the sale of tax-delinquent housing is designed to provide homes for the poor, selling such housing at auction at a very high price would defeat the purpose. Public agencies measure their success in terms of their mission, their financial resources, the size of their staffs, and the satisfaction of their clientele. If the agency comes under fire for high costs or low revenues, these indicators of successful operations rarely make for a good defense. In fact, in the public sector, incentives to limit service are often strong. Fewer services usually mean saving scarce public resources. In the private sector it might mean a costly loss of business.[13]

Management of public agencies is also made more difficult because decisions about funding, personnel, and policies frequently are dictated by partisan motifs rather than the merits of the case that agency officials may plead.

Another reason for lack of control over information and poor morale is the fact that many top administrators are political appointees who are unlikely to stay a long time compared to the tenure of subordinates with civil service protection. The average political executive in the United States at the cabinet or subcabinet level remains in office for a scant twenty-two months—scarcely enough time to know the agency intimately, let alone gain control over information flows.

Many political concerns that shape the public sector are also shared by the private sector. Private firms operate subject to rules issued by the government and must therefore respond to political pressures. Like public agencies, they may have to expose their activities to public scrutiny through reports to the government or public relations releases. But as Box 1–1 suggests, the differences remain major and are reflected in their respective communication needs and options.

Fish Bowl Effects

From an organizational communications perspective, a crucial difference between public and private organizations springs from the fact that public organizations operate or are presumed to operate in an atmosphere of transparency. Internal and external communications of public agencies, unlike private sector organizations, are potentially, if not always actually, subject to public scrutiny. A hostile press and dissatisfied public interest groups are the chief critics. Scrutiny may also come from members of legislatures who eagerly seek plaudits for spotlighting what appear to be bureaucratic failings. In most instances, humiliating administrators is "not so much an exercise in sadism as a byproduct of pursuing other goals," such as self-glorification.[14]

Open organizational communication in the public sector is particularly important in democratic societies, which venerate the full and free flow of information. This is partly a matter of principle, springing from the belief that democracy must conduct its business openly so that all citizens can know what is happening. It is also partly an efficiency issue, grounded in the belief that open communication is beneficial because it exposes a multiplicity of concerns and opinions that then become available for decision making. Based on these beliefs, promotion of open communication has become enshrined in America's fundamental laws, such as the constitutionally protected rights of freedom of assembly, speech, and the press. Public access to information has been eased through sunshine laws that open the meetings of public bodies to the citizenry and through freedom of information laws that permit private citizens to scan information files collected by the government. Of course, there are also laws that impede free access to information. Examples are privacy laws that prohibit government agencies from unauthorized disclosure of personal data or gag rules that bar access to information during litigation.

Freedom and openness have a price. Upholding the principle of the free flow of information has posed many difficult problems for governmental organizations. The most dramatic of these involve the conflict between protecting national security secrets from the nation's enemies and at the same time avoiding undue limits on access to and circulation of information. Even when national security is not involved, forced disclosure of information can be troublesome. When agencies negotiate agreements internally or with outside agencies, full control over information can be a significant asset. Having to share information with the opposing side may severely limit the ability to strike favorable bargains. It may foster conflict by publicizing clashing values and alerting opponents, as has happened in the areas of environmental and nuclear safety. It may also lead to a dual decision-making process, with the formal level out in the open, accessible to the public, and the informal level taking place behind closed doors.

To avoid the risks of potentially dangerous adverse publicity, public managers tend to adopt cautious, conservative operating styles. They choose stability and adherence to the letter of the law rather than flexibility and innovativeness. If they follow the rules closely, they are less likely to be blamed when things go wrong. To ensure accountability, managers in the public sector emphasize strict controls and rules for employees. They are less inclined to delegate authority or to solicit group decisions. This type of defensive management often creates an atmosphere of hostility and mistrust that hampers agency achievements.

Wrestling with Giants

The size and diversity of public institutions and the requirements of checks and balances of power built into these institutions create unique challenges for public sector managers. As Box 1–1 records, these top executives enjoy far less control over their organizations than is true of their private sector counterparts. Secretary of the Treasury W. Michael Blumenthal (1977–1979), who had been a corporation president, voiced a typical complaint: "Even though I'm technically the chief executive of the Treasury, I have little real power, effective power, to influence how the thing functions."[15] As a public official, he felt helpless and exasperated about responsibility unmatched by powers of control.

Anthony Frank, postmaster general from 1988 to 1992, recruited from running the nation's sixth largest savings institution, explained to reporters how the disparities of scale between private and public bodies make control difficult.[16] In the public sector, instead of two million customers, he served 200 million; instead of 400 branches, there were 40,000; instead of a work force of 8,000 employees, he now headed an army of 800,000. Instead of making policies independently, he now had to be sensitive to the ideas of fifteen different constituencies, including members of Congress and their staffs, the Postal Rate Commission, four unions, and three management associations. Most troubling, independent commissions controlled the pricing of products and services sold by the Postal Service, and it took up to a year to get rate changes to match the activities of private competitors.

Because superior–subordinate relationships are vastly more complex in public agencies, top personnel do not have the strong control over organizational communication flows enjoyed by their private sector counterparts, as Box 1–1 indicates. Administrators' power to hire and fire is limited because employees are either protected under a merit system or selected on a patronage basis, putting them under the wing of a political mentor. Many employees who perform important support services belong to central staff agencies, such as the Office of Management and Budget, that are beyond the control of the organizations they serve. Staff agencies have their own priorities, which may differ sharply from their client organizations. Communication efforts to bring about mutual understanding and cooperation are rarely entirely successful.

Promotions and pay may be predetermined by seniority or other rules. This makes it difficult to reward merit or take disciplinary action except for the most serious infractions. Preferences for minorities and veterans further remove control over personnel and may produce resentment among people who do not enjoy these special benefits. Morale at the lower levels of government service also frequently suffers because jobs lack prestige and pay may be poor compared with unionized jobs in the private sector. As discussed more fully in Chapter 5, this limits the possibility for leadership and makes it more difficult to use various communication techniques to generate high levels of morale.

Coordination of the policies and activities of the vast array of public agencies at all governmental levels presents an almost insurmountable challenge. It is therefore not surprising that conflicts between personnel in different agencies or even departments within an agency are endemic in the public sector. Congress and state legislatures act like remote boards of directors, making little effort to integrate the operations of diverse agencies, even when their policies vary substantially while their jurisdictions overlap. For political reasons, public agencies often represent strange aggregations of tasks and goals under one organizational roof. Accordingly, agencies have to generate very diverse types of information and messages to meet internal and external needs.[17]

Control over information is also difficult because information needs are extremely diverse in large public agencies. Information is required for policy formulation, planning, decision making, and implementation in a vast number of areas such as international trade, education, and public safety.[18] Political considerations may force top-level administrators to structure their information intake and use in ways that run counter to their preferences and often counter to the norms of professionalism, which are based on nonpolitical criteria. For instance, the wish of a local member of Congress to locate a military airport in a particular town may have to be accommodated even when transportation studies indicate that it should go elsewhere.

From a broader perspective, organizational communication issues in the public sector, to a greater extent than in the private sector, have ramifications far beyond concerns about operating efficiency. They entail the distribution of power in government and society. People who control important messages circulating within an organization have the opportunity to be powerful within that organization. They may be able to determine policies that have major societal consequences.[19]

Although the challenges faced by public-sector communicators seem daunting, steady improvements have been made. Numerous commissions at all levels of government have tackled public-sector communication problems. That includes the National Partnership for Reinventing Government (NPR) that started in 1993 under the aegis of then Vice President Albert Gore.[20] This long-term initiative has improved the government's communication with clients through simplifying the language of government documents and facilitating computer-based interchanges between bureaucrats and citizens.[21] In the past, administrative reform efforts usually drew on private-sector experts assembled in blue-ribbon commissions, such as the Grace Commission Report created by President Ronald Reagan in 1982 to examine federal government operations from a private business perspective. When it became clear that public business cannot be run like private business, a new combination approach, called quality management, became popular. It tempered the business know-how of the private sector with the sense of political realism of public-sector officials.

Nearly half the states, as well as the federal government and many localities, now have programs and institutions to improve all phases of their operations, including communication, through private–public quality management operations. Among them are large states such as California, New York, and Florida, as well as smaller ones such as Minnesota, Iowa, South Carolina, and Washington. The use of Web sites has mushroomed at all levels of government and the private sector and has vastly expanded opportunities for information dissemination and collaboration.

The Foundations of Organizational Communication Studies

The study of organizational communication is plagued by a number of problems typical of many social science fields. It lacks an overarching theory. In fact, there are heated disputes about what theoretical approaches are best.[22] There is controversy about the best level for studying information management in public or private organizations. Should it be a macro look or a micro look—a bird's eye view or a close-up view? Each of these perspectives has its plusses and minuses. A systems-wide macro perspective permits a total overview, displaying individual organizations in their contexts while blurring details. A subsystem-level micro perspective allows details to emerge but at the expense of the context included in the larger picture. In this book, I attempt to finesse this dilemma by combining macro perspectives in the general discussions with a micro focus in specific examples.

A second level of controversy relates to the theoretical and ideological lenses through which organizational communication should be viewed. I lean toward positivist perspectives, searching for measurable phenomena and for practical recommendations for solving observable problems. Nonetheless, I have great respect for the contributions made by proponents of more subjective orientations who contend that reality is plural and not necessarily observable and measurable. What matters in human interactions, these scholars argue, is how people interpret their perceptions of their environments and how they mentally construct the particular realities that guide their actions.

Social scientists can be hegemonic and claim rightful dominance for their preferred theories, or they can be catholic, accepting a variety of perspectives as legitimate. I belong to the latter category. Although the choices of situations and problems addressed in this book reflect my positivist orientation, the discussion also takes other perspectives into account. In fact, I firmly believe that the insights gleaned by social scientific research are on firmest ground if they are informed by findings gained from diverse theoretical perspectives using a multiplicity of research strategies.

Unfortunately, from my point of view, most organizational communication research has represented single theoretical perspectives and a meager array of research strategies. Most of the research has been static, looking at organizational communications at one point in time in one or more institutions. Dynamic approaches, using time-series analyses to discover long-range patterns, have been relatively rare. Field studies involving observations of actual communication behaviors have also been scarce. There has been little "soaking and poking" in the vein of Richard Fenno's intensive observations of members of Congress.[23]

The validity of the few controlled experiments that have been conducted is suspect because laboratory studies cannot effectively simulate the social structure in which organizational communication takes place. Samples of organizations that were observed have been too small to establish norms. Case studies of individual organizations, which predominated before the 1970s, were not conducive to building generalizations because they dealt mainly with specific communication problems. Most of these studies paid insufficient attention to the internal structures of organizations and to situational variables that might affect their communication behavior. As mentioned, no special efforts were made to focus on organizational communication problems in public institutions. Nonetheless, despite these failings, these earlier studies provide important insights into public-sector organizational communication that are well worth exploring.[24]

Systems-Level Studies

Viewed from a positivist perspective, analyses of systems-wide communication flows have made the most important contributions to an understanding of the challenges confronting information management in the public sector. These comprehensive analyses of all aspects of information generation and communication trace how messages are generated and circulated in political systems to guide operations. Karl Deutsch's path-breaking study, *The Nerves of Government: Models of Political Communication and Control,* is the classic and still best example.[25] Deutsch argued that the functions of the body politic, like those of the human body, are triggered by its communication system, which he called the *nerves* of government.

Many systems-level studies deal with the most powerful political body—the state—because scholars believed that the nature and quality of a state's political communication system determined the overall performance of all of its units.[26] However, these studies are also relevant for smaller types of organizations, such as public agencies within states. Deutsch, for instance, pointed out that all political systems, regardless of their size, require constant flows of information about what is going on inside and outside the system if they are to function well.[27]

New information entering a system is combined with information already present in the system's organizational memory so that organizational decisions represent an amalgamation of old and new information. When messages are communicated to various parts of a political system, including multiple layers of bureaucracy, they generate further communications as well as actions. All messages that pass through a system must be comprehensible to the intended recipients. In the process of preparing and transmitting appropriate messages, much information may be lost. The original meaning intended by the sender may also become distorted when intermediaries at various levels of hierarchies reframe the information in line with their prejudices and preferences or when new information is combined with what is stored in organizational memory.

To permit members of organizations to learn from past decisions, feedback messages must be generated. Policy evaluation studies in public agencies, periodic reports, spot-checks, or internal and external polls are examples of feedback procedures. When they reveal performance inadequacies, government officials can make corrections that steer the system in the right direction. The term *cybernetic system* describes organizations that use feedback to adjust their policies in accordance with changing needs and human and material resources. Instead of striving to maintain or restore the status quo, the goal is conscious guidance toward system improvement. Cybernetic information flows in political and other types of organizations are circular. Information reaching the organization produces action, which in turn generates information that the system uses as a means for constant adaptation. Figure 1–1 shows a crude model.

Figure 1-1 A Crude Diagram of Information Flow in a Political System

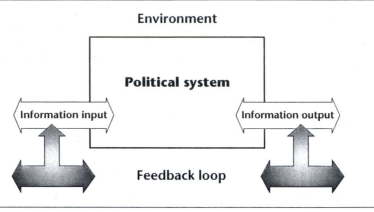

SOURCE: Author.

To allow for the fact that political systems are in constant flux—rather than in equilibrium as postulated by earlier theories—Deutsch explained that decision makers must anticipate developments. Their decisions must take into account that there are always time *lags* between the receipt of information on the one hand and the response to this information on the other. If no allowances are made for these time lags, decisions may provide solutions geared to conditions that no longer exist. Closure of underused elementary schools, for example, may come years after they were no longer needed. It may fail to anticipate the renewed need for the schools when birthrates skyrocket following the influx of young immigrant populations with large families.

To compensate for unavoidable lags in the communication process, decisions must *lead,* or be ahead of, current goals. Monitoring birth and immigration statistics may be essential to anticipate changing demands for classrooms and teachers. Most of the time, governments are not very effective in anticipating the leads needed to solve problems. Frequently there are gaps between information available to intelligence-gathering agencies and information available to operating agencies. When leads are excessive, overly large *gains* may ensue so that the target is missed. Such oversteering is uncommon in the United States, where most changes are incremental and slow because bureaucrats lean toward undue caution and because the wishes of numerous conflicting pressure groups need to be considered in many public policy decisions.

Deutsch's analysis of communication flows in public organizations also points out that information passes through a variety of channels whose configuration is highly significant for the system. Messages cannot reach their destination if communication channels are unavailable or if they lack the capacity to handle the flow of essential messages. This is well-illustrated in crises such as earthquakes or floods when rescue services may be unable to communicate with victims because telephone channels are jammed with messages or disrupted. This is what happened following the terrorist bombing of New York's World Trade Center in September 2001. Phone lines were so jammed that many callers were unable to make connections. Lives might have been saved if the calls had been successful.

If units within a political system are improperly connected, messages may miss their targets. This is why President George W. Bush created an Office for Homeland Security in 2001. It was charged with making sure that officials at all levels of government would receive security-related messages in a timely fashion so that they could coordinate their responses.

The structure of the network of communications within an organization determines message diffusion patterns. In general, leaders are at the hub of communications and therefore receive comparatively large amounts of information. People who are not connected to the channels through which essential information flows may be unable to participate effectively in organizational activities, including decision making. Channels of communication vary in the number of people they connect and in the character of the information flows they carry. Flows may be predominantly in one direction, taking the form of commands, or they may be reciprocal, involving exchanges of information among individuals. Communication characteristics may indicate how well political organizations function. For instance, performance is affected by the time it takes for messages to reach their targets and to elicit responses.

One of the most potentially fruitful aspects of Deutsch's analysis of political communication systems is his discussion of likely problems that can cause serious political difficulties, such as overloads in communication channels and message distortions. Problems can be discovered by tracing the paths of communication flows, by examining the substance of meanings conveyed, and by analyzing how the information is used. Communication problems can spring from the structural characteristics of public organizations as well as from imperfect functioning. Functional problems are often caused by the manner in which people ordinarily process information. We will be discussing these problems in later chapters.

The broad overviews entailed in a systems approach facilitate the comparison of communication patterns in various types of political organizations. One may judge how simple or complex these patterns are relative to other organizations and how cultural, social, economic, and political factors affect the nature of organizational communication systems. One can compare how organizations allot resources to communication functions and how they distribute them among information production, reception, and dissemination. Allocation patterns thus reveal where the organization's priorities lie. One can also assess differences among various organization members in access to information and ability to disseminate their views to various potential receivers. The findings may provide clues to the degree of democracy within the organization and the extent of internal cohesion. Cohesive organizations are able to transmit information accurately about a wide variety of topics to most of their members without major losses or distortions and without a great deal of noise.

Chaos theory is a promising newcomer to the array of extant systems theories. It is based on the supposition that complex systems, like those found in modern governments, often go astray because of unforeseen, unpredictable happenings. Simply amassing additional information in line with feedback and previous assumptions, as cybernetic systems theories would suggest, will not work. The unforeseen events—the chaos—have changed the situation so materially that entirely new approaches based on fresh information and assumptions are required to cope.[28] For example, the unexpected outbreak of war in neighboring countries may require a complete revision of previous plans for new trade agreements with these countries.

More generally, chaos theory, which originated in the physical and biological sciences, focuses on inherently unstable dynamic systems whose behavior occurs irregularly and is nonlinear. Information flows in large organizations exhibit these characteristics. They are often unpredictable, moving alternately forward and backward in unintended and unexpected directions. This means that information systems based on notions of stability and regular repetitions are prone to multiple failures. In Neil McBride's words:

> In attempting to provide a concrete form to organisational activities which are often tacit, indistinct and evolving in nature, these systems ignore the dynamic flux of organisational form and activity. They try to provide certainty in the face of uncertainty, objectivity in the face of subjectivity, uniformity in the face of multiple contexts and views, and static, designed processes in the face of dynamic, evolving processes.[29]

Chaos theory lends itself to analyses that use narrative techniques to discern patterns of influence and behavior over time. With these qualitative approaches, investigators can track major system changes that may be the unintended and unpredictable consequences of even minor technological or managerial developments. Chaos theory thus sheds light on hitherto confounding organizational events. It is an example of the benefits that may flow from using new theories to solve riddles that had previously stumped researchers.

Subsystems-Level Studies

Rather than analyzing political communication systems in their entirety, many scholars concentrate on specialized aspects of information management. *Decision-making studies* are one example. These studies focus on ways in which information is collected, processed, and guided to ensure that the appropriate people are involved, the right kind of information is conveyed at the proper time, and various common problems that lead to information distortion and faulty decisions are avoided. These works provide the foundation for the analysis of decision making presented in Chapter 8, although most of them do not focus on problems encountered in the public sector.[30]

Other subsystems-level studies are concerned primarily with the management of information flows in individual institutions, focusing on messages that will motivate workers to perform well.[31] Historically, three major theoretical approaches have dominated these studies, each based on a different view of the human motivations and types of behavior that should be considered in devising effective internal communication systems. Based on these theories and their ethical implications, organization leaders have adopted different management and communication strategies and styles. For example, some managers believe that people perform best in a restrictive, rule-dominated environment. Therefore, they provide close supervision and restrict communication flows. Other managers believe that an environment fostering personal growth is best. Therefore, they strive to humanize the workplace by encouraging communication between superiors and subordinates. Finally, some managers, adapting Japanese models, emphasize that organizations are social bodies. They see the creation of participatory organizational cultures as their main challenge.[32]

Analyses of internal organizational communications often encompass all three approaches simultaneously. The Senate's investigation of President Bill Clinton's conduct in the Monica Lewinsky affair is a case in point. The president had been accused of sexual misconduct involving a White House intern and of misconduct during various court cases related to the affair. Focusing on formal communication rules, Senate sleuths examined the hierarchical communication structure of the White House, the formal duties assigned to White House aides, and the nature and flow of directives from the president's office. But the Senate also used a human relations approach when it asked various defendants about the personal motives that prompted their actions. The social systems approach, which focuses on the entire setting in which communication occurs, was evident in questions probing the relationship between the Lewinsky affair and other charges of improprieties leveled against the president. The investigation revealed a complex web of interrelationships between the president and various White House staffers, high-level government employees and advisers, and various citizens.

In recent decades, positivist theories about public sector information management have come under attack on theoretical and ideological grounds. *Interpretist* and *postmodern* theories have come into vogue, especially in Europe and Latin America.[33] Many critical researchers believe that current approaches to studying and practicing information management serve to perpetuate a repressive capitalist system.

Compared to positivist theorists, who focus inquiry on observable phenomena, interpretive theorists believe that there is no organizational reality. It is all a matter of human interpretations that evolve from group interactions.

The interpretive school is bifurcated into naturalistic and critical approaches. Naturalists are concerned with recording existing interactions and the perceptions they generate. They observe actual organizational behavior much as anthropologists would, and then describe and explain what they have seen.

Critical theorists are concerned with what interactions ought to be.[34] They decry the fact that past theories have been anchored in capitalist notions of productivity and efficiency that deem work accomplished in line with the agency's mission as most important. Instead, these critics argue, the welfare of human beings, as they perceive it, should be the focus of organizational concern as well as the chief object of organizational communication studies. Organizational health and efficiency are secondary. Critical theorists are chiefly interested in ascertaining the meanings and patterns of domination created through human interaction. They believe that greater sensitivity and responsiveness to workers' feelings and perceptions will lead to more egalitarian organizational relationships and to a better society overall.[35] Information management must vary depending on the goals to be achieved. Therefore roles, norms, and values must be studied subjectively by observing and interacting with workers rather than by so-called objective criteria interpreted from the researcher's perspectives. Descriptions and interpretation are deemed more significant than traditional hypothesis testing.[36]

The latest turn of the theoretical wheel has landed on a space called *postmodern theory*. Like chaos theory, it is based on the defensible assumption that the world is a nonrational place in which the old organizational models based on traditional rationality frequently do not work. The most challenging human issues are beyond the grasp of science. Contrary to the views of many other social scientists, postmodernists contend that human identities are not based on fixed social roles and traditions, that ethical and moral concepts are not absolute, and that art and culture are constantly reinvented. Finally, unprecedented interchanges of information and unprecedented human mobility create a truly global civilization that is in a constant state of flux.[37]

Because modern society is constantly changing to remain in tune with technological advancements, theories about the best ways to manage information must be fluid. Chaos and postmodern theories are important because they remind scholars that social science theories deal with probabilities, rather than certainties. The march of time may erode underlying premises and crucial contexts can change suddenly and unpredictably. However, judging from past trends, the perspectives from which public sector information management will be viewed will continue to be a mixture of old and new theories. Positivist theories will remain dominant, but they will be tempered by humanistic concerns and respect for uncertainties that are the main contributions made by newer theories.

Despite the pleas of many researchers that theorists should find common ground, the quest for one overarching theory remains elusive.[38] The basic assumptions underlying the various theories are too antagonistic. One cannot simultaneously argue that there is and that there is *not* a real world beyond the perceptions in human minds and that social scientists' observations should and should *not* reflect and serve their social values. Still, it is possible to combine the insights from disparate perspectives to shed light on specific organizational issues and problems because " . . . organizational communication demands to be approached through multiple perspectives, and even those will be inadequate to fully understand its mysteries."[39]

Where Do We Go from Here?

What lessons can be drawn from this chapter? It seems clear that collecting essential information and communicating it appropriately are increasingly crucial for attaining the goals of the public sector in American society. It seems equally clear that the efficiency and effectiveness of organizational performance hinge on well-designed and well-executed information management. Despite its importance and its relevance to the distribution of political power, and despite the fact that administrators have long paid heed to its significance, information management in the public sector remains neglected by scholars of the political scene. The time is ripe for a change.

This chapter has shown that a variety of useful theories can guide scholars in selecting facets of information management for careful analysis. Major information management problems will always plague the public sector because of its complexity. When such problems occur, public attention should focus on resolving them rather than on bashing public agencies, as happens all too often. This is why the story told in the chapters that follow covers problems as well as solutions. Chapter 2 starts the journey with an analysis of typical information selection issues.

NOTES

1. Mars Climate Orbiter Failure Board Report, 1999 (Nov. 10), http://mars.jpl. nasa.gov/msp98/news/mco991110.html
2. Barbara S. Romzek and Melvin Dubnick, "Accountability in the Public Sector: Lessons from the Challenger Tragedy," *Public Administration Review* 47 (May/June 1987): 227, 233. The full report is available in U.S. Congress, House, Committee on Science and Technology, *Investigation of the Challenger Accident,* Report, 99th Cong., 2d sess. (Washington, D.C.: U.S. Government Printing Office, 1978).
3. John M. Stevens and Robert P. McGowan, *Information Systems and Public Management* (New York: Praeger, 1985), 7.
4. Daniel Katz and Robert L. Kahn, *The Social Psychology of Organizations* (New York: Wiley, 1978), 431–432.
5. Harold D. Lasswell, "The Structure and Function of Communication in Society," in *Mass Communications,* ed. Wilbur Schramm and Donald F. Roberts (Urbana: University of Illinois Press, 1971), 84; Claude E. Shannon and Warren

Weaver, *The Mathematical Theory of Communication* (Urbana: University of Illinois Press, 1949).

6. Everett M. Rogers and Rekha Agarwala Rogers, *Communication in Organizations* (New York: Free Press, 1976), 6–7.

7. Raymond L. Falcione and Allyson Downs Adrian, "Communication Practices in Public Administration," in *Handbook of Administrative Communication,* ed. James L. Garnett and Alexander Kouzmin (New York: Marcel Dekker, 1997), 717–746.

8. David Sadofsky, *Knowledge as Power: Political and Legal Control of Information* (New York: Praeger, 1990); Joseph P. Viteritti, "The Environmental Context of Communication: Public Sector Organizations," in *Handbook of Administrative Communication,* ed. James L. Garnett and Alexander Kouzmin (New York: Marcel Dekker, 1997), 79–100; Uriel Rosenthal, "The Relevance of Administrative Communication to Democratic Politics: Communicating in Democracies," in *Handbook of Administrative Communication,* ed. James L. Garnett and Alexander Kouzmin (New York: Marcel Dekker, 1997), 153–168.

9. For arguments that the differences between public and private organizations have nearly disappeared because all are public now, to a degree, see Barry Bozeman, *All Organizations Are Public: Bridging Public and Private Organizational Theories* (San Francisco: Jossey-Bass, 1987), and Michael A. Murray, "Comparing Public and Private Management: An Exploratory Essay," *Public Administration Review* 34 (July/August 1975): 364–371.

10. James L. Garnett, "Trends and Gaps in the Treatment of Communication in Organization and Management Theory," in *Handbook of Administrative Communication,* ed. James L. Garnett and Alexander Kouzmin (New York: Marcel Dekker, 1997), 21–57.

11. Barbara S. Romzek and Melvin Dubnick, "Accountability in the Public Sector, Lessons from the Challenger Tragedy," *Public Administration Review* 47 (May/June 1987): 233.

12. Ibid., 227, 233. The full report is available in U.S. Congress, House, Committee on Science and Technology, *Investigation of the Challenger Accident,* Report, 99th Cong., 2d sess. (Washington, D.C.: U.S. Government Printing Office, 1987).

13. James Q. Wilson, *Bureaucracy: What Government Agencies Do and Why They Do It* (New York: Basic Books, 1989), 135.

14. Herbert Kaufman, *The Administrative Behavior of Federal Bureau Chiefs* (Washington, D.C.: Brookings Institution, 1981), 28.

15. W. Michael Blumenthal, "Candid Reflections of a Businessman in Washington," *Fortune,* January 29, 1979, 39.

16. Nathaniel C. Nash, "New Postal Chief Looks at the Really Big Picture," *New York Times,* July 27, 1988.

17. William Eddy, *Public Organization Behavior* (Cambridge, Mass.: Winthrop, 1982), 4–15.

18. Stevens and McGowan, *Information Systems and Public Management,* 5.

19. John Rawls, in *A Theory of Justice* (Cambridge: Belknap Press of Harvard University Press, 1971), argues that social harmony is fostered when individuals or groups possess complementary information.

20. Al Gore, *From Red Tape to Results: Creating a Government that Works Better and Costs Less.* Report of the National Performance Review (Washington, D.C.: U.S. Government Printing Office, 1993).

21. National Partnership for Reinventing Government, 2000. "Reinvention @work-foryou," http://www.npr.gov/library/announc/040700.html

22. Steven R. Corman and Marshall Scott Poole, eds., *Perspectives on Organizational Communication: Finding Common Ground* (New York: Guilford Press, 2000). Essays in the book focus on the interpretive, postpositivist, and critical perspectives.

23. Richard F. Fenno, *Homestyle: House Members in Their Districts* (Boston: Little, Brown, 1978).

24. Representative works include Harold D. Lasswell et al., *The Language of Politics: Studies in Quantitative Semantics* (Cambridge: MIT Press, 1965); Edward Sapir, *Culture, Language and Personality: Selected Essays,* ed. David Mandelbaum (Berkeley: University of California Press, 1962); Kenneth Burke, *Language as Symbolic Action* (Berkeley: University of California Press, 1966); Ernst Cassirer, *Language and Myth* (New York: Harper, 1946); Alfred North Whitehead, *Symbolism: Its Meaning and Effect* (New York: Macmillan, 1958); Susan Langer, *Philosophy in a New Key: A Study in the Sociology of Reason, Rite, and Art* (Cambridge: Harvard University Press, 1951); Kenneth Boulding, *The Image: Knowledge in Life and Society* (Ann Arbor: University of Michigan Press, 1956); Murray Edelman, *The Symbolic Uses of Politics* (Urbana: University of Illinois Press, 1964).

25. Karl W. Deutsch, *The Nerves of Government: Models of Political Communication and Control* (New York: Free Press, 1966).

26. Among these scholars, Lucian Pye, *Communication and Political Development* (Princeton: Princeton University Press, 1963); Daniel Lerner, *The Human Meaning of the Social Sciences* (New York: Meridian Books, 1959); and Wilbur Schramm, *Mass Media and National Development: The Role of Information in Developing Countries* (Stanford: Stanford University Press, 1964), studied communication patterns in governmental systems as a whole, and Richard Fagen, *Politics and Communication: An Analytic Study* (Boston: Little, Brown, 1966), and Gabriel Almond and James Coleman, eds., *The Politics of the Developing Areas* (Princeton: Princeton University Press, 1960), focused on parts of political systems from a communications perspective. Also see David Easton, *A Systems Analysis of Political Life* (New York: Wiley, 1965).

27. Part III of Deutsch, *Nerves of Government,* is most relevant.

28. Sam E. Overman and Donna T. Loraine, "Information for Control: Another Management Proverb?" *Public Administration Review* 54 (March/April 1994): 193–196; Lucas D. Introna, *Management, Information and Power* (New York: Macmillan, 1997); Haridimos Tsoukas, "Chaos, Complexity and Organisation Theory," *Organization* 5 (1998): 291–313.

29. Neil McBride, "Chaos Theory and Information Systems," Track 4: *Research Methodology and Philosophical Aspects of IS Research* (June 23, 2000), http://www.cms.dmu.ac.uk/~nkm/CHAOS.html

30. These studies are based on a variety of decision-making theories. See Robert P. Abelson and A. Levi, "Decision-Making and Decision Theory," in *Handbook of Social Psychology,* 3d ed., Vol. 1, ed. Gardner Lindzey and Elliott Aronson (New York: Random House, 1986), 231–310, for an overview. Also see Herbert A. Simon, *Administrative Behavior: A Study of Decision Making Processes in Administrative Organizations,* 2d ed. (New York: Macmillan, 1957); Rogers and Rogers, *Communication in Organizations* (New York: Free Press, 1976); R. Wayne Pace

and Don F. Faules, *Organizational Communication,* 2d ed. (Englewood Cliffs, N.J.: Prentice-Hall, 1989); Gerald M. Goldhaber, *Organizational Communication,* 3d ed. (Dubuque, Iowa: Wm. C. Brown, 1983); Katherine Miller, *Organizational Communication: Approaches and Processes* (Belmont, Calif.: Wadsworth, 1995); Eric M. Eisenberg and H. L. Goodall, Jr., *Organizational Communication: Balancing Creativity and Constraint,* 2d ed. (New York: St. Martin's Press, 1997); Katz and Kahn, *The Social Psychology of Organizations;* Jeffrey Pfeffer, *Power in Organizations* (Marshfield, Mass.: Pitman, 1981); and Karl Weick, *The Social Psychology of Organizing,* 2d ed. (Reading, Mass.: Addison-Wesley, 1979).

31. James L. Garnett, "Administrative Communication: Domains, Threats, and Legitimacy," in *Handbook of Administrative Communication,* ed. James L. Garnett and Alexander Kouzmin (New York: Marcel Dekker, 1997), 1–20.

32. Eisenberg and Goodall, Jr., *Organizational Communication,* 83–84.

33. Dennis K. Mumby, "Critical Organizational Communication Studies: The Next 10 Years," *Communication Monographs* 60 (March 1993): 18–25.

34. The Institute for Social Research at the University of Frankfurt in Germany has been the intellectual fountainhead of critical theory. It became the home of the Frankfurt School in the 1920s, guided by philosophers such as Jürgen Habermas and scholars such as Max Horkheimer. Jürgen Habermas, *Toward a Rational Society: Student Protest, Science, and Politics* (Boston: Beacon, 1970); Max Horkheimer, *Critical Theory: Selected Essays* (New York: Herder, 1972). In the late 1970s Robert B. Denhardt and several colleagues applied Habermas's ideas to the field of public administration. Robert B. Denhardt, "Toward a Critical Theory of Public Organization," *Public Administration Review* 41 (1981): 628–632; Michael T. Harmon and Richard T. Mayer, *Organizational Theory for Public Administration* (Boston: Little, Brown, 1986), 326.

35. See Harmon and Mayer, *Organizational Theory for Public Administration,* for details.

36. Weick, *The Social Psychology of Organizing;* David Silverman, *The Theory of Organisations* (New York: Basic Books, 1971).

37. Walter Truett Anderson, *The Truth about the Truth* (New York: Tarcher/Putnam, 1995), 10. Also see Eisenberg, and Goodall, *Organizational Communication,* chap. 7.

38. Steven R. Corman, "The Need for Common Ground," in *Perspectives on Organizational Communication: Finding Common Ground,* ed. Steven R. Corman and Marshall Scott Poole (New York: Guilford Press, 2000).

39. Kathleen J. Krone, "Becoming Deeply Multiperspectival: Commentary on Finding Common Ground in Organizational Communication Research," in *Perspectives on Organizational Communication,* ed. Corman and Poole, 146.

Chapter 2 **Building Information Bases:**
Resources and Obstacles

In the past, social scientists have been more concerned about misuse of power by public agencies than misuse of information. Yet control over information gives power. It may enable the knowledgeable to set organizational goals, make decisions, and control the performance of activities within the organization. Hence acquisition, use, and misuse of information should be major concerns.[1] In this chapter we will examine the types of information that public agencies need to operate effectively and the problems they face in finding and acquiring high-quality information.

Information Needs

All complex organizations require a great deal of technical and political information. The Environmental Protection Agency (EPA), for example, deals with literally millions of toxic substances that threaten the soil, water, and air. EPA personnel must know what these substances are and what millions of public and private enterprises should do to keep them under control. The agency must monitor its own programs and evaluate how well it is doing in its own estimation and in that of salient others. The Department of Defense needs technical information to predict how many missiles of various types potential enemies of the United States are likely to deploy over specified periods of time. Billions of dollars of defense expenditures, along with the security of the country, hinge on the accuracy of such forecasts. The Department of Veterans Affairs serves 30 million former members of the armed forces and their families. Its more than 200,000 full-time employees administer a vast array of programs ranging from education and medical and disability benefits to low-interest home loans for veterans and their 50 million dependents and survivors. Running these agencies efficiently requires a vast amount of technical information.

Technical and Political Data

Technical needs are "exceeded only by the need for political information." Take the example of the EPA. Because the agency's mandate and funding depend on Congress, its policymaking officials must know what types of activities will please influential congressional leaders and what will anger them to the point of retaliating against the agency. When the EPA decides to attack pollution problems in a particular industry or company, it must be aware of the political connections of that industry or company. It may harm the agency to undertake projects to which there is powerful, politically well-connected opposition.[2] For instance, the EPA may well shy away from investigating pollution charges leveled against companies with close ties to the White House or appropriations committees in Congress. It is never wise to bite the hand that feeds you.

Executives in public agencies require information about the political climate in which agencies operate, about the resources that are potentially available, and about the tactics that spell the greatest success, especially under adverse conditions. The Clinton years, for example, were a period of bureaucratic contraction. Officials needed to know how much contraction was politically feasible and in which areas expansion remained possible. When programs concern groups whose interests may clash, such as business and labor, bureaucrats must know how to steer a middle course between the interests of these groups. They must know what kinds of appeals are most suitable for attracting support for a policy, how these appeals should be framed to capture the attention and backing of appropriate publics and how to avoid unduly antagonizing potentially hostile groups. Even the choice of technical information is often a political decision. For example, the Department of Education may be loath to collect data showing that infant education is more beneficial than nursery-school training when it is trying to gain support for an expanded nursery-school program.

Political considerations rather than analyses of technical data determine how an agency formulates and implements goals. Decisions about who will collect information about prospective action, and from whom, are also political. Which experts are chosen matters very much, especially when they are summoned while the problem is still being formulated. The way issues are defined shapes what information will be gathered and narrows the options for dealing with them. For example, information needed to cope with problems of alcoholism varies considerably depending on whether alcoholism is defined as a disease, a personal vice, or a problem caused by societal deficiencies.

Information needs differ at various management levels. Table 2–1 illustrates how divergent goals require tapping into different information pools. At the top levels, where broad organizational strategies are devised, information about the organization's external controllers may be most crucial. Mid-level administrators, responsible for implementing the strategies, must draw on information supplied by the top levels to draft operational plans. At the operational level, the officials' primary task is to provide specific directives and monitor the actual operations to ascertain whether or not they are in line with organizational goals.[3]

The Information Environment

To a degree, public agencies create their own information environment by selecting information sources and deciding what to ignore and what to heed.

Table 2-1 Information Systems Needs for Public Managers

Management level	Type of information needed	Primary sources	Decisions supported	Goals
Organizational—institutional—agency strategic level	Statutory authority, charter, long-term economic and budget resources, forecasting information on political uncertainty, social and technological trends	Executive, legislative, and judicial controllers Charter/laws Economic forecasts Technology forecasts Political environment Constituencies	Overall objectives Budgetary allocations Authority allocation Overall organization structure Level of differentiation and integration External coordination Intergovernmental relations	Acquire statutory authority Acquire budgets Achieve goals, support organizational stability and survival Ensure overall organizational independence
Management—midlevel or coordinating	Control objectives, resources available, long-term needs, operational capability, resource potential	Internal resources Top-level management Operational environment Past performance Financial sources	Allocate financial and personnel resources Ensure alignment of strategy and operations Reallocation of tasks	Resolve organizational conflict Achieve organizational objectives Align goals and set standards
Operational task/supervisory	Task technology, process requirements, resource availability, performance data, financial support, standards development, service impact	Technology requirements Past performance Personnel resources Budget forecasts Clients/recipients Top-level information	Evaluate and monitor operations Task design Procedures Measures needed for evaluation Efficiency determination Cost reduction	Support objectives Efficient operations Low cost Meet standards Align top-, mid-, and operational-level objectives

SOURCE: John M. Stevens and Robert P. McGowan, *Information Systems and Public Management* (New York: Praeger, 1985), 16. Reprinted by permission of Greenwood Publishing Group, Inc., Westport, Conn.

Table 2–2 illustrates the preference for different information sources expressed by staffs of various types of congressional committees. It demonstrates that most agencies must rely on outsiders for information, including "the very actors upon whom they are to confer benefits or harm," and whose information may be slanted accordingly.[4] Staffers on eight congressional committees were asked, "How would you rank the following information sources in terms of importance for your work on this committee staff?" Response options were "very important," "somewhat important," and "not very important." The answers reflect widely varying preferences.[5]

If preferences reflect actual choices accurately, then all staffers relied heavily on information from executive agencies. The majority of staffers on clientele-oriented committees, such as Merchant Marine, Interior, and Public Works also relied heavily on interest-group information, whereas committees such as Armed Services, Budget, and Appropriations slighted these sources. Committee staffers also differed in their regard for information from congressional support agencies, from other committees, and from the staffs in their own offices. In addition, they varied in the extent to which they used information generated during public hearings. Nearly all of the staff members of the Armed Services, Government Operations, and Appropriations Committees claimed to make ample use of information from such hearings.[6] These patterns suggest differential use of sources and, because sources are unique in the information they provide, differential exposure to information. The consequences can be profound.

The array of information sources that public officials consult is in flux. Members of Congress, for example, rely increasingly on outside specialists such as lobbyists from inside and outside government, on expert consultants, and on their own staffs for information inputs. These specialists filter information, provide facts and opinions, and often initiate proposals. Each congressional office, as well as each congressional committee and even subcommittee, tends to develop its own group of experts who determine what information needs to be considered and how it should be evaluated. Consequently, political subsystems often are isolated from each other, constructing and living in their own communication ghettoes and basing decisions on their unique information bases, including their lists of preferred Web sites.

For example, in the health care field, it has been difficult for states to ensure that citizens pay fair prices for treatments, regardless of where they live. Healthcare organizations in the various states use different accounting methods so that comparable statistics are unavailable. To ameliorate the problem, many states have created health data collection agencies whose findings are published. Still, major obstacles to interstate comparisons remain because states vary in the kinds of data they collect and in their data collection specifications.[7]

There is also much duplication of effort in data collection. From an efficiency perspective, legislators should use the same information sources to

Table 2-2 Percentage of Congressional Committee Staffers Calling Various Information Sources "Very Important"

Question: "How would you rank the following information sources in terms of importance for your work on this committee staff?" (Close-ended responses provided: very important, somewhat important, not very important.)

	Merchant Marine	Budget	Interior	Armed Services	Public Works	Government Operations	Ways & Means	Appropriations
Executive agency	87%	88%	78%	100%	87%	94%	78%	94%
Interest groups	53	12	67	7	57	39	53	18
Congressional support agencies	53	83	39	36	52	39	59	23
Other committees	20	39	22	29	30	28	12	12
Personal offices	0	12	22	29	17	17	18	0
Total number	15	18	18	14	23	18	18	17

SOURCE: Adapted from Edward I. Sidlow and Beth Henschen, "The Performance of House Committee Staff Functions: A Comparative Exploration," *Western Political Quarterly* 38 (Sept. 1985): 486–487. Reprinted by permission of the University of Utah, copyright holder.

NOTE: In the spring of 1982, 305 questionnaires were mailed; 140 were returned for a response rate of 46 percent. The response rate did not vary significantly across committees.

ensure a uniform base for decision making and to avoid duplication. But sharing sources would also reduce diversity and impoverish the information pool available for decisions. Moreover, major turf battles are apt to develop about control over information gathering and processing and the choice of experts. People on opposite sides of the political fence are likely to want dissimilar experts and data and are likely to arrange the data in self-serving patterns. It is akin to contending sides in a lawsuit who reach widely disparate conclusions by constructing their arguments from different pieces of the evidence.

Agencies lack complete control over their information environment. Political considerations may force them to rely on sources that they would not freely choose. Time and money stringencies may put limits on information gathering, as may difficulties in locating desired sources. Because they are not fully familiar with technological information, agency personnel often become pawns of technical experts. For example, during the early years of the space flight program, NASA deferred almost completely to the judgments and recommendations of technical experts whose conclusions could not be challenged because of the complexity of the enterprise. Social and political concerns may be slighted when technical experts dominate decision making.[8]

Capture by technical experts is not the only information trap in which government agencies may get caught more or less unwittingly. Stereotypes held by members of organizations or circulating in their environment may preclude open-minded information searches. "Francis Bacon's warning that man converts his words into idols that darken his understanding is as pertinent today as it was three centuries ago."[9] For instance, once safety engineers have labeled nuclear energy plants inherently unsafe, agency personnel may think only about shutting them down. Information searches for less drastic measures are unlikely to be encouraged. Likewise, once agency personnel have made a policy choice, information searches and interpretations will focus primarily on data supporting the choice rather than on countervailing information.[10]

Symbolic and Tactical Data

Most of the information collected by public agencies relates to their mission. It is "instrumental." However, it may be necessary to collect information for symbolic and tactical purposes as well. For instance, agencies frequently collect information from diverse publics primarily to symbolize that government is run democratically. The informational base for a particular policy or issue under consideration may already be firmly established. Nonetheless, a series of public hearings may be held. These hearings, in addition to symbolizing democratic procedures, are a valuable tactic that permits people to let off steam.

Similarly, many of the data solicited from experts are used largely as window dressing. When decisions misfire, and highway surfaces crumble prematurely or computer systems fail to function, expert testimony may help save face for executives. They can absolve themselves by blaming the problem on faulty expert advice. Reports by bureaucrats are often structured primarily to promote their agency's long-range goals, such as enhancing its funding, obscuring its shortcomings, or creating an overly rosy image of successful performance. Exaggerating budgetary needs in anticipation of routine budget trimming by funding bodies has become a pervasive ritual.[11]

Many study reports are commissioned merely to symbolize governmental concern about problems, with no expectation that they will lead to action of any kind. As one wit put it, members of Congress want "vindicators" rather than "indicators." For example, to quiet concerns about U.S. military policy, the Reagan administration commissioned a study of long-term strategies, which took a year to complete and cost $1.6 million. It featured a star cast of investigators, including high military brass, two former secretaries of state, and well-known scholars of defense policy. Although its recommendations were cautious, the administration knew that the report was doomed to join the huge array of similar reports gathering the dust of oblivion.

In addition to the usual reasons for burying reports, this particular one faced the additional handicap of being commissioned by a lame-duck administration. Incoming administrations, for tactical reasons, are rarely willing to base their operations on information packages assembled by their predecessors. To compound the problem, the State Department had been alienated early on when the Defense Department, rather than State, was selected as sponsor of the study. Besides, influential Pentagon officials disagreed with the basic concepts of the report. Given such formidable opposition, the recommendations made in the report were predictably stillborn. Its sole value was favorable political symbolism, a value often bought at high costs that are nonetheless deemed defensible.[12]

Efforts to make government reports politically palatable to diverse constituencies often doom their usefulness. When report writers who represent many different interests must combine many points of view, the "result is seldom a forceful analysis or a strong presentation of a position. Positions and analyses are watered down. Obtaining consensus on the report often means either leaving out so many points that the paper is bland or putting in so many points that it is wishy-washy."[13] As a consequence, many reports requested by legislative bodies and other oversight agencies, while placating their constituencies, are useless for decision making or problem solving.

Tactical considerations frequently determine what structures will be created to collect and process information. Such structural decisions may have profound, often unexpected consequences for information flows. For example, transacting congressional business through task-specific rather than geographically organized committees has put the focus on nationwide policy concerns rather than on policy geared to the needs of individual states or regions. Tactical maneuvers to control structures to shape functions are discussed more fully in the next chapter.

Whether information will be used instrumentally or tactically often depends on the phase of policymaking. A study of congressional committees' use of information available from the Office of Technology Assessment (OTA) documents that policymakers are most likely to make instrumental use of technical information when they are not yet committed to a particular solution to a problem and are groping for an acceptable policy.[14] This is most common during the early stages of deliberation. If policymakers are partially committed, they use information largely to support, extend, and refine the preferred policy. If they have made a strong commitment to a well-defined position, they use information tactically to reconfirm the merits of their position and to advocate it.

The level of political conflict surrounding particular decisions is also crucial. When conflict is high, tactical use of information increases to support the positions that have already been taken. When the conflict level is low, information is more likely to be used instrumentally to adopt or to extend and refine a chosen policy. Overall, the greater the concern about an issue, the greater is the use of information for all purposes.[15]

Information-Gathering Strategies

Gathering information is complex and requires careful planning to obtain the most useful data at the lowest cost. Usually there are many search design options, each with different advantages and drawbacks. Selecting the best is partly science, partly art and intuition, and partly plain, old-fashioned luck.

Finding and Choosing Information

The explosive growth of available information confronts all types of organizations with a number of difficult choices. In the first place, they must decide how to locate potentially salient information. All along they must keep in mind that information gathering, processing, and storing is costly in time, money, and human resources. It is expensive to provide facilities where communication can take place, such as meeting rooms, broadcast studios, communication equipment, supplies, and labor. It takes time for agency personnel to compose, transcribe, and present data. It also takes time and effort to receive messages and interpret them, particularly when they are very complex. Preparing reports and publications is costly, even for making contact with informants or attending hearings. In fact, the high cost of gathering information may be an incentive for retaining past policies whenever possible and preferring incremental changes to major policy revisions. Limiting message input has the added advantage of avoiding information that might disturb a carefully constructed prior consensus.[16]

Possibilities for collecting information include retrieving it from recent and long-term organizational memory, generating it through reading or research, or contacting others who may have the information. When political scientist Herbert Kaufman observed six federal bureau chiefs in action over a one-year period, he found that they used all three tactics for intelligence gathering. Conferring singly or in group meetings with knowledgeable people including consultants, lobbyists, and pollsters took up 60 to 75 percent of their time.[17] Much of it was spent receiving and giving information over the telephone. Reading old and new reports came next, and direct observation of crucial situations was last. In addition, bureau chiefs gathered information through their own reflections and during special briefings before meetings, press conferences, and congressional inquiries. The chiefs were from the Forest Service, the Social Security Administration, the Food and Drug Administration, the Internal Revenue Service, the Customs Service, and the Animal and Plant Health Inspection Service in the Department of Agriculture.

Once they have gained access to information, officials must determine what is essential and then ignore or discard what is not. The remainder must be encoded into messages that convey particular meanings. This usually entails considerable paring of the information and is done at the lower organizational levels. As a consequence, top executives work with extracts selected and condensed by their subordinates rather than with the complete set of data. If these subordinates are savvy and attuned to their chief's needs and desires, the process benefits the organization because it would be impossible for top officials to deal effectively with the copious stream of raw data. But if subordinates do a poor job, especially if they omit or distort important information, the top echelon's effectiveness is seriously compromised.

Although it is essential to be highly selective to avoid overloading the information transmission and processing channels, it is also important for organizations to keep as fully informed as seems advantageous. Multiple sources must often be tapped for the same information to guard against depending on a single source that might be biased or otherwise flawed. To conserve resources, decisions need to be made through "satisficing"—gathering enough information to make a reasonably good choice likely—rather than "optimizing" procedures, which would entail gathering or using all the data that might possibly affect the decision. The bureau chiefs observed by Kaufman seemed to place the highest priorities on three types of information: data related to important pending decisions, information to appraise their agency's performance in relation to its goals and resources, and information needed to avoid embarrassment should questions about it arise.[18]

The last category reflects the fact that many executives in the public sector must endure innumerable interrogations by political superiors and often by journalists as well. This forces them to keep on top of a great deal of information that they might otherwise ignore because it is not directly germane to their jobs. In particular, they believe that it is essential to be informed about incipient problems so that corrections can be made before outside agencies become alerted and publicize these problems.

Selecting information to make decisions usually involves examining various options prepared by staff members, along with projections of their positive and negative consequences. Chiefs appraise the agency's internal performance largely by studying the periodically required reports of its activities and by direct observation during occasional visits undertaken by agency executives for other reasons. Because so many decisions need to be made about general policy directions, as well as specific programs, budget, and personnel matters and the like, top-level executives must handle vast amounts of information even though data collection and initial processing have been done at lower levels.[19] How information can be reduced to manageable proportions will be discussed more fully in Chapter 6.

Intelligence gathering is usually best during the early years of an organization's life, before routines have hardened. During these years organizations tend to hire innovative leaders. Once policies are established, the emphasis is on continuity, and people are chosen and socialized accordingly. Except during periods of rapid technology changes, like the proliferation of computers and the creation of the Internet, new approaches to information gathering often face resistance. The early innovators cast their information nets widely to resolve the many uncertainties faced by new organizations. By contrast, in established organizations, well-socialized professionals and bureaucrats follow in the tracks already laid out for them.

Access Barriers

Gaining access to needed information frequently poses serious difficulties for public organizations. Information storage and retrieval practices may be to blame. For example, high turnover of key personnel, which is common at the executive levels of the public service, means loss of organizational memories about important past events. So do reporting systems that are inadequate or improper for the kind of information retrieval that is needed. A study of tainted food shipped to school lunch rooms across the United States revealed that national and state food safety inspection agencies rarely notified schools about serious contamination problems in the food supplier's kitchens.[20] Similarly, when records of AIDS patients are filed according to disease symptoms to protect the individual's privacy, rather than by name and social security number, these records may be useless for retrieving information on particular patients. Information stored on e-mail only can be easily wiped out when computer systems are changed or become corrupted. This allegedly happened to White House files that were subpoenaed during President Bill Clinton's second term. Methods to restore deleted files exist, but they are costly.

Resistance to Disclosure. It is often very difficult for regulatory agencies such as the Justice Department's Anti-Trust Division, the EPA, the Occupational Safety and Health Administration (OSHA), or transportation safety agencies to secure potentially incriminating information from major industries subject to their control. These industries are understandably reluctant to surrender their records. Microsoft, for example, did not want to submit internal e-mail requested by the Justice Department in 1999 and 2000 to facilitate punishing the company severely for alleged antitrust violations.

The Firestone Tire and Rubber Company was equally reluctant to inform the National Highway Traffic Safety Administration (NHTSA) about tire failures that caused numerous serious accidents in 1977–1978 and again in 1999–2000.[21] Firestone blamed the problems on mishandling by consumers but refused in the earlier case to comply with a NHTSA request to make its complaint records available. It took a court order to force the release of the data. Firestone then supplied massive amounts of raw data shortly before the deadline set by the court, putting a tremendous burden on NHTSA to scrutinize it. When analyzed, the data showed that Firestone knew of the problems long before NHTSA entered the fray.[22] New federal laws that mandate reports to NHTSA about customer complaints about tire failures may prevent similar problems in the future.

The magnitude of information involved in many regulation cases is illustrated by the government's attempts to secure information from General Motors about the safety of the brakes on some of its models. There had been complaints that the brakes locked, causing more than 1,500 accidents, 322 injuries, and 17 deaths.[23] NHTSA used its subpoena power to force a reluctant General Motors to release the required information. Ultimately, the government's case came to rest on more than 100,000 documents supporting the charge that General Motors had falsely denied having data about problems with the braking system.

The problems of getting essential information for regulatory policies are not solely a result of private sector intransigence. Agency inefficiencies, many of them caused by understaffing and lack of adequate facilities, are also to blame. The EPA's pesticide-control program provides a case in point. Before pesticides can be sold, the agency must certify that pesticides are safe and effective when used properly. But the EPA lacks the staff to carry out the testing program to obtain required information on the nearly 50,000 certifiable products manufactured by 10,000 firms. It must therefore rely on the experimental results provided by manufacturers. If these results or the underlying tests are flawed, EPA certification about product safety and effectiveness is flawed.[24]

The Food and Drug Administration (FDA) faces similar problems. It relies on physicians to report adverse reactions to approved drugs. But most doctors are unaware of reporting procedures or reluctant to use them. Still, the agency gets roughly 200,000 reports of adverse reactions annually. It has a staff of only fifty people to examine these complaints, hardly enough to deal even with the 10 percent of cases that involve life-threatening situations.[25] The federal government's Centers for Disease Control and Prevention

(CDC), charged with tracking food-born illnesses, records about 15,000 cases a year. Estimates are that the number represents one out of 5,000 of the 76 million actual cases. If all were reported to the CDC and logged, the information load would be overwhelming.[26]

Faulty transmission and withholding of information may also be a problem within agencies. Information is a strategic resource that agency managers hoard because they do not wish to lose control over it.[27] For example, when internal disagreements developed in the EPA about the best way to control air pollution from power-plant emissions, proponents of various approaches deliberately withheld information from each other. The office favoring scrubbing of emissions kept its proposals from the EPA planning office because it knew that the EPA opposed it. In turn, the planning office, instead of consulting internal staffs who might offer undesired advice, commissioned an outside consulting firm to provide information supporting the policies that the EPA leadership favored.[28]

Opting Out. Information-withholding problems of a different kind arise from the frequent political tensions between the government and the academic and nonacademic science community. For example, to implement the building of the Strategic Defense Initiative, a space-based nuclear defense system initially proposed by the Reagan administration, the government needed scientific information already available, or likely to be generated, within the private sector science community. But many American scientists and many universities refused to make their know-how and creative capabilities available to the government because they opposed the project.

Several issues are involved in such refusals. Many scientists face the dilemma of balancing their obligation as citizens to make knowledge available to the government against their convictions that they must refuse to cooperate with a policy they oppose on moral, ethical, or even economic grounds when the research has high commercial value. The government faces the dilemma of needing the expertise of such citizens to carry out controversial policies but lacking acceptable means to compel their cooperation. Its only recourse lies in persuading reluctant scientists that the policy deserves support or using the government's carrot-and-stick policies of financial support for the science community to elicit cooperation.

Shielding Sensitive Information

Privacy Concerns

Privacy rights raise yet another information-gathering problem. The Privacy Act of 1974 was adopted to protect individuals against undue invasion of privacy by disclosure of their records on file with various government agencies (see Box 2–1). The act has changed the nature of government information

Box 2-1 **The Privacy Act**

Public Law 93-579: The Privacy Act of 1974

Be it enacted by the Senate and House of Representatives of the United States of America in Congress assembled, That this Act may be cited as the "Privacy Act of 1974."

Sec. 2.

(a) The Congress finds that—

(1) the privacy of an individual is directly affected by the collection, maintenance, use, and dissemination of personal information by Federal agencies;

(2) the increasing use of computers and sophisticated information technology, while essential to the efficient operations of the Government, has greatly magnified the harm to individual privacy that can occur from any collection, maintenance, use, or dissemination of personal information;

(3) the opportunities for an individual to secure employment, insurance, and credit, and his right to due process, and other legal protections are endangered by the misuse of certain information systems;

(4) the right to privacy is a personal and fundamental right protected by the Constitution of the United States; and

(5) in order to protect the privacy of individuals identified in information systems maintained by Federal agencies, it is necessary and proper for the Congress to regulate the collection, maintenance, use, and dissemination of information by such agencies.

(b) The purpose of this Act is to provide certain safeguards for an individual against an invasion of personal privacy by requiring Federal agencies, except as otherwise provided by law, to—

(1) permit an individual to determine what records pertaining to him are collected, maintained, used, or disseminated by such agencies;

(2) permit an individual to prevent records pertaining to him obtained by such agencies for a particular purpose from being used or made available for another purpose without his consent;

(3) permit an individual to gain access to information pertaining to him in Federal agency records, to have a copy made of all or any portion thereof, and to correct or amend such records;

(4) collect, maintain, use, or disseminate any record of identifiable personal information in a manner that assures that such action is for a necessary and lawful purpose, that the information is current and accurate for its intended use, and that adequate safeguards are provided to prevent misuse of such information;

(5) permit exemptions from the requirements with respect to records provided in this Act only in those cases where there is an important public policy need for such exemption as has been determined by specific statutory authority; and

(6) be subject to civil suit for any damages which occur as a result of willful or intentional action which violates any individual's rights under this Act.

SOURCE: 5 U.S.C., 552 A (1974).

collection and use of such records. It sets out guidelines for sharing personal data files among agencies. It outlines procedures by which individual files and records are maintained by government agencies and gives individuals the right to inspect their files and ask for corrections. Agencies are required to report annually about the character of their record system and are subject to civil and criminal penalties for violations.[29]

New electronic technologies pose ever-increasing challenges to personal privacy. There is as yet no foolproof way to protect information provided by citizens who use the Web sites of various government agencies to search for information or submit information required by the agency to tailor its services to the needs of the client. In fact, many government agencies have been slow to follow the guidelines for privacy protection that they urge business enterprises to follow, aside from warning Web site visitors that the site's information is not secure.[30]

Various government agencies acquire extensive dossiers about individual citizens. They may come from other databases, such as medical records gathered by hospitals, or directly from citizens. Welfare clients, for example, must disclose data about family composition and living arrangements, education and training, economic resources, employment history, job searches, medical status, nationality and citizenship, and past recourse to welfare. Some of these data are germane to the work of other agencies, such as the Immigration Service, various health agencies, the Department of Education, and the Internal Revenue Service (IRS). Yet privacy considerations have long barred many of these public bodies from sharing data. For instance, state welfare agencies have found it difficult in the past to gain access to the records of the IRS to check whether a welfare client has concealed paid employment. In most jurisdictions, the records of welfare clients are kept confidential to spare them the embarrassment of having their economic needs becoming public knowledge.

In 1984 the Senate finally passed legislation requiring the IRS to share income data about recipients of government aid with a variety of federal and state agencies.[31] The legislation affects the financial records of many millions of people in programs such as Medicaid, aid for dependent children, food stamps, and unemployment compensation. Despite cutbacks in some programs such as food stamps, Medicaid, and unemployment compensation, the numbers of recipients continue to grow, raising new data-sharing and privacy issues.

To skirt the Privacy Act, the 1984 data-sharing law stipulated that information about aid recipients would *not* come from individual tax returns, which were deemed confidential. Instead, they would come from reports of payouts made by employers, banks, brokerage houses, and similar private sources. The government collects such records to cross-check individual returns. The legislation authorized computer-matching programs to detect discrepancies in information received by government agencies. The goal was to reduce fraud in various programs providing medical care for the poor, unemployment benefits, and aid to dependent children. Aid could not be terminated under the law until the information released by the IRS for matching had been verified and until recipients had the opportunity to protest the cutoff.

Congress had previously authorized the sharing of income information in connection with state and local efforts to track down parents who were delinquent in paying child support. The benefits flowing from these efforts to discourage fraud have to be weighed against the threats to constitutionally protected privacy and due process rights of individuals. The IRS has been accused of acting on the basis of these matches without the safeguards of cross-checking and allowing rebuttal. Moreover in many instances the data are not entirely suitable for the purposes to which the secondary users put them, with unfortunate results. Health benefits may be denied, for example, when individuals earn substantial incomes but are forced to divert them to creditors as part of a bankruptcy settlement. Also the costs of collecting such information may exceed the sums saved by preventing cheating.

Ethical dilemmas abound as well. For instance, when government agencies collect data for one purpose, such as welfare payments, should they be used for another, like tracking down parole violators? People may volunteer information for one purpose, such as getting rent subsidies, for example, but would not do so for another, such as sending a relative to prison. If information is used for an unforeseen purpose, must people be at least notified that disclosure will occur or has occurred? The Social Security Administration maintains files on most Americans, which cover their age, sex, race, yearly earnings, work and benefit history. Some files also contain information on alcoholism or drug addiction and financial resources other than earned income.[32] Is it ethical to share such data with other agencies without the consent of the individuals whose lives are bared to the gaze of unknown observers? Finally, where does the balance lie between privacy and national security concerns? Should personal records such as e-mails, library and Web site visits, or credit card statements be open to government inspection when that might be helpful in tracking potential serious criminals or terrorists? If so, should it require a court order as a check on government abuse of search powers?

National Security Concerns

Aside from clashes between privacy and national security concerns, the need to shield sensitive information from other agencies and from the public is another formidable information access problem. Technological advances have made it relatively easy to gain access to confidential government documents. Invisible electronic listening devices can be implanted in computers and other electronic appliances. The computer files containing nuclear secrets that disappeared from the Los Alamos Weapons Laboratory in 2000 were the size of a deck of cards, easily concealed in someone's pocket. Passing their content into unauthorized hands and then restoring the complete or altered files to their safe location would have been easy. It required costly scanning operations to check the integrity of the tapes when they suddenly reappeared.

As discussed more fully in Chapter 8, politically inspired leaking of sensitive information has become rampant and may constitute a threat to national security. The problem is further complicated by the often difficult and always controversial task of determining which information is genuinely sensitive and which is not. In the past, the sensitivity label has been misused regularly to hide information that should be open to scrutiny. Security problems become particularly difficult to handle when sensitive and nonsensitive information is intermingled so that one cannot be disclosed without damaging the other. For example, the Justice Department in the 1980s tried to prosecute National Security Council staff members for illegally diverting funds from arms sales to Iran to antigovernment forces in Nicaragua. Its efforts were partially stymied because much of the crucial information was either unavailable to the prosecution and defense or could not be disclosed in open court, forcing prosecutors to drop a number of charges. Similar issues were involved in the 2002 trial of terrorism suspect Zacarias Moussaoui. His request to conduct his own defense raised the specter of having to reveal classified information in open court.

Over the years, the tightness of government secrecy rules has see-sawed. The Clinton administration released massive amounts of classified information after executive orders changed the burden of proof. Protection of information, rather than its release, now required special permission. Agencies must declassify documents held for more than twenty-five years—ten years for new documents—or prove to an appeals panel that they warrant continued secrecy. Previously, declassification hinged on proving that secrecy was no longer needed.[33] That rule led to huge backlogs of classified information. The Energy Department, for example, tended to classify nearly all incoming information about nuclear weapons as secret. By 1996, it had accumulated more than 100 million pages of documents that it wanted to release. But it could not do so because it lacked the resources to scan them so that they could be certified as safe for declassification.[34]

Excessive secrecy is dangerous in an era when public agencies collect increasingly huge amounts of information that may require checking to ascertain its accuracy. Many secret files, such as the Federal Bureau of Investigation (FBI) records, are full of unchecked information, much of it defective. It may come from small numbers of informants without the benefit of open discussion and possible challenges. When its authors remain anonymous, their credibility cannot be checked. Access to secret information is usually granted only to safe, compliant people unlikely to challenge its accuracy. However, the Freedom of Information Act (FOIA) of 1966, as amended in 1996, has eased access to classified files in recent years, facilitating corrections (see Box 2–2). Combined with President Clinton's declassification

Box 2-2 **Statement Issued by President Clinton on Signing the "Electronic Freedom of Information Act Amendments of 1996"**

. . . Enacted in 1966, the Freedom of Information Act (FOIA) was the first law to establish an effective legal right of access to government information, underscoring the crucial need in a democracy for open access to government information by citizens. . . . Since 1966, the world has changed a great deal. Records are no longer principally maintained in paper format. Now, they are maintained in a variety of technologies, including CD ROM and computer tapes and diskettes, making it easier to put more information on-line.

The legislation I sign today brings FOIA into the information and electronic age by clarifying that it applies to records maintained in electronic format. This law also broadens public access to government information by placing more material on-line and expanding the role of the agency reading room. As the Government actively disseminates more information, I hope that there will be less need to use FOIA to obtain government information.

This legislation not only affirms the importance, but also the challenge of maintaining openness in government. In a period of government downsizing, the numbers of requests continue to rise. In addition, growing numbers of requests are for information that must be reviewed for declassification, or in which there is a proprietary interest or a privacy concern. The result in many agencies is huge backlogs of requests.

In this Act, the Congress recognized that with today's limited resources, it is frequently difficult to respond to a FOIA request within the 10 days formerly required in the law. This legislation extends the legal response period to 20 days.

More importantly, it recognizes that many FOIA requests are so broad and complex that they cannot possibly be completed even within this longer period, and the time spent processing them only delays other requests. Accordingly, H.R. 3802 establishes procedures for an agency to discuss with requesters ways of tailoring large requests to improve responsiveness. This approach explicitly recognizes that FOIA works best when agencies and requesters work together.

Our country was founded on democratic principles of openness and accountability, and for 30 years, FOIA has supported these principles. Today, the "Electronic Freedom of Information Act Amendments of 1996" reforges an important link between the United States Government and the American people.

SOURCE: U.S. Department of Justice, Office of Information and Privacy, H.R. 3802, http://www.usdoj.gov/oip/f...dates/Vol_XVII_4/page2.htm

orders, it has also increased the danger that genuinely sensitive information will be jeopardized.

Access to guarded information is most difficult when it is controlled by multiple intelligence agencies or police departments. The generally cautious behavior of public agencies fosters a tendency to exaggerate security threats. Bureaucrats know that it is safer to be overzealous in classifying documents as secret than to permit access to them and be reprimanded for exposing secrets. Once the information cat is out of the proverbial bag, it is irretrievable. In the past, courts have usually supported refusals to disclose information when they were based on claims that disclosure might endanger national security. The *Pentagon Papers* case may have changed that permanently: The court sanctioned media coverage of foreign policy documents about U.S. activities in war-torn Vietnam that the Nixon administration had tried to shield.[35] The judges disagreed with the government's claim that national security was at stake.

Nonetheless, when the United States has become involved in military operations, such as attacks on Taliban strongholds in Afghanistan in 2001, the Persian Gulf War in 1991, the Panama intervention in 1989 to 1990, and the Grenada intervention in 1983, military censors severely restrict access to information. In the Persian Gulf War, for example, reporters were allowed to observe front-line operations only as members of pools arranged and supervised by the military. Most of the time, top-level military commanders refused to answer questions that would shed light on plans and operations, claiming that responses would endanger the conduct of the war. Under such circumstances, journalists have little chance to contest such policies.

During the Reagan years, controls were especially tight to protect scientific information that had military applications and to limit the right of foreigners to obtain research data on technological breakthroughs such as high-temperature superconductors. Numerous U.S. scientists, concerned about what they considered excessive government secrecy, were therefore leaving research jobs with the government or refusing to take such positions. They feared that military reviewers might veto publication of their findings from sensitive but unclassified research. They were also concerned about the damaging consequences of throttling unhampered scientific dialogue.[36]

Therapeutic Ignorance

Although secrecy is a problem, uncontrolled access to information coupled with excessive publicity can be equally damaging to the public welfare. Many institutions, such as drug firms, grocery chains, and stock exchanges depend on public confidence. When reports drawn from government investigations into the safety of their services and products suggest that they may have betrayed the public trust, such institutions can be ruined because the reports enjoy credibility and usually receive wide publicity. Being exonerated of the charges does not restore losses suffered or even restore confidence. Suspicions linger. This happened, for example, in 1989 in the wake of news that the EPA was investigating the safety of Alar, a potentially cancer-causing chemical used by apple growers to enhance the quality of the fruit. Although the cancer danger proved groundless, apple sales declined sharply, hurting the economies of apple-growing states. Industry representatives estimated the losses in 1989 at more than $100 million, roughly 10 percent of total sales. A portion of this loss was expected to be permanent because it came from cancellations of orders by school districts unwilling to take any chances with children's health.[37] Financial markets are particularly vulnerable to damage when rumors circulate.

Certain types of knowledge may actually harm organizations by undercutting morale or paralyzing actions. "Therapeutic ignorance," as Harold Wilensky calls it, may indeed be bliss.[38] For instance, a survey of top administrators of sixty-two social service agencies in central Iowa disclosed that knowledge about imminent budget cuts led to drastic, often unwarranted service curtailments.[39] By contrast, when budget cuts were only a possibility, rather than a certainty, administrators developed creative strategies to manage with fewer resources. Similarly, when agency members were unaware of major threats facing their agency, they were less likely to be paralyzed by fear.

It may also be good for subordinates to be unaware of the foibles of their superiors so that they retain faith, respect, and high morale. This accounts for the common practice of explaining high-level personnel changes in terms of innocuous reasons such as illness or the executive's personal wishes rather than disclosing his or her incompetence or dishonesty. Similarly, to keep up morale, it may even be essential to maintain false stereotypes about the organization that enhance its image and that of its personnel. Finally, many organizations benefit from concealing information about salaries paid to various staff people, thereby avoiding jealousies and possible difficulties with workers, either singly or collectively.

Information may be particularly harmful at certain times. For instance, controversial legislation—such as tax increases, immigration issues, or abortion limitations—often is postponed during election years because news about incumbents' positive votes could harm their political fortunes.

Similarly, some information may be too politically sensitive for open discussion during a particular historical period. When a White House conference on civil rights in June 1966 wanted to focus on the problems of the black family, the organizers canceled it when they were warned that critical remarks might be construed as racism. By 1984 this sensitivity to criticism had lessened so that a conference called by the National Association for the Advancement of Colored People (NAACP) and the National Urban League could schedule the topic for discussion.

The Carter and Reagan administrations shied away from discussing the emotionally explosive issue of artificial insemination of a woman willing to produce a child for a sperm donor and his wife. The two presidents avoided the debate by refusing to appoint members to an unstaffed federal ethics advisory committee.[40] Congress, equally timorous, allowed its own commission on bioethics and its fourteen-member advisory commission to remain inactive. The failure to discuss and agree on national public policies in this controversial area of human reproduction has led to a maze of conflicting state regulations and has paralyzed publicly financed fetal and embryo research. But it has allowed federal agencies to delay action in the probably vain hope that societal consensus about these matters will eventually evolve.

Rather than stopping discussion entirely when politically touchy issues are involved, agencies may opt for partial suppression of information or for framing it in ways that reap political benefits. Several techniques have been widely used.[41] Agencies can report information selectively, omitting those parts that might harm their cause. In making reports, they can turn to favorable "experts" to support their claims and avoid unfavorable experts. They can also bury important information in low-level reports that are unlikely to arouse the attention of decision makers. Finally, agencies can submit so much information that the receivers are swamped and cannot digest it.

The latter tactic recognizes the fact that an oversupply of information creates serious problems. Too much information is as bad as—and sometimes even worse than—too little. This fact is often forgotten in American culture, where the mantra is that "more is better" and that ample information about problems permits their solution. This is false, of course. As James Q. Wilson pointed out, a large amount of information does not necessarily constitute "a full, accurate, and properly nuanced body of knowledge about important matters." Rather, it may be "a torrent of incomplete facts, opinions, guesses, and self-serving statements about distant events."[42] The overload can overwhelm an organization's processing capacities and grind operations to a halt. Moreover, piles of data may merely reinforce what is already known about a problem. Military and police intelligence services, for example, are particularly prone to accumulating unmanageable amounts of redundant information about security problems. Much of it sits in unopened files where nuggets of vital data languish along with the chaff. Horror stories about available information that might have prevented the 1941 attack on Pearl Harbor and assaults on the World Trade Center in 1993 and 2001 are part of a long list of examples.

Overload sometimes springs from excessive internal communication. To prevent units of various organizations from inundating each other with messages, restrictions on the number, length, or subject matter of interoffice memos may become necessary. Without such restrictions, officials may find that their other duties suffer. For example, President Richard Nixon estimated that 42 million documents passed through his office during his tenure and that he personally attended to some 200,000.[43] The draconian whittling still left him with an obvious overload. The nearly universal use of e-mail has made the problem infinitely worse since the Nixon era.

Surmounting Information Hurdles

Legislation

Congress has tried to address various information-gathering problems that plague the public sector. The Paperwork Reduction Act of 1980, revised in 1995, is designed to reduce excessive paperwork, which is costly in terms of money and labor and produces information overloads that delay governmental activities (see Box 2–3).[44] The revised act sets annual reduction targets in the public's paperwork burden of 10 percent for 1996 and 1997 and 5 percent annually until new goals are set in 2002. The act establishes clear accountability for managing information resources by mandating the designation of chief information officers for federal agencies.[45] A council composed of some of these officers and chaired by the deputy director of the Office of Management and Budget (OMB) serves as an interagency forum to develop and coordinate overall information policies. The act also establishes an implementing Office of Information and Regulatory Affairs (OIRA) in OMB. The OIRA reviews tests, inspection procedures, labeling, and disclosure requirements, as well as records, questionnaires and forms used for applications, census data, and taxes.[46]

On its face this appears to be a nonpolitical office, but the facts are otherwise. Choosing messages for elimination can be highly political. For example, OMB embroiled itself in a major political battle when it proposed to eliminate thirty questions from the 1990 census. OMB claimed that the information duplicated data collected at state and local levels about the nation's housing supply, energy consumption, population fertility, migration, and participation in the labor force. Groups that had benefited from using federal data about these matters for their own benefit argued otherwise. Such conflicts have often been adjudicated in the federal courts. In 1990, in a case involving communications about hazards in the construction industry, the Supreme Court ruled that the reach of the Paperwork Reduction Act was far narrower than OMB had contended. OMB control extends only to information solicited by government for itself, not to information that government requires private parties to furnish to each other.[47]

Excessive paperwork, producing unneeded information, is common in government because of politically inspired caution. Check, double-check, and triple-check are the watchwords designed to guard against dishonesty and poor performance. To protect their turf and guard against challenges of their performance, agencies may engage in numerous costly and time-consuming studies and analyses to forestall external review or scrutiny. Other contributing

Box 2-3 **Excerpts from the Paperwork Reduction Act of 1995**

Sec. 3508. Determination of necessity for information; hearing

Before approving a proposed collection of information, the Director shall determine whether the collection of information by the agency is necessary for the proper performance of the functions of the agency, including whether the information shall have practical utility. . . . To the extent, if any, that the Director determines that the collection of information by an agency is unnecessary for any reason, the agency may not engage in the collection of information.

Sec. 3510. Cooperation of agencies in making information available

(a) The Director may direct an agency to make available to another agency, or an agency may make available to another agency, information obtained by a collection of information if the disclosure is not inconsistent with applicable law. (b)(1) If information obtained by an agency is released by that agency to another agency, all the provisions of law (including penalties) that relate to the unlawful disclosure of information apply to the officers and employees of the agency to which information is released to the same extent and in the same manner as the provisions apply to the officers and employees of the agency which originally obtained the information. (2) The officers and employees of the agency to which the information is released, in addition, shall be subject to the same provisions of law, including penalties, relating to the unlawful disclosure of information as if the information had been collected directly by that agency.

Sec. 3511. Establishment and operation of Government Information Locator Service

(a) In order to assist agencies and the public in locating information and to promote information sharing and equitable access by the public, the Director shall—(1) cause to be established and maintained a distributed agency-based electronic Government Information Locator Service (hereafter in this section referred to as the "Service"), which shall identify the major information systems, holdings, and dissemination products of each agency; (2) require each agency to establish and maintain an agency information locator service as a component of, and to support the establishment and operation of the Service; (3) in cooperation with the Archivist of the United States, the Administrator of General Services, the Public Printer, and the Librarian of Congress, establish an interagency committee to advise the Secretary of Commerce on the development of technical standards for the Service to ensure compatibility, promote information sharing, and uniform access by the public; (4) consider public access and other user needs in the establishment and operation of the Service; (5) ensure the security and integrity of the Service, including measures to ensure that only information which is intended to be disclosed to the public is disclosed through the Service; and (6) periodically review the development and effectiveness of the Service and make recommendations for improvement, including other mechanisms for improving public access to Federal agency public information. . . .

SOURCE: U.S. Department of Commerce, National Oceanic and Atmospheric Administration, http://www.rdc.noaa.gov/~pra/pralaw.htm

factors, as previously noted, are the vagueness of directives and inadequate communication among agencies, which results in duplication of work.

Another law designed to ease communications is the Information Technology Management Reform Act of 1996. The act requires the director of OMB to monitor and guide the acquisition of information technology by federal government agencies. Agencies must appoint a chief information officer to manage information technologies and report to OMB to ensure intragovernment standardization.

The FOIA of 1966, as mentioned earlier, has eased disclosure of information. It counteracts the tendency of government agencies to keep information secret. Its 1996 version clarifies to what extent the rules apply to electronic communication. However, many uncertainties remain about the duties of public officials to preserve e-mail records electronically or in print and to allow citizens access to them.[48] Nine categories of information are specifically exempted from disclosure under FOIA laws: (1) designated information on national defense or foreign policy; (2) internal personnel rules and practices; (3) information exempted by statute; (4) trade secrets and commercial or financial information obtained as privileged or confidential; (5) interagency and intraagency memoranda or letters that would not otherwise be available by law; (6) personnel and medical files when disclosure would constitute an unwarranted invasion of personal privacy; (7) investigatory files compiled for law enforcement; (8) various reports required of financial institutions; and (9) geological and geophysical information and data about wells. If enemies of the United States used this information to destroy important resources, national security might suffer.

Freedom of information laws at the state level parade under diverse names, such as public records, public information, right to know, open government, and uniform information practices acts. They are similar to the federal laws, although some state laws are somewhat more restrictive and rules about availability of e-mails are not universally included. The fact that these laws exist and are drafted to make access to information easy does not necessarily mean that they are carried out according to the letter and spirit of the law. A study conducted to ascertain whether the city of Chicago had implemented a mayoral freedom of information executive order first promulgated eight years earlier disclosed numerous compliance gaps. Moreover, several freedom of information officers whose job called for easing the public's access to information refused to respond to inquiries. Telephone calls to the appeals office also remained unanswered.[49] Such noncompliance has been common at all levels. When serious issues are involved, requesters of information have repeatedly taken the matter to court, usually successfully.

Freedom of information laws are helpful in providing access to otherwise hidden information, but only when investigators know that the information exists and search it out and publicize it. A good example are the files of President Ronald Reagan's Secretary of Housing and Urban Development,

Samuel R. Pierce Jr. Normally this treasure trove of evidence of corrupt dealings would have remained buried and untouched in storage boxes and computer files. There is no regular scrutiny of the mountains of information accumulated year by year by public agencies at all levels of government. In Pierce's case, charges of massive corruption in the office happened to surface. Newspeople then requested and received access to these files, thanks to the FOIA.[50] (Several HUD officials went to prison for misappropriating low-cost housing loan funds. Pierce took responsibility for misconduct by HUD personnel but was never indicted.)

Judicial Proceedings and Other Remedies

As discussed earlier, government agencies often encounter resistance when they seek high-quality information. Most agencies have limited resources and often insufficient authority to conduct full-scale investigations on their own. They are forced to depend on the willingness of sister agencies and private-sector companies to share their databases. That may entail secondary uses of information that often has been gathered for different purposes. Getting unbiased information is especially difficult for regulatory agencies trying to investigate harmful behaviors by powerful private-sector enterprises.

Government agencies have several ways to extract information when other organizations deny access to their data.[51] *Judicial proceedings* are one approach. Agencies may seek a court order to obtain information—but only when their opponents are obligated by law to disclose it. When that avenue is foreclosed, the government may sue recalcitrants, although that process is not ideal for getting complete information. In a lawsuit the contending parties define the issues narrowly, as do courts. That tends to disclose less than the full picture. In many cases it may be evident from the start that full disclosure will be elusive, so that attempting to elicit it may not even be worthwhile. When private-sector agencies have near-monopoly status, as the Bell telephone system did before its breakup, it becomes particularly difficult to get the necessary information to regulate them appropriately.

Public agencies can also try to get at the truth through *expert testimony*. This route, too, entails problems. Scientists often have political motivations, so that their testimony corresponds to their own or their employer's political orientation. In fact, the most highly regarded scientists in many technical fields are paid consultants for industry or have received research grants from industry that may create a conflict of interest when government requests their services. The nature of the specialized knowledge brought to bear on particular situations may also color the outcome. If, for example, psychiatrists are invited as consultants in a court case involving the adequacy of safety devices, a psychiatrically based solution is far more likely than if engineers or economists are the chief consultants. Thus the nature of the expertise that is tapped shapes the nature of the truth that will be found.

Although expert testimony is not infallible, it is tempting to accept it uncritically. When special-interest groups provide information on issues of concern to them, countervailing intelligence is essential but often unavailable. For example, transportation lobbies have often made an excellent case and received resources for highway construction. At the same time, mass transit has been starved for resources because it lacked a good lobby to present its case effectively.

Legislative investigations are yet another avenue to discover information. Legislators draw on a broad array of informants who have access to more knowledge than would be available to individual experts. They also often capture wide public attention through media coverage, which may elicit input from previously untapped sources. The problem with legislative investigations is that much of the information submitted and widely publicized may be unverified and even unverifiable. The mere fact that the proceedings are publicized may affect what will and will not surface. Witnesses may try to play to the galleries rather than focus on the truth. Moreover, there is no assurance that all views that ought to be exposed are represented in public hearings.

Fact-finding commissions are a British contribution to truth-finding devices. Although they limit themselves to investigations, taking no action, they frequently have led to major social reforms. British royal commissions often explore the feasibility of policies with people who are the targets of prospective policies, allowing them input into policy formation. This makes nongovernmental elites part of the policy process. Commission findings arouse public attention, but that does not usually harden policy proposals because binding decisions are far off.

A final way of discovering truth consists of building *countervailing information* sources. President Franklin D. Roosevelt did this by overlapping the responsibilities of various agencies and individuals; Congress has done it by duplicating presidential information sources. The information provided by OMB, for example, can be checked against comparable data collected by the Congressional Budget Office. This tactic will be discussed more fully in Chapter 6.

Judging Information Quality and Quantity

Quality Indicators

Finding needed information is not the only problem. One must also be concerned with the quality of the information collected. Harold Wilensky, in his pioneering studies on gathering information (which he refers to as "intelligence"), indicates that high-quality information must have six characteristics.[52] It must be clear, timely, reliable, valid, comprehensive, and diverse. If it lacks these qualities, policies will suffer, as will the millions of citizens whose lives are shaped to varying degrees by these policies.[53]

Clarity. Above all, information must be clear to those who use it. Enough information must be made available so that it can be interpreted in a meaningful context. Clarity also means that it must be encoded, either by the original source or by those who transmit it to the organization, in ways that can be readily understood by the users. It must avoid typical bureaucratic jargon, in which cutbacks are "resource reallocations" and tax increases become "revenue enhancements."

The complexity of the public business and the diversity of its clientele are the chief barriers to clarity, though deliberate obfuscation also plays a part. For example, real estate agents must be informed about complex open-housing laws, contractors have to learn about building and zoning codes, and tax consultants have to administer constantly changing tax laws. Lack of clarity in the directives transmitted by government to such business groups creates major problems in implementing public policies effectively.

Much important information intended for various clientele remains unused because it is encoded in ways that are ill-suited to the capacities of the intended users. For example, the FDA requires warning labels to be attached to medicines to alert consumers to potentially serious problems, but the warnings are largely ignored because they are too detailed and couched in excessively technical language. Bulletin boards at public agencies describing available services remain unread because their messages are too complicated. The directions provided by the IRS to its millions of clients are a prime example of government instructions that are far too complex to be useful to average citizens. No wonder that cartoonists regularly poke fun at the notorious density of the typical income tax form. (See the cartoon in Chapter 7.)

Fuzziness is particularly serious when it occurs in communications between legislatures and public agencies. Legislative directives concerning the activities of public agencies are often exceedingly vague. That makes it difficult to discern the precise legislative intent and also easy to evade it if bureaucrats so desire, as they frequently do. Interest groups commonly take advantage of flexibility in interpretation to push bureaucrats to make decisions in their favor. A typical example of a vague power grant is the congressional mandate to the Federal Communications Commission (FCC) to exercise its regulatory powers to "serve the public interest, convenience and necessity."[54] Over the years, the meaning of the phrase has sparked countless debates whenever FCC policies have been challenged as contrary to these goals and defended as complying with them.

A 1989 survey of 1,075 county and municipal officials responsible for hiring decisions revealed that the concept of "affirmative action," which was to guide employment policies, was widely misunderstood. Fifty-six percent of the officials wrongly thought that affirmative action requires preferential treatment for women and minorities. In effect, the law requires employers only to alert minorities to job opportunities and to give them an equal chance to be hired. The widespread misunderstanding produced faulty employment decisions and unequal application of the law in different cities and counties.[55]

The reasons for vague legislative directions are manifold. Besides the complexity of the issues with which governmental institutions must deal, they include the unpredictability of future circumstances. When language must cover unforeseen and unforeseeable contingencies, it cannot be specific and to the point. Moreover, consensus is often lacking about the best ways to accomplish desired objectives. This is especially true when the area of government activity is new, such as environmental protection policies, and when the expertise to devise appropriate solutions is still questionable. Precise guidelines may be technically and politically difficult to frame.

Legislators often choose vague language to protect their political hides by avoiding clear choices that could alienate constituents. They believe that bureaucrats can make unpopular decisions with more impunity because they do not face elections. In return for avoiding the wrath of constituents and interest groups, they are willing to pay the price of bestowing nearly unlimited discretion on bureaucrats. Vague legislative directions lead to more or less welcome second-guessing by bureaucrats about what the legislators had in mind. These guesses, molded by the bureaucrats' own preferences, often stray far from the legislators' intentions.

Timeliness. In addition to being clear, good messages also must be timely. They must be available when needed and be kept up-to-date. For instance, vulnerable citizens must know about the availability of an immunization program to protect them from the influenza many months before an epidemic strikes. Similarly, people who are trying to influence decision making in governmental agencies, including legislative bodies, must make sure that their information reaches these bodies before the decision process has hardened and narrowed down to a few options.

The stereotypical image of public agencies working at a snail's pace is widespread because it is reinforced by a steady succession of examples. For instance, when top-secret computer hard drives carrying nuclear secrets disappeared from the Los Alamos Weapons Laboratory in 2000, the loss was not discovered for two months. It took nearly another month before Energy Secretary Bill Richardson, the official responsible for U.S. nuclear safety, learned about the missing data and informed Congress. Department of Energy regulations specify an eight-hour deadline for reporting security breeches.[56] When the FBI announced in 2001 that it urgently needed Arab-language specialists, it took several months to prepare and administer tests and several more months to get security clearance for prospective employees.

Reliability. Good intelligence must also be reliable. This means that it should be correct, unambiguous, and consistent so that bureaucrats do not receive contradictory messages. For example, in 1987 the chief of the IRS's field branch in Baltimore issued a directive instructing agents to seize property promptly when taxpayers failed to honor a demand for payment. He indicated that promotions would be linked to the number of property seizures made by IRS agents and the amount of money they collected. These instructions ran directly counter to directives issued by IRS commissioner Lawrence Gibbs, which prohibited linking employee rewards to the harshness of enforcement measures. The case is typical of instances when written directives from the central administration clash with verbal instructions passed on to field staffs.[57] The staffs are torn between relying on agency directives or on those issued by their immediate superiors. They usually obey the people with whom they have the most direct contact.

Validity. Good information must also be valid. Concepts and measures used must be logically consistent and reflect the real world, rather than totally unrealistic conditions. The reports must be free from pressure to distort information, as happened in reports about security at the Los Alamos National Laboratory. After security breeches had been reported at the top-secret nuclear research facility, sizable numbers of employees acknowledged slanting their safety survey responses to make the lab look good.[58] Validity may also be threatened by the biases of the information source. Much information flows to public agencies from interest groups that present data and analyses structured to favor particular conclusions.[59] For example, air pollution measurements may be recorded on an exceptionally windy day when noxious elements are less likely to be detected.

Even information from specially commissioned research is often flawed. Thus a careful validity check of a report on a multicity survey, commissioned to determine the causes of juvenile delinquency, found twenty-five common errors, omissions, and ambiguities.[60] They included inaccurate factual claims, faulty sampling procedures in selecting juveniles for study, and deemphasis of problematic aspects of the research findings. The investigators attributed these faults to the research agency's desire to gloss over flaws in the execution of the project and to produce a politically pleasing report likely to lead to future research contracts. Some of the flaws had resulted from bureaucratic procedures mandating rigid research guidelines as part of the original contract award. Such guidelines are common in government-sponsored research. They may take the form of fixed timetables for each phase of the research, requirements regarding the hiring of research personnel and subcontractors, and precise specification of the issues to be addressed by the final report.

Research reports may also convey incorrect messages when the raw data produced by external researchers are presented without adequate contextual information. Managers with limited training in statistics may misinterpret the raw data. For example, managers may conflate statistical and practical significance of the data. They may not be alert to the intricacies of comparing groups of varying sizes.[61] Flawed research reports result in invalid information for policymaking and difficulty in replicating improperly reported projects.

Depth. Wilensky's remaining two points relate to the ampleness of the information gathered. He points out that intelligence must be adequate, including all essential facts about the situation. It must also be wide-ranging so that a broad array of options are presented. By and large, feedback about an agency's activities and even about the helpfulness of its reports is what is most lacking. When the eye is on the here and now, an in-depth focus on the past and the future tends to get lost. A National Research Council report, for example, noted that the EPA, despite its concern with excellence in data collection, had failed to develop systematic self-evaluation measures.[62] Wilensky's stipulation that all essential facts must become available begs the difficult question of which facts are essential and which merely contribute to information overload. For instance, when prospective employees are screened for jobs in a particular agency, is it essential to know their policy preferences or party affiliation? A good case can be made for either a yes or a no answer. It may be good that they are ideologically attuned to the policies that the agency is trying to promote. Or it may be valuable that they take a critical stance, questioning the pet theories of the agency's old-timers.

Judgments of adequacy also hinge on the goals sought by bureaucrats and on their operating styles. Many agencies are interested primarily in planning policy for the short-term, ignoring information that would be important for long-term estimates. Some users of intelligence, such as lawyers and military professionals, want primarily "facts," shunning interpretations. Other officials deem information inadequate if it is presented without context and fails to suggest an appropriate interpretation. Members of Congress, for example, do not want undigested, unprocessed information. Instead, they like a combination of facts, values, and suggestions for action.[63]

As Table 2–1 illustrates, the information needs of people in an organization may vary widely, especially at different levels of the hierarchy. Agency heads may want the very information that their subordinates are least willing to provide. An example might be information about a new computer program that can perform the tasks currently done by workers whose jobs could be eliminated. Problems of adequacy may also spring from transmission difficulties. Information that is available in the system may fail to reach the parties needing it. The pipe bomb explosion in Atlanta during the 1996 Olympics that killed two people and injured more than a hundred is a good example. A warning about the impending attack that safety officials had received was never released to security forces on duty at the explosion site.[64]

Wilensky's recommendation that information should come from a wide range of sources to present decision makers with various alternatives raises difficulties. It may lead to delays that make the information untimely. It may be hard to determine who should be consulted and what kinds of information should be solicited. Are interested or disinterested parties best? What kinds of experts should be consulted? Should ordinary citizens be included? If so, to what extent should their beliefs prevail over the advice of experts? There are no easy answers.

It is difficult to devise objective evaluation criteria assessing the quality of information in terms of all six variables. Evaluations of the quality of information, therefore, are largely subjective. Consequently, officials find it difficult to determine whether available information is good enough to permit valid inferences and to serve as the basis for action. Wilensky's estimates of the quality of information are disquieting, to say the least. He contends that generally only big, costly, urgent decisions activate high-quality intelligence. Such decisions tend to be made outside "channels" by top-level generalists who are advised by technical experts.[65]

Even if messages are initially accurate, clear, timely, and relevant, they may still become distorted by intermediate receivers. As Gordon Tullock pointed out, when information gathered at the bottom level of the hierarchy is filtered upward through several intermediate levels, most of it is lost.[66] If, for instance, 5,000 bits of information are received at the entry level, and if one assumes that half of the information is omitted each time it is passed on to the next level, less than 80 bits will survive a trip through six levels. That is less than 2 percent. (See Figure 2–1.) Intelligence thus deteriorates routinely between initial collection and its final use in a policy decision.

Moreover, the weeding-out process is rarely random. Successive receivers along the line, intentionally or unintentionally, screen out message elements that do not fit their preconceptions or the accepted collective wisdom of the agency. James March and Herbert Simon call this "uncertainty absorption." Instead of passing on messages as received, the transmitters may pass on the inferences that they have drawn from these messages. Transmitters also screen out information that comes from sources that they distrust. In addition, they may change the emphasis given to various parts of the message, thereby altering its overall thrust.[67]

How Much Is Enough?

The information requirements of an organization and its need for professional help in securing and disseminating this information hinge on four factors, according to Wilensky.[68] The first factor is the degree of conflict, competition, or systematic contact with the external environment. The more an agency is in constant contact or conflict with or dependent on its environment, the more it requires information about this environment and about possible ways to reduce conflict and friction. For instance, if the agency's goals are closely monitored by Congress, as happens with the EPA, or if it is likely to be in open conflict with Congress, as happened with the Federal Trade Commission, it needs to have more information about the interests

Figure 2-1 Tullock's Model of Hierarchical Distortion

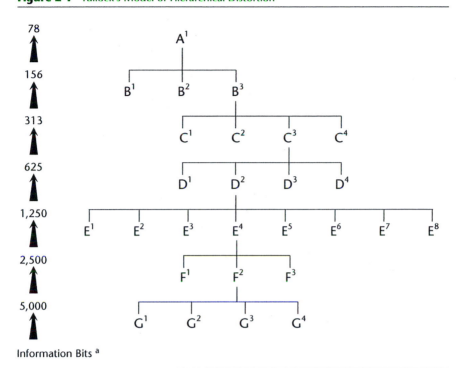

Information Bits [a]

SOURCE: Anthony Downs, *Inside Bureaucracy* (Santa Monica, Calif.: RAND, 1967), 117. Reprinted with permission.

[a] Half of the information is lost as it passes from level to level.

motivating Congress at that particular time than would be necessary if relations with Congress were placid. The organization may have to hire press officers, lobbyists, legislative representatives, or legal counsel to gather and disseminate information. Public corporations such as the Postal Service, which interact constantly with their environment, need regular and continuous contacts with Congress, the executive branch, and the public.

The second factor is the degree of dependence on internal support and unity. When internal support and unity are needed, specialists may be required to transmit information from the leadership to members of the organization. In the military or in social service organizations, for example, it may be necessary to monitor the opinions, feelings, and morale of lower level personnel. When people join the organization, they may have to be instructed about its culture. It may also be essential to train leaders so that they can attain a willing following and maintain morale in crisis situations.

The third factor is the need for information and advice, which varies, depending on the degree to which the organization's internal and external environments require scientific data. If internal and external relationships depend heavily on scientific data, there may be a constant need to stay ahead of new developments. The FCC, for example, must cope with extremely swift major technological changes that often make rules obsolete. That happened when many rules about telephone emergency services, designed for wired communication, became outdated because cell phones had become a major communication tool. The FCC needs vast amounts of technical information for internal governance and for effective communication with its clients and relevant public institutions. It often requires scientifically targeted public relations efforts to achieve its goals.

The fourth factor is a direct correlation between the size, structure, and heterogeneity of an organization and its information needs. Increases in size, heterogeneity of personnel, tasks, and clients, and complexity of structure all generate greater communication demands. Organizations must have information about the public they are serving, their regulatory agencies, and about the indirect effects of their operations. They must know about relevant professional associations, citizens' groups, and potential support groups such as the financial community and educational institutions that train personnel.

The amounts of information needed for particular decisions differ depending on the decision stage. The start-up of programs may require large amounts of new information. When decisions must be made rapidly, time pressures may limit the amount of information sought and the number of sources consulted. During crises executives are more likely to rely on trial and error and precedent than on scientific advice, except when decisions are purely technical.[69] They have learned to question the opinions of experts, who often lack political insights. When stakes are high, more information is usually sought, although there is also a temptation to cling to the tried and true. Increased information then enhances the likelihood of overload and its attendant problems. Decisions about what is and is not needed are difficult to make and organizations tend to err in the direction of oversupply.

Intelligence Disasters

Given the vastness of the governmental enterprise, it is easy to find horror stories of botched communication that present multiple examples of violations of the canons set forth by Wilensky.

A Litany of Military Debacles

In the spring of 1999, for example, U.S.-led NATO forces mistakenly bombed the Chinese embassy in Belgrade. There were deaths and injuries as well as major property damage. The action severely strained U.S. relations with China. What had gone wrong? Apparently there were three major communications failures.[70] The National Imagery and Mapping Agency, responsible for supplying accurate map information, had provided outdated maps. Agents of the Central Intelligence Agency (CIA) had misidentified the target, a Yugoslav foreign trade agency, and their errors were missed by CIA officials responsible for checking the accuracy of this type of information.

"Operation Urgent Fury" is another example that ranks with the best—or worst—of intelligence horror stories. It heavily involved the Department of Defense and the CIA, two agencies that are especially geared to securing adequate intelligence. Operation Urgent Fury was the code name for the 1983 military invasion of Grenada, a small Caribbean island that was experiencing political turmoil in the wake of a pro-Communist coup détat. Six hundred American medical students on the island were presumed to be in danger and in need of rescue by their compatriots. Serious communication problems surfaced almost immediately. The landing forces lacked adequate information about the location and strength of enemy positions. The information they had was unreliable and did not warn them adequately about the resistance they were likely to face. They paid in lives for that mistake.

Three branches of the military were involved in the invasion: the Navy, the Army, and the Marines. This raised numerous problems in coordinating information. For example, the three branches operated from different maps, and therefore could not coordinate their assaults. In one instance, because of unclear information, a Marine aerial attack destroyed an Army command post, killing one soldier and wounding seventeen. An air attack destroyed a local mental hospital that did not appear on the map used for the attack, killing and wounding more than a score of patients and staff.[71]

Marine and Army ground units used different radio frequencies and could not talk directly with one another even when deployed in the same area because they did not know each other's frequencies. When the Army needed aircraft support for ground troops from Navy and Marine units, the request had to be relayed through headquarters at Fort Bragg, North Carolina, because the naval units at the scene lacked modern communication equipment. This caused delays and distortions. One lieutenant used his telephone credit card in a public telephone booth to request air support from his stateside commanding officer.[72]

The soldiers involved in Operation Urgent Fury were supplied with outdated tourist maps, published by the Grenada tourist board, which were useless for directing artillery fire. High-quality maps were delivered when the operation was nearly over, fully nine days after the initial assault, hardly a timely delivery of information.[73] The mission called for rescuing the medical students. Yet the Defense Department had never bothered to find out where they were located, even though school authorities had been in touch with the State Department and the CIA and presented maps showing campus locations and student distribution. Moreover, the assumption that the students were endangered by the political turmoil and needed rescue was never adequately validated. School authorities had been in touch with the State Department, indicating that the Grenadan government was eager to keep the medical school in operation and to protect the students.[74] Similar intelligence failures have led to disaster for U.S. military forces in Lebanon and Iran. However, such failures should not obscure the fact that many military missions have been carried out successfully, with precision and foresight.

Common Causes of Failure

Intelligence failures occur when organizations are unable to muster the information needed for the successful pursuit of their goals because essential information is not readily available or it is inaccurate, untimely, or poorly interpreted. The Belgrade bombing and the Grenada situation are excellent examples. Wilensky ascribed most intelligence failures to six causes.[75] One of them, *secrecy,* has already been discussed. Three others—*hierarchy, specialization,* and *centralization*—are inherent in the nature of complex organizations. They will be discussed more fully in Chapter 3. Here it suffices to mention that, for technical as well as psychological reasons, the *hierarchy* of roles often causes poor communication links between the various levels of the organization. *Specialization* of functions, such as dividing the military into Army, Navy, and Air Force components, may lead to disabling interagency rivalries that prevent proper exchange of information and resistance to accepting information gathered by other agencies. *Centralization* becomes a problem when too much information is diverted to the top levels of an organization, causing overload, while lower levels are deprived of the information needed to function efficiently.

Wilensky also mentioned *anti-intellectualism* and *narrow empiricism*—a tunnel view of a limited number of factual data—as common causes of intelligence failures.[76] People conducting the business of government often scorn theories as abstract and impractical, designed for eggheads in ivory towers. They fail to realize that theories help to make sense of the mass of information received by the organization, enabling it to discern trends and anticipate future developments. Narrow empiricism may also lead to intellectual myopia. When agency personnel insist on collecting only verifiable, objective data, many valuable insights may be lost. For example, much important information is ignored when personnel officers concentrate only on objective facts about recruiting expenditures, hiring, and retention rates, without assessing how people feel about the organization and without considering the societal benefits of hiring transient workers. Interpretist, critical, and postmodern theorists have called attention to these problems.

The nature of organizations and data are not the only hurdles to acquiring the information needed to function effectively. Human personality traits, information-processing capabilities, and interactions are other potential obstacles. The dynamics of individual, group, and organizational behavior are particularly likely to create problems.[77] Individual behavior elements include biopsychological factors and information-processing capabilities. The dynamics of group behavior include internal group processes, group structure, and leadership factors. These problems, as well as the dynamics of organizational behavior, will be discussed in Chapter 6.

The major lessons to be drawn from this chapter are threefold. Public administrators must never lose sight of the political environment in which they operate. First, they must gather information about politics for political reasons and disseminate it to accomplish political purposes vital to their agency's welfare. It is unfortunate that American political culture holds politics in such disdain that public officials often feel compelled to hide political motivations behind a skimpy cloak of excuses, apologies, and often outright lies.

Second, all information is not equal in value and less can be better than more. Administrators need to scrutinize sources and learn to distinguish between the wheat and the chaff. This is extraordinarily difficult in the public sector, where vast amounts of information are needed, much unwanted information is submitted, and much needed information is withheld or controlled by self-interested outsiders.

Third, obtaining and using high-quality information is costly. It requires more time, effort, and money than most administrators and their congressional funding sources are willing to acknowledge. More resources need to be allocated to attend to these vital activities.

Securing good information is only the first step in information management. The second crucial step requires structuring the organization so that information flows smoothly to the destinations that need it. Chapters 3 and 4 address these issues.

NOTES

1. Charles E. Lindblom and David K. Cohen, *Usable Knowledge: Social Science and Social Problem Solving* (New Haven: Yale University Press, 1979).
2. Harold F. Gortner, Julianne Mahler, and Jeanne Bell Nicholson, *Organizational Theory: A Public Perspective* (Chicago: Dorsey, 1987), 301.
3. John M. Stevens and Robert P. McGowan, *Information Systems and Public Management* (New York: Praeger, 1985), 111.

4. Edward O. Lauman and David Knoke, *The Organizational State: Social Choice in National Policy Domains* (Madison: University of Wisconsin Press, 1987), 191.

5. Edward I. Sidlow and Beth Henschen, "The Performance of House Committee Staff Functions: A Comparative Exploration," *Western Political Quarterly* 38 (September 1985): 487. The committees were Appropriations, Armed Services, Budget, Government Operations, Interior and Insular Affairs, Merchant Marine and Fisheries, Public Works and Transportation, and Ways and Means. They were chosen to represent committees varying in environment and prestige.

6. Ibid., 488.

7. E. Sam Overman and Anthony G. Cahill, "Information, Market Government, and Health Policy: A Study of Health Data Organizations in the States," *Journal of Policy Analysis and Management* 13 (1994/3): 435–453.

8. Barbara S. Romzek and Melvin Dubnick, "Accountability in the Public Sector: Lessons from the Challenger Tragedy," *Public Administration Review* 47 (May/June 1987): 231.

9. Quoted in Harold L. Wilensky, *Organizational Intelligence: Knowledge and Policy in Government and Industry* (New York: Basic Books, 1967), 22.

10. Martha S. Feldman, *Order without Design: Information Production and Policy Making* (Stanford: Stanford University Press, 1989), 7–9.

11. Jonathan Bendor, Serge Taylor, and Roland Van Gaalen, "Politicians, Bureaucrats, and Asymmetric Information," *American Journal of Political Science* 31 (1987): 797.

12. Bernard E. Trainor, "Another U.S. Study Down the Drain?" *New York Times,* Jan. 13, 1988.

13. Feldman, *Order without Design,* 2–3.

14. David Whiteman, "The Fate of Policy Analysis in Congressional Decision Making: Three Types of Use in Committees," *Western Political Quarterly* 38 (June 1985): 298.

15. Ibid., 304–307.

16. Anthony Downs, *Inside Bureaucracy* (Boston: Little, Brown, 1967), 249–252.

17. Herbert Kaufman, *The Administrative Behavior of Federal Bureau Chiefs* (Washington, D.C.: Brookings Institution, 1981), 33.

18. Ibid., 26–33.

19. Ibid., 31.

20. David Jackson, "School Lunches: Illness on Menu," *Chicago Tribune,* Dec. 9, 2001.

21. The first request for information was made on Dec. 22, 1977. The National Highway Traffic Safety Administration's Defects Panel announced a formal investigation on Feb. 28, 1978.

22. For similar problems faced by the EPA in collecting data about industrial wastes, see Wesley A. Magat, Alan J. Krupnick, and Winston Harrington, *Rules in the Making: A Statistical Analysis of Regulatory Agency Behavior* (Washington, D.C.: Resources for the Future, 1986), 26–40.

23. *New York Times,* Apr. 17, 1984

24. Magat et al., *Rules in the Making,* 36–40.

25. Gina Kolata, "The F.D.A. Approves a Drug. Then What?" *New York Times,* Oct. 7, 1997.

26. Jackson, "School Lunches."
27. Hugh Heclo, *A Government of Strangers: Executive Politics in Washington* (Washington, D.C.: Brookings Institution, 1977), 205.
28. Bruce A. Ackerman and William T. Hassler, *Clean Coal/Dirty Air* (New Haven: Yale University Press, 1981), 84.
29. The implications of the act are discussed in Jay A. Sigler, "Legal Issues Surrounding Administrative Communications," in *Handbook of Administrative Communication,* ed. James L. Garnett and Alexander Kouzmin (New York: Marcel Dekker, 1997), 171–186.
30. Jeri Clausing, "Few Federal Web Sites Observe Federally Proposed Privacy Rules," *New York Times,* Aug. 31, 1998.
31. *New York Times,* May 3, 1984.
32. Stevens and McGowan, *Information Systems and Public Management,* 197.
33. David H. Morrissey, "Disclosure and Secrecy: Security Classification Executive Orders," *Journalism & Mass Communication Monographs* 161 (February 1997).
34. Matthew L. Wald, "Millions of Secrets Burden Energy Agency," *New York Times,* Feb. 7, 1996.
35. *New York Times Co. v. United States,* 403 U.S. 713 (1971).
36. "Pentagon's Scientist Curb Hit," *Chicago Tribune,* Apr. 27, 1984.
37. James Warren, "CBS-TV's Apple Scare Is Costly to Growers," *Chicago Tribune,* May 11, 1989.
38. Wilensky, *Organizational Intelligence,* ix–x.
39. Frederick O. Lorenz, Betty L. Wells, Charles L. Mulford, and Daisy Kabagarama, "How Social Service Agencies React to Uncertainty: Budget Cuts Need Not Curb Creativity," *Sociology and Social Research* 71 (October 1986): 29–30.
40. Timothy J. McNulty, "Ethics Run Weak 2d to Birth Technology," *Chicago Tribune,* Oct. 18, 1987.
41. Gortner et al., *Organizational Theory,* 187–189.
42. James Q. Wilson, *Bureaucracy: What Government Agencies Do and Why They Do It* (New York: Basic Books, 1989), 228.
43. Hugh Heclo, "Issue Networks and the Executive Establishment," in *The New American Political System,* ed., Anthony King (Washington, D.C.: American Enterprise Institute, 1978), 99.
44. Pub. Law No. 96-511 (1980). The original act expired on September 30, 1989, but was subsequently renewed. Earlier laws included the Federal Reports Act of 1942 under which paperwork requests by the executive branch were scrutinized by the Bureau of the Budget to make sure that costs to the government and private sector were justifiable. Kitty Dumas, "Congress or the White House: Who Controls the Agencies?" *Congressional Quarterly Weekly Report,* Apr. 14, 1990, 1131.
45. NCMA (National Contract Management Association) (1996), http://www.mckennacuneo.co...archive/GC02419960901.html.
46. Pub. Law No. 96-511 (1980), 1133.
47. *Dole v. Steelworkers,* 494 U.S. 26 (1990). The case is discussed in Linda Greenhouse, "High Court Decides Budget Office Exceeded Power in Blocking Rules," *New York Times,* Feb. 21, 1990.

48. Tina Kelley, "Behind Closed E-Mail: Politicians Grapple with Public Scrutiny of their Electronic Communications," *New York Times,* Apr. 1, 1999.

49. The research was conducted by the author's graduate students.

50. Philip Shenon, "The Freedom of Information Act and Its Role in Disclosing Influence Peddling," *New York Times,* Aug. 28, 1989.

51. Wilensky, *Organizational Intelligence,* 151–171, provides additional detail.

52. Ibid., viii–ix.

53. David Sadofsky, *Knowledge as Power: Political and Legal Control of Information* (New York: Praeger, 1990).

54. Telecommunications Act of 1996, Pub. Law No. 104-104, 110 Stat. 56 (1996).

55. Joseph Michael Pace and Zachary Smith, "Understanding Affirmative Action: From the Practitioner's Perspective," *Public Personnel Management* 24 (1995): 139–147.

56. "Grand Jury to Examine Case of Nuclear Secrets," *Chicago Tribune,* June 22, 2000.

57. Rose Gutfeld, "Employees Pressured by Managers to Seize Property, Senate Panel Told," *Wall Street Journal,* June 23, 1987.

58. James Risen, "Report Says Los Alamos May Mislead on Security," *New York Times,* June 26, 2000.

59. Carol Weiss, "Congressional Committee Staffs as Problematic Users of Analysis," 1984 American Political Science Association paper, 14.

60. David R. Maines and Joseph Palenski, "Reconstructing Legitimacy in Final Reports of Contract Research," *Sociological Review* 34 (August 1986): 575–589; also see Carol H. Weiss and Michael Bucuvalas, "Truth Tests and Utility Tests: Decision-Makers' Frames of Reference for Social Science Research," *American Sociological Review* 45 (1980): 302–303.

61. Frank P. Williams III, Marilyn McShane, and Dale Sechrest, "Barriers to Effective Performance Review: The Seduction of Raw Data," *Public Administration Review* 54 (1994: 6): 537–542.

62. National Research Council, *Decision Making in the Environmental Protection Agency,* Vol. II (Washington, D.C.: National Academy of Sciences, 1977), 119–121.

63. Carol Weiss, "Congressional Committee Staffs as Problematic Users of Analysis," 1984 American Political Science Association paper, 21.

64. CNN Interactive, "Who Planted the Bomb?" (July 27, 1996), http://www.cnn.com/US/ 9607...t.investigation/index.html

65. Wilensky, *Organizational Intelligence,* 173–191.

66. Downs, *Inside Bureaucracy,* 117.

67. This is discussed in Charles A. O'Reilly III, "The Intentional Distortion of Information in Organizational Communications: A Laboratory and Field Investigation," in *The Study of Organizations,* ed. Daniel Katz, Robert L. Kahn, and J. Stacy Adams (San Francisco: Jossey-Bass, 1982), 328–344.

68. Wilensky, *Organizational Intelligence,* 8–16.

69. Ibid., 80–81.

70. Robert M. Gates, "In War, Mistakes Happen," *New York Times,* May 12, 1999.

71. James G. March and Roger Weissinger-Babylon, *Ambiguity and Command* (Boston: Pitman, 1986), 295.

72. Richard Gabriel, "Scenes from an Invasion," *Washington Monthly* (February 1986): 40.
73. March and Weissinger-Babylon, *Ambiguity and Command,* 293.
74. Frontline #602 Broadcast, "Operation Urgent Fury" (Boston: WGBH Educational Foundation, 1988), 14.
75. Wilensky, *Organizational Intelligence,* 41–74.
76. Ibid., 62–63.
77. Alexander L. George, *Presidential Decisionmaking in Foreign Policy: The Effective Use of Information and Advice* (Boulder: Westview, 1980), 11–12.

Chapter 3 **Channeling Bureaucratic Information Flows**

The Interface of Structure and Function

What happens when unwise decisions are made about channeling information flows? We begin our discussion about structuring organizations so that information moves smoothly to appropriate destinations with a tale about a conspicuous failure that had serious consequences. Charges of widespread sexual abuse in large public institutions are always shocking, particularly when the abuse has been reported repeatedly over decades without eliciting adequate remedies. This is why a 1996 poll of women at U.S. Army bases that suggested inaction in the face of serious abuses stirred a lot of anger in the nation. Army leaders, eager to integrate females into the primarily male organization, worried how recruiting efforts might be affected by the report that a majority of the poll respondents mentioned encountering sexual harassment and alleged that their complaints had met with indifference, ridicule, or retaliation.[1]

Investigations showed that the structures set up to funnel information about abuses to high-level officers were flawed. Women had to appeal first to their immediate unit commander who lacked power to enforce remedies and whose record would be tarnished if the charges proved correct. It is no wonder then that more than two thirds of all complaints to low-level officers were dismissed as unsustainable. Army chaplains might have been able to circumvent the lower level command structure by passing the information directly to top echelons. But there were too few chaplains to do this job. When the Army changed the appeals structure so that women could forward information directly to the Army's Criminal Investigation Command, the number of complaints reaching their target and eliciting action increased sharply. Many women who had previously refrained from filing complaints because they thought it would be useless—if not harmful to their careers—felt encouraged to voice their allegations, putting potential abusers on notice that their actions might be severely punished.

To function well, organizations must have structures that are appropriate to organizational goals. *Structure,* as we shall use it in this context, refers to the patterns of information flow inherent in formal organization charts and reflected in work manuals. Redesigning the structure for reporting sex abuse in the Army is just one example. Similarly, when President George W. Bush wanted to make antiterrorism actions a primary goal of the federal government in 2002, he proposed a massive restructuring of federal agencies. A new cabinet-level Department of Homeland Security would draw units from eight cabinet departments to unify antiterrorist activities. The purpose sparked a heated, nationwide dialogue about the merits of various structure options and the changes in functionality that they might generate. Different structures reflect officials' intent to privilege particular policies or constituencies. Organizational structure thus became an essential guide for organizational behavior, including communication behavior.[2] As James March and Herbert Simon, pioneers in the study of organizations, have noted, without prescribed structures, human beings would find it difficult to coordinate their efforts to achieve common goals.[3] Thanks to the nature of the structure in which they work, employees know what their particular position requires and with whom they are supposed to communicate. The official structures provide a restricted, standardized communication environment that enhances the stability and predictability of organizational behavior.[4]

When messages do not move well in the existing structures, these structures may be altered to better serve the communication flow patterns. Again, the Army case and the new Department of Homeland Security are good examples, as is the reorganization of the Federal Aviation Administration's (FAA) terrorism warning system for airlines. When a Pan-American flight exploded over Lockerbie, Scotland, in December 1988, killing 270 people, flaws in the transmission of danger messages were highlighted. The Department of Transportation, which oversees the FAA, ordered major structural changes to improve the agency's aircraft warning system, expecting that the altered structures would lead to better communication in the future.[5]

What Structures Are Best?

In the public sector, basic options for designing organizational structures include emphasis on geographical divisions, functional divisions, line and staff functions, or client types. Various mixtures of these elements are also possible. Which of these structures is best, considering the functions to be performed, has remained a matter of some controversy. Some analysts contend that communication flows best if work is functionally divided, so that units are concerned with a single project or task or deal with only one problem. For example, the Illinois Public Health Department is divided into units dealing with Consumer Health Protection, Geriatrics and Long Term Care, Reduction of Infant Mortality, Parents Too Soon, and Nuclear Safety, among others. Divisions by discipline, as is common in universities, or skill, as done for work involving the building trades, or clientele, as in veterans' affairs, also work well. Dividing work by geographical unit, according to this view, is least conducive to good information flows because political boundaries become barriers to information exchange. Police departments, which are geographically organized, are examples. They often experience communication difficulties attributable to political boundary problems.

By and large, the difficulties encountered in creating effective communication systems mount with increasing size of the organization and increasing complexity of the functions to be performed. It then becomes harder to design a standardized system. More improvisation becomes necessary, guided by feedback about ongoing and past activities of the organization.[6] Appropriate structures do not guarantee that information flows will be perfect. Human error is an ever-present likelihood. Even when special efforts have been made to ensure flawless communication, serious information-flow lapses occur routinely, like the failures of the FAA warning system in the Lockerbie case, failures in the Army's personnel administration structure, and breakdown of the communication chain that should have carried warnings about a pipe bomb attack during the 1996 Olympics in Atlanta and failure to prevent the 2001 terrorist assault on the United States.[7]

Political Implications of Structure Designs

The public sector is prone to developing structures that are not adequately adapted to the needs they must serve. This happens because political concerns often dominate decision making. When power struggles determine the outcome, they often produce "organized anarchies"—structures that may look sensible even though they are quite inappropriate. Frequently they reflect outdated phases of the organization's life because entrenched stakeholders resist changes that are likely to reduce their power and control. It is legendary in government circles that it is practically impossible to close down unneeded services and agencies. The state of Illinois, for instance, maintained an agency dealing with horseshoe inspections for decades after streetcars had stopped the use of horses.[8]

Structuring information flows effectively is particularly difficult when it comes to the many services provided jointly by public and private sector organizations. Public health issues, like the influenza vaccination program, offer prime examples. New strains of the vaccine must be produced each year, making it essential to match each year's supplies to estimated demands. Unused vaccine cannot be stored for use in subsequent years. Vaccine shortages occur regularly because the communication channels connecting the private companies that supply the vaccine and public health authorities are flawed. Health authorities do not share their data about prospective needs with vaccine suppliers in timely fashion, and suppliers do not share their prospective production figures with health authorities. Suppliers inform the Food and Drug Administration about vaccine production, but that agency is barred by law from disclosing these trade secrets to anyone, including other government agencies. No organizational structures have been responsible for monitoring the distribution and use of flu vaccine. As a consequence, even when total vaccine supplies are adequate in a particular year, health authorities in areas with too much vaccine rarely know where the shortage areas are to which vaccine could be redistributed.[9] The Internet provides many inexpensive options for coping with such problems.

Speedy action may be crucial to accomplish structural reforms of administrative agencies. Gov. Terry E. Branstad of Iowa, who was able to reduce departments from sixty-eight to twenty and to eliminate forty boards and commissions, attributed his success to "Compression of time [that] allowed us to build enough momentum to reduce the drag caused by the opposing interest groups during this entire process. If we had waited longer to devise or to accomplish the plan, the interest groups would likely have simply picked it apart."[10]

General Considerations. All levels of organizational life require decisions about structure. They range from determining what new structures will be created and which existing structures will be abolished to resolving how existing structures should be modified to alter the directions of information flows. All of these decisions are vulnerable to political influence because they affect how government business is done—who benefits and who loses and who has power and who does not. The incentive to control decisions about structure is particularly strong in the public sector because these decisions are usually formalized through laws or administrative regulations that are difficult to modify.

Political leaders spend considerable time and effort on creating the kinds of structures deemed best for accomplishing their purposes.[11] It is particularly important to structure who has access to top-level decision makers when crucial decisions are under way and who prepares the final reports that explains the rationale for decisions. For example, foreign policy decisions are based on the National Intelligence Estimates prepared by the intelligence agencies in the State Department, Defense Department, and Central Intelligence Agency (CIA). The estimates presumably represent a consensus among the contributing bodies but, in reality, they often disagree substantially about facts and their implications. The CIA dominates the process because the CIA director chairs the meetings and edits the joint report. As a consequence, the report reflects CIA views.[12]

Prospective changes in communication patterns tend to arouse opposition when they are viewed as a reallocation of influence. This happened when the Carter administration wanted to create a separate Department of Education. Secretary of Health, Education and Welfare Joseph A. Califano opposed the move, arguing that the new department would mean an extra voice with direct access to the president. It would add to the overload of messages with which the executive office was already struggling.[13] From a departmental perspective, the separation would make it much more difficult to coordinate health and welfare matters with education because previously internal messages would now become external communications. The proposed structural changes would also radically change the responsiveness of the educational bureaucracy to various elected officials and interest groups. Despite Califano's arguments, the new department was established in the waning years of the Carter administration.

Structuring Legislatures. The legislative committee system prevalent in Congress, state legislatures, and city councils illustrates particularly well how structure shapes function. Most American legislatures are organized along functional lines. They deal with specialized areas of concern, like education or transportation, even though one might expect them to be geographically organized when they are elected to represent geographically defined districts. Information flows and the resulting patterns of influence therefore reflect the specialized tasks. For instance, congressional committees and their subordinate units deal with concerns of agriculture or banking or air transportation predominantly on a nationwide basis, although individual legislators do remain attuned to pressing needs of the people who elected them.

In line with the old adage that "you stand where you sit," legislators' policy positions vary, depending on the bundles of concerns reflected in the committee structure. For example, legislation to provide access to transportation for handicapped people is likely to be viewed from quite different perspectives if proposals are routed through Health and Human Services committees than if they are channeled through transportation committees. The former are likely to stress human needs; the latter tend to be concerned with efficiency and costs in public transportation systems.[14] The number of committees created to deal with specialized needs has escalated at all governmental levels. Legislators' workloads accordingly have become heavier and more fragmented. Therefore more of the work underlying legislators' decisions has to be based on work by their staffs and by respected colleagues and experts who draw on their own information sources.[15] The structural changes have altered how legislators function.

Overall, because the congressional structure is decentralized and nonhierarchical, it offers numerous access points where outsiders can convey information and pressure for consideration. They will vary the information contained in their appeals depending on which formal or informal structural units they are approaching. A group of African American citizens seeking help to combat racial discrimination in their hometown will use different arguments when contacting their senator's office, the offices of the Congressional Black Caucus, or a civil rights lobby group.

Money available to members of Congress for hiring information-gathering staffs has risen sharply over time, restructuring information-intake patterns.[16] Previously, much of the information, of necessity, flowed from interest groups and their lobbyists. The new money allows Congress members to rely most heavily on their committee and personal staffs for advice and information.[17] These young, well-educated professionals are intellectually and ideologically far removed from the former ranks of lobbyists and special-interest pleaders. Similar pattern changes are evident in many state legislatures.

This does not mean that special-interest groups and their lobbyists are unable to communicate with Congress. Most legislators feel compelled to consider information offered by interest groups because these constituencies can provide campaign resources and votes. Moreover, despite the growth in staffs, resources for gathering information remain insufficient, so that legislators must still rely to a substantial degree on data provided by outside sources. That means that organizations and individuals who control relevant information and who manage to channel it to Congress remain influential.[18] Those who do not control salient information, or who lack access to channels that lead to Congress, tend to be low on the congressional-influence scale. As Table 2-2 in Chapter 2 shows, the extent to which various staffs rely on information submitted by interest groups differs significantly. Among the eight House committees studied by Edward Sidlow and Beth Henschen, the staffs in clientele-oriented committees such as Merchant Marine, Interior, and Public Works were more concerned with interest-group information than were committees such as Ways and Means, Budget, or Government Operations.[19] Wise interest group managers know such matters.

Structuring Information Flows

The congressional example shows that "who" and "how" questions are the two main decisions that administrators face when they adapt structures to the functions that need to be performed. The "who" question concerns personnel. Which individuals, with all the intellectual baggage they carry, will be major cogs in the communication process? The "how" decision relates to the rules that organizations devise to cope with their communication processes. We will first discuss "who" and "how" issues and follow this with a discussion of major structural constraints on information flows in typical organizations.

Designating Personnel

Organizations increasingly need staff members who devote all or most of their time to gathering information because so much is needed and because so much potentially crucial information is available to deal with the complex internal and external issues handled by governments. Appropriate personnel structures range from assigning information functions as sidelines in jobs primarily concerned with other matters to hiring part- or full-time communication specialists or setting up attached or freestanding organizational units solely devoted to information functions. The organizational chart of the Department of Interior in this chapter is typical of the specialized structures used by modern organizations. Some government agencies specialize in gathering information systematically. The Bureau of the Census, which collects demographic information, and the Federal Bureau of Investigation (FBI), which collects crime data, are examples.

Internal information managers include personnel directors who monitor the organization's work force. They are primarily concerned with human relations aspects of organizational communication, with the technical expertise of internal dialogue, and with the efficient transmission of work-related information throughout the organization. Their work may be supplemented by education and training staffs who continuously develop the organization's human resources in line with changing needs and by staffs who prepare publications for internal circulation. In recent decades public agencies have drawn on a much wider array of skills to satisfy their communication needs. For instance, the military now uses psychologists to guide training operations; it also uses sociologists to study internal communication and aspects of organizational climate, such as morale.[20]

To mesh the information-processing structures of a multitude of agencies and overcome excessive fragmentation, coordinating structures, like the Office of Management and Budget (OMB) at the federal level may be needed. Among its many functions, OMB monitors reports by federal agencies to make sure that uniform procedures are used. It also keeps tabs on the amount of time that citizens must spend to complete government forms and encourages creation of briefer and simpler forms. All federal agencies must obtain OMB approval before collecting information from the public.[21]

Organizations also need structures for preserving organizational memories so that past experiences can guide actions. Information storage and retrieval of stored information have become major concerns in an age of overabundant messages. Someone has to decide what to store and how to store it so that it can be readily recaptured when needed. This job may be assigned to an archivist, but most public agencies lack the funds for such a position. In fact, little formal attention has been given to creating structures for preserving organizational memories aside from legal requirements that mandate retention of designated information, such as contracts, financial data, or client files that must be kept for a specified number of years. These record-keeping requirements, coupled with a fair degree of job stability in the lower civil service ranks, keep organizational memories in the public sector in better shape than might be expected. To save physical and electronic filing space, many organizations destroy information about intermediate steps in decision making and aborted transactions. It is thus often difficult to track major considerations that entered into decisions and thereby learn from past experiences.

For external communication, organizations may have to create public relations staffs, along with lobbyists, legislative representatives, and supporting legal personnel. Such staffs funnel information about the organization to outsiders and gather needed technical, organizational, and political information. Managing information successfully may require hiring a research staff, planners, analysts who monitor internal proceedings, economists, statisticians, and management consultants, as well as lawyers who negotiate, arbitrate, and litigate. Public agencies often falter when it comes to scanning the external environment to mesh it with the agency's work. Research and development personnel tend to be technologically oriented and rarely produce the broader picture that is needed to keep the organization in balance with its environment.

Concern about obtaining information about the general public's reactions to government programs has led to the establishment of many new liaison structures in recent decades. A number of states now appoint advocates for the public interest.[22] Wisconsin, for example, has a public intervenor, located in the attorney general's office, who has successfully represented the views of citizens on environmental issues considered by state agencies. The office also helps build and sustain public interest in environmental issues. Other states have created offices that counsel consumers and have appointed ombudsmen who funnel citizens' concerns to public agencies.[23] Similarly, the White House and many executive departments and agencies now have public liaison offices to provide two-way channels of information for various publics. Many of these offices can be reached through readily accessible Web sites. The impact of these access structures in bringing public views to bear on decision making is discussed more fully in Chapter 6.

Compared with large private enterprises, the public sector generally is not well-supplied with personnel dispensing and gathering information. The State Department is an example. American diplomats stationed abroad have always lacked sufficient personnel to gather the large amounts of information that they need to function effectively. That makes them heavily dependent on press reports and on contacts with a small number of informants who may not represent mainstream interests in their societies. The difficulties of setting up appropriate liaison structures in foreign countries and keeping in touch with people who belong to often vastly different cultures also militate against effective information management.

Personnel shortages are made more serious by the penchant of government agencies to collect excessive amounts of information, often at great expense. As a consequence, government resources are drained needlessly, as are the resources of millions of citizens who must report to the government. When Congress initially passed the Paperwork Reduction Act in 1980 to improve information-collection procedures and ease the burden of handling government paperwork, it took citizens an estimated 12.7 billion hours annually to fill out federal government forms.[24] Despite regular tightening of the constraints imposed by the act, that figure has escalated. Just one form, the 1040 personal income tax form completed annually by more than half of all Americans, requires nearly thirteen hours, according to IRS estimates. Directions for completing the form grew from half a million words in 1955 to six million words in 2000.

Drafting Communication Rules

Turning to the "how" issue, administrators must formulate a variety of rules to guide the flow of information within their organization. These include descriptions of the communication duties encompassed in each job and descriptions of reporting routes to be followed in ordinary and extraordinary circumstances. Once established, the patterns of formal communication flows tend to be relatively stable because they become hardened in custom and are buttressed by the power relationships that they create. The network of contacts established among members of a group determines its structure and the group's shared knowledge about group procedures becomes its culture. Stabilizing these relationships fosters regularity and predictability, so that people within the organization as well as outsiders find it easy to know the routines that must be followed. If asked to funnel their requests through "channels," they know precisely what that means.

Organizational charts usually indicate for each position who communicates with whom and who has authority over whom. The position thus furnishes a frame of reference that its occupant quickly learns to adopt. For example, during the Nixon administration, the director of the White House Office of Communication reported directly to the White House chief of staff. That changed during the Ford administration when the Office of Communication was put under Press Office jurisdiction. Following the Carter years, the Office of Communication was either separated from the Press Office or made superior to it in the hierarchy. Each of these changes had a strong impact on the office's operations.[25]

A person's position within an organizational structure serves as an extremely strong social constraint that determines likely actions. A study of business executives, for example, showed that their attitudes were better explained by their position within the organizational structure than by their self-interest or ideology.[26] Accordingly, officials who hold different jobs in different subsystems within an organization will seek out different information and respond quite differently to a given message. The chief financial officer, charged with keeping budgets low, looks for different information to make her case than the research and development chief who wants to advocate new programs.[27]

Once political power relationships have hardened as part of the established communication game, it is difficult to switch to new rules that change these relationships. An example from politics in Chicago is relevant. Harold Washington, the city's first black mayor, faced grave difficulties during the early years of his administration in controlling city politics. Many aldermen opposed his leadership. Washington therefore decided to curb their power by rerouting communications away from aldermanic offices to positions controlled by his allies.

Chicago aldermen have traditionally derived political power from their ability to secure city services for their constituents.[28] The heart of aldermanic operations is the ward office where people telephone their requests for services from city government, such as repairing gutters, planting trees, or installing street lights. The aldermen then relay these demands to the appropriate offices in the city and capture the plaudits—and the votes—when the service is rendered. Mayor Washington proposed to eliminate the aldermanic hub in the communication system, suggesting that city residents seek help directly from City Hall, which was controlled by the mayor and his allies.

As typically happens in such political battles, Washington denied that his proposal was an effort to reduce the power of aldermen and increase City Hall clout. Instead, he justified the proposed changes as a streamlining of communication circuits. Similarly, the aldermen put their opposition on technical grounds, skirting the political issue that was at the heart of the move. They argued that the capacity of City Hall to handle such messages was already strained because the Mayor's Office of Inquiry and Information already handled 25,000 telephone calls each month. Besides, City Hall would not know the neighborhoods well enough to render services efficiently. Predictably, a political battle royal ensued and the mayor's proposals died. Similar battles about potential losses of turf are common when proposals surface to conduct business via Web sites that bypass the officials who formerly handled these tasks. As in the Chicago case, the real motives are usually hidden behind technical and managerial arguments.

Problems faced by the FAA illustrate how tough it is to make rules for adequate information flows. The FAA is charged with monitoring airline safety. Therefore, it receives numerous reports about terrorist threats against aircraft. Many of these reports are exceedingly vague, indicating only that some unidentified terrorist group is planning an attack on American aircraft in some imprecisely specified area of the globe. Lacking its own overseas investigation staff, the FAA must rely on military and CIA information and on warnings supplied intermittently by foreign governments. Most of the time the information is too sketchy to verify the credibility of these reports. If they contain specific information, the FAA must subsequently conceal details that could identify secret intelligence sources.

Even though the data may be shaky, the FAA must inform threatened airlines soon enough to take precautions but not so hastily that they respond to false alarms. It is difficult to pinpoint the ideal time. Moreover, airlines need far more specific data than the FAA is usually able to provide initially. The outcome is frustration all around. Even worse, the outcome may be major disasters such as the failed warnings about the possibility of a bomb aboard the Pan-American flight that exploded over Scotland in 1988 and the inability in 2001 to interrupt the terrorist flights targeted on New York's World Trade Center and the Pentagon as soon as suspicions about a hijacking had been aroused.

Office Landscaping

Communication flows are also affected by the physical structures of offices, including locations assigned to offices, room layouts, and color schemes. Experiments performed by psychologists Abraham Maslow and Norbert Mintz, for example, showed that research participants seated in a beautiful room reacted more positively to stimulus pictures than did participants situated in an ugly room.[29] Warm reddish room colors stimulated people to interact, whereas cool bluish colors produce more restrained communication patterns.[30]

German and Swedish management scientists have developed the concept of "office landscaping" to facilitate communication. For example, research shows that intraoffice face-to-face communication is sparse among people whose work stations are separated by more than seventy-five feet.[31] Hence, it is important to structure office space so that people who should continuously meet in person are located close to one another, particularly at the start of their working relationship. Once communication ties become established, personal and professional attraction serve to overcome physical distance. The fact that a goodly portion of congressional committee staffs are dispersed among spatially distant offices may be detrimental to their performance, though the ease of sending e-mails has markedly alleviated the problem.

In recent years the importance of office landscaping has been forcefully impressed on American managers in the private sector who have compared Japanese management styles with their own. The Japanese office structure is designed to keep people as close to one another as possible to encourage communication. Up to fifty members of a department may be arranged in one big room with desks closely crowded together.[32] Such an office landscape makes supervision easy. Departmental executives share these same rooms, although their desks may be on a raised dais to provide more visibility and allow them to keep in better visual contact with their work force. There is no privacy. All transactions, whether business or personal, are readily observable by coworkers. The Japanese office design encourages gossip and idle chatter, but most Japanese managers believe that this loss of time is more than compensated by high morale and team spirit.

These office layouts reflect a distinct management philosophy. The emphasis is on teamwork and group performance. In the American system, where individual offices and privacy are much more common, the emphasis is on clearly defined specialties and job assignments. This creates "turfs" that their owners try to protect by keeping information to themselves.[33] The Japanese system seems dismaying to American managers who put high values on privacy, individual achievement, and competition.

The psychological impact of architectural settings has been well-known throughout history. It has been implemented by using opulent interiors as organizational status symbols and erecting awe-inspiring buildings to house heads of state or high courts. But these insights are rarely given sufficient consideration in planning the offices of less-exalted public agencies. As John Crompton and Charles Lamb noted,

> When discussing facility development or renovation, government and social service agencies frequently think only in terms of functional considerations and minimum costs. Economies are made on such items as carpeting, drapes, furnishings, lighting and landscaping because they are considered peripheral items that can be cut from the budget without adversely impacting the basic service. In fact, however, these are often the most critical ingredients in a new facility. They are the very things that create the welcoming atmosphere necessary to encourage potential clients to use the service. . . . Even if they are added later, the initial image of the facility has been established in the minds of its potential clientele. . . . You never get a second chance to make a first impression.[34]

The physical setting of an agency communicates messages about its professionalism to employees and clients alike.

> People use visual and audio cues to generalize about the entire agency. Overflowing waste baskets, filled ash trays, temporary signs, and outdated posters may lead a client to infer that (1) this is "just a job" for the staff and they do not take pride in their agency, (2) the manager is ineffective, or (3) the agency is not concerned about its clientele. If an environment is perceived as desirable, relaxing, comfortable, nonhostile, and hence rewarding, it is likely that the activities that take place in that environment will also be perceived as desirable and rewarding.[35]

A welfare client interviewed in a homelike setting, with appropriately placed seating facilities, is likely to feel more relaxed, making communication easier, than when the interview takes place in a crowded office where clients have to stand in front of a counter and discuss their personal affairs within earshot of a multitude of strangers.[36] All too often in the public service, the physical setting of agencies is unattractive, dowdy, and even dirty and neglected, making users feel uncomfortable and degraded.

Bureaucratic Structure Handicaps

It should be clear by now that organizational structure may facilitate communication flows or it may impair them. We now turn to several problems that are endemic in organizations because they arise from the very nature of bureaucratic structure. According to Max Weber, the main characteristics of a bureaucracy include (1) a hierarchy of formal positions that makes task performance more rational; (2) division of tasks by specialization; and (3) central direction and coordination of tasks. All of these essential characteristics produce major challenges for information management in public bureaucracies.

Hierarchy

In hierarchical structures, superiors direct the work and subordinates carry out the superiors' commands. Instructions flow downward from top-level personnel to the lower echelons in stepwise progression. The lower echelons, which carry out these commands and instructions, in turn are told what kind of information and reports they must provide to upper-level personnel. Several problems ensue.

The number of levels through which information must pass is a problem per se. In Chapter 2 we discussed why distortions occur when messages travel through a series of intermediaries in the hierarchy. Major information loss is likely at every transmission point. The hierarchical layers through which information must pass also produce delays that are detrimental to efficiency and may lead to inaction. There is much evidence that multiple clearances and consultations stultify action in government agencies. An FBI whistle-blower in the Minneapolis office whose action requests were sidelined put the blame on being located eight levels below the FBI director. Her pleas might have foiled the 2001 terrorist attacks. Multiple levels may also discourage innovation because it is easier to persist in old ways that require no further communication than to initiate and implement changes. Each bureaucratic level becomes a hurdle to be cleared or a trap for the innovator. Proposals for changes may never reach the people who have the power to initiate them. Hierarchical communication also impedes the flow of information that does not fit precisely into the formally established patterns.

Political scientists Robert O'Conner and Larry Spence warned that "hierarchical communication systems may be 'rational' in some abstract sense but, according to human communication theory, they deny rules basic to the successful exchange of information."[37] O'Connor and Spence contend that only face-to-face interactions can capture the implicit messages conveyed through voice, tone, gestures, vocabulary, and style. Yet such interactions are largely lacking in the typical bureaucratic situation, making it difficult to discern the real intentions of message senders. According to O'Conner and Spence, "the neglect of implicit messages makes bureaucratic organizations ponderous, inefficient, and unable to learn from their mistakes."[38]

The depersonalization common in hierarchical communication makes it especially difficult to know to what extent messages are meant to lead to action and to what extent they are tactical or purely symbolic. Hugh Heclo titled one of his books *A Government of Strangers*, referring to communication among bureaucrats who do not know one another. He commented about the difficulty of transmitting meanings accurately under such conditions: "Those on the receiving end of messages from political executives are accustomed to applying a heavy discount factor to mere proclamations." Heclo quoted a typical comment by a line official that "over the years you see that a lot of the instructions aren't intended to be carried out. It takes extra effort to make it clear to people down the line that something is meant, not just another statement for the record or some speech writer's inspiration."[39]

The extra effort to overcome doubts may take the form of structures and functions designed to build additional redundancy into the system. Examples are complex information-management systems, written reminders, beefed-up reporting structures, and the like. But, in Heclo's view, "none of these techniques are substitutes for personalized networks and discussions." However, this inability to capture all the nuances transmitted in face-to-face interactions can be advantageous. It makes it easier for organization members to interpret messages to fit their own predilections. It also facilitates turning down requests for help or ignoring them because impersonal messages are stripped of the emotional force that face-to-face interactions supply.

Several scholars have pointed out that hierarchical structuring is conducive to concealment and misrepresentation.[40] In turn, this may encourage "whistle-blowing," where employees bypass the hierarchy and take their concerns directly to higher authorities or to the public. When subordinates manage to pierce the middle layers and reach the top of the hierarchy, superiors are often unreceptive, especially in the face of status differences and their own contrary beliefs. The much-told story of the Japanese attack on Pearl Harbor in 1941 is illustrative. The attack planes were spotted by an army private nearly one hour before the bombing started. He notified his lieutenant who, "knowing" that no attack was in the offing, told his underling to "forget it."[41]

Even when good information transmission channels exist among various levels of the hierarchy, subordinates are often disinclined to use them because they feel intimidated by the trappings of hierarchy and are fearful of being perceived as troublemakers. Subordinates who want to look good to receive favorable evaluations may be reluctant to report problems because bad news often taints the messenger. Hence, bad news often does not flow upward. This unfortunate yet understandable yielding to self-interest occurs even when outside experts are hired. Such experts prefer to pass on messages that please rather than disturb the top echelons of the bureaucracy. Subordinates also lean toward withholding potentially disturbing information when they do not want to be saddled with extra work to correct problems. If there is fierce competition for promotions, subordinates seeking to increase their own chances may restrict information to keep it from coworkers. Where promotion and tenure are protected by a civil service system, such concerns become less acute.

Acculturation to the organization is yet another factor that stifles the upward flow of information within hierarchies. Organizations emphasize loyalty, adherence to rules, and enthusiastic support for the agency's mission. They indoctrinate their staffs and often convince the public to believe that the agency's performance is excellent even when there are problems. This discourages critical questions and reduces the number of proposals for fresh initiatives. In most political cultures, it is deemed improper to contradict people in higher organizational ranks. When President Bill Clinton in 1999 admitted to sexual misconduct in the White House, most members of his administration cautiously abstained from adverse comments. The veil of silence extended even to high-ranking Democrats in Congress. When the press reported that military appraisals made by Gen. Norman Schwarzkopf, commander of American forces in the Persian Gulf War, conflicted with President George Bush's views, Schwarzkopf promptly recanted. Top-level officials may feel that they must resign from their jobs before they can legitimately criticize their boss. For example, President Gerald Ford's press secretary, J. F. ter Horst, resigned so that he could protest Ford's pardoning of former President Richard Nixon without facing accusations of disloyalty.

Several structural and procedural changes may help to surmount the hurdles posed by hierarchy.[42] Making lines of communication available that are outside the normal hierarchical channels is one possibility. For instance, top-level administrators may periodically spend time in the field to observe and contact employees at all levels, rather than relying on reports. Alternatively, they may establish direct contacts with rank-and-file employees, bypassing intermediate levels. When that happens, intermediate levels should be consulted before they are bypassed, lest both morale and efficiency suffer.

Top bureaucrats may also talk with external contact people such as reporters and researchers who may be studying their organization. They may call on experts such as consultants or statistical analysts to investigate what is going on at remote lower levels. However, it is not clear how useful such unofficial sources are compared with more readily available inside sources. As one close observer of the Peace Corps described it:

> Unfortunately, neither the congressmen nor the press display much enthusiasm for visits to the mines. Yet this is what I found to be the key to getting the real story about the Peace Corps. I had to go to Ouagadougou and talk to the volunteers at their sites before I could really know what the Peace Corps was doing and what its problems were. I wasn't going to find out by asking the public affairs office. But that's where most reporters go and sit all day. . . .[43]

Other possibilities for reducing the ill effects of hierarchy include rearrangement of structures to reduce the number of bureaucratic layers through which information has to travel. Hierarchies then become flatter. This is particularly important in bureaucracies in which lower level employees are faced with complex nonroutine decisions. Case workers in social welfare agencies, for example, can make better decisions about an individual client's case after observing the situation directly than is possible for higher-ups who have no contact with the client. Psychological barriers to superior-subordinate communication also are easier to bridge when the hierarchy is flatter.

In response to the Reinventing Government reforms of the Clinton administration, many federal agencies have flattened their hierarchies by eliminating midlevel bureaucracies and allocating more control over decisions to street-level bureaucrats. Vice President Al Gore's initial report on Reinventing Government cited an example from the Forest Service as a model.[44] Flattening bureaucracies in a pilot project in the twenty-two-state Eastern region had increased productivity by 15 percent over a two-year span thanks to simplified budgets, elimination of layers of middle-management, and paring of central headquarters staffs by 20 percent. Functionally oriented "strategy teams" were created to serve the entire region's need in human and capital resources work, public relations, and natural and information resource development. Front-line employees had been empowered to make their own decisions about street-level business, such as granting grazing permits. That change had reduced the time needed to process a permit from thirty days to just a few hours.[45]

Still, as discussed previously, despite important successes, major restructuring remains extremely difficult to accomplish because it alters power relations and often requires cumbersome changes in the law or in official rules. It may be somewhat easier to arrange for teams of experts representing various specialties and ranks to work together as a task force for specific projects. The informality of this type of organization encourages exchange of information irrespective of the bureaucratic ranks of the members. The team approach also spurs innovations. "Quality circle" programs, discussed in Chapter 6, have become popular to improve performance, bringing together individuals from a cross-section of hierarchical levels to brainstorm solutions to problems.[46] It may also help to rotate experts and executives among jobs to break down barriers.

Specialization

Specialization is another source of communication problems related to the structure of organizations. Agencies may be divided into numerous highly specialized units that speak in mutually unintelligible jargons. Definitions of key terms such as what constitutes "unemployment" may be so incompatible that data about the same phenomenon may be useless for comparisons. One agency may call part-time workers, students, and retirees "unemployed," whereas another excludes them from that category. The National Bureau of Standards, the Maritime Administration, the Patent and Trademark Office, and the Economic Development Administration have their own language and interpretations, although all are part of the Department of Commerce. When research units are highly specialized and often physically remote from the organization they serve, specialization may be a serious communication barrier. Researchers may not fully understand what the ultimate users of their findings need and how it should be packaged for greatest usefulness. Much academic research is structured and presented in ways that make potential users in public agencies shy away from it as "purely academic," which translates to "operationally useless."

Specialization often produces unhealthy competition among units to control aspects of the work that each specialty sees as primarily within its domain. An example is the conflict between the Census Bureau, eager to retain previously used housing questions in the 1990 Census, and OMB's edict that these questions must be scrapped as superfluous paperwork. Each group claimed jurisdiction and insisted that its concerns were so weighty that they must prevail. Subunits often engage in overblown rhetoric that overstates the advantages of their case and exaggerates the risks of other options. They may also selectively pass information to top executives to boost their particular unit. These maneuvers are difficult to penetrate when they involve highly specialized knowledge. Competing units may not want to communicate with others to avoid betraying weakness or incurring obligations to release information they would rather keep for their own exclusive use. Substantial waste occurs when units do not share information and the analyses based on them. It is therefore not surprising that specialization often leads to parochialism and failure to reach out to sister units.

Damaging rivalries among specialized units are more common in the public than in the private sector because people tend to remain affiliated with the same unit over lengthy time periods. Bureaucratic rigidities make it difficult to circulate easily among various units, thereby learning to identify with them, as is more common in the private sector. The perennial tensions between the Bureau of Mines and the Army Corps of Engineers and between the Department of State and the Department of Defense are examples of damaging rivalries among organizations whose functions overlap. In the past, coordination of intelligence among Foreign Service agencies, the military, and intelligence agencies has been especially poor. Each has considered its own methods superior to those of its competitors.

Remedies for parochialism born of specialization and mutual ignorance require bringing specialists and their clients into closer contact. Rotating assignments to familiarize people with all branches of their organization, as has been done in the Forest Service, may be useful.[47] Conferences of various types that bring generalists and specialists together are another method. The many White House conferences organized around such problems as child welfare, pornography, or drug abuse are examples.

Centralization

Centralization is another structural barrier to good communication.[48] In many organizations most of the important communications are directed to top-level officials who are faced with message overloads. The consequences are undesirable, sometimes disastrous, delays before the information is processed and appropriate decisions made and neglect of the information requirements of line agencies and bottom levels of the organization. For example, when the head of a large agency orders all staff complaints to be funneled through his or her office, lower levels, well-equipped to deal with complaints, may not become aware of them in a timely fashion. On the other hand, if there is no centralization, much duplication of effort may result. More costly experts may be hired and cohesive, uniform planning for the entire organization may be impeded.

When it becomes physically impossible for top administrators to scan all information, how much and what kind should be diverted to other levels of the organization? How does one balance the need for central control and accountability with the need for procedural efficiency? How can one devise appropriate structures and guidelines for channeling information most effectively? The answers remain elusive. After studying practices at the Internal Revenue Service (IRS), the U.S. Customs Service, the Food and Drug Administration, the Social Security Administration, the U.S. Forest Service, and the Animal and Plant Health Inspection Service over the period of a year, Herbert Kaufman reported that subordinates "could not always explain fully how they decided whether to handle things themselves or pass them on to their bosses for signature; 'you just know' was a common answer. Within a few months after a new chief took over, it seemed to be a reflex action, apparently satisfactory to the subordinates and the chiefs alike."[49]

Kaufman pointed out that the quality of a bureau chief's leadership hinged on avoiding excessive centralization. "If great numbers of matters were referred to them for decision, other vital parts of their jobs would have been neglected and backlogs of matters awaiting decision would have accumulated." The fear of backlogs provided "strong incentives to install fine-mesh screens around the chiefs to hold down the number of things they decided personally."[50] However, when decentralization is excessive, so that subordinates make too many important decisions, their chiefs may become figureheads. The flow of intelligence to them may dry up when informants discover that the chiefs are not handling their messages.

Decisions are likely to move to the top level when subordinates are risk-averse, when they believe that the top administrator has contextual information that they lack, when they respect their boss's knowledge or cannot resolve differences of opinion, and when bureau chiefs worry about the judgment and reliability of subordinates. Pressure to make uniform policy decisions throughout an agency or throughout the country also forces decisions upward. Decisions are likely to remain at lower levels when subordinates have special expertise, are highly committed to the outcome of particular programs, when speed is essential and subordinates are competent, and when bureau chiefs want to encourage employee self-reliance and innovation.[51]

These various, sometimes contradictory, factors make it hard to predict which decisions will end up at top levels. Kaufman found that decisions reaching the top ranged from the trivial to the very important. To strike a balance between overload and isolation at the top, decisions affecting the internal management of the agency were often made by subordinates because they believed they knew the agency better than the chief. The chief could then concentrate more on external communication, an especially important arena in the public sector because democratic norms demand ready access to public officials. Kaufman found that in the agencies he studied access to top administrators was fairly automatic when calls came from politically well-connected individuals. Among the privileged were members of Congress, the White House staff, top officers of the departments in which the agencies were housed, civic leaders or clientele or professional groups, other government agencies, and journalists.[52]

Centralization of information seems to work best in single-purpose organizations such as the Forest Service, particularly when there is good rapport throughout the organization. But when organizational missions are diverse, centralization may be inefficient. Top officials may not fully understand the problems faced at lower levels that deal with areas outside their competence. In that case, centralization may have to be limited sharply to the few areas that concern all levels of the organization and require uniform policymaking. The results may be a hybrid organization that combines centralized with decentralized authority.

The increasing complexity of the tasks performed by public organizations and the mushrooming of information especially on the Internet have exerted strong pressure to decentralize information intake and decision making. The trend has been enhanced by emphasis on responsiveness to clients and employee participation in decisions—hallmarks of the Reinventing Government reforms.[53] Decentralization makes lower level officials feel more important and may expedite decision making. But it also creates problems of consistency and integration within organizations and may make large-scale planning more difficult. When implementation of decisions is decentralized, it may be more difficult to communicate with all the units involved in carrying out tasks. Again, Internet technologies have been a tremendous boon to resolving such problems.

The Direction of Communication Flows

The discussion of hierarchy, specialization, and centralization indicates that communication flow problems vary, depending on the direction of the flow. This makes it important to focus more specifically on problems related to the direction of message flows. As the arrows in Figure 3–1 indicate, flows may be directed upward, downward, or laterally. The Bureau of Indian Affairs may send messages upward to the assistant secretary for Indian Affairs who may relay them to higher ups, such as personnel in the Office of the Special Trustee for American Indians, or the inspector general, or the secretary of the Interior. Downward flows travel in reverse order. Information flows laterally if the Minerals Management Service contacted the Bureau of Land Management or, in a cross-channel trip, if the Bureau of Indian Affairs communicated with

Figure 3-1 U.S. Department of the Interior

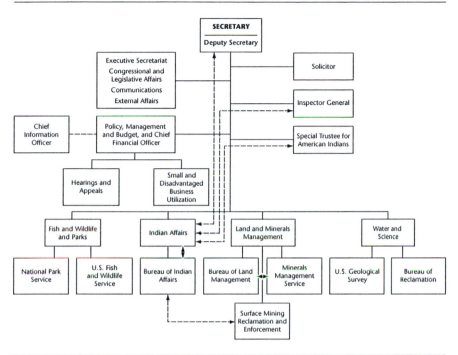

NOTE: The Office of Insular Affairs also reports to the Assistant Secretary, Policy, Management, and Budget.

the Office of Surface Mining Reclamation and Enforcement. The structure of the Department of the Interior is typical for complex modern government agencies. The department has nineteen major divisions and multiple subdivisions, including an Office of Information Resources Management and multiple information officers.

Downward Flows

Superiors tend to communicate more freely and more often with subordinates than the reverse. In general, the greater the differences in status and power and the more formal the procedures in an organization, the more likely it is that downward communication will predominate and upward communication will be inhibited. This can become troublesome.[54] If subordinates receive many orders and have little opportunity for feedback, the atmosphere may become authoritarian, breeding resentment. Therefore, it is very important for executives to take time to establish rapport with their subordinates and create an atmosphere of mutual respect.[55] Chief executives who have brief tenures in huge agencies find this very difficult to do.

Top-level politically appointed executives in the public sector are at times particularly handicapped in communicating with lower echelon personnel. There are several reasons. These executives, who owe their appointment to political skills, frequently lack the necessary technical and managerial knowledge to provide task directives. Because of the typically short tenure of political executives, they may be unfamiliar with organizational procedures and practices and often with the rationales for doing certain kinds of jobs. The area in which politically appointed executives generally communicate most effectively is indoctrination about organizational goals. Yet this is the area where they are likely to encounter the most resistance from long-term civil service personnel who have formed their own ideas about the best goals for the agency. In fact, lower level bureaucrats are generally able to resist policy directives from higher authorities, including legislators and top executives, through their control over day-to-day operations and their intimate knowledge of the agency's operations. For example, lower level bureaucrats kept established stricter policies fairly intact despite the Reagan administration directives to ease enforcement of clean air legislation.[56]

When labor–management problems erupt in the public sector, inadequate downward communication is a frequent complaint. The perennial teachers' strikes in major American cities are good examples. Because teachers often believe that their superiors bestow too little praise for their achievements and fail to address problems that impede teachers' performance, they feel alienated. They also think that policies are often imposed on them by administrators who are unfamiliar with classroom realities. Many of the problems that surface during contract negotiations, when the atmosphere is heated and not conducive to settlement, could be better resolved through establishing permanent communication channels between school administrations and school boards on the one hand and teachers and teachers' unions on the other.

A study of the Pennsylvania Department of Public Welfare furnishes a good example of problems in downward communication and the difficulties they can cause.[57] The study was undertaken to discover the reasons for excessively high rates of psychosomatic disabilities and pervasive low morale in the agency. The job turnover rate was also high, especially among well-educated employees.[58] Responses to a questionnaire administered to 1,313 case workers indicated that they deemed the agency's system of communication seriously flawed and that they thought that their superiors were preoccupied with bureaucratic rules and did not understand their problems (see Table 3–1). They felt overloaded with often vague messages from the top while their upward messages received inadequate attention.

Fifty-five percent of the case workers also complained that they received inconsistent requests. Conflicting federal, state, and local regulations may be the explanation. Workers were unhappy about excessive checking of their records, repetitive messages, and frenzied and overbearing responses to upward messages sent by subordinates to superiors. They also complained about

Table 3-1 Percentage of Workers Perceiving Specific Communication Disturbances

Disturbance	Percentage reporting
Messages do not result in prompt responses	80.3
Too many messages to read or digest	76.6
Officials do not understand daily casework problems	75.6
Officials preoccupied with enforcing bureaucratic rules	63.2
Messages inconsistennt	55.0
Failure to acknowledge messages	46.9
Responses frenzied and overbearing	44.5
Messages vague	44.4
Messages surprising	44.3
Records checked excessively	42.2
Instructions not meant seriously	38.3
Messages difficult to interpret	35.6
Messages repetitive	30.7

SOURCE: Robert E. O'Conner and Larry D. Spence, "Communication Disturbances in a Welfare Bureaucracy: A Case for Self-Management," *Journal of Sociology and Social Welfare* 4 (1976): 186. Reprinted with permission.

limited opportunities for lateral communication whereby workers performing the same tasks could exchange ideas and benefit from one another's experience. Seventy-one percent of the workers said that it had not been made clear to them what was expected of them. They complained that downward messages took little account of workers' information needs or the need to validate their performance. The messages were therefore viewed as disorienting and dysfunctional. Thirty-eight percent of the workers believed that the instructions issued by their superiors were not intended to be carried out. This is a common complaint in public agencies where laws and rules often spell out in excessive detail what should be done, even though the superiors know that these regulations are ill-adapted to the realities of field situations.

Workers also considered it demeaning when superiors conveyed implicit messages through styles of interaction and body language. Much bureaucratic communication is therefore ignored or circumvented because employees consider it unnecessary and burdensome reporting that seriously interrupts their work. Two thirds of the Pennsylvania workers admitted that they violated explicit rules despite the risk of disciplinary action. Fifty-seven percent said that they withheld helpful information because of communication difficulties.

The analysts who studied communication patterns in the Pennsylvania Department of Public Welfare recommended that decision making about clients should take place largely at the caseworker level to make it more client centered and to reduce downward communications. Decentralization would increase upward communication of information and suggestions by case workers, enhancing their sense of self-worth. The study's concluding observations noted, "While all this may violate traditional ideas about hierarchical organization and the necessity of status differentiation, that only means the time has come to question and criticize those ideas."[59]

Lateral Flows

Lateral (horizontal) communication occurs among individuals who are positioned at the same organizational level. When it involves members of functionally distinct organizations, it is often called "cross-channel" communication. Lateral flows are used mainly to coordinate the work of various units and usually take the form of meetings, telephone conversations, memos, notes, and even social activities. Coordination may also occur through establishing functionally oriented teams staffed by people from different units. When drug enforcement task forces are created within the criminal justice system, for example, they often combine personnel from police departments in different jurisdictions.[60] The effectiveness of such task forces hinges on how they are structured in terms of the units that are included and the channels designated for interagency communication.

Lateral communication tends to be rapid, facile, and often quite informal. It is more likely to occur in organizations with diverse structures and much task specialization so that specialists in one unit want to communicate with their counterparts in other units. Nuclear physicists may benefit more from communicating with other nuclear physicists than with electrical engineers in their own units. Similarly, when administrators go outside their own organizations to coordinate activities with related organizations, they often concentrate their contacts at a peer level where communication needs are likely to be similar.

Lateral communication in the public sector is often more constrained than in the private sector because of the sheer size of the governmental enterprise and because public agencies compete more directly for the same scarce resources. The fact that bureaucrats are less likely to belong to professional associations and unions than their counterparts in the private sector is an additional damper. Top administrators often view lateral communication with concern because it has the potential for reducing their power. Talking with their peers gives people insights that might otherwise be available only to the top leadership. Accordingly, top administrators are tempted to restrict lateral communication, insisting that all communication pass through them.

A case in point occurred in 1979 when Patricia Harris became secretary of health, education, and welfare. Because she inherited a staff that was not of her choosing and apt to be hostile, she curbed lateral communication as a possible threat to internal efficiency.[61] Meetings, calls, and staff contacts between her subordinates and members of Congress, congressional and White House staffs, and the Office of Management and Budget were forbidden without previous authorization. In this way she could be sure that only authorized personnel would present departmental views. Other cabinet secretaries have issued similar directives.

Although beneficial in some respects, restraints of lateral flow can impede coordination among public agencies performing related functions. It can lead to much duplication of intelligence-gathering efforts. Coordination between the State and Defense departments, for instance, has been notoriously poor, often with dire consequences. A typical situation occurred in 1989 when a Pentagon report listed South Africa's African National Congress as a dangerous terrorist group. This happened at a time when the State Department was trying to build ties to the militant antiapartheid organization and had endorsed some of the ANC's objectives. Better communication might have avoided this embarrassing divergence in policies.

Upward Flows

Upward flows are mainly used to provide feedback on operations within the organization. They encompass (1) self-reports by subordinates about work they have performed or about their problems and grievances; (2) reports about others and their problems; (3) messages concerning organizational practices and policies in general; and (4) normative messages, suggesting how actual or potential tasks should be performed.[62]

Upward communication is important for assessing the effectiveness of internal communications. It indicates whether downward messages reached their targets, were understood, and led to appropriate actions. Given the vagueness of many directives and the wide geographic dispersion of many government offices, upward feedback is essential for sound decision making. It taps important internal data that are unavailable from other sources. Upward flow also boosts morale and provides a safety valve for potentially explosive gripes. Unfortunately, as the numbers and diversity of internal and external messages increase, structuring adequate upward feedback becomes problematic.[63]

As discussed earlier, upward communication is often restrained. One reason is the simple fact of hierarchy. People feel inhibited about communicating with their superiors, especially at levels above their immediate supervisors. Even if top management keeps an open door, this opportunity to communicate upward remains largely symbolic. Upward communication also suffers when subordinates use it to manipulate superiors for personal or group advantage. As Daniel Katz and Robert Kahn stated, "It is not only that they tell the boss what he or she wants to hear, but what they want the boss to know. . . . Full and objective reporting might be penalized by the supervisor or regarded as espionage by peers."[64] Hence, the messages that flow upward often provide skewed versions of reality.

To avert such problems, executives must be receptive and sensitive listeners and must acknowledge legitimate demands. Placing suggestion boxes throughout the organization or rewarding helpful suggestions may be useful. When Adm. Elmo Zumwalt assumed command of the U.S. Navy, for example, he encouraged employee correspondence by regularly publishing selected letters in the Navy newspaper, along with his responses. This symbolized that the letters were valued and that the top commander was interested enough in their content to answer them personally.[65]

To prevent top officials from drowning in an excess of upward information flows, organizations must often condense them despite the danger that superiors may become insulated. Insulation is a major problem for key leaders, such as presidents, governors, mayors of large cities, and their inner-circle advisers. Although many feedback messages can be properly processed at lower levels, top-level administrators must remain aware of operations throughout their agency. Overly zealous shielding to conserve their energies for other tasks may come to haunt them if troubles erupt and they are forced to plead ignorance.

Grapevine Connections

Formal communication patterns, which mirror an organization's formal authority structure, are always supplemented by informal systems. The formal and informal structures are usually complementary. They can also serve as substitutes for each other so that many messages can pass through either one. People within the organization thus can bypass formal rules or go through "channels." Informal communication—christened *grapevine* during the Civil War because of the configuration of makeshift telegraph lines—is needed because formal structures tend to be restrictive and often out of date because of the slow pace of changes. By contrast, informal channels can be quickly established when needed.[66]

Formal channels generally are limited to routine messages, such as relaying policy directives, correspondence, and reports. The grapevine, in addition, carries information that would be unsuitable for formal channels, including social and personal messages. Similarly, formal rules provide general fixed frameworks for sending messages; informal communication adapts to specific situations, as needed. The formal network tends to be dominated by top executives, whereas control over informal communication is dispersed more widely. Grapevine communication can ignore positional roles and move helter-skelter, depending on the situation.

Grapevine messages usually travel by word of mouth or via e-mail. Presumably, face-to-face communication fosters trust, social support, and rapid feedback. It is still uncertain to what extent e-mail does the same. Although grapevine communication may not give a complete picture, researchers agree that usually 75 to 90 percent of the information traveling via grapevine channels is accurate.[67] Informal communication also encourages change and innovation because feedback is immediate and situation specific. It does not prematurely alert opposition that might try to fight changes.[68] Because its paper trails are less obvious and often absent, it can be officially denied when this is advantageous.[69]

Grapevine communication also has several drawbacks. It is unsystematic and generated and driven largely by individual self-interest. Grapevine channels are often restricted to privileged groups or long-term members of the organization. When such "old boy" networks develop informally, laws against discrimination are usually powerless to force inclusion of disadvantaged groups. Grapevine may also degenerate into rumor, which involves the circulation of unsubstantiated, often erroneous information, particularly in times of crisis when information is scarce.

The main message of this chapter is that the structure of organizations is far more influential in determining how well they will function than is generally acknowledged. The role that organization designs play in shaping information flows and determining who controls organizational intelligence therefore deserves much more attention, experimentation, and careful planning than it has received from practitioners and scholars thus far. Constantly changing situations and technologies preordain that it will be forever debatable what structural arrangements are best for effective communication flows.

One aspect of this quest for more effective structures that has long intrigued scholars and practitioners is networking. How should structures be connected? How do complex communication networks arise within and between organizations? How do they function and what are the consequences? We turn to that message flow issue in the next chapter.

NOTES

1. Peter T. Kilborn, "Sex Abuse Cases Stun Pentagon, But the Problem Has Deep Roots," *New York Times*, Feb. 10, 1997.
2. For a differentiation between structural analysis and network analysis, see J. David Johnson, "Approaches to Organizational Communication Structure," *Journal of Business Research* 25 (1992): 99–113; the impact of structure on interorganizational functions is discussed by Laurence J. O'Toole, Jr., "Inter-organizational Communication: Opportunities and Challenges for Public Administration," in *Handbook of Administrative Communication*, ed. James L. Garnett and Alexander Kouzmin (New York: Marcel Dekker, 1997), 61–77.
3. James G. March and Herbert A. Simon, *Organizations* (New York: Wiley, 1958), 158–169.
4. Robert D. McPhee, "Formal Structure and Organizational Communication," in *Organizational Communication: Traditional Themes and New Directions*, ed. Robert D. McPhee and Phillip K. Tompkins (Beverly Hills, Calif.: Sage, 1985), 152. Also see Anselm Strauss, "The Articulation of Project Work: An Organizational Process," *The Sociological Quarterly* 29 (1988): 163–178.
5. "Terrorism Alerts: The FAA's Dilemma," *Wall Street Journal*, Apr. 3, 1989.

6. Jerald Hage, Michael Aiken, and Cora B. Marrett, "Organization Structure and Communications," in *The Study of Organizations,* ed. Daniel Katz, Robert L. Kahn, and J. Stacy Adams (San Francisco: Jossey-Bass, 1982), 304.

7. Parveen P. Gupta, Mark W. Dirsmith, and Timothy J. Fogarty, "Coordination and Control in a Government Agency: Contingency and Institutional Theory Perspectives on GAO Audits," *Administrative Science Quarterly* 39 (1994): 264–284.

8. "Sunset" laws now provide an automatic expiration for many laws. They may be part of a specific piece of legislation or they may cover multiple laws.

9. Lawrence K. Altman, "Gaps Shown in Flu Fight," *New York Times,* Dec. 3, 1991.

10. Terry E. Branstad, "Restructuring and Downsizing," in *Governors on Governing,* ed. Robert D. Behn (Washington, D.C.: National Governors' Association, 1991), 148–149.

11. Charles Walcott and Karen M. Hult, "Organizing the White House: Structure, Environment, and Organizational Governance," *American Journal of Political Science* 31 (February 1987): 122.

12. Stephen Engleberg, "Doubts on Intelligence Data: Iran Affair Renews the Issue," *New York Times,* Aug. 31, 1987.

13. David Stephens, "President Carter, the Congress, and NEA: Creating the Department of Education," *Political Science Quarterly* 98 (winter 1983–1984): 645.

14. Robert Katzmann, *Institutional Disability* (Washington, D.C.: Brookings Institution, 1986), chaps. 2–5. Also see Keith Krehbiel, *Information and Legislative Organization* (Ann Arbor: University of Michigan Press, 1991).

15. For examples, see Michael J. Malbin, *Unelected Representatives: Congressional Staffs and the Future of Representative Government* (New York: Basic Books, 1980), 232–233. Also see Stephen Kelman, *Making Public Policy* (New York: Basic Books, 1987), 54.

16. Edward I. Sidlow and Beth Henschen, "The Performance of House Committee Staff Functions: A Comparative Exploration," *Western Political Quarterly* 38 (September 1985): 485.

17. David Whiteman, "The Fate of Policy Analysis in Congressional Decision Making: Three Types of Use in Committees," *Western Political Quarterly* 38 (June 1985): 295–296; David Whiteman, *Communication in Congress: Members, Staff, and the Search for Information* (Lawrence: University Press of Kansas, 1995), chap. 2.

18. For insights into lobbying practices of major corporations, see Conference Board, *Managing Federal Government Relations,* Research Report No. 905 (New York: Conference Board, 1988).

19. Sidlow and Henschen, "The Performance of House Committee Staff Functions," 487.

20. Daniel Katz and Robert L. Kahn, *The Social Psychology of Organizations* (New York: Wiley, 1978), 455.

21. Richard F. Fenno, *Homestyle: House Members in Their Districts* (Boston: Little, Brown, 1978).

22. William T. Gormley, Jr., "The Representation Revolution: Reforming State Regulation through Public Representation," *Administration and Society* 18 (August 1986): 181.

23. William T. Gormley, Jr., "Intergovernmental Conflict on Environmental Policy: The Attitudinal Connection," *Western Political Quarterly* 40 (June 1987): 300.
24. Pub. Law No. 104-13 (1980). http://www.rdc.noaa.gov/~pra/pralaw.htm
25. John Anthony Maltese, *Spin Control: The White House Office of Communications and the Management of Presidential News,* 2d ed. (Chapel Hill: University of North Carolina Press, 1994), appendix.
26. Raymond A. Bauer, Ithiel de Sola Pool, and Lewis A. Dexter, *American Business and Public Policy* (New York: Atherton, 1963).
27. Everett M. Rogers and Rekha Agarwala Rogers, *Communication in Organizations* (New York: Free Press, 1976), 78–80.
28. David Axelrod, "New City Services Plan Threatens Political Truce," *Chicago Tribune,* May 3, 1984.
29. Abraham H. Maslow and Norbert L. Mintz, "Effects of Esthetic Surroundings: Initial Effects of Three Esthetic Conditions upon Perceiving 'Energy' and 'Well-Being' in Faces," *Journal of Psychology* 41 (1956): 253. Also see Sherry Devereaux Ferguson and Stewart Ferguson, "The Physical Environment and Communication," in *Organizational Communications,* 2d ed., ed. Sherry Devereaux Ferguson and Stewart Ferguson (New Brunswick, N.J.: Transaction Books, 1988), 183–187.
30. The impact of physical settings is discussed fully in Charles T. Goodsell, *The Social Meaning of Civic Space* (Lawrence: University Press of Kansas, 1988); Fred I. Steele, *Physical Settings and Organizational Development* (Reading, Mass: Addison-Wesley, 1973); and Ferguson and Ferguson, "The Physical Environment and Communication."
31. Rogers and Rogers, *Communication in Organizations,* 102.
32. Terence R. Mitchell and James R. Larson, Jr., *People in Organizations: An Introduction to Organizational Behavior,* 3d ed. (New York: McGraw-Hill, 1987), 237.
33. Ferguson and Ferguson, "The Physical Environment and Communication."
34. John L. Crompton and Charles W. Lamb, Jr., *Marketing Government and Social Services* (New York: Wiley, 1986), 212.
35. Ibid., 211.
36. Gerald M. Goldhaber, *Organizational Communication,* 3d ed. (Dubuque, Iowa: Wm. C. Brown, 1983), 200. Also see Clyde Haberman, "The Injustice of Incivility in Civic Duty," *New York Times,* Aug. 2, 2000.
37. Robert E. O'Conner and Larry D. Spence, "Communication Disturbances in a Welfare Bureaucracy: A Case for Self-Management," *Journal of Sociology and Social Welfare* 4 (1976): 182.
38. Ibid., 183.
39. Hugh Heclo, *A Government of Strangers: Executive Politics in Washington* (Washington, D.C.: Brookings Institution, 1977), 207.
40. Harold L. Wilensky, *Organizational Intelligence: Knowledge and Policy in Government and Industry* (New York: Basic Books, 1967), 42–48; Janet Fulk and Sirish Mani, "Distortion of Communication in Hierarchical Relationships," in *Communication Yearbook* 9, ed. Margaret L. McLaughlin (Beverly Hills, Calif.: Sage, 1986), 483–510.
41. Quoted in Harold F. Gortner, Julianne Mahler, and Jeanne Bell Nicholson, *Organizational Theory: A Public Perspective* (Chicago: Dorsey, 1987), 165.

42. Wilensky, *Organizational Intelligence*, 42–48; Alexander L. George, *Presidential Decisionmaking in Foreign Policy: The Effective Use of Information and Advice* (Boulder: Westview, 1980), 148–159.

43. Charles Peters, "From Ouagadougou to Cape Canaveral: Why the Bad News Doesn't Travel Up," *Washington Monthly* 18 (April 1986): 31.

44. Al Gore, *From Red Tape to Results: Creating a Government that Works Better and Costs Less.* Report of the National Performance Review (Washington, D.C.: U.S. Government Printing Office, 1993), 5–6.

45. Ronald E. Yates, "Total Quality Management: A Forest Service Resource," *Chicago Tribune,* Feb. 15, 1993.

46. Terrance L. Albrecht and Vickie A. Ropp, "Communicating about Innovation in Networks of Three U.S. Organizations," *Journal of Communication* 34 (summer 1984): 79–80, and sources cited therein.

47. Herbert Kaufman, *The Forest Ranger: A Study in Administrative Behavior* (Baltimore: Johns Hopkins Press, 1967).

48. Wilensky, *Organizational Intelligence*, 58–62.

49. Herbert Kaufman, *The Administrative Behavior of Federal Bureau Chiefs* (Washington, D.C.: Brookings Institution, 1981), 21–22.

50. Ibid., 21.

51. Ibid., 21–22.

52. Ibid., 35.

53. Gore, *From Red Tape to Results,* chaps. 2 and 3.

54. Gortner et al., *Organizational Theory,* 160.

55. Ibid., 162.

56. B. Dan Wood, "Principals, Bureaucrats, and Responsiveness in Clean Air Enforcements," *American Political Science Review* 82 (March 1988): 213–234.

57. O'Conner and Spence, "Communication Disturbances in a Welfare Bureaucracy."

58. Ibid., 181–182.

59. Ibid., 198.

60. Edmund F. McGarrell and Kip Schlegel, "The Implementation of Federally Funded Multijurisdictional Drug Task Forces: Organizational Structure and Interagency Relationships," *Journal of Criminal Justice* 21 (1993): 231–244.

61. Kaufman, *The Administrative Behavior of Federal Bureau Chiefs,* 167.

62. Katz and Kahn, *The Social Psychology of Organizations,* 446.

63. Ibid., 432.

64. Ibid., 447.

65. Goldhaber, *Organizational Communication,* 159.

66. Ibid., 164; Katz and Kahn, *The Social Psychology of Organizations,* 449.

67. Goldhaber, *Organizational Communication,* 164, and sources cited therein. Also see R. Wayne Pace, *Organizational Communication: Foundations for Human Resource Development* (Englewood Cliffs, N.J.: Prentice-Hall, 1983), 58.

68. Albrecht and Ropp, "Communicating about Innovation in Networks of Three U.S. Organizations."

69. Lori A. Fidler and J. David Johnson, "Communication and Innovation Implementation," *Academy of Management Review* 9 (1984): 704–711; and David Whiteman, *Communication in Congress: Members, Staff, and the Search for Information* (Lawrence: University Press of Kansas, 1995).

Chapter 4 Constructing Networks

The Whys and Hows of Network Formation

"Networking" has become a buzzword of our time. Individuals network, interest groups network, countries network, and members of public and private organizations network. The chief goal of networking is always the same—to establish communication links with significant others to share information about mutually relevant situations. The chief goal of network analysis is to examine the communication roles played by organization members and the consequences for the performance of the organization.

General Patterns

Networks have been formally defined as relatively stable patterns of information flows within organizations that develop when individuals and groups of people—called "nodes" in network jargon—generate and exchange information on a regular basis.[1] Because people live and work in groups, networks are omnipresent throughout society. They are, as Ithiel de Sola Pool said, "the thread that holds any social organization together."[2] Besides exchanging work-related information, people use communication networks to enhance their power and influence and to gratify their desire to affiliate with a group and enjoy affection and warm interpersonal relations.[3]

Within organizations, networks should be tailored for the tasks to be performed. If networks are larger than needed, participants may be burdened with unnecessary information; if they are too small, organizations may be unable to gather and process all the data they require for sound operations. Once established, networks tend to maintain their patterns over long periods of time. Such stability can be troublesome when organizations are changing rapidly. In times of flux, it is essential to keep network structures open enough so that changing patterns reflect evolving information requirements. An expanding school district, for example, needs to incorporate new families into its communication networks, especially when the newcomers represent unique demographic characteristics.

When organizational components become too unwieldy or functionally diverse to satisfy the needs of all members in a single communication circuit, networks linking only selected individuals tend to develop spontaneously. Small networks of five to twenty-five people embedded in a larger network are often called "cliques." Most public agencies operate through multiple networks because they carry out many diverse functions and employ large numbers of people who need not be in touch on a regular basis with everyone else in the organization.

Analysis of typical information-flow patterns within most organizations clearly shows that information does not circulate freely to everyone. Some groups are regularly privy to the most important information. Dubbed "old boy" or "insider" networks, these groups often develop close personal ties as well as shared values and expectations. Networks beyond insider circles usually share less important information, and their members often differ substantially in outlook from insiders so that intergroup communication may become difficult. Participation in the insider network confers status and power whereas deliberate or inadvertent exclusion from insider networks reduces opportunities for influence. Network configurations thus determine and reflect the organizational power structure. This is why the study of networks is crucial for understanding how organizations function.

Information-flow problems can often be diminished or corrected through deliberate network restructuring. A case involving the issuance of European Community passports by the Dutch government is in point.[4] When networks within the two ministries charged with overseeing the printing of new passports could not agree on the terms because the ministries were linked to different interest groups, the prime minister assigned the project to one of the contestants, the Foreign Affairs Ministry. That ministry abandoned earlier compromise plans and created a totally new network of groups that reflected foreign affairs concerns. When that network failed because it was not inclusive enough, the other contestant, the Ministry of Home Affairs, was put in charge. It was able to assemble a successful network to manage the new passport system along the lines favored by the Home Affairs Ministry.

Network structures can be changed in various ways. Instead of creating an entirely new structure, executives can change the roster of network participants by adding or dropping members. They can also increase or decrease or merely alter the resources available to a network and they can change the operational rules, such as requiring public hearings or approval of decisions by an outside agency.[5]

Adding new people to a network may produce major changes in the substance and framing of information streams because newcomers often introduce perspectives drawn from other networks. For example, when environmental analysts were added to the staffs of the Army Corps of Engineers and the Forest Service to help them prepare environmental impact statements, environmental considerations became part of the deliberations of these agencies. Because these concerns were introduced during the very early stages of planning various projects, before any plans had crystallized, implementation was likely.[6]

Networks may reflect the formal structure of the organization. More commonly, they are dictated by functional needs and interpersonal chemistry. Although influenced by formal structures, networks tend to be less structured. They often cut in unpredictable ways across hierarchical levels and interorganizational barriers.[7] Networks may also be deliberately created by political leaders who want to control who the insiders and outsiders will be.

Friendship Networks

Presidential cabinets are good examples of networks based on both formal and friendship patterns. Structural arrangements determine the formal cabinet membership because occupants of specified offices automatically become cabinet members. But it is not uncommon for presidents to add personally chosen informal networks of advisers. These have been known as "kitchen cabinets."[8] On the positive side, networks based on friendship permit executives to tap into congenial information networks that they might not reach through formal organizational networks. On the negative side, tapping into groups of soul mates decreases opportunities for hearing detached criticism and diverse thoughts.

The Kennedy administration's imprudent decision in 1961 to invade Cuba's Bay of Pigs shows the disastrous consequences that may follow when friends talk only to friends.[9] CIA director Allen Dulles and CIA deputy director Richard Bissell who favored the ill-conceived plans had many friends in high places. Dulles and President Kennedy had become friends through common acquaintances. This made it easy for Dulles to gain access to the president and get a sympathetic hearing for his views. McGeorge Bundy, the president's special assistant for national security affairs, knew Bissell through friendship networks formed as an undergraduate at Yale University. He admired Bissell's intellect. White House aide Arthur Schlesinger Jr. had known Dulles in the Office of Strategic Services during World War II and had become Bissell's friend when Bissell worked for the Marshall Plan for European recovery in the post–World War II years. Assistant Secretary of State for Latin American Affairs Thomas Mann was a personal friend of both Dulles and Bissell.

Opponents of the ill-considered invasion plans, such as the joint chiefs of staff, were unlikely to voice their reservations, knowing that the CIA leadership was closely linked to the president's network. Friendship ties thus may discourage other voices from expressing contrary views that might have forestalled the blunder. The obvious drawbacks of friendship networks are balanced by major advantages. Among friends, interaction is easy because it is based on shared experiences, values, and mutual trust and understanding.

Issue Networks

Just as friendships can become the magnet that draws people together into communication networks, so shared interests in particular issues often generate network structures. Overlapping jurisdictions over various issues have become the rule in policy areas such as occupational health and safety, air and water pollution, consumer protection, and energy production. The nature of the issue, rather than the more formal ordinary relations among agencies, then determines what shape this network will take and what its members will do to foster their shared concerns.[10] In many instances, issue networks encompass public agencies, private groups, technical experts, and policy activists concerned about the issue. When network members disagree about the appropriate policies for dealing with an issue, they may subdivide into coalitions that share information to foster preferred goals.[11]

Once formed, these networks tend to grow whenever issues move onto the public policy agenda and new groups decide to join. This has happened in areas such as energy policy, where oil interests, conservationists, and consumer groups were joined by tax reformers, nuclear power specialists, and civil rights groups eager for energy-related jobs. Each new group contributed fresh information and perspectives. In many respects, this diversity of interests and information makes it more difficult to construct policy coalitions within the networks. In other respects, the proliferation of players eases coalition building because it offers new opportunities "to split and recombine the many sources of support and opposition that exist on policy issues."[12] Public hearings often serve as a way to recruit new groups into coalitions. Because the life of these networks is limited to the life of particular issues, network construction has become a perennial task for political leaders.[13]

When issue networks involve complex technical problems, as often happens, information contributed by technical experts with political savvy tends to become dominant. Political scientist Hugh Heclo refers to such experts as "technopols." They are activists with specialized knowledge, which includes knowing people who share an interest in the particular issue. Because they serve as experts in a variety of different networks, they are extremely influential. In time, they become so well-known that they are repeatedly consulted, which gives them entry to an exceptionally wide array of issue networks. As Heclo put it, "More than ever, policy making is becoming an intramural activity among expert issue-watchers, their networks, and their networks of networks. In this situation any neat distinction between the governmental structure and its environment tends to break down."[14]

The prevalence of issue networks has several adverse consequences for American political life. Like all concentrations of decision power by exclusionary groups, it runs counter to the democratic values of open access to power and to significant information and dealings. Technopols, more than generalists, tend to ignore average people who lack expertise in the issue under discussion. Accordingly, public influence on policy outcomes diminishes because of the deference accorded technical expertise and because of the difficulty of divining what transpires in complex networks. Whenever various groups of technopols do compete for the support of average citizens and each group emphasizes its own perception of "truth," people can become totally confused and often cynical about the possibilities of knowing where the truth lies. Disagreements among experts also hamper consensus within an issue network, particularly when political considerations run at cross purposes with scientific verities. Technocrats cannot usually be bought off with the kinds of material rewards that have been the coin of the realm in politics.

When issue debates become battles over the merits of scientific findings, such as the safety levels of mercury in drinking water, it becomes difficult to reach closure so that action can take place. There is always just one more study that needs to be done or one more player who needs to be heard. Afterward, the additional information must be fully considered, reopening many previously reached decisions. Political executives who try to push for urgently required action may find it hard to oppose the delays recommended by the "experts" and by disgruntled network partners. Occasionally they can successfully appeal to nonpolitical values such as efficiency and the need for the service, but more often than not, action is delayed and important goals are frustrated.

Despite their drawbacks, issue networks are here to stay because they are bridges between the various branches and levels of government.[15] They fill the void left by the weakening of party-based networks. "For example, on energy policy," according to Heclo,

> regardless of one's position on gas deregulation or incentives to producers, the policy technocracy has established a common language for discussing the issues, a shared grammar for identifying the major points of contention, a mutually familiar rhetoric of argumentation. . . . Like experienced party politicians of earlier times, policy politicians in the knowledge networks may not agree; but they understand each other's way of looking at the world and arguing about policy choices.[16]

The new focus on issue networks dominated by technical experts has led all branches and levels of government to hire issue experts for their staffs. Pressure groups, too, have become more oriented to joining issue networks.

Network Analysis

Measurement Issues

Network analysis, as noted, aims to capture the interactive aspects of communication. Unlike survey research, "The network paradigm refocused researchers' preoccupations with individuals as independent senders and receivers of messages toward a concept of individuals as nodes in a network of interdependent relationships. Instead of analyzing average values of aggregated individual-level variables, network analysis focuses on patterns of relationships among individuals."[17]

Network analysis does not pool the information gathered from organization members to arrive at a generalized description of the organization, like traditional multivariate descriptive techniques. Instead, it preserves the data sets of individual members and describes each person's placement in the organization. Besides indicating who communicates with whom in the formal or informal communication network, either reciprocally or nonreciprocally, network analysis also indicates the importance of each of these communication links for the work of the organization. Studies of the reliability of such sociometric data show that patterns of group interaction are quite stable, even though individual behaviors may vary considerably over time.[18]

However, some caution is in order when using sociometric data based on a one-time survey that may not capture customary interaction behavior. Moreover, behavior may depend on the nature of the issue that is the focus of information exchanges. Major and minor crises may alter network patterns temporarily or permanently.[19] A single-shot investigation is thus bound to miss a variety of network routines that come into play periodically. Ideally, studies should be repeated, covering multiple points in time. The patterns detected are also determined in part by the nature of the questions asked by the investigator. It is therefore wise to phrase questions in different ways to tap diverse thinking patterns.[20]

Level of Analysis Choices. Analysts must determine the level of network structures within the organization on which the analysis will focus. They can study the entire organization as a network or smaller subgroups of structurally equivalent members—those who show identical, or nearly identical, patterns of network relationships.[21] Alternatively, researchers can focus on the personal networks of particular individuals, noting the people with whom the chosen individuals interact most. Small-group specialists often focus their research on cliques of five to twenty-five people. "The implicit proposition motivating clique analysis," according to David Knoke and James Kuklinski, "is that actors who maintain especially cohesive bonds among themselves are more likely to perform similarly (e.g., to share information, to develop similar preferences, to act in concert)."[22]

Network analysts may face difficult decisions when they must specify the boundaries of organizational networks. There are no obvious limits to social networks.[23] Analysts may define the boundaries of organizations in accordance with the perceptions of all or most of its members, or they may allow the purpose of their investigation to guide their boundary definition. For example, the analysis could be limited to networks of civil servants at a particular grade. If investigators use a snowball-sampling approach to network analysis, in which they trace with whom a particular respondent communicates and then trace the contacts of these contacts, where should they stop? After the second level, the fifth, the tenth? There is no pat answer.

Knoke and Kuklinski recommend that "the decision about where to draw the boundary must ultimately be set by social-theoretic considerations of the phenomenon under investigation."[24] Because restricted samples lead to distortions, it is always wise to err in the direction of broadening the network depending, of course, on available resources. If the focus is too narrow, it may capture only truncated network structures. On the other hand, if the focus is too wide, it may be impossible to collect and handle all the data. For example, when a network includes 5,000 people, it encompasses 25,000,000 linkage possibilities. Many computer programs cannot handle such massive data sets effectively.[25]

Sociometric Measures. Networks are best studied through sociometric measures that reveal how communication travels among senders and receivers. Data about who interacts with whom about what and how often are usually derived from questionnaires, interviews, diaries, focus groups, and on-site observations. They are normally gathered from each member of an organization, *not* merely a random sample. Researchers ascertain how often the members communicate with specific colleagues inside and outside the organization and how this information moves through the network. Researchers may also inquire about who ordinarily initiates the information exchange and the nature and importance of network messages.[26] To ease the task, the respondents may receive name lists of all members within the organization. Very large organizations do not usually supply a complete name list because its length would be overwhelming.

In place of self-reports, which some investigators distrust as potentially flawed, it is, of course, possible to obtain contact data through direct observations or through scanning records of past communications. Using archival data has the added advantage of covering long time periods, which may provide insights on networking in diverse settings such as major changes in the economic, political, and personal situations faced by network members.

Data Analysis. After the data about links among organization members have been collected, computer programs can identify formal and informal networks. Data analysis poses several difficult problems. One is the fact that data collections have to be massive because network analysis requires receiving data from all members of the organization, or at least from 90 percent of them, to obtain a sufficiently clear picture of interrelationships. A moderately sized network of 1,000 people could have as many as half a million links.[27] This problem may be alleviated when suitable sampling programs are developed.[28]

Network data can be processed in many different ways. Possibilities include sociometric analysis, graph-theoretical analysis, matrix analysis, factor analysis, block-modeling techniques, multidimensional scaling techniques, and cluster analysis.[29] Conventional statistical methods can be used to describe the properties of various aspects of the network structures.[30] However, because network data violate the random sampling assumptions that underlie statistical inference, conventional statistical analyses are problematic.[31] The results of network analysis can be presented as matrixes or sociograms.[32]

The analysis can focus on dyadic (two-person), group, or organizational relationships. It can identify the individuals who occupy key roles in organizations, such as gatekeepers, liaisons, or isolates. It can also stress network characteristics, such as the centrality of various nodes within the network; the accessibility of particular nodes to other nodes; and the reciprocity, strength, and frequency of relationships.[33]

Common indexes that can be derived from network data include an index of *network cohesion* that shows the proportion of network relations that are reciprocated. One can also derive an index of *network multiplexity,* which indicates multiple types of relationships, such as communication about a variety of issues among nodes. An index of *communication intensity* can be created that combines measures of frequency of contacts, average frequency of individual contacts, response satisfaction, and response importance. An *ego network density* index measures the density of networks clustering around a particular individual, presumably supporting his or her ego. There are also indexes of *network centrality* that measure the degree to which an official is enmeshed in various relationships occurring within the network. Finally, indexes of a *member's prestige* have been devised. For example, network members who receive more communications than they send are generally considered to have high prestige. This is especially true if their contactors also enjoy high prestige.[34]

The various indexes permit analysts to determine how well coordinated the communication network is overall and within various units of the organization. They can tell which communication roles are adequately handled and where additional liaisons and gatekeepers are required. The charts developed from the data show who needs to be integrated into the communication system. Finally, a combination of network data and other communication data can provide answers to many intriguing questions about the relationship between an individual's network roles and position and other communication behaviors and evaluations. This is why small-group researchers, sociometricians, political scientists, and anthropologists have long been interested in network analysis.[35]

Network Analysis Payoffs

To fathom who enjoys power and influence in an organization and what kinds of information are likely to be transmitted or excluded, one needs to know who is part of a particular network and who is excluded. Political scientist John Kessel, for example, studied communication networks at the top levels of the Carter and Reagan administrations to assess who was in close touch with the president and how information traveled among top White House advisers and to more remote parts of the executive branch.[36] Kessel's findings demonstrate that even relatively minor variations in communication network patterns can produce substantial differences in information flows and in the distribution of political influence. The two White House staffs varied considerably in the number of people included in the network, the quality of their interpersonal relations, the frequency of their internal and external communications, and the substance of their interactions. Network analysis provided a tool for comparing the effectiveness of network structures and identified dominant members whose views were likely to prevail.

Knowledge about an organization's network structure is essential for interested outsiders such as lobbyists, legislators, and concerned citizens who want to deal with the organization. They need to understand where the key points are for introducing certain types of information and which networks should be avoided as unproductive for particular transactions. In fact, knowledge of how various government networks are structured and operate is the chief asset of ex-officials turned lobbyists. Former Reagan aide Michael Deaver, for instance, worked on the acid rain problem during his government days. Knowing the network for this issue helped him become a consultant on acid rain for the Canadian government.[37]

Understanding network structures also may be the key to unraveling how citizens develop their political views in mutual discussions and how they gain access to decision makers. A team of researchers who conducted the Redwood Project in the San Francisco Bay area in the 1980s therefore questioned citizens about their normal conversational networks. They asked whose help their respondents would seek about problems such as crime, objectionable industrial development, book censorship, and excessive federal taxation. Some citizens participated in tightly structured networks whose members communicated almost exclusively with each other. These citizens reinforced each other's opinions but lacked contacts with people with access to public officials. Other citizens had loosely structured communication networks through which they were able to reach public officials directly or through an intermediary. Citizens with connections to the right networks could share in making governmental decisions. Citizens without these connections could not.[38]

Power Configurations—An Example

Power configurations created through local interorganizational network patterns can be illustrated by the hypothetical urban hospital network shown in Figure 4–1. Besides the five hospitals designated by blackened circles, the network contains a supporting academic network cluster indicated by triangles. The academic cluster encompasses a state university, a medical school, a nursing school, and the National Institutes of Health (NIH), a major source of government grants, as well as the private Ford Foundation. There is also a cluster of regulatory and special interest groups, identified by stars. This cluster includes a state health

Figure 4-1 Hypothetical Urban Hospital Network

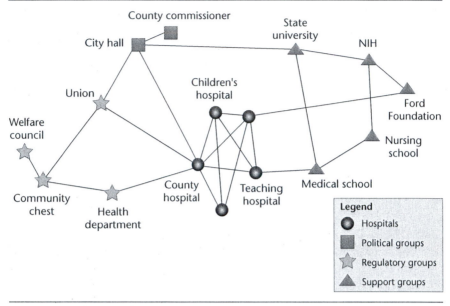

SOURCE: Adapted from Charles Perrow, *Complex Organizations: A Critical Essay*, 2d ed. (Glenview, Ill.: Scott Foresman, 1979), 222.

department, a labor union to which employees of the county hospital belong, the community chest that raises money for local charities, and a citizen-run welfare council. Finally, city hall and the county commissioner's office, identified by boxes, are the political bodies involved in the network.

The figure depicts strong ties only, which represent the organization's influence structure, omitting unimportant connections that convey routine and symbolic messages.[39] Figure 4–1 illustrates how the density of communication links can vary considerably in different parts of an interorganizational network. Some units are tightly connected, others loosely, and still others are barely coupled at all even though they are part of the network. The five hospitals are tightly coupled, as shown by the dense pattern of interconnecting communication channels that links each unit directly to all others within the hospital cluster. By contrast, the five support groups, which deal with training and research, are loosely coupled. Some communicate within the group; others do not. Hence, these groups are only partially interactive. Only one of the support units, the medical school, is in direct contact with the teaching hospital, and there is only one additional direct link between the hospital cluster and the support units.

The scarcity of ties across the boundaries of various organizations that are part of the network may suggest a lack of sufficient interunit connections and may indicate that additional links are needed. For example, the state university lacks strong direct ties to the county hospital. If it wants to influence the level of care at that hospital, it must go through city hall, or it could ask the medical school to use its ties with the teaching hospital to influence the county hospital.

The regulatory and special interest groups are hardly coupled at all, suggesting that they do not collaborate despite their often complementary interests. The welfare council and community chest have no direct lines into the hospital system. Only the union and the state health department are linked to the hospital cluster, and then only through the county hospital link. When the state health department makes rules for the county hospital, such as requiring the use of generic drugs to reduce the cost of health care, these rules may spill over to other hospitals because of their tight linkage to the county hospital network. Tightly coupled networks are prone to fast, often unpredictable interactions and changes in response to shared information. However, a three-step flow is unlikely whereby a rule regarding the use of generic drugs would be transmitted from one of the second-step hospitals to the support groups, such as the medical school.

City hall has the greatest reach and centrality of all the organizations in the hospital network because it can dip directly into the county hospital network or approach the hospital cluster indirectly through its contacts among the interest groups or its ties to the supporting agencies that flow through the state university. The teaching hospital and medical school are well insulated from the interest groups and the state health department. If the medical school wishes to influence care at the county hospital, it can go either through the teaching hospital or through city hall via the state university. To increase its influence, it might try to gain direct ties to city hall, lessening its dependence on the state university.

Although this is a hypothetical urban hospital network system, the relationships described are very real and common. They are the gist of most activities that fall under the heading of "organizational politics." Much time, effort, and scheming is directed toward structuring appropriate networks, placing supporters in key positions, or wooing key network figures who are already in place. It takes a lot of sleuthing to learn which are the right networks to join, to gain entry to them, and to use these connections to the organization's advantage. But building productive networks can be extraordinarily rewarding for administrators.

The Significance of Network Positions

Network Patterns

The network diagrammed in Figure 4–2 illustrates typical network interactions, though on a smaller scale than would be true for most public sector

Figure 4-2 Information Flows in a Three-Group Network

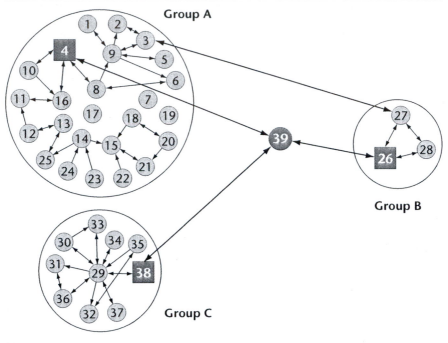

SOURCE: Author.

agencies. The figure diagrams information flows inside three small groups as well as the communication links among these groups. The more groups a system has, the more differentiated it can be. A large number of groups makes it easier for individual groups to specialize and experiment.[40] However, the gains from specialization and expertise may be outweighed by the losses from fractionalizing organizational activities and the problems of interclique coordination. One-headed arrows in Figure 4–2 show predominantly one-way message flows, while two-headed arrows show two-way communications. Arrows are plentiful within each unit, indicating ample internal communication. However, patterns vary.

Interaction Patterns. Although Figure 4–2 does not illustrate this, four patterns of interaction among network members have been identified in small groups.[41] They are the chain, the wheel, the circle, and all-channel interrelationships shown in Figure 4–3. In the *circle* pattern, information travels round-robin style, with each person passing messages to the next person. The final person completes the circle by contacting the message originator, either to acknowledge that the message was circulated or to report various types of

Figure 4-3 Small-Group Interaction Patterns

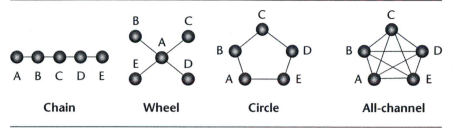

| Chain | Wheel | Circle | All-channel |

SOURCE: Author.

responses or feedback by network members who are reacting to the substance of the message. Absent this last step, the pattern is called a *chain* that reaches from the first to the last link. If the message has become distorted in its passage through the chain, which is common, the last person, who may be the individual charged with taking message-related actions, is apt to receive the most tainted information. Therefore, circle patterns are preferred whenever accuracy is essential.

In the *wheel* pattern, all communications pass through one centrally located node, which may be one individual or a cluster of individuals. When individuals within the wheel-type network also interact with each other, the wheel becomes an *interlocking* network; otherwise it is *radial*. Most networks are a mixture, but interlocking ones are more common. Because the wheel configuration centralizes information flows, the center may become overloaded and inefficient, and people at the periphery may feel dominated and dissatisfied.

In the *all-channel* pattern, messages circulate freely among all members. The pattern is ideal from the standpoint of openness because all share information. However, in complex organizations, the price of openness may be debilitating communication overloads for all network members. When the organizational climate is friendly, wheel patterns appear to be most efficient, followed by circle patterns. However, once groups learn how to communicate efficiently, all of the patterns can produce good results. Unfortunately, the external validity of most of the studies on which such findings rest is questionable because they have been done under artificial laboratory conditions. Researchers have worked with groups of strangers and asked them to perform unfamiliar, often meaningless tasks. They have not worked with groups whose members know each other and have learned to cooperate as would be the case in more natural settings.[42]

Group Cohesiveness. Figure 4–2 illustrates that some groups show more internal two-way communication and hence greater cohesiveness than others. Such variations are commonly related to the functions performed by a group and the characteristics of its members and the physical environment in which the group operates. Individuals whose offices are near each other are more likely to communicate. When analysts compare actual with potential message flows, they can construct indexes of group connectedness that reveal the degree to which network channels are used and how information travels inside the network. They can also examine the relationship between group connectedness and other organizational behaviors. For example, investigators have studied how the flow of communication increases or decreases productivity and have recommended changes to improve network functioning.

In Group A in Figure 4–2, individuals 7, 17, and 19 are not connected to the other members of the network, which makes them *isolates*. Possible reasons for isolation include personality-interaction barriers, deliberate discrimination, or lack of shared interests with other members of Group A. When individuals belong to several networks, they often play an isolate role in at least some of them either because other ties occupy them fully or because these ties mark them as outsiders.

Many organizations are concerned about isolates as evidence of major problems in organizational structure and functioning. There is also evidence that isolates perform poorly because they often lack information that is important for doing their assigned tasks.[43] Conversely, there is solid research evidence that participation in organizational networks is advantageous to their members. It may enhance their power and prestige, increase their productivity, and make them feel more satisfied with their jobs.[44]

In Figure 4–2, individual 39 is in touch with all the groups but is not part of them. In network-analysis jargon, No. 39 is a *liaison* who links groups. The functions entailed in the liaison role, as well as other network roles, will be discussed more fully once the overall network pattern has been set forth. Liaison among groups A, B, and C could be No. 39's main function. For instance, social service agencies within a state or city are often linked through a coordinator. Alternatively, No. 39 may be the boss who controls all three units. If No. 39 performs the liaison function while also part of a network, she or he serves as a *bridge*. No. 3 and No. 27 are bridges between Groups A and B. Liaisons and bridges are also referred to as *boundary spanners* or *cosmopolites* when their communication reaches beyond the boundaries of their own network. Some boundary spanners may even be members of several networks, which would then be depicted as overlapping circles.

Within each group in Figure 4–2, the official head is identified by a square box, and other members are encased in circles. All heads contact other groups through liaison No. 39. In Group C, No. 38 is the only individual connected to the other networks via the liaison. Therefore, all information flowing into the network from the outside must pass through a single individual. That makes No. 38 a *gatekeeper* with complete control over the information entering or leaving the network. However, No. 38 seems peripheral to intraunit communication, being in regular touch only with No. 29 who is the central figure within the unit. This suggests that No. 38, although the formal unit leader and the contact person to outside groups, has been replaced by No. 29 as the actual leader of intragroup communication.

In Groups A and B, the head's gatekeeping control is weaker because it is shared with the boundary spanners, who are in touch with each other. The boundary spanners, in this case, each have direct access to one group, compared with the heads who are connected to two other groups, but only indirectly through the liaison. Whether direct access to one group conveys more gatekeeping control than indirect access to two groups depends on the circumstances involved in each case.

The individual whose control is most diverse, thanks to being in touch with all three groups, is the liaison, No. 39. Because of its ready access to information, such a position of centrality used to be automatically equated with power. More recent research has called this power equation into question. Proponents of exchange-network theory argue that control over information resources that are valuable because others desire them, rather than central location in a communications network, is the major source of power. Individuals in the network who hold the most coveted information are dominant because others depend on them.[45] Their ability to influence other network members with some regularity may cast such individuals into the informal role of *opinion leader.*

Some opinion leaders function only in one specialty area, while others play more diverse roles. For example, an official in a city's police department may be the opinion leader when it comes to treatment of all types of criminals or only when juvenile offenders are involved. Opinion leaders are usually experts whose knowledge and experience give them high credibility and status. Their reputation allows them superior access to internal as well as external information sources, even when they are not members of the top hierarchy. If opinion leaders conform to organizational norms, they are valuable to the system, enhancing organizational coordination and control by motivating others to behave in approved ways. When they do not conform to norms, the organization may be in trouble because the opinion leader may carry it in directions that are not approved by the organization's leadership.

Central location within a communication network has been linked to the ability to innovate. Centrally located individuals and groups are exposed to most of the information entering the network, including information coming from people beyond their own immediate network.[46] Even though such information may constitute only a very minor part of the total information flow, it is often crucial because it introduces fresh ideas into a network. Sociologist Mark Granovetter calls it "The Strength of Weak Ties."[47] Although it is debatable whether they are innovative because they are centrally located, or whether they are centrally positioned because they are innovative, it is clear that people eager to exercise power strive to be centrally located within communication networks.[48] Whether or not a potentially powerful network position will actually convey power hinges on the personal attributes of the incumbent, such as intelligence, interpersonal skills, prestige, and professional qualifications. Network positions provide opportunities but no guarantees of success.

Network Roles

We are now ready to take a closer look at individual positions within networks to assess their significance for information management in organizations.[49]

Gatekeepers

As the name suggests, gatekeepers control the flow of information into communication networks. Strictly speaking, every individual who controls message transmission is a gatekeeper, but the term is generally reserved for individuals who routinely perform gatekeeping functions within a particular network. Executive secretaries who scan incoming information and determine whether it should be passed on to network members, sent elsewhere, or ignored are good examples. Gatekeeping is an extremely sensitive role because wrong decisions—whether excessive openness or undue barriers—can lead to major malfunctions. Often gatekeepers' greatest value lies in protecting network members from information overloads. Organizations may also assign the information control function to designated specialists or groups of specialists. For instance, at the Department of Defense, specialists in aircraft procurement or nuclear submarine deployment serve as gatekeepers who screen information in their respective areas of expertise.

Gatekeepers make four types of potentially crucial decisions: (1) admitting messages to the network or rejecting them; (2) determining how quickly they will be transmitted; (3) editing them; and (4) routing them to specified or unspecified receivers. When messages or messengers seek entry to a network's communication channels, gatekeepers may grant or refuse it. In the past, unless there were multiple gatekeepers, refusal usually kept these messages out of the network, which could be helpful or harmful. The ready availability of e-mail messages has greatly weakened this insulation. Although it is still possible to shield organization members from unwanted messages, many prefer unshielded access to their e-mail address to the safety of a gatekeeping shield. Gatekeeping also involves the sensitive issue of responsiveness to the public. If gatekeepers lack the interpersonal skills to convey openness, if they shield top personnel too much, public agencies may seem unduly unresponsive. Problems posed by overzealous gatekeepers have been only marginally improved by structural remedies, such as creating ombudsman offices.

Gatekeepers may also select message routes. Again, this is a crucial decision. Messages routed to inappropriate or unsympathetic targets may be doomed. For instance, messages about the need for tax rebates for gasoline used in farm machinery are apt to receive better treatment if they are referred to an agriculture committee in Congress than to a highway traffic committee.[50]

Gatekeepers usually can decide whether to paraphrase messages or transmit them verbatim. If they decide to paraphrase, they are usually free to rephrase the message, interpret it, shift its focus, abbreviate it, or even lengthen it. In the process they can frame the message in ways that affect how it will be perceived. Here again, Web technology portends greater openness. Gatekeepers are more likely to forward e-mail messages, including links to additional information, in their entirety because that is simplest. Search functions ease and systematize the effort required to scan lengthy documents for specific types of information.

A story from Chicago illustrates how gatekeeping routines can lead to catastrophe when a message requiring well-chosen, expeditious routing is poorly handled.[51] A major flood in April 1992 could have been prevented if an engineer's memorandum to the head of the city's Department of Transportation had been promptly transmitted. The engineer had reported a rupture in a tunnel wall that required immediate repairs to prevent flooding throughout the inner city. Unfortunately, gatekeepers routed the message through the sluggish city hall interoffice mail system and retyped the handwritten note, leaving out underlining that stressed the urgency of immediate action.

The memo reached the transportation commissioner a day later. He concluded from the altered version, and the fact that it had arrived by regular interoffice mail, that it was not urgent and could be handled through routine inspection. While the request for repairs moved at the normal snail's pace through bureaucratic channels, river water broke through the damaged tunnel wall. The ensuing flood, which reached a depth of 40 feet in some places, shut down the inner city for days and caused losses estimated between $1 billion and $2 billion. One million people had to be evacuated. Miraculously, there was no loss of lives.

As discussed fully in Chapter 2, the most recalcitrant problems encountered in gatekeeping relate to suitable methods for gauging the importance of messages and channeling them appropriately. How can gatekeepers judge the significance of incoming messages, label them accordingly, and route them in timely fashion to the appropriate parties inside or outside the communications network? These problems are particularly acute because most gatekeeping decisions are made by people who lack sufficient information to judge the urgency of messages. The staff member who retyped and routed the flood-warning message in Chicago lacked the engineering training to recognize the urgency of the situation.

Placing gatekeeping responsibilities at low levels in the hierarchy has been called a regrettable "information asymmetry."[52] For example, at the National Labor Relations Board (NLRB) low-level officials make crucial initial decisions about accepting cases for adjudication. These decisions, which are usually final, often do not reflect the views of upper-level personnel in the NLRB's hierarchy. Efforts to monitor or control decisions made by nonprofessional gatekeeping staffs have generally been only moderately successful. Yet switching this function to individuals in the network holding higher level jobs is also un-desirable because of the burdens it places on them when gatekeeping decisions are numerous and mostly are routine. It is, indeed, a dilemma.

Bridges and Liaisons

Although networks in large organizations make communication more man-ageable and efficient, they also tend to balkanize information flows. There-fore, various networks must be linked horizontally and vertically through per-sonnel acting as bridges or liaisons. Like other gatekeepers, liaisons usually serve as two-way channels who receive as well as transmit information. In Fig-ure 4–2, for example, liaison No. 39 both receives and sends information to all three groups. Bridges No. 3 and No. 27 are also two-way channels be-tween Groups A and B. In the absence of such linkages, organizations disin-tegrate into uncoordinated subsystems.[53]

Unlike ordinary gatekeepers, employees involved in bridging and liaison functions are more likely to be drawn from higher professional levels because decisions about disseminating information to and from other agencies or de-partments usually are difficult to routinize. In the average organization, 5 to 20 percent of the personnel are likely to be formally involved in liaison work steadily or intermittently.[54] The ease of communicating via e-mail and Web pages has decentralized bridging and liaison functions because many more members of organizations have intermittent informal contacts with peers in related organizations. In the process, organizational boundaries have become highly permeable. The short- and long-term effects on matters such as orga-nizational efficiency, cohesiveness, internal power relationships, and morale remain unclear.

Bridges and liaisons, like gatekeepers, are prone to becoming bottlenecks, particularly when they link multiple units, as liaison No. 39 does in Figure 4–2.[55] Bottleneck problems are most serious when agencies are faced with major crises. It is almost impossible to plan adequate reserve transmission ca-pacity when the nature and extent of such crises are unforeseeable. For ex-ample, when the United States became involved in the Persian Gulf military operations in 1990, the Defense Department was swamped with inquiries by reserve personnel and National Guard units who were anxious to know their status. It was impossible to provide rapid, individualized responses under these unexpected circumstances.

Overwhelming bottleneck problems can spring from the requirement for openness that forces public agencies to comply with sometimes excessive and unwarranted demands for information whenever there is a hint of wrongdo-ing. A false rumor that contracts awarded by a municipality have excluded mi-nority enterprises, for instance, may spark a flood of requests to inspect the lists of the city's contractors. Compared with overload problems, sparse in-formation flows are a fairly uncommon problem for bridges and liaisons, but

Figure 4-4 Linking Pin Model of a State School System

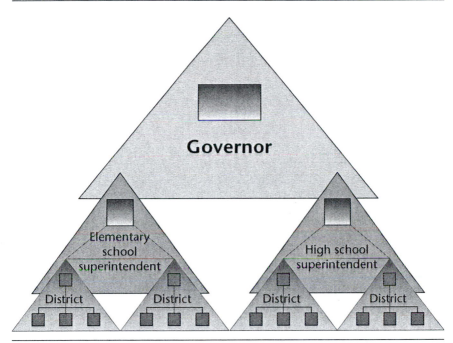

SOURCE: Author.

NOTE: The triangles are networks with overlapping memberships. The shaded squares are organizational units within a network. Bottom squares represent individual schools.

they do occur. When that happens, network members may find it difficult to obtain necessary information.

Formal leaders within a given agency or department often become ad hoc members of a network of leaders at the next higher level. Their dual roles make these individuals the *linking pins* that knit the various parts of the hierarchy together. Figure 4‑4 shows a linking-pin organizational structure for a hypothetical state school system. The governor is the linking pin and individual schools are at the bottom of the pyramid. How efficiently various tasks are handled when they require coordination among multiple networks depends on the nature and compatibility of the individual networks, the characteristics of the coordinating structures and their leaders, and on the resources available for coordination.[56]

Public agencies often do not make formal assignments to bridging or liaison roles because the mission of the organization is defined largely in terms of separate group tasks. Agency executives then assume bridging and liaison roles informally. Given the importance of these roles and the explosive growth of messages that provide essential information to organizations, it seems wise to assign liaison work to career officials.[57] Ensuring stability at professional levels is particularly critical in public bodies because of the rapid turnover among top political appointees.

A White House Example. To be responsive, a president's staff should scan the political environment constantly to pick up cues from relevant actors like Congress members, bureaucrats, and interest group leaders. If several White House units are affected by a particular decision, they must have some means of consulting with each other. If the decision is sufficiently important to require presidential action, there must be a flow of information from staff units to the Oval Office. Once a decision has been made, it must be communicated to those within and without the White House who have to implement it.[58]

How these intelligence-gathering, transmission, and liaison functions are performed hinges very much on the types of networks established among White House staff members. To assess and compare the flow of communication during the Carter and Reagan administrations, political scientist John Kessel asked White House aides then serving in the Carter and Reagan administrations to identify the people with whom they spent the most work-related time.[59] From the responses, Kessel constructed communications matrices tracing direct contacts between people as well as indirect communication through third parties. The analyses covered members of the National Security Council (NSC), major economic policy advisers, the domestic policy staff, heads of miscellaneous executive units, members of the Office of Congressional Liaison, and the presidential press secretary's office. These units varied widely in terms of sending and receiving messages. For example, Carter's domestic policy staff received the largest number of messages by far, followed by the legislative liaison staff. The economists and the domestic policy staff were the most prolific message senders. Reciprocal message flows were uneven, indicating that traffic is not necessarily balanced with inflow matching outflow, even though liaison channels are two-way.

Kessel found that staff members fell into two distinct groups—an inner network that maintained regular liaison with the president, mostly about domestic legislation, and an outer circle that maintained only sporadic contact. Members of the inner network were more likely to be generalists and communicated mostly with members of their own unit. In fact, the most striking finding in both administrations was that members of four of the six units communicated more internally than externally. Staff in the outer circle were usually handling specialized assignments and maintained liaison with networks that had the same substantive concerns.[60] Outer-circle staff, such as the NSC staff and the press office in the Carter White House, were relatively isolated from the internal network because they were kept busy communicating with outsiders.

A comparison of the Carter and Reagan White House staffs revealed much greater liaison activity in the Reagan administration and hence much greater cohesion. There were 55 percent more contacts with other units than had been the case for Carter's staff. The chief reason was structural. The Reagan White House had added four senior staffers to coordinate communication.[61] Message contacts, which had gone directly to the White House in the Carter years, now went to these coordinators: James Baker, Edwin Meese, Michael Deaver, and Craig Fuller. Besides receiving a flood of messages, the coordinators were also in constant contact with each other because they held each other in high regard.[62] Placing the coordinators between himself and the various White House units shielded Reagan from much of the kind of information that had reached Carter directly in his less centralized network structure. It made Reagan's coordinators extremely powerful because they monopolized access to the top level of the hierarchy.

There were other significant differences as well as similarities in the communication patterns of the two presidencies. The Carter White House kept in much more frequent contact with the legislative liaison staff about the content of the president's legislative program. In the Reagan White House, this staff was rarely consulted because there was a separate legislative strategy group that made these decisions. The legislative liaison staff was thus free to devote its time to making contacts with Congress.[63] Overall, in both administrations the domestic staffs were tied most closely to the White House communication network, and the NSC staff was most isolated. Nonetheless, the NSC staff was highly influential in White House decision making, indicating that a central position in the communication network, although helpful, is neither a prerequisite for nor a guarantee of influence. Kessel concluded that influence within the White House hinged on a combination of factors, including position within the hierarchy, seniority, and personal attributes.

The magnitude of the liaison function at the presidential level emerges from data collected about Lyndon Johnson's administration, for which exceptionally complete records of presidential communications are available. During the first twenty-five months of his administration, Johnson was directly involved in more than 28,530 interactions with more than 2,000 different people. The 158 people whose face-to-face and telephone interactions with the president are recorded in Table 4–1 were fairly regular contacts, speaking with him at least five times during a given month.[64] The president kept in closest touch by far with the twenty-nine members of the White House staff, composed of Kennedy holdovers and Johnson appointees. However, 73 percent of his staff interactions were with his own appointees, who were close personal friends, rather than with Kennedy's appointees. Overall, 75 percent of Johnson's contacts were with people characterized as political elites rather than ordinary citizens. As time progressed and the president became disenchanted with many of his advisers, this circle contracted sharply.

Table 4-1 Total Number of "Elite" Interactions, by Group, During Johnson Administration

Group	Number of staffers	Number of interactions	% of all interactions	% of elite interactions
Congress	22	1,832	6.4	8.6
White House staff	29	11,319	39.7	53.2
Kennedy appointments	15	2,985		
Johnson appointments	14	8,334		
Executive Office of the President	17	1,269	4.4	6.0
Executive branch	18	1,120	3.9	5.3
Cabinet	15	2,532	9.9	11.9
Inner cabinet	6	1,949		
Other	57	3,205	11.2	15.1
Total elite	158	21,277	74.6	100.1
Total interactions		28,530		

SOURCE: James A. Best, "Who Talked to the President When? A Study of Lyndon B. Johnson," *Political Science Quarterly* 103 (fall 1998): 536–537. Reprinted with permission from *Political Science Quarterly* 103 (fall 1998): 531–545.

Boundary Spanners

General Features. Boundary spanning occurs when duties of various individuals cut across organizational barriers. For example, in Table 4–1 Johnson's contacts with Congress and with personal friends who were not part of the executive branch were boundary spanning rather than liaisons because they reached into the environment surrounding the executive branch. Other examples occur when labor unions and agency executives need to settle conflicting claims or when jurisdictionally distinct units decide to share and exchange information.[65] Designating contacts as boundary spanning raises tricky issues about defining the level of analysis. If the entire government is considered one unit, then contacts between the executive and Congress, for example, are internal liaisons rather than external boundary spanning. Alternatively, one could consider the cabinet or the White House staff or the executive office of the president as the unit of analysis and relations among them as boundary spanning. Choices of analysis levels are wide and hinge on the purposes of a particular investigation.[66]

Boundary spanning is a daily event in the life of bureaucrats.[67] As political scientist Herbert Kaufman noted, after studying federal bureaucracies, "Programs intersect at innumerable points, and staff functions cut across each other and all line operations in comparable profusion. Hardly anything can be done anywhere that does not quickly involve other agencies, committees, and interest groups in sister triadic clusters. . . ." Government business is "much more interdepartmental than departmental," giving rise to innumerable interagency committees that nobody really wants.[68]

The increased sharing of information among government units has been called the "convergence" model.[69] The concept alludes to the fact that units that interact frequently in a shared communication environment tend to develop shared vocabularies and often shared understandings about the nature of problems and what needs to be done to cope with them. Even without a formal merger, their perspectives and policies are likely to converge. Although convergence may increase efficiency, the openness of the system may suffer so that it becomes less hospitable to new ideas and new conceptual frames. In a nutshell, the system becomes less democratic.[70]

The array of interconnections among government agencies is vast and growing because it is essential to coordinate matters if they affect more than one agency. In some parts of government, boundary-spanning offices have become routine. Their primary function is intelligence gathering and dissemination. For example, the NSC gathers information from the State and Defense departments, multinational corporations, and foreign governments and transmits it to various agencies concerned with foreign policy so that they can operate from a common information base when dealing with shared problems. The Bureau of the Census collects a vast array of economic and demographic data that is then mined by government agencies and the private sector. Similarly, the Library of Congress is a huge repository for government information, available in print or on the Web, which serves agencies and citizens irrespective of their institutional affiliation. Despite the growth of boundary-spanning offices, most boundary-spanning networking is done by individual agencies in a decentralized fashion. Still, it has proved virtually impossible to achieve adequate coordination of information disseminated at various governmental levels. When internal networks absorb a great deal of energy and resources, to what extent can scarce resources be diverted from internal networking to more costly boundary spanning? Viable answers are tough to find for these difficult questions in times when the stakes are extraordinarily high.

In a government that depends heavily on public support and prizes the principle of public accountability, boundary-spanning ties with various representatives of the public are deemed particularly important. Numerous agencies have been created for this purpose. Examples at the presidential level are the Office of Public Liaison, which provides linkage to interest groups, and the Office of Intergovernmental Relations, which provides ties to governors and mayors and liaison with minority groups such as Hispanic and African Americans.[71] Besides instrumental services, like explaining an agency's goals to outsiders or mollifying competing interest groups, boundary-spanning offices often render symbolic services, like signaling concern for particular groups. When administrators must have public support for burdensome policies, soothing boundary-spanning messages can be crucial.[72]

Boundary-Spanning Challenges. Situations that cut across federal and state agencies and also involve the private sector pose exceptionally difficult boundary-spanning problems. An example is the situation that occurred more than twenty-five years ago at Love Canal, a toxic waste site in New York State that began to leak noxious vapors twenty years after the last dumping ceased. In the most active stages of investigating the problem, nineteen separate agencies were involved. At the state level they included the Departments of Health, Environmental Conservation, Transportation, Housing, Social Services, Banking, Insurance, the Office of Disaster Preparedness, and the Division of Equalization and Assessment. Joining these nine were the federal Environmental Protection Agency, the Niagara County Health Department, the local civil defense unit, the police and fire departments, the city of Niagara Falls, and the Niagara Falls school board. There also were three private sector agencies: the Red Cross, the United Way, and the Love Canal Homeowners' Association. "No wonder that, although by 1976 government authorities were aware of the toxic infiltration at Love Canal, the problem was tossed among agencies like a hot potato. No one agency was in charge, no agency had responsibility for coordination."[73] Nobody had kept track of waste disposal sites; nobody had studied medical reports about miscarriages and birth defects that could have triggered an earlier investigation. It took organized pressure by concerned residents to finally get the investigation under way. In the wake of its findings, large parts of the area were evacuated and there were major clean-up operations to make it livable again.

Boundary-spanning networks may arise from task forces created to solve particular problems that overlap jurisdictional borders. They may develop informally and almost spontaneously in response to a problem or high-impact disaster that cuts across geographic jurisdictions or functional lines or becomes too large to be handled locally. The 1982 Air Florida jet crash into the Potomac River in Washington, D.C., exemplifies a disaster where rescue efforts by agencies from various localities were hampered because no interagency networks were created or arose spontaneously.[74] Although the crash demonstrated the need for interagency coordination in disasters, it took many months before effective communication channels were instituted. Disagreements about power sharing caused the problem.

Differences in the goals of various agencies sometimes prevent money-saving sharing of services across agency boundaries. Relations between the Agricultural Marketing Service (AMS) and the Food and Drug Administration (FDA) provide an example.[75] The AMS, which grades fruits and vegetables, did not wish to share inspectors with the FDA, fearing that the FDA, in line with its mandate, would take action against food adulteration discovered during the grading process. The main reason was the difference in goals. The FDA's objective was to prevent the distribution of adulterated foods, whereas the AMS's chief objective was the improvement of marketing and distribution of agricultural products. The AMS feared that fruit and vegetable processors, who pay for its grading services, would be unhappy if the information collected for grading were used to disqualify their products from the market. They might cancel grading services, thereby reducing job opportunities for AMS personnel. The intrinsic conflict of interests was unbridgeable.

Finally, it is a common complaint that top administrators engaged in boundary-spanning all too often function as official spokespersons for their agency without consulting their communication staffs until after miscommunication has occurred. At critical times, executives routinely bypass liaison staffs and concentrate their personal efforts on communicating with key individuals with whom satisfactory contacts are essential. If these efforts are poorly coordinated with the work done by regular boundary-spanning staffs, trouble may ensue. In fact, coordination of boundary-spanning activities is a major problem in the White House and elsewhere. Congress has tried to foster boundary-spanning through passage of the 1970 Intergovernmental Personnel Act, which was revised in 1997.[76] This act encourages federal, state, and local agencies to exchange personnel for up to a year. It has not been widely used.[77]

The Press as Boundary-Spanner. When essential contacts among public officials are neither mandated nor established by custom, formal or informal boundary-spanning arrangements may fail to develop. In that case, the press may partially fill the void. American court systems have been particularly deficient in interagency communications. Judges of higher level courts lack institutionalized means for communicating with lower courts. The U.S. Supreme Court, for example, transmits its decisions only to the lower court from which the case originated.[78] Whether other judges learn about these decisions depends on their own efforts and professional contacts and the diligence of the press in transmitting these decisions. Unfortunately, coverage of court decisions, even at the Supreme Court level, is spotty and often inaccurate.[79]

Insufficient boundary-spanning also plagues other governmental units. For example, local government agencies such as police departments and school boards are often uninformed about court decisions that undoubtedly affect their operations. Aside from trade journal reports of varying quality and completeness, there simply are no regular, reliable network structures to transmit these decisions. Political scientist George Edwards reports that "only a few police departments have legal advisers or officers assigned to transmitting information from the courts to the police. For these reasons, police administrators have had to rely primarily upon newspapers for information on judicial decisions, when they involve officers in their own departments."[80]

To increase the opportunities for effective as well as favorable boundary-spanning by the media, most government agencies now assign specially trained personnel to handle media contacts. Presidents, governors, mayors, as well as major departments and agencies, employ expert press secretaries. To collect the necessary information for transmission to the media, press secretaries must be able to tap into large numbers of governmental networks. David Gergen, who served Presidents Reagan and Clinton as communications director, for instance, participated in senior staff meetings. He learned a great deal about pending domestic and foreign developments through regular contacts with congressional leaders, the NSC, the State and Defense departments, and the U.S. Information Agency. Press office personnel also monitor the media to be fully aware of what governmental news is covered and how it is being appraised. Press relations are discussed more fully in Chapter 7.

The media are important boundary-spanners because many governmental units, as well as the general public, depend on media monitoring and publicizing of governmental actions. Unfortunately, news media do not cover governmental events systematically. Instead, they select stories based on their newsworthiness rather than their intrinsic political importance. Exciting and appealing stories get published while duller or highly complex ones about laws and regulations do not. In fact, a survey of 287 reporters and news executives showed that 77 percent would avoid stories that audiences might consider dull, and 52 percent would be inclined to skip highly complex stories.[81] When the news media cover complex stories, the information contained in the story is rarely comprehensive and adequately detailed. It often contains substantial errors.

Network analysis may seem like a new approach to studying organizational communication, especially because many technical details remain to be worked out. But, in fact, it is a case of pouring old wine into new bottles. The English poet John Donne reminded us many centuries ago that "No man is an Iland, intire of itselfe; every man is a peece of the Continent, a part of the maine." Wherever human beings congregate and need to cooperate, they must create channels to convey the messages that lead to coordinated behavior.

Donne did not say it, but it is implied in his message. If everyone is "part of the maine," everyone must know the culture that prevails there and the climate of public opinions in which messages are sent, received, and interpreted. In Chapter 5, we turn to these crucial contextual factors.

NOTES

1. For various other definitions of networks, see Rolf T. Wigand, "Communication Network Analysis: History and Overview," in *Handbook of Organizational Communication,* ed. Gerald M. Goldhaber and George A. Barnett (Norwood, N.J.: Ablex, 1988), 321; Evelyn M. Fenton and Andrew M. Pettigrew, "Theoretical Perspectives on New Forms of Organizing," in *The Innovating Organization,* ed. Andrew M. Pettigrew and Evelyn M. Fenton (London: Sage Publications, 2000), 19–21; and Robert D. McPhee and Phillip K. Tompkins, eds., *Organizational*

Communication: Traditional Themes and New Directions (Beverly Hills, Calif.: Sage, 1985), 60, and sources cited therein.

2. Ithiel de Sola Pool et al., eds., *Handbook of Communications* (Chicago: Rand-McNally, 1973), 3. For the argument that networks are the key to understanding individual political preferences, see Robert Huckfeldt and John Sprague, "Networks in Context: The Social Flow of Political Information," *American Political Science Review* 81 (1987): 1197–1216; and Robert Huckfeldt and John Sprague. *Citizens, Politics, and Social Communication: Information and Influence in an Election Campaign* (New York: Cambridge University Press, 1995), chap. 7.

3. R. Wayne Pace, *Organizational Communication: Foundations for Human Resource Development* (Englewood Cliffs, N.J.: Prentice-Hall, 1983), 136–137.

4. Erik-Hans Klijn, Joop Koppenjan, and Katrien Termeer, "Managing Networks in the Public Sector: A Theoretical Study of Management Strategies in Policy Networks," *Public Administration* 73 (1995): 437–439.

5. Ibid., 444–446.

6. Serge Taylor, *Making Bureaucracies Think: The Environmental Statement Strategy of Administrative Reform* (Stanford: Stanford University Press, 1984).

7. Everett M. Rogers and Rekha Agarwala Rogers, *Communication in Organizations* (New York: Free Press, 1976), 110–111. Also see Morgan, 1997, chap. 4.

8. James E. Anderson, "A Revised View of the Johnson Cabinet," *Journal of Politics* 48 (February 1986): 534.

9. Lucien S. Vandenbrouke, "Anatomy of a Failure: The Decision to Land at the Bay of Pigs," *Political Science Quarterly* 99 (fall 1984): 482.

10. Hugh Heclo, "Issue Networks and the Executive Establishment," in *The New American Political System,* ed. Anthony King (Washington, D.C.: American Enterprise Institute, 1978), 103.

11. Paul A. Sabatier and Neil Pelkey, "Incorporating Multiple Actors and Guidance Instruments into Models of Regulatory Policymaking," *Administration and Society* 19 (August 1987): 236–263.

12. Heclo, "Issue Networks and the Executive Establishment," 117.

13. For a detailed discussion of all aspects of issue network construction and operation, see David Knoke, *Political Networks: The Structural Perspective* (New York: Cambridge University Press, 1990).

14. Heclo, "Issue Networks and the Executive Establishment," 105–106.

15. Laurence J. O'Toole, "Interorganizational Communication," 66–68; also see Erik-Hans Klijn, "Analyzing and Managing Policy Processes in Complex Networks: A Theoretical Examination of the Concept of Policy Network and Its Problems," *Administration and Society* 28 (1996/1): 9–19.

16. Heclo, "Issue Networks and the Executive Establishment," 117.

17. Frederick Williams, Ronald E. Rice, and Everett M. Rogers, *Research Methods and the New Media* (New York: Free Press, 1988), 164. Surveys could, of course, use sociometric questions to reflect social realities. But they rarely do. Even when individuals are the unit of response, they need not be the unit of analysis.

18. Louise H. Kidder, *Seltiz, Wrightsman and Cook's Research Methods in Social Relations,* 4th ed. (New York: Holt, Rinehart and Winston, 1981), 191. For more nuts and bolts details see Knoke, *Political Networks,* 235–240.

19. James A. Danowski and Paul Edison-Swift, "Crisis Effects on Intraorganizational Computer-Based Communication," *Communication Research* 12 (April 1985): 259–270.

20. Network analyses often miss important nonroutine relationships that may yield exceptionally valuable new information. What is involved is the concept of "the strength of weak ties" mentioned in Chapter 5.

21. David Knoke and James H. Kuklinski, *Network Analysis* (Beverly Hills, Calif.: Sage, 1987), 59–60.

22. Ibid., 56.

23. Ibid., 22.

24. Ibid., 23.

25. William Richards and George Lindsey, "Social Network Analysis: An Overview of Recent Developments," in *Communication and Control in Society,* ed. Klaus Krippendorff (New York: Gordon and Breach, 1982), 59. Also see John Scott, *Social Network Analysis: A Handbook* (Thousand Oaks, Calif.: Sage, 2000).

26. Examples can be found in Rogers and Rogers, *Communication in Organizations,* 124–125.

27. Gerald M. Goldhaber, *Organizational Communication,* 3d ed. (Dubuque, Iowa: Wm. C. Brown, 1983), 165.

28. Peter R. Monge and Eric M. Eisenberg, "Emergent Communication Networks," in *Handbook of Organizational Communication,* ed. Gerald M. Goldhaber and George A. Barnett (Norwood, N.J.: Albex, 1988), 330; also see Knoke and Kuklinski, *Network Analysis,* 26–30, for a discussion of attempts at sampling large populations.

29. Rolf T. Wigand, "Communication Network Analysis: History and Overview," in *Handbook of Organizational Communication,* ed. Gerald M. Goldhaber and George A. Barnett (Norwood, N.J.: Ablex, 1988), 328–336. The author provides brief descriptions of the use of these techniques for network analysis. The possibilities of graphic computerized representations of networks are discussed and illustrated in J. David Johnson, "On the Use of Communication Gradients," in *Handbook of Organizational Communication,* ed. Gerald M. Goldhaber and George A. Barnett (Norwood, N.J.: Ablex, 1988), 361–383.

30. Richards and Lindsey, "Social Network Analysis," 64–69; Wigand, "Communication Network Analysis," 337–342.

31. Knoke and Kuklinski, *Network Analysis,* 30.

32. For a discussion of the advantages and disadvantages of various types of sociograms, see Wigand, "Communication Network Analysis," 328–331.

33. Gerald M. Goldhaber and Donald P. Rogers, *Auditing Organizational Communication Systems: The ICA Communication Audit* (Dubuque, Iowa: Kendall/Hunt, 1979), 411.

34. Knoke and Kuklinski, *Network Analysis,* 50–56.

35. For an extensive list of earlier studies relevant to political science research, see the bibliography in Edward O. Lauman and David Knoke, *The Organizational State: Social Choice in National Policy Domains* (Madison: University of Wisconsin Press, 1987), and the bibliography in Knoke and Kuklinski, *Network Analysis.*

36. John H. Kessel, "The Structure of the Carter White House," *American Journal of Political Science* 27 (August 1983): 431–463; John H. Kessel, "The Structure

of the Reagan White House," *American Journal of Political Science* 28 (May 1984): 231–258.

37. Phil Gailey, "Deaver Stirs a Hornet's Nest," *New York Times,* Apr. 5, 1986.

38. Heinz Eulau, "The Redwood Network Project: Small-Scale Research at the Local Level," *ICPSR Bulletin* (January 1984): 4, app. A. Also see Robert Huckfeldt and John Sprague, "Networks in Context: The Social Flow of Political Information, *American Political Science Review* 81 (1987): 1197–1216.

39. Karen S. Cook et al., "The Distribution of Power in Exchange Networks: Theory and Experimental Results," *American Journal of Sociology* 89 (1983): 276–279.

40. Rogers and Rogers, *Communication in Organizations,* 144.

41. Ibid., 120.

42. Ibid., 122–123.

43. Ralph Katz, "The Effects of Group Longevity on Project Communication and Performance," *Administrative Science Quarterly* 27 (1982): 81–104.

44. Alicia A. Marshall and Cynthia Stohl, "Participating as Participation: A Network Approach," *Communication Monographs* 60 (1993): 137–157.

45. Toshio Yamagishi, Mary R. Gillmore, and Karen S. Cook, "Network Connections and the Distribution of Power in Exchange Networks," *American Journal of Sociology* 93 (1988): 833–851; Phillip Bonacich, "Power and Centrality: A Family of Measures," *American Journal of Sociology* 92 (1987): 1170–1182; Cook et al., "The Distribution of Power in Exchange Networks," 275–305.

46. Terence R. Mitchell and James R. Larson, Jr., *People in Organizations: An Introduction to Organizational Behavior,* 3d ed. (New York: McGraw-Hill, 1987), 306, and sources cited therein.

47. Mark S. Granovetter, "The Strength of Weak Ties," *American Journal of Sociology* 78 (1973): 1360–1380. Information flows leading to the adoption of innovations are discussed in Marc L. Lame, "Communicating in the Innovation Process: Issues and Guidelines," in *Handbook of Administrative Communication,* ed. James L. Garnett and Alexander Kouzmin (New York: Marcel Dekker, 1997), 187–193.

48. Judith R. Blau, "Prominence in a Network of Communication: Work Relations in a Children's Psychiatric Hospital," *Sociological Quarterly* 23 (1982): 236.

49. Rogers and Rogers, *Communication in Organizations,* 132–140. This presents a good discussion of individual network roles.

50. Steven Kelman, *Making Public Policy* (New York: Basic Books, 1987), 48.

51. David Jackson, "Memos an Art Form at City Hall," *Chicago Tribune,* Apr. 26, 1992.

52. Terry M. Moe, "Control and Feedback in Economic Regulation: The Case of the NLRB," *American Journal of Political Science* 79 (December 1985): 1094–1116.

53. Rogers and Rogers, *Communication in Organizations,* 136, and sources cited there.

54. Ibid., 137.

55. Daniel Katz and Robert L. Kahn, *The Social Psychology of Organizations* (New York: Wiley, 1978), 450.

56. For relevant case studies see Edmund F. McGarrell and Kip Schlegel, "The Implementation of Federally Funded Multijurisdictional Drug Task Forces: Organizational Structure and Interagency Relationships," *Journal of Criminal Justice* 21 (1993): 231–244. The study deals with cooperation among crime-fighting agen-

cies. Also see Keith G. Provan and H. Brinton Milward, "A Preliminary Theory of Interorganizational Network Effectiveness: A Comparative Study of Four Community Mental Health Systems," *Administrative Science Quarterly* 40 (1995): 1–33, which deals with cooperation among health care providers.

57. Harold F. Gortner et al., *Organization Theory: A Public Perspective* (Chicago: Dorsey, 1987), 175.
58. John H. Kessel, *Presidential Parties* (Homewood, Ill.: Dorsey, 1984), 90.
59. Ibid., 90–108. Some sample answers are provided.
60. Kessel, *Presidential Parties,* 93.
61. Richard Darman and William Clark were also members of the group at times.
62. Kessel, "The Structure of the Reagan White House," 238.
63. Kessel, *Presidential Parties,* 97.
64. James J. Best, "Who Talked to the President When? A Study of Lyndon B. Johnson," *Political Science Quarterly* 103 (fall 1988): 531–545.
65. Raymond A. Friedman and Joel Podolny, "Differentiation of Boundary Spanning Roles: Labor Negotiations and Implications for Role Conflict," *Administrative Science Quarterly* 37 (1992): 28–47.
66. Relevant theories that attempt to explain why organizations engage in boundary-spanning and how they interact have dealt primarily with the private sector. For an attempt to expand these theories to public sector organizations, see Mark Kessler, "Interorganizational Environments, Attitudes, and the Policy Outputs of Public Agencies: A Comparative Case Study of Legal Services Agencies," *Administration and Society* 19 (1987): 48–73.
67. Office of Technology Assessment, *Informing the Nation: Federal Information Dissemination in an Electronic Age* (Washington, D.C.: U.S. Government Printing Office, 1988), 27.
68. Herbert Kaufman, *The Administrative Behavior of Federal Bureau Chiefs* (Washington, D.C.: Brookings Institution, 1981), 190.
69. Lame, "Communicating in the Innovation Process," 196–198.
70. Laurence J. O'Toole, Jr., "Interorganizational Communication: Opportunities and Challenges for Public Administration," in *Handbook of Administrative Communication,* ed. James L. Garnett and Alexander Kouzmin (New York: Marcel Dekker, 1997), 61–77, 70.
71. Kessel, *Presidential Parties,* 97.
72. Joseph A. Pika, "Interest Groups and the White House under Roosevelt and Truman," *Political Science Quarterly* 102 (winter 1987–1988): 647–648.
73. John A. Worthley and Richard Torkelson, "Managing the Toxic Waste Problem: Lessons from the Love Canal," *Administration and Society* 13 (1981): 152.
74. Gortner et al., *Organizational Theory,* 169.
75. Ibid., 170. Also see David M. Boje and David A. Whetter, "Effects of Organizational Strategies and Contextual Constraints on Centrality and Attributions of Influence in Interorganizational Networks," *Administrative Science Quarterly* 26 (1981): 378–395.
76. Pub. Law No. 91-648 (1971).
77. William T. Gormley, Jr., "Intergovernmental Conflict on Environmental Policy: The Attitudinal Connection," *Western Political Quarterly* 40 (June 1987): 301.
78. George C. Edwards III, *Implementing Public Policy* (Washington, D.C.: CQ Press, 1980), 22.

79. Doris A. Graber, *Mass Media and American Politics,* 5th ed. (Washington, D.C.: CQ Press, 1997), 307–322, and sources cited there.

80. Edwards, *Implementing Public Policy,* 23; also see Stephen L. Wasby, *Small Town Police and the Supreme Court: Hearing the Word* (Lexington, Mass.: Lexington Books, 1976), 35–50.

81. Pew Research Center for the People and the Press, "Journalist Report," (2000), http://www.people-press.org/jour00rpt.htm.

Chapter 5   Designing Climates and Accommodating Cultures

W hen in Rome, do as the Romans do" is an old saying. This sage counsel is based on the well-established fact that cultures differ substantially
in their behavioral norms. Seemingly unimportant customs, like who speaks
first in a formal encounter, can set the tone of a meeting, ensuring its success
or dooming it to failure. The fact that it is vital to be sensitive to the beliefs,
norms, and customs of the people in one's environment explains why information management entails more than gathering information and channeling
it so that it reaches its destination as quickly and cheaply as possible. Sound
information management must be attuned to an organization's culture and
must strive to create and maintain an appropriate organizational climate.

Organizational Climates

We shall begin by discussing how messages generate the internal and external
climates in which organizations operate. Because of their size and rigidity and
the diverse cultural backgrounds of organization members, public sector
agencies find it especially difficult to create productive organizational climates. We shall then turn to an analysis of the larger organizational culture in
which agencies operate, examining formal and informal rules that dictate the
behavior of organization members. We shall focus on two important aspects
of bureaucratic culture in the public sector. They are the use of bureaucratic
symbols to convey an aura of importance to bureaucratic activities and the
major intended and unintended cultural changes produced by evolving communication technologies, particularly computers and the Internet.

Climate Facets

Psychological Facets. Organizational climate is a psychological construct. Human minds can sense it but it is hard to measure precisely because it leaves few
physical traces.[1] Simply defined, climate is the psychological atmosphere
members of an organization perceive. Climates have been characterized as
hostile or friendly, employee- or management-oriented, sexist, liberating,
tense, or relaxed. Such characterizations refer to the atmosphere of an entire
system whose boundaries may extend to the whole organization or may be
limited to an organizational subunit or even a specific organizational activity.
A variety of different climates may prevail in an organization at different

times, depending on the nature and pace of its activities and on personnel factors. For example, a laid-back atmosphere may prevail at an Internal Revenue Service branch office following a hectic, high-pressure climate during the spring when most tax returns are filed. Some supervisors may be able to maintain islands of serenity in a subunit, surrounded by a sea of turmoil; others may heighten the sense of pressure. When climates are friendly and supportive or hostile and tense, trusting or mistrusting, these qualities are diffused throughout particular units largely through verbal and nonverbal communication. The end product involves widely shared perceptions, not just one individual's reactions to the unit or its activities.

Questionnaires have been the usual way to ascertain which perceptions are shared by members of an organization. Surveys are often supplemented or replaced by participant-observer techniques borrowed from anthropology or by less formal observations.[2] Because this research focuses on people's feelings about their environment, measurements are inherently subjective. Climate measurements may involve aggregating individuals' perceptions of various climate factors or asking them for an overall evaluation of climate conditions. Alternatively, employees may be asked to judge how others in the organization are experiencing the climate. An organization may receive high ratings on individual aspects of climate but still receive poor overall evaluations when employees rate it in terms of their expectations or compare it with other organizations. For example, employees whose pay and benefits may be above established norms may still feel deprived when they measure themselves against comparable workers whose total pay seems higher.

People typically use idiosyncratic cues when they assess organizational climates. When gauging a superior's interest in subordinates' views, some may consider the time it takes to receive a response to a question and its degree of formality. Others may judge interest by the number of employee suggestions that have been implemented. Still others may use promotions and budget allocations to judge whether their comments are valued. The criteria chosen by organization members to assess the organizational climate thus determine their conclusions.[3]

The degree of individual recognition and autonomy and the sense of importance conveyed by an agency are particularly important yardsticks for gauging climate. When superiors are supportive and warm, when they reinforce appropriate behavior, and when coworkers inspire trust and liking, employees feel in tune with the goals of the organization and judge its climate favorably. It is important for employees to believe that they are well-informed and that they can communicate adequately with superiors and fellow workers.[4] The organizational climate also benefits when subordinates become involved in making decisions about how their work is conducted.

The verbal as well as nonverbal cues that affect climate may relay their messages directly or indirectly. For instance, a threat to cut an agency's budget for noncompliance with demands can be expressed explicitly—"we will cut your budget"—or obliquely—"we expect to be short on funds." Nonverbal cues can indicate the seriousness with which various situations and demands for performance are viewed. A suggestion that the agency should discontinue a service that has become troublesome may have little or no follow-through if it is given in an informal memo that suggests trivial significance or is accompanied by disconfirming body language, like a wink of the eye or a shrug of the shoulders. The receiver may even confirm intent by an equivocal remark such as "You didn't really mean that, did you?"

Nonverbal cues transmitted through everyday interactions also constitute a significant aspect of climate. Clothing and hair and make-up styles can signal formality or informality in interactions within and across levels of the hierarchy. Arriving late for an important meeting, thereby forcing others to wait, can symbolize power and disdain for wasting associates' precious time.[5] Lack of esteem is commonly communicated nonverbally or inferentially rather than explicitly. This often happens to minorities and to women in organizations. They may be snubbed during organizational meetings by receiving less time than their equals to present ideas, by being interrupted more often, and by being treated in patronizing fashion.[6] They may be excluded from important social channels, such as lunch-time get-togethers and after-work social events. Low esteem can be communicated by assigning disrespected groups to tasks in occupational backwaters, by excluding them from the top levels of management, and from planning sessions about programs for which they will be responsible. Women and minorities have been barred from field assignments involving travel or from technologically demanding jobs. Consequently, they have felt "tolerated but not necessarily welcomed."[7] It is difficult to cope legislatively or even through education with climates of discrimination created and maintained through such indirect messages.[8]

Women and minorities also are more often the butt of jokes than others, signaling their lower power status. In fact, humor plays an important role in the social dynamics of organizations. It contributes to an egalitarian climate when the organizational culture allows joking to be symmetrical so that people can kid each other irrespective of organizational rank. By contrast, it enhances hierarchy cleavages when higher-ups can tease lower-level workers whom the culture constrains from reciprocating.[9] Humor can also ease tensions and take the edge off of otherwise disturbing remarks.

Structural Facets. Climate is often related to structural variables, such as the number of employees under a single manager's jurisdiction, the division of labor, or provisions for on-the-job social interactions. It may also be shaped by communication network structures that determine which individuals or groups interact, thereby affecting decisions and inter- and intragroup relations.[10] The hierarchical structures that are common in public agencies inhibit the flow of upward communication, making it difficult to create collegial climates. Usually superiors are responsible for many employees, so that inter-personal contacts are minimized. Extensive division of labor gives individuals an atomized view of the organization's work. On-the-job social interactions are rare because they cannot easily be included in organizational budgets. The ready availability of e-mail can be a further damper on face-to-face encounters. However, rank-based hierarchical barriers are partly overcome in U.S. agencies because the mechanisms for keeping social distance are weak. Subordinates are more likely in the United States than in other societies to act like social equals of their bosses.

Failure to communicate across organizational lines is a common cause of hostile climates. For example, reciprocal misunderstandings led to a climate of distrust and disenchantment when citizens were appointed to Environmental Protection Agency (EPA) advisory committees to help the agency plan for improved water quality in their communities. Citizens felt that they were merely completing meaningless paperwork and interpreted the long delays in implementing water improvement programs as a sign of the EPA's lack of respect for their advice. Unlike the citizens who expected to play an active advisory role, EPA officials viewed the citizens' role as largely symbolic. For them, the long delays in the implementation of programs were standard for bureaucratic cultures. In-depth interviews of citizens who served on advisory committees made it clear that the EPA had failed to communicate its goals and constraints.[11]

Environmental Facets. An organization's external climates may be shaped through interaction with its environment. For example, much of the working environment of the State Department has been created through publicizing slogans and metaphors, such as referring to enemies as "rogue nations" and to military occupations as "peace-keeping" missions. Cold-war rhetoric created a climate of distrust for Soviet-bloc countries in the decades following World War II. This climate proved inimical to reaching any kind of disarmament agreement with these countries. Similarly, the United States described its 1990 invasion of Panama as an effort to stop drug dealing, so that it would be viewed as part of the government's well-publicized "war on drugs." This reduced the level of anxiety that might have been created by characterizing the action as military intervention or an effort to police the Western Hemisphere.

Efforts to control the climate of interrelationships are common during various types of negotiations. Attractive physical surroundings may be chosen as meeting sites and language may be deliberately restrained, even friendly, to create a climate that encourages agreement. Alternatively, threatening language and austere physical surroundings, along with timely hostile incidents, may be used to coerce an opponent into accepting particular terms.[12]

The negotiating agenda may also be structured with climate concerns in mind. Items on which agreement seems most likely may be placed at the beginning to create a favorable momentum for solving problems, or at the end, to conclude on a strong, unifying note. Difficult items may be scheduled when the prevailing mood is likely to be most receptive to new ideas that may promote a settlement. Accurate timing is essential, requiring such maneuvers as stalling through lengthy speeches and delays in opening sessions or rearranging meeting agendas to speed decisions.

Climate Types

Climate can be described in terms of various general typologies, or the focus can be on climate factors that affect specific activities, such as job performance or interactions among employees. At the general level, one can distinguish between democratic and authoritarian climates. A democratic climate fosters open communication and is oriented toward individuals.[13] Leaders feel accountable to the rank and file and care about their opinions and preferences. By contrast, an authoritarian climate is dominated by the leader. Because it is penalty-oriented, the temptation to conceal and distort may be greater. A lot of guessing and spying may occur because fewer data are readily available in authoritarian settings. Stress levels can be used to classify organizational climates and compare agencies or various levels within the same agency. At the top of the hierarchy, public-agency climates are typically characterized by high stress levels. These often reach danger points at which they harm individuals and impair work performance. Burnout is common, leading to physical and psychological distress and high job turnover.[14] High stress climates in the public sector have been attributed to executives' feelings of inadequacy about solving complex problems, fear that policy outcomes cannot be successfully controlled, and apprehension about media and public criticism. Tension at the top tends to radiate downward to mid- and lower-level officials. Conversely, high stress levels at the bottom of the hierarchy may radiate upward when they arouse concern at the top.

When attitude toward job performance is the focus, climate has been assessed in terms of factors like morale, crispness of task performance, and policy consensus. According to Herbert Kaufman,

> Morale is the level of unity, pride, confidence, dedication, enthusiasm, conscientiousness, and industry displayed by an organization's members. Crispness is a comprehensive term for the speed, accuracy, efficiency, and competence with which members do their jobs. Policy consensus means the absence of sharp divisions among the members about the values emphasized in the organization's operations.[15]

Climate can also be characterized in terms of the perceived qualities of interaction among organization members. Six styles of interaction have been identified. When organization members are intensely *competitive* with each other, the climate may become tense. Members may become uncooperative or even hostile. Friction may spring from divergent political, policy, or personal goals or from interpersonal incompatibilities. The reverse is a *collaborative* climate in which members believe that they share goals and are personally compatible. Collaborative behavior can be encouraged through rotating the roles of various people and keeping them well-informed about organizational goals and their relation to those goals. Combining a climate of competition with a climate of collaboration is considered ideal. Verbal behavior can help in achieving that difficult goal.

Some organizations emphasize teamwork. Teams are more likely to thrive when hierarchies are flat, with line and staff distinctions blurred—an uncommon condition in public sector agencies except for ad hoc task forces that often cut across hierarchical lines. Other characteristics favoring teamwork include extensive face-to-face interaction among members of the organization about nonroutine decisions and fairly close consensus about values. It also helps if members have a deep appreciation of the organization's mission and goals.[16] Research and development laboratories often have such a *concertive* climate, as do highly professional agencies like the Corps of Engineers or the Central Intelligence Agency (CIA). When members have internalized the values of the organization, no other control mechanism is needed. Concertive climates are fairly rare because the personal values of organization members or the values of unions and other interest groups with whom they identify often conflict at least partially with the values of the organization.

When members differ in their goals and perceptions of organizational policies but are willing to compromise, relationships become *conciliatory*. The ability to develop a compromise position often hinges on the leadership skills of dominant individuals within a particular communication network. Some organizations may have several leaders, each with a group of followers. In such cases, a *supportive* relationship exists between each leader and his or her followers, although the overall climate of the organization may be competitive. Finally, intergroup relations may foster a climate that can be characterized as *detached*. Members of the organization accept whatever is decided and feel little or no personal involvement. Such a neutral climate is hardly conducive to enthusiastic job performance, but it comes closest to the Weberian notion of appropriately detached bureaucratic attitudes.

Over time, organizational climates often change. Different stages have been identified as organizations move through typical life cycles. Organizational life begins with a *forming*, or developmental stage during which there is likely to be a great deal of cooperation as members learn what their tasks are and how to perform them. The climate is either collaborative, conciliatory, or supportive. A *storming* stage follows, during which open conflict is common about structural concerns such as operating rules, the arrangement of the organizational agenda, and leadership roles. A competitive organizational climate prevails. During the third phase, called *norming,* the organization returns to a more collaborative and conciliatory climate. The group tends to reach consensus about rules and procedures, and members identify more closely with group norms. During the final phase, called *performing,* the organization functions smoothly because rules and routines have become second nature. The climate is predominantly collaborative.[17] In the public sector, a postfinal phase, *adjourning,* is rare. It involves the disintegration of the organization after its tasks have been completed and the agency shuts down fully or partially.

How Internal Climates Shape Organizations

Organizational climate, according to Marshall Scott Poole, "represents the linkage between the organizational situation and members' cognitions, feelings, and behaviors."[18] Most important for organizational life, it affects job satisfaction and performance. Employees work harder or less hard, and better or less well, depending on the impact of internal climates.[19] Improvements in climate may have a spiral effect. The satisfactions flowing from these improvements may enhance the quality of the climate even more.

Job Satisfaction and Performance. It is particularly important for public agencies to create climates that motivate employees to high performance, because the penalty and reward structures that are powerful motivators in the private sector are weak in the public sector. Aside from a few special projects, the public sector's civil service system largely precludes rewarding excellence through increased benefits and pay or promotion unless there are open positions that have not been claimed by aspirants under seniority rules. Similarly, it is almost impossible to penalize unsatisfactory performance through pay reduction, demotion, or dismissal. The plight of a police captain in a large metropolitan department is a case in point. The captain could offer neither financial rewards nor job retention nor promotion as incentives to motivate young police officers to prepare adequate arrest reports. Even creating team competitions failed because there were no prizes. "No one," the captain complained, "was getting any type of reward for winning the competition, and they figured why should they bust a gut when there was no payoff."[20]

Performance evaluations and appraisals for promotion are areas in which formal communications are frequently mishandled in public agencies, with destructive consequences for organizational climate. Neither managers nor employees like personal evaluations, especially when feedback about job performance has to be negative. There are many reports of undercurrents of "envy, fear, and hostility" on the part of subordinates who typically feel "insecure, powerless, vulnerable and dependent" in hierarchical settings where rewards are uncertain. This may produce a "pervasive lack of enthusiasm, boredom, low productivity, red tape, and officious compensatory behavior to achieve recognition and respect."[21] When employees are doing well, managers may be overly eager to praise, often giving employees more credit than is due. To maintain morale, they may overstate chances for promotion. Ultimately, such lack of candor results in disillusionment and a climate of distrust.

When top executives are replaced, as happens frequently in the public sector, dramatic changes in organizational climate may follow. Herbert Kaufman cites the example of the Food and Drug Administration following the accession of Donald Kennedy in 1977. The "agency's drug unit had been rent by internal conflict and division, assailed by both the industrial and the consumer wings of its clientele, afflicted with demoralization, and at war with the commissioner at the time. Some employees denounced it in congressional testimony."[22] Kennedy was able to turn the agency around. Two years later, there was no evidence of internal warfare in the agency. "At meetings, the atmosphere was businesslike, cordial, open, and relaxed, and at informal gatherings there was obvious camaraderie."[23] Kennedy's management style was a major factor in his success. "He treated his colleagues with respect, was receptive to their ideas, encouraged inventiveness, and did his homework assiduously when they put proposals before him. He helped create a collegial environment."[24]

The benefits of skilled leadership may evaporate quickly when leaders leave an organization. For instance, when Wernher von Braun, the charismatic leader of NASA's Marshall Space Flight Center in Huntsville, Alabama, left the agency, the legendary communications climate that he had created deteriorated rapidly.[25] Job satisfaction and performance quality plummeted.

Climate can foster a high moral tone in an agency, but it can also do the reverse. When there is a pervasive sense that flouting the rules is condoned or even encouraged, many members succumb, pushing aside personal scruples. Jeb Magruder, a Nixon official involved in the Watergate scandal, testified that the organizational climate inspired his illegal actions. "Because of a certain atmosphere that had developed in my working at the White House, I was not as concerned about its illegality as I should have been."[26] Pervasive corruption in police departments and even court systems has often been linked to a climate of "everybody does it, why shouldn't I?" The remedies for such social evils go beyond prosecuting the guilty and removing them from office. What is needed is a profound change in the organizational climates and cultures that condone corruption.

Profound climate and culture changes are difficult and often painful. *Whistle-blowing* provides many graphic examples.[27] Whistle-blowers who reveal their agency's transgressions break with the prevailing institutional climate that condones these practices. Whistle-blowers may be motivated by combinations of altruistic and selfish concerns. Irrespective of motivations, they risk severe retaliation such as censure, dismissal, and public scorn for tattling and disloyalty that many cultures abhor. Because of disdain for whistle-blowing, the chances are slim that their complaints will lead to major reforms.

Whistle-blowing is important because it discloses otherwise unavailable information needed to correct serious deficiencies in the public service or by private contractors serving the government. For example, whistle-blowing revealed age discrimination by the National Aeronautics and Space Administration (NASA), price fixing and excessive charges by major corporations dealing with the government, and defrauding of Medicare by health care providers.[28] In 1989 Congress passed the Whistle-Blower Protection Bill to encourage unauthorized disclosures by diminishing their risks. The bill makes it faster and easier for whistle-blowers to fight against dismissal.[29] A 1983 government poll had shown that 70 percent of federal employees who knew that their agency's climate condoned waste, fraud, and other abuses were unwilling to blow the whistle because they feared the consequences.[30] Besides dismissal and acts of revenge by the exposed wrongdoers, whistle-blowers also reap personal scorn because American political culture detests stool pigeons. At best, even when whistle-blowers are respected, they are rarely liked.

Developing Loyalty and Morale. Loyalty, morale, and a sense of mission are important aspects of organizational climate that boost work performance and employee retention. Agencies can develop these sentiments among their employees through personal ties between superiors and subordinates or through charismatic leadership or through creating stimulating, challenging working environments.[31] Developing and disseminating effective mission statements may also help.[32]

In large multifaceted organizations, the size of the workforce makes it nearly impossible for managerial personnel to develop personal relationships with their employees by keeping in close touch with most of them. Loyalty, morale, and sense of mission must therefore be developed through formal training or through working in a climate pervaded by these qualities. Indoctrination about the organization's mission generally must circulate throughout the entire organization, with adaptations geared to the special needs of various organizational levels. Indoctrination messages may be conveyed through handbooks, briefings, office newsletters, internal rotations, apprenticeships, and the like. They may also be disseminated informally by word of mouth. This informal approach is often the most important introduction to the organizational climate.

Loyalty and morale can also grow from ideological commitment to the organization's policies. The Department of State, the EPA, and the CIA have been able to attract ideologically committed individuals to their ranks because they are allowed to be highly selective in choosing applicants and testing them for appropriate value structures as well as for technical proficiency. However, ideological commitment is a mixed blessing. It runs counter to the bureaucratic culture ideal that public servants, although loyal to their agency, must be ideologically neutral technicians who carry out whatever mandate a changing cast of partisan superiors requires.

Fostering a Climate for Innovation. Although anxiety about major changes in tasks and their execution is universal, changes are made fairly readily in the private sector. This is not so in the public sector, where maintaining consensus about established policies is preferable to risking its breakdown to accomplish needed changes. The varied constituencies with vested interests in public policies almost ensure that there will be sharp conflicts over the goals of innovation and the means to reach these goals.[33] Conflicts of interests between administrators and legislators often become major obstacles to innovation.[34] Would-be innovators find it exceedingly frustrating to appear at hearing after hearing to justify their proposals when they must face staunch defenders of the status quo or eager rivals for the resources available for innovations.

Even when changes are within the power of a single agency, the mere fact of large size is a major obstacle, as is the tendency of job descriptions to be too detailed to allow for major reallocations of duties. When innovations interfere with employees' lifestyles, vocal resistance is usually high. For instance, when New York City tried to change police officers' assignments so that more would be on duty during peak crime periods, officers complained bitterly.[35] A climate of resentment was unavoidable because it was impossible to make the innovations palatable to most members of the force.

Earlier we noted the tendency of bureaucrats to adhere strictly to established rules because of their vulnerability to media criticism, political pressures, complaints, and threats of litigation about inequities. This is the hallowed rule that one should never be the first to do anything unusual. It is part of what is indelicately known as a CYA (cover-your-ass) maneuver. Such sentiments are not conducive to creating a climate that encourages new initiatives.[36] So it is not surprising that a government agency in Atlanta paid $40 for mowing a lawn to a landscaping firm that had competed for the contract in the kind of formal bidding that is customary in awarding government contracts. At that time, it would have cost just $10 to hire an eager neighborhood teenager, possibly risking a reprimand for violating the rule that all work must be bid competitively. Teenagers are unlikely to submit such bids.[37]

Many private sector measures for enhancing the climate for innovation are unavailable to public agencies. They include structuring the reward system to foster innovation, selecting leaders committed to innovation and removing obstructionists, providing needed financial and psychological resources for retraining and restructuring or for new ventures and personnel, and improving communication so that information about innovations and their relevance to the agency's mission is widely circulated.[38] To lower the barriers to innovations, the legal base of some agencies has been changed to transform them into government corporations with increased control over making and altering their own rules and procedures. The U.S. Postal Service is one example.

Despite the obstacles, many governmental units do make concerted efforts to encourage their own as well as private sector innovations and reinventions.

The latter is a term that is used when innovations that have already been tried out in other organizations are adapted to the particular circumstances of a new adopter of the innovation.[39] The most massive reinvention effort in recent U.S. history has been the National Partnership for Reinventing Government launched under the sponsorship of Vice President Gore in 1993. The official report, *Creating a Government that Works Better and Costs Less,* made specific reinvention proposals for twenty-one government departments and agencies. As the recommendations for the Federal Emergency Management Agency in Box 5–1 indicate, many of these suggested changes constitute major innovations in the operations of the agency. To increase the chances for adoption of these far-reaching proposals, they had been discussed with the affected organizations before including them in the report. These organizations had also been asked to create their own reinvention teams. In addition, the federal government instituted the Hammer Awards to recognize the reinvention achievements of teams of employees. Four years after the start of reinvention, federal agencies claimed that they had successfully implemented two thirds of the initial recommendations and that innovations were continuing.[40]

Many innovations are suggested by communication with people from outside the organization. Such external contacts are usually less frequent than internal contacts and often involve parties that have little in common. Rather than being weaker, such contacts can be extraordinarily stimulating because they dip into new networks where different ideas are circulating. This is why such contacts demonstrate *the strength of weak ties.* System openness to the external environment produces a climate favoring innovation. Such openness often lags in the public sector because there is less boundary-spanning networking and less internal networking than in the private sector and because joint ventures cutting across agencies are less common.[41] Political appointees in the top echelons who might provide fresh insights rarely spend enough time with an agency to implement innovations.[42]

Within organizations, information about innovations is most likely to be exchanged by people who are familiar with each other and who have the same status.[43] When the climate for circulating innovative ideas is restrictive because of fears of criticism and ridicule or concern that change will put fellow workers' jobs at risk, innovations may not circulate widely enough to gain legitimacy. They may also fail to benefit from discussion and scrutiny.

Organizational Cultures

Organizational culture refers to the written and unwritten and explicit and implicit rules of behavior that each organization develops and to the unique myths and symbols that guide the behavior of individuals within the organization. Organizational culture is thus, as Dennis Mumby states, "a complex web of socially constructed experiences which embodies various and heterogeneous organizational meaning structures."[44] James Wilson defines it as a

Box 5-1 **National Performance Review: Major Recommendations By Agency**

Federal Emergency Management Agency

Shift Emphasis to Preparing for and Responding to the Consequences of All Disasters

FEMA's early focus was on preparedness for nuclear war. The current world situation and recent natural disasters highlight the need for FEMA to continue to shift its resources to respond to all hazards.

Develop a More Anticipatory and Customer-Driven Response to Catastrophic Disasters

These recommendations should make FEMA respond faster and more effectively to catastrophic disasters.

Create Results-Oriented Incentives to Reduce the Costs of a Disaster

The Midwest floods, Hurricanes Hugo and Andrew and the Loma Prieta Earthquark all illustrate the enormous costs of disaster to society. These recommendations will move toward reducing that cost.

Develop A Skilled Management Team Among Political Appointees and Career Staff

Leadership has been the weak link in FEMA's mission as the federal government's emergency management coordinator. These recommendations strive to improve FEMA leadership to successfully implement its new, all-hazards mission.

SOURCE: Al Gore, *From Red Tape to Results: Creating a Government that Works Better and Costs Less.* Report of the National Performance Review (Washington, D.C.: U.S. Government Printing Office, 1993), *140*

"persistent, patterned way of thinking about the central tasks of and human relationships within an organization."[45] It develops in response to the organization's need to perform its mission in a particular environment. Organizational leaders determine how that mission is interpreted and what approaches should be used to achieve organizational goals. In the process, they shape or implement organizational cultures.[46] Figure 5–1 exemplifies the interaction between the general culture in which organizations operate and various subordinate cultures. These include the political culture that pervades the public sector, the organizational culture, as well as the subculture or subcultures of particular organizations.[47]

Figure 5-1 Circles of Culture

General Culture

Political culture   Subculture

Organizational culture

SOURCE: Author.

Culture Facets

A shared organizational culture does not mean that members are in total agreement. They can take organized action even when they have different reasons for acting and assign very different "equifinal" meanings to their common experiences. Dissimilar interpretations can produce similar behaviors.[48] Postal workers, for example, may share in a culture that believes that mail must be delivered as fast as technology permits. For some, this may be a matter of professional pride and tradition, whereas others see it as a chance to collect overtime bonuses that they view as a perquisite of postal jobs.

Rules of organizational culture may be thematic, relating to the basic belief structure and values—the ethos—of the organization, or they may be tactical, designed to ease life within the organization. For example, a thematic rule that hierarchy distinctions must be respected can be accompanied by the purely tactical command "Don't argue with your boss!"[49] At times, thematic and tactical rules may be contradictory. For example, it is a general thematic rule that public agencies must keep their dealings open to public scrutiny. However, within agencies such as the CIA and the FBI there are numerous tactical rules that prescribe exceptions to the culture of openness. When such exceptions become pervasive, it may indicate a change from a culture of openness to one of secrecy and possibly deception.

Cultural rules influence the types of goals that agencies may seek and also the types of behavior that will achieve them. For example, the political culture of the United States is oriented toward the preservation of biological families.

A child care agency would run counter to cultural constraints if it advocated the large-scale removal of children from their biological families to raise them in foster homes or institutional settings. Given the culturally sanctioned inviolability of the home, it would probably be impossible to authorize an agency to monitor parenting behavior inside private residences over parental objections. Theorists who espouse a critical interpretive perspective have claimed that political elites who control an organization's material resources also control the symbol system that creates and maintains organizational culture.[50] These elites design cultural rules to maintain existing power structures for their own benefit.

Learning Cultural Rules

Because the myths, symbols, rules, and values constituting the organizational culture or cultures are unique to particular contexts, they must be communicated verbally and behaviorally so that members can learn and share them. Learning is easiest and the impact strongest when these cultures correspond to the personnel's existing values and ethics.[51] Even then complete acculturation may take a long time, and it may always remain incomplete even for long-term workers because "[m]eanings do not reside in messages, channels, or filters; rather, they evolve through social interaction and sense-making activities of people."[52] Incomplete acculturation may impair the effectiveness of the agency and lead to numerous personnel problems, including high turnover rates.

One can learn cultural rules through observing behavior and social interaction within the organization—what is done and not done and the social consequences. According to Michael Thompson and Aaron Wildavsky "the key question is 'In what way would which people, sharing which values, legitimating what practices, act to strengthen their own organization and/or to weaken their adversaries?' How do they select data so as to convert it into information that will support the mode of organization they prefer?"[53] Answers to these questions may be elusive. One can rely on word-of-mouth instructions from people in the organization who have been socialized to its cultures, or one can glean a number of cultural rules from personnel department publications. In general, such publications cover only a fraction of the rules, symbols, myths, values, and perspectives that make up an organization's culture. Full acculturation is left to on-the-job experience.

Organizations with clear missions generally find it easiest to convey their organizational culture. For example, Forest Service personnel could be easily indoctrinated because the values, perspectives, and rules governing work performance were clear and unvarying throughout the agency.[54] The fact that personnel wore distinctive uniforms helped to convey a sense of identity among widely dispersed officials. Most government agencies are too large and diversified in their mission to have a single culture.

In fact, there has been a steady increase in cultural diversity in organizations in the United States, particularly in the public sector. It has given rise to a veritable flood of studies of cultural integration problems faced by multicultural organizations. Most large organizations have specialists on board periodically or permanently to instill the values of multiculturalism into the work force. They must battle against the culture's most recently targeted demons, such as racism, sexism, ageism, and discrimination against the disabled. These practices were once tolerated by the culture, but no longer are, at least officially.[55]

The greatest difficulties in bridging cultural differences arise in external communications involving culturally different countries. As difficult as it is to take climates and cultures into account in framing communication on the domestic scene, it is infinitely harder when national and ethnic barriers must be breached. Studies by famed Dutch organizational anthropologist Geert Hofstede explain some of the reasons. Hofstede examined survey data about the values of IBM employees in more than fifty countries worldwide. Statistical analysis of their answers revealed shared problems but fundamental differences in resolving them. The differences were most prominent in five areas: (1) social inequality, including relations with authorities; (2) relations between individuals and their group; (3) the social implications of masculinity and femininity; (4) control of aggression and emotion when dealing with uncertainty; and (5) long-term versus short-term orientation toward life.[56]

Table 5–1 summarizes some of the key cultural differences between citizens living in collectivist or individualist societies. How difficult it must be for people subscribing to such different views of political life to work together in ways that serve their respective interests and goals! For example, the table lists self-actualization by every individual as an ultimate goal. A Chinese student, exposed to this concept, told a group of visiting Americans that "the idea of 'doing your own thing' is not translatable into Chinese." In collectivist societies people belong to strong, cohesive groups that expect unquestioning loyalty in exchange for protecting group welfare.[57] You do the "group thing," no matter the personal sacrifice that it may entail. A survey of British and Egyptian technical education managers led researchers to the conclusion that "different national cultural characteristics make the hypothesis that it is possible to transfer management ideas, concepts and theories usefully between nations highly questionable."[58] Of course, this does not mean that people from these nations cannot work satisfactorily together as long as their interactions are culturally sensitive and as long as they are willing to compromise rather than insist on uniform cultural standards.

How Cultures Shape Organizations

A few examples illustrate the importance of organizational culture in shaping the character and performance of various public agencies. For instance,

Table 5-1 Key Differences between Collectivist and Individualist Societies' Politics and Ideas

Collectivist	Individualist
Collective interests prevail over individual interests	Individual interests prevail over collective interests
Private life is invaded by group(s)	Everyone has a right to privacy
Opinions are predetermined by group membership	Everyone is expected to have a private opinion
Laws and rights differ by group	Laws and rights are supposed to be the same for all
Low per capita GNP	High per capita GNP
Dominant role of the state in the economic system	Restrained role of the state in the economic system
Economy based on collective interests	Economy based on individual interests
Political power exercised by interest groups	Political power exercised by voters
Press controlled by the state	Press freedom
Imported economic theories largely irrelevant because unable to deal with collective and particularist interests	Native economic theories based on pursuit of individual self-interests
Ideologies of equality prevail over ideologies of individual freedom	Ideologies of individual freedom prevail over ideologies of equality
Harmony and consensus in society are ultimate goals	Self-actualization by every individual is an ultimate goal

SOURCE: Geert H. Hofstede, *Cultures and Organizations: Software of the Mind* (Berkshire, UK: McGraw-Hill Book Company, 1991), 73. Reprinted with permission.

the FBI's culture calls for calm and deliberate procedures. Agents know that painstaking collection and analysis of evidence are more important than speed. By contrast, local police departments usually prize speedy action. Calming community fears by announcements that offenders have been apprehended or at least identified is an important goal. Depending on the particular culture of a department, police may be instructed to treat suspected offenders sternly or to try to resolve law infractions with a minimum of confrontation.[59]

Organizational culture norms may be quite influential in determining how communication flows between dissimilar parties such as superiors and subordinates, service providers and clients, or males and females. In a NASA unit charged with preparing astronauts for space flight, the basic unit has to be the work group rather than the individual. Individuals are recruited with an eye toward keeping the organization harmonious. When they are assigned to the organization, they are explicitly indoctrinated into its culture. Friendliness and teamwork are stressed and short tempers are disdained.[60] On a more mundane level, organizational culture generally dictates that superiors support mid-level executives against claims from bottom-level personnel, regardless of the merit of the claim. Hence, it is a tactical rule for employees at the bottom of the hierarchy to avoid complaining about mid-level managers. The penalty for ignoring the rule may be dismissal of the subordinate.

Cultural rules are important in defining the nature of conflicts and the appropriate methods for seeking solutions.[61] Strategies and tactics must be constructed with these rules in mind. For example, in a labor dispute between unionized government workers and the labor relations section of a county government, each side tried to present its case in a way designed to win a favorable ruling from the panel of adjudicators.[62] They geared their appeals to the presumed cultural expectations of all parties to the dispute. For instance, they referred to shared moral and rational standards, such as the importance of treating people equally.[63] The opponent's perspectives were depicted as irrational or unwarranted. Appeals made during the hearings were impersonal, because cultural constraints inhibit requesting personal favors and partisan rulings by judicial bodies.

Box 5–2 provides an outline of the various types of appeals that were used. For instance, within the prevailing U.S. cultural context, few would argue with the moral command that people should be treated fairly or with the rational imperative that people should behave logically. Few would contest a standard of responsibility that prescribes that people who are at fault should be punished. Other arguments called the credibility of the opponent into question and confirmed the credibility of the claimant because it is culturally customary to assess the relative credibility of the parties in legal proceedings. By presenting their pleas in line with such well-accepted frameworks, the contestants hoped to make them irrefutable.

Bureaucratic Symbols

Organizational culture commonly requires that bureaucrats communicate in ponderous, often incomprehensible styles.[64] This is done to satisfy the requirements of equally ponderous legislative and judicial language and to lend an air of authority to bureaucratic transactions. Simple yes or no responses have been shunned despite rigorous government efforts to translate bureaucratic jargon into plain English. Normally, bureaucrats will not call a spade "a spade" when it can be called "a soil-rotation facilitator." When Rep. Jack Kemp asked Budget Director Bert Lance whether the Carter administration could terminate a missile project without prior permission from Congress, the simple answer would have been "yes." Instead, Lance responded in classic bureaucratic style:

> As you know, the Impoundment Control Act of 1976 does not contain any provision governing the obligation or deobligation of funds proposed for recision during the forty-five-day period. A recision message is awaiting congressional action. There is no prohibition on terminating existing contracts, thereby deobligating funds, during this period.

> In the absence of express requirements with respect to obligation or deobligation of funds and in view of the recognition by Congress that funds could be withheld, there is no legal basis for precluding the Department of Defense from either refraining from obligating additional funds or terminating existing contracts during the forty-five-day period the related recision message is pending in the Congress.[65]

Box 5-2 **Content-Level Coding System**

Moral standards—A standard or principle of morality is invoked in support of the sender's position.
> *Debt:* People should pay their debts.
> *Equality:* People should be treated equally/consistently.
> *Empathy:* People should treat others as they would like to be treated themselves.
> *Equity:* People should be treated fairly/justly.[a]

Rational standards—A standard or principle of reason is invoked in support of the sender's position.
> *Law:* People should obey the law/rules/contract.
> *Authority:* People should obey authority/courts/arbitrators.
> *Efficiency:* People should behave efficiently/practically.
> *Logic:* People should behave logically/sensibly.[a]

Standards of responsibility—A standard of responsibility is invoked in support of the sender's position.
> *Blaming:* People who are at fault should be punished.
> *Second chance:* People who admit they have done wrong should be given a second chance.
> *Mistake:* People should not be punished for honest mistakes and misunderstandings.

Credibility comparison—The credibility of the opponent is called into question while the sender's credibility is assured.
> *Truth:* They are not being honest, we are.
> *Motivation:* They have hidden motives, we do not.
> *Knowledge:* They do not know what they are talking about, we do.
> *Competence:* They have not done their job, we have.

Perspective manipulation—The adjudicator is directed to view the conflict from a perspective that supports the sender's position.
> *Issue definition:* The issue or question before the adjudicator is framed in a way that favors the sender's position or detracts from the opponent's position.
> *Minimization:* The strength of the opponent's position is minimized by the sender.

SOURCE: Elizabeth A. Martin and Louis P. Cusella, "Persuading the Adjudicator: Conflict Tactics in the Grievance Procedure," in *Communication Yearbook 9*, ed. Margaret L. McLaughlin (Beverly Hills, Calif.: Sage, © 1986), 541. Reprinted with permission.

[a]Tactic was identified during coding of data.

Bureaucratic culture mandates that announcements of organizational changes maintain the appearance that the power structure is intact and functioning properly. "It will not do to admit that your top executives have been performing inadequately. And it certainly will not do to point out that an effective executive has been removed because he lost out in political infighting."[66] When changes result from conditions that the culture deems inappropriate or embarrassing, official explanations usually hide the real facts. They "save face" by presenting socially acceptable explanations that sustain the legitimacy of the organization and its goals. Most changes are depicted as progress that will enhance the efficiency and effectiveness of the agency. Insiders who publicly discuss the organization's shortcomings are likely to find themselves ostracized by their colleagues and may be dismissed from their jobs. Destroying an image is treated as a major transgression, because it is likely to undermine morale internally and cause external difficulties for the agency.

Organizational rituals are also useful for maintaining desired images. For example, to maintain the image of a busy top executive, incumbents of high offices rarely grant interviews on short notice even when they have open time. The culture may also demand restricting information intended for higher level executives to a small corps of especially trustworthy people. Excluding lower level personnel from decision-making meetings serves to set upper-level officials apart as more knowledgeable and hence more competent. The symbolism narrows the information input into decisions but it surrounds top executives with an aura of mystery. Presumably it also creates awe for the participants of these sessions and facilitates maintenance of the existing authority structure.[67] An organization's dominant norms and values tend to be reflected in the way meetings are conducted. Meetings are also the place where cultural norms may be contested, negotiated, or changed.[68]

Red Tape Rationale

The cultures of government bureaucracies mandate that procedures follow explicit rules whenever possible. Organizations therefore develop detailed, complex guidelines for their various activities. The term "red tape" is used to refer to the sum total of these guidelines, procedures, and forms, which political folklore stigmatizes as excessive and wasteful. The name commemorates the fact that official documents were tied with red tape during the nineteenth century.

When the Chicago Transit Authority wanted to sign contracts exceeding $5,000 during the late 1980s, red tape required fifty-four separate steps.[69] As a consequence, processing a contract took more than six months. In the wake of public complaints about too much red tape, nineteen steps were eliminated, thereby reducing processing time to three months. That horror story can be duplicated endlessly at all levels of government. This is why the 1993 National Performance Review devotes an entire chapter to cutting red tape.

Government performance, according to the reform proposal, should be judged by its substantive results rather than by compliance with a raft of procedural rules.[70] Many Gordian knots of red tape have been cut under the Reinventing Government program thus far, but not without major political battles. Standardizing record keeping among government offices is one example, and creating central registries so that all records can be searched simultaneously is another.

How many rules and procedures are necessary safeguards to keep administrators accountable and honest and how many are excessive remains a matter of controversy. Political scientist Raymond A. Rosenfeld therefore defines red tape in subjective terms as "guidelines, procedures, forms, and government intervention that are *perceived* as excessive, unwieldy, or pointless in relationship to decision-making or implementation of decisions."[71] Barry Bozeman, a red tape expert, goes further and limits red tape to "Rules, regulations, and procedures that remain in force and entail a compliance burden but do not advance the legitimate purposes the rules were intended to serve."[72] The definition acknowledges that many complex rules and duplicate procedures are justifiable because they protect citizens from abusive discriminatory treatment and force government to be open and accountable. In addition to these benefits, bureaucrats prize detailed rules that absolve them from using their own discretion in making decisions and thereby risking censure. A multiplicity of complex rules that the public labels as red tape also makes bureaucracies more powerful in the public's eyes. The bureaucrat is the all-powerful professional who knows the magic formulas that will unlock the agency's resources.

Even though the term red tape carries pejorative connotations of needless, time-wasting procedures, citizens want checks and balances because they distrust government. Distrust is part of America's political culture, embedded in the Constitution, which mandates multiple checks and balances to prevent the reckless or corrupt use of power by government officials. Unfortunately, all these safeguards, which are red tape, albeit labeled with a positive name, greatly complicate government. They cause delays, prevent innovation, curb needed discretion in decisions, and increase expense. At the same time, they also accomplish their purpose of diminishing hasty and ill-considered government actions as well as fraud and other illegal behaviors.[73]

The federal system makes American government particularly prone to red tape because its multiple levels lead to multiple rules for various shared activities. When state legislatures pass laws, they rarely consider the impact of the many layers of often superfluous regulations that may be necessary to comply with their collective mandates. The requirements of periodic reports to Congress and state legislatures to meet criteria of accountability force agencies to collect and keep very extensive records that are rarely used and therefore largely a waste of bureaucratic energy that could be spent in more productive pursuits. The Administrative Procedure Act and the Freedom of Information Act and their state-level counterparts have also resulted in massive amounts of red tape.[74] As programs age, red tape mounts because new regulations are added to the existing old ones. This happens even in administrations eager to reduce red tape. The fear that freedom from restraints may lead to license and corruption is too strongly embedded in the American political psyche.

How New Communication Technologies Transform Bureaucracies

The Internet, satellites, computers, fax machines, and similar technologies are new means of communication that have a strong bearing on organizational cultures and climates. Some of the changes brought about by these technologies are inherent in their nature; others flow largely from the ways in which new tools are used by various organizations.[75] In many instances, they generate significant changes in established cultures. Conventional practices must be revised and new norms created to guide behavior in the new environment. These changes have improved organizational performance and the organizational climate in many respects, but there have also been major drawbacks.

The wide dispersion of computing facilities has made it increasingly necessary to develop elaborate information policies and plans. Data sharing requires a high degree of compatibility among systems. The Johnson Space Center, to use just one example, had to set up a permanent planning committee, composed of designers, users of the system, and upper-management representatives, to create information technology policy guidelines for the entire organization. However, operational control remained decentralized because the majority of users of the system preferred that.[76]

The George W. Bush administration created the office of Associate Director of Information Technology in the Office of Management and Budget (OMB) in the summer of 2001 to lead an interagency task force to facilitate interagency coordination.[77] Subsequently, a director of information technology was chosen to oversee the integration of new information technologies into the operations of the federal government.[78] These officials were given a fourfold charge. With the help of an interagency task force, they were asked to identify areas where information technology would enhance performance in service to individuals, service to businesses, the handling of intergovernmental affairs, and the efficient and effective conduct of the internal affairs of government organizations.

Among possible priorities in services to individuals, OMB listed portals where citizens can access high-quality government services without searching through multiple Web sites. Simplicity and speed would be the chief goals. Businesses might be served by using Internet protocols and by consolidating redundant reporting requirements. Similarly, intergovernmental affairs could benefit from easier reporting requirements and more uniform performance measurements. To aid internal agency management, the government would draw on information technology developed in the private sector to enhance the handling of supplies, finances, and information.

Advantages and Disadvantages of "Powering Up"

The Positives. On the plus side, for the most part "powering up"—the use of new information technologies to manage organizations more effectively—creates more open communication climates. The new technologies make it easier to contact agency members even when message senders do not know them personally and even when large numbers of employees are involved. Widespread ready access to computerized information is a distinct advantage, making it easier for isolates to tap into organizational networks. However, the knowledge required to use the new technologies may create a new crop of isolates. This is likely to happen whenever the development of complex new ways of managing information exceeds the capacity and willingness of change-resistant personnel to use the new tools. Older workers and the inadequately educated are most likely to be isolated and disadvantaged.

The new technologies simplify sending and receiving lengthy messages at any time in a variety of locations beyond the traditional office settings. Messages can be stored for later retrieval whenever the intended receivers are not at the point of reception and cannot be reached by cell phones. This flexibility allows employees in agencies with far-flung branch offices or staffs whose work requires travel away from their offices to stay in much closer touch than was previously possible. Messages intended for a variety of receivers, whose needs and comprehension levels may vary, can be easily issued in multiple versions. They can now be personalized even for mass mailings. A seemingly personalized message presumably enhances the quality of the relationship between agencies and constituencies. Interconnected computers can disseminate messages extremely rapidly, facilitating prompt action. Faster action generally improves responsiveness to client needs. Organizational effectiveness tends to increase when time and distance constraints become less formidable, unless a flood of messages overwhelms the capacity of the system or its users to process the information adequately.

The electronic revolution has also had a major impact on the climate for organizational decision making.[79] Computer data storage capabilities have broadened the information base available for decision making, including ample data from external sources. Costs for collecting, processing, and storing information have plummeted. The additional information can be circulated to all parties involved in a particular decision, making sound judgments and appropriate actions more likely because relay points, which can be sources of distortion, are eliminated. An instantaneous, readily accessible, accurate record stored in the computer's memory is an added benefit.

Computers serve as boundary spanners par excellence, fostering collaborations across organizational boundaries. They can be particularly helpful in making innovations because external databases may contain stimulating ideas. They also transcend the barriers often created through hierarchies and friendship circles. Overall, computers make it possible to reap the benefits of centralization and decentralization simultaneously and at comparatively low cost. Data archives combine information that was widely dispersed and therefore often inaccessible before the advent of modern computers. Moreover, computerized information has become so user-friendly that people with minimal computer skills can use it without the aid of information technology experts.

By disseminating knowledge more widely, computers also facilitate more input from lower levels of the organization. In many instances, decision making can even move from higher to lower levels so that it is closer to field operations and clients.[80] Such decentralization promotes greater responsiveness to local conditions, albeit at the cost of decreased uniformity.

Computers with Internet access can be extraordinarily useful for communication between average citizens and government agencies. Benefits accrue in four important areas. Computers allow citizens to (1) explore services that they need from government; (2) conduct business with government agencies online; (3) send comments about government policies and services to bureaucrats, elected officials, and fellow citizens; and (4) monitor what government agencies are doing. A few examples follow drawn from the rapidly growing record of electronic communication between citizens and their government.

All major federal government departments and agencies now have Web pages that list the services available. For instance, as a public service, the Department of Labor posts continuously updated job listings for the benefit of prospective employers and employees. The agency also stores records of applicants for federal jobs and forwards them to departments with job openings. The Internal Revenue Service (IRS), along with many other agencies, now encourages clients to complete forms on line. This saves clients time-consuming trips to government offices and allows them to complete the forms at times of their own choosing. Agencies dealing with automobile, airline, and hospital safety are benefiting from reports of problems submitted by clients nationwide. The wealth of information allows them to improve their activities. It also permits clients to tap into this type of information and become more knowledgeable consumers.[81] Finally, clients, including journalists, now have inexpensive access to the records of government agencies, putting real teeth into the watch-dog function of the press and the public.[82]

As with any new technology, many of the electronic contacts between the public and government agencies are still beset with problems, and many people remain out-of-contact. Web design and browser functions are only at the toddler stage. Problems of privacy and confidentiality pose tricky technical and political challenges because it has been difficult to block unauthorized access to computerized information. Even intelligence agencies like the FBI are not immune from major damage caused by security breeches. That became painfully evident when FBI double agent Robert Hanssen confessed to breaking into secret files to spy for the Soviet Union.[83] Still, progress in linking government agencies and citizens electronically is moving at a swift pace, propelled by steady technological advances and spreading computer literacy.[84]

The Negatives. On the negative side of the technological revolution, when machine communication takes the place of face-to-face or even telephone contacts, important nonverbal message cues are absent. This impairs the ability to judge the meaning of messages and to learn from visual and aural cues when individuals interact or when public meetings are conducted electronically.[85] Also absent are elements of instant reciprocity in synchronous communications that can clear up misunderstandings and lead discussions into productive paths. Brief electronic messages may seem curt, and the ruffled feelings are unlikely to be soothed by subsequent face-to-face interaction. Diminished interpersonal contacts may also impair morale and the sense of belonging.

The sheer volume of new information available through computerized data and messages may lead to serious information overloads. The ease of sending electronic mail to large numbers of people simultaneously also fosters a culture where communication is excessive. "Computers seem almost to serve as a pernicious nutrient for bureaucracies, allowing their structures and their flaws to grow gigantic." Instead of generating thirty useless pieces of paper, the computerized bureaucracy may generate three hundred. In sum, "Automating a mess yields an automated mess."[86] The increased ability to communicate may actually reduce the time available for productive work. It also makes bureaucratic communication systems more vulnerable because the possibilities for communication breakdowns mount when more information must be manipulated and shared. To make matters worse, many government agencies still use incompatible systems and find it difficult to agree on standardization. The blessings of ease of access to more information may thus turn out to be disabling curses as well.

Many issues of open access to public information stored in computerized formats remain to be resolved.[87] Who should have access at what cost and at what price? Who will be excluded from access to sensitive information such as personnel data or payroll accounts? If people have access to government files, how can sensitive personal data about their health, their finances, and even their social security number be protected? Will most people be able to master the technical skills required to process information held in government files? The answers await legislation, rule making, and court decisions, as well as public education and technological improvements.

New text-searching capabilities may have to be created. For example, tapes of the *Congressional Record* could not be searched efficiently until full text-searching capabilities were developed. Rapidly changing technologies may make existing data not only obsolete but unusable. The National Archives already has scores of unreadable computer files, including Vietnam War data collected by the Pentagon, NASA's early scientific observations of the earth and planets, and voluminous public health records.[88]

Does a climate of openness require that all government documents be made available in formats that will permit computer searches? The implications of allowing everyone to search documents systematically could be enormous in light of the wide access to documents permitted under the Freedom of Information Act.[89] This is why several federal agencies removed sensitive documents from their sites after the September 2001 terrorist strikes against the United States. For example, the EPA pulled information on risk management programs that contain information about potential risks from the operations of 15,000 U.S. industrial plants. The Transportation Department removed information pinpointing the location of the country's pipelines, and the Nuclear Regulatory Commission did the same for information about the location of nuclear plants.[90] It will be very difficult to devise an effective, culturally acceptable system that allows citizens to monitor government activities while still protecting security and privacy interests.

Aside from the external security concerns, if access to computer files is made easy, agencies may feel compelled to keep information off record to shield themselves from fishbowl effects. Agencies may wish to omit damaging information from databases accessible to members of Congress and the public. It is not particularly flattering to the Immigration and Naturalization Service, for example, to disclose that its sophisticated system for tracking illegal immigrants works well at individual stations but that these stations remain unconnected, or that new airport passenger-checking facilities are not cost-effective and that other innovations are years behind schedule.[91] As discussed more fully in Chapter 7, public officials know that the government's good reputation with the public and with its employees must be maintained at all costs. It may be impossible to achieve that goal without excluding sensitive information from computer systems where it can be retrieved easily. Policy options that have not been adopted may have to be concealed. Such issues of information management raise important ethical questions about the emerging communication culture.

Lack of resources is one of the greatest obstacles to using the new electronic technologies to best advantage in the public sector. Agencies are often barred by law from charging clients for the extra costs of online transactions. Rapid turnover of top executives before cohesive policies can be formulated, political sensitivities, and turf protection by managers are other problems.[92] Older employees in particular resist the new technologies that may threaten their authority, possibly even their jobs, and that they may regard as undesirable pressures to change their established methods of operation. Given the difficulties in rearranging civil service jobs within an agency, it is not easy to overcome resistance to change. Fears have been expressed that use of computerized data depersonalizes the public service even beyond current levels and that cross-matching of computer files will lead to undue invasions of privacy when individuals are under scrutiny.[93]

Mixed Consequences. Many consequences of the new technologies cannot be easily classified as primarily positive or negative. Rather, they are a mixture of both. Changes in organizational networks belong in that category. As mentioned, computers make it easier to integrate isolates into existing networks but may create new types of isolates. Overall, networking has become simpler through e-mail, computer program sharing, and the like, although information overloads have caused bottlenecks and slowdowns. E-mail distribution lists have created new networks and cliques and have changed existing networks in beneficial and detrimental ways. External boundaries can be crossed more readily. Computers also encourage decentralized communication. Some scholars have documented a decrease of intraorganizational messages compared to interorganizational ones. Formally designated bridges and liaisons have become less essential.

In the process, the new technologies may change the roles and hence the possibilities for influence of large numbers of public officials. Role distinctions and jurisdictional boundaries have eroded. The implications for morale and other climate factors are vast. When information circulates freely throughout an organization, filtering operations diminish. This spells a loss of power for previous gatekeepers. It also becomes more difficult to ascertain who introduced certain information into the system, how this information was processed, and who is responsible for taking action. Computerization may thus increase problems of accountability.

Formal distinctions among levels of the hierarchy diminish when computers provide subordinates access to everyone.[94] Status blurring has advantages as well as disadvantages. Greater social interaction through computerized communication may lead to greater social integration. It may also lead to more social disintegration as organizational boundaries become more indistinct and crumble.[95] Dominant leaders are less likely to emerge. Status, power, personal appearance, charisma, past achievements, and ability to communicate mean much less than before. This frees network members from possible intimidation by higher status members of the organization. However, because computer messages often fail to identify their information sources, anxieties may develop about the status of the message sender because reactions to messages are conditioned in part by the sender's status.

The ease of sharing databases encourages the creation of special task forces to handle problems as they arise, thereby undermining the powers of formally established agencies. It has also permitted moving more decisions to lower level employees without diminishing oversight powers at top levels of the organization. The most far-reaching unintended consequence of such power shifts has been the elimination of mid-level jobs. This raises an as yet unanswered question: How flat can and should hierarchies be in the new information age? How often new communication technologies produce profound changes in organizations remains uncertain because organizations resist major power shifts and try to use new technologies to reinforce the status quo. But the current tide of change seems too strong and swift for effective long-term resistance.

The Pace of Change

The establishment and development of new technologies inevitably give rise to serious turf battles, especially when an important power resource such as control over information is involved. When officials at the Johnson Space Center in Clear Lake, Texas, decided to use computers for making operational and management decisions about the space station and space shuttle programs, managers and clients, along with computer vendors, pushed for buying particular systems.[96] More than twenty principal contractors and a host of subcontractors and consultants also asked for consideration of their divergent proposals. Such competing demands may make the organizational climate tense, hostile, and excessively competitive. Because many of the problems are cultural, stemming from conflicting motivations and values, compromises may be difficult. Agency officials worry that technicians' advice may become overly dominant; technicians complain about oversight by nonexperts. Tensions between high-level line officials and data-processing personnel often arise because they do not speak the same language.[97] These tensions are serious because there is no agreement about who should have the final word when politically relevant decisions about computer policies need to be made.[98]

In the end, are the changes brought about by computers and the Internet merely altered versions of established practices that leave the basic system unchanged, or are they major cultural shifts? My crystal ball shows the latter. The changes in information flows discussed in this chapter are having a major impact on public agency structures and functions. On balance, the system is becoming more transparent and democratic because more people within government and outside it have access to information and an opportunity to add to it. Public officials can enhance the quality and speed of their decisions by tapping into enormous databases that were hitherto unavailable. Computers aid in the management of these databases and allow public officials to manipulate the data in a variety of ways to meet the needs of the moment. Indeed, a treasure trove of new information and new tools to turn it into knowledge is now within reach of masses of potential users.

Although it is clear that the new message transmission technologies are producing major changes in cultures and climates, their long-range consequences for organizational welfare may not be apparent for many years. In the meantime, governments continue to cope with their responsibilities by blending familiar and novel approaches. Among their perennial challenges, none is more pervasive and important than managing information to produce sound decisions. What bearing do the issues discussed thus far have on the ability of government officials to make decisions that cope with ongoing problems in ways that are fair and effective from the government's as well as the public's perspectives? The next chapter addresses that question.

NOTES

1. Everett M. Rogers and Rekha Agarwala Rogers, *Communication in Organizations* (New York: Free Press, 1976), 73–74. For an overview discussion of organizational climates see Raymond L. Falcione, Lyle Sussman, and Richard P. Herden, "Communication Climate in Organizations," in *Handbook of Organizational Communication,* ed. Frederic M. Jablin et al. (Newbury Park, Calif.: Sage, 1987), 183–227.
2. Edgar H. Schein, "Culture: The Missing Concept in Organization Studies," *Administrative Science Quarterly* 41 (1996): 229–240.
3. Jeffrey Pfeffer, *Power in Organizations* (Marshfield, Mass.: Pitman, 1981), 186; for some examples, see 191.
4. R. Wayne Pace and Don F. Faules, *Organizational Communication,* 2d ed. (Englewood Cliffs, N.J.: Prentice-Hall, 1989), 121–126.
5. Gareth Morgan, *Images of Organization,* 2d ed. (Thousand Oaks, Calif.: Sage, 1997), 189–191.
6. Clyde Haberman, "The Injustice of Incivility in Civic Duty," *New York Times,* Nov. 2, 2000. Also see Martha Glenn Cox, "Enter the Stranger: Unanticipated Effects of Communication on the Success of an Organizational Newcomer," in *Organization–Communication: Emerging Perspectives I,* ed. Lee Thayer (Norwood, N.J.: Ablex, 1986), 41.
7. Robert Pear, "Blacks and the Elitist Stereotype," *New York Times,* Sept. 29, 1987.
8. Eric M. Eisenberg and H. L. Goodall, Jr., *Organizational Communication: Balancing Creativity and Constraint,* 2d ed. (New York: St. Martin's Press, 1997), 159–162.
9. Dean L. Yarwood, "Humor and Administration: A Serious Inquiry into Unofficial Organizational Communication," *Public Administration Review* 55 (1995): 81–90.
10. Falcione et al., "Communication Climate in Organizations."
11. John P. Plumlee, Jay D. Starling, with Kenneth W. Kramer, "Citizen Participation in Water Quality Planning: A Case Study of Perceived Failure," *Administration and Society* 16 (February 1985): 455–473.
12. Doris A. Graber, *Verbal Behavior and Politics* (Urbana: University of Illinois Press, 1976), 258–269.
13. Marshall Scott Poole, "Communication and Organizational Climates: Review, Critique, and a New Perspective," in *Organizational Communication: Traditional Themes and New Directions,* ed. Robert D. McPhee and Phillip K. Tompkins (Beverly Hills, Calif.: Sage, 1985), 86–91.
14. Lloyd Etheredge, "Government Learning: An Overview," in *The Handbook of Political Behavior,* vol. 2, ed. Samuel L. Long (New York: Plenum, 1981), 110–113.

15. Herbert Kaufman, *The Administrative Behavior of Federal Bureau Chiefs* (Washington, D.C.: Brookings Institution, 1981), 139–141.
16. Phillip K. Tompkins and George Cheney, "Communication and Unobtrusive Control in Contemporary Organizations," in *Organizational Communication: Traditional Themes and New Directions,* ed. Robert D. McPhee and Phillip K. Tompkins (Beverly Hills, Calif.: Sage, 1985), 184.
17. Raymond S. Ross and Jean Ricky Ross, *Small Groups in Organizational Settings* (Englewood Cliffs, N.J.: Prentice-Hall, 1989), 64–65.
18. Poole, "Communication and Organizational Climates," 86–91.
19. For evidence that climate affects performance when other factors are held constant, see David M. Hedge, Donald C. Menzel, and George H. Williams, "Regulatory Attitudes and Behavior: The Case of Surface Mining Regulations," *Western Political Quarterly* 41 (June 1988): 323–340.
20. Terence R. Mitchell and James R. Larson, Jr., *People in Organizations: An Introduction to Organizational Behavior,* 3d ed. (New York: McGraw-Hill, 1987), 184.
21. Etheredge, "Government Learning," 111–112.
22. Kaufman, *The Administrative Behavior of Federal Bureau Chiefs,* 139–141.
23. Ibid., 142.
24. Ibid., 143.
25. Phillip K. Tompkins, "Management Qua Communication in Rocket Research and Development," *Communication Monographs* 44 (March 1977): 1–26.
26. Poole, "Communication and Organizational Climates," 79.
27. Philip H. Jos, Mark E. Tompkins, and Steven W. Hays, "In Praise of Difficult People: A Portrait of the Committed Whistleblower," *Public Administration Review* 49 (November/December 1989): 555–558.
28. Bruce Japsen, "The Secret Inside the Box," *Chicago Tribune,* July 18, 1998; Ronald E. Yates, "Whistle-Blowers Pay Dearly for Heroics," *Chicago Tribune,* July 23, 1995.
29. Robert Pear, "Whistleblowers Likely to Get Stronger Federal Protections," *New York Times,* March 15, 1999.
30. "Congress Sends Bush Bill to Protect Whistle Blowers," *Chicago Tribune,* Mar. 22, 1989.
31. James Q. Wilson, *Bureaucracy: What Government Agencies Do and Why They Do It* (New York: Basic Books, 1989), 95–101. The Forest Service story is detailed in Herbert Kaufman, *The Forest Ranger: A Study in Administrative Behavior* (Baltimore: Johns Hopkins Press, 1967); the FBI story is told by Thomas Gid Powers, *Secrecy and Power: The Life of J. Edgar Hoover* (New York: Free Press, 1987); and the story of the Social Security Administration can be found in Martha Derthick, *Agency under Stress: The Social Security Administration and American Government* (Washington, D.C.: Brookings Institution, 1991) and Derthick, *Policymaking for Social Security* (Washington, D.C.: Brookings Institution, 1979).
32. W. Jack Duncan, Peter M. Ginter, W. Keith Kreidel, "A Sense of Direction in Public Organizations: An Analysis of Mission Statements in State Health Departments," *Administration & Society* 26 (1994): 11–26; Jane E. Dutton, Janet M. Dukerich, and Celia V. Harquail, "Organizational Images and Member Identification," *Administrative Science Quarterly* 39 (1994): 239–263.

33. Robert T. Golembiewski, *Humanizing Public Organizations* (Mount Airy, Md.: Lomond, 1985), 14–17.

34. Ibid., 24.

35. Steven Kelman, *Making Public Policy* (New York: Basic Books, 1987), 169–170. For various communication hurdles plaguing innovations see Lame, 1997, 190–191.

36. Wilson, *Bureaucracy*, 221.

37. Al Gore, *From Red Tape to Results: Creating a Government that Works Better and Costs Less. Report of the National Performance Review* (Washington, D.C.: U.S. Government Printing Office, 1993), 4.

38. Jerald Hage, Michael Aiken, and Cora B. Marrett, "Organization Structure and Communications," in *The Study of Organizations,* ed. Daniel Katz, Robert L. Kahn, and J. Stacy Adams (San Francisco: Jossey-Bass, 1982), 302–315.

39. Marc L. Lame, "Communicating in the Innovation Process: Issues and Guidelines," in *Handbook of Administrative Communication,* ed. James L. Garnett and Alexander Kouzmin (New York: Marcel Dekker, 1997), 193–195.

40. http://www.npr.gov (July 11, 2000). An earlier appraisal by the Brookings Institution was somewhat less enthusiastic: Donald R. Kettl, *Reinventing Government: A Fifth Year Report Card* (CPM 98-1) (Washington, D.C.: Center for Public Management, Brookings Institution, 1998), 2–5.

41. See Chapter 4 in this volume.

42. Wilson, *Bureaucracy*, 229–230.

43. Terrance L. Albrecht and Vickie A. Ropp, "Communicating about Innovation in Networks of Three U.S. Organizations," *Journal of Communication* 34 (summer 1984): 78–91.

44. Dennis K. Mumby, *Communication and Power in Organizations: Discourse, Ideology and Domination* (Norwood, N.J.: Ablex, 1988), 8. For a fuller discussion of the communication aspects of organizational culture see Charles R. Bantz, *Understanding Organizations: Interpreting Organizational Communication Cultures* (Charleston: University of South Carolina Press, 1993), especially chap. 2; Eric M. Eisenberg and H. L. Goodall, Jr., *Organizational Communication: Balancing Creativity and Constraint,* 2d ed. (New York: St. Martin's Press, 1997), especially chap. 5; Mary Leslie Mohan, *Organizational Communication and Cultural Vision* (Albany: State University of New York Press, 1993); and Linda Smircich and Marta B. Calás, "Organizational Culture: A Critical Assessment," in *Handbook of Organizational Communication,* ed. Frederic M. Jablin et al. (Newbury Park, Calif.: Sage, 1987), 228–263.

45. Wilson, *Bureaucracy*, 91.

46. Stanley A. Deetz, Sarah J. Tracy, and Jennifer Lyn Simpson, *Leading Organizations through Transition* (Thousand Oaks, Calif.: Sage, 2000), provide an excellent guide for constructing and changing organizational cultures.

47. Maryan S. Schall, "A Communication Rules Approach to Organizational Culture," *Administrative Science Quarterly* 28 (1983): 557. The importance of the macroculture is discussed in Virginia Hill Ingersoll and Guy B. Adams, "Beyond Organizational Boundaries: Exploring the Managerial Myth," *Administration and Society* 18 (November 1986): 360–381.

48. Ann Donnellon, Barbara Gray, and Michel G. Bougon, "Communication, Meaning, and Organized Action," *Administrative Science Quarterly* 31 (1986): 44.

49. Schall, "A Communication Rules Approach to Organizational Culture," 562.
50. Mumby, *Communication and Power in Organizations,* 95–125.
51. Schall, "A Communication Rules Approach to Organizational Culture," 575.
52. Smircich and Calás, "Organizational Culture," 231.
53. Michael Thompson and Aaron Wildavsky, "A Cultural Theory of Information Bias in Organizations," *Journal of Management Studies* 23 (May 1986): 277.
54. Kaufman, *The Forest Ranger.*
55. Eisenberg and Goodall, *Organizational Communication,* 212–214.
56. Geert H. Hofstede, *Cultures and Organizations: Software of the Mind* (Berkshire, England: McGraw-Hill, 1991), 3–19.
57. Ibid., 73.
58. Andrew D. Brown and Michael Humphreys, "International Cultural Differences in Public Sector Management: Lessons from a Survey of British and Egyptian Technical Education Managers." *International Journal of Public Sector Management* 8 (1995): 5; also see Hale N. Tongren, Leo Hecht, and Kenneth Kovach, "Recognizing Cultural Differences: Key to Successful U.S. Russian Enterprises," *Public Personnel Management* 24 (1995): 1–18; and Jim D. Rhody and Thomas Li-Ping Tan, "Learning from Japanese Transplants and American Corporations," *Public Personnel Management* 24 (1995): 19–32.
59. Kelman, *Making Public Policy,* 152–153.
60. Tom F. Carney, "Organizational Communication: Emerging Trends, Problems, and Opportunities," in *Organization–Communication: Emerging Perspectives I,* ed. Lee Thayer (Norwood, N.J.: Ablex, 1986), 9.
61. Karen A. Jehn, "A Multi-Method Examination of the Benefits and Detriments of Intragroup Conflict," *Administrative Science Quarterly* 40 (1995): 256–282.
62. Elizabeth A. Martin and Louis P. Cusella, "Persuading the Adjudicator: Conflict Tactics in the Grievance Procedure," in *Communication Yearbook 9,* ed. Margaret L. McLaughlin (Beverly Hills, Calif.: Sage, 1986), 533; for a similar analysis, see Elihu Katz et al. "Petitions and Prayers: A Method for the Content Analysis of Persuasive Appeals," *Social Forces* 47 (1969): 447–463; and Cheryl Zollars and Theda Skocpol, "Cultural Mythmaking as a Policy Tool: The Social Security Board and the Construction of a Social Citizenship of Self Interest," in *Research on Democracy and Society,* vol. 2, ed. Frederick D. Weil and Mary Gautier (Stamford, Conn.: JAI Press, 1994).
63. Martin and Cusella, "Persuading the Adjudicator," 540.
64. Murray Edelman, *The Symbolic Uses of Politics* (Urbana: University of Illinois Press, 1964), 134–146.
65. Quoted in Gerald M. Goldhaber, *Organizational Communication,* 3d ed. (Dubuque, Iowa: Wm. C. Brown, 1983), 133.
66. Ibid.
67. Lee Clarke, *Mission Improbable: Using Fantasy Documents to Tame Disaster* (Chicago: University of Chicago Press, 1999), chap. 6.
68. Rick Iedema and Ruth Wodak, "Organizational Discourses and Practices," *Discourse and Society* 10 (1999): 11–13.
69. Gary Washburn, "Red Tape Bogs Down CTA, Report Says," *Chicago Tribune,* Aug. 17, 1988.
70. Gore, *From Red Tape to Results,* 14–41.

71. Raymond A. Rosenfeld, "An Expansion and Application of Kaufman's Model of Red Tape: The Case of Community Development Block Grants," *Western Political Quarterly* 37 (December 1984): 603.

72. Barry Bozeman, *Bureaucracy and Red Tape* (Upper Saddle River, N.J.: Prentice Hall, 2000), 12.

73. Herbert Kaufman, *Red Tape: Its Origins, Uses, and Abuses* (Washington, D.C.: Brookings Institution, 1977), 29; also see Kaufman, *The Administrative Behavior of Federal Bureau Chiefs*, 42.

74. Rosenfeld, "An Expansion and Application of Kaufman's Model of Red Tape," 604–605.

75. John W. Linker, "Utilizing Communication and Information Technologies in Government and Business," in *Handbook of Administrative Communication*, ed. James L. Garnett and Alexander Kouzmin (New York: Marcel Dekker, 1997), 329–342. Also see Stephen Frantzich, "Legislatures and the Revolution in Communications and Information Processing: Untangling the Linkage between Technology and Politics," 1990 American Political Science Association paper.

76. E. Sam Overman and Don F. Simanton, "Iron Triangles and Issues Networks of Information Policy," *Public Administration Review* 46 (November 1986): 585.

77. Office of Management and Budget, "OMB Memorandum 01-28, 2002" http://www.whitehouse.gov/omb/memoranda/m01-28.html.

78. Diane Frank, "Bush Hires First CTO," *Federal Computer Week*, Jan. 11, 2002, http://www.fcw.com/fcw/articles/2002/0107/web-cto-01-11-02.asp

79. Sharon L. Caudle, "Information Technology and Managing Public Management Choices," 1987 American Political Science Association paper.

80. Richard K. Caputo, *Management and Information Systems in Human Services* (New York: Haworth, 1988), 6. Also see G. David Garson, ed., *Handbook of Public Information Systems* (New York: Marcel Dekker, 2000); and Katherine Barrett and Richard Greene, *Powering Up: How Public Managers Can Take Control of Information Technology* (Washington, D.C.: CQ Press, 2001).

81. Cheryl Jensen, "Watchful Eye," *Chicago Tribune*, July 20, 2000.

82. Jo Bardoel and Valerie Frissen, "Policing Participation: New Forms of Participation and Citizenship and their Implications for a Social Communication Policy," *Communications & Strategies* 34 (1999): 203–227; Paul Frissen, "The Virtual State. Postmodernisation, Informatisation and Public Administration," in *The Governance of Cyberspace*, ed. Brian D. Loader (London: Routledge, 1997); Patricia B. Wood, "Public Management in a dot-gov World," 2000 paper, Spring Conference of the National Capital Area Chapter, American Society for Public Administration. For examples at the state and local levels see Andrew Bluth, "Wire It, and They Will Come," *New York Times*, Dec. 24, 1998; Dennis Marstall, "Local Government Internet Policies: Kent County's Experience," *Public Management Magazine* (January 1998): 12–15.

83. Mike Dorning, "Accused Spy Reportedly Exploited Computers," *Chicago Tribune*, Mar. 1, 2001.

84. G. David Garson, *Information Technology and Computer Applications in Public Administration: Issues and Trends* (Hershey, Pa.: Idea Group, 1999).

85. Mitchell and Larson, *People in Organizations*, 315.

86. James L. Gibson, John M. Ivancevich, and James H. Donnelly, Jr., eds., *Organizations Close-up: A Book of Readings*, 5th ed. (Plano, Texas: Business Publications, 1985), 263.
87. Frank James, "Watchdog Group: Federal Agencies Need a Policy for their Web Sites," *Chicago Tribune*, Aug. 28, 1997.
88. "Years of Computer Data May Be Lost in Old Tapes," *Chicago Tribune*, Jan. 2, 1991.
89. Office of Technology Assessment, *Informing the Nation: Federal Information Dissemination in an Electronic Age* (Washington, D.C.: U.S. Government Printing Office, 1988), 207.
90. Charles Ornstein and Deborah Schoch, "Agencies Remove Some Data from the Web," *Chicago Tribune*, Oct. 5, 2001.
91. Eric Schmitt, "Immigration's Automation Plan Criticized," *New York Times*, Feb. 27, 1997.
92. Caudle, "Information Technology and Managing Public Management Choices," 6.
93. Sharon S. Dawes, "Human Resource Implications of Information Technology in State Government," *Public Personnel Management* 23 (1994): 31–46. Oscar H. Gandy, Jr., "The Surveillance Society: Information Technology and Bureaucratic Social Control," *Journal of Communication* 39 (summer 1989): 61–76.
94. Sara Kiesler, "The Hidden Messages in Computer Networks," *Harvard Business Review* 64 (1986): 46–60.
95. Benjamin D. Singer, "Organizational Communication and Social Disassembly," in *Organization–Communication: Emerging Perspectives*, ed. Lee Thayer (Norwood, N.J.: Ablex, 1986), 223.
96. Overman and Simanton, "Iron Triangles and Issues Networks of Information Policy," 585.
97. Caputo, *Management and Information Systems in Human Services*, 106.
98. Caudle, "Information Technology and Managing Public Management Choices," 13.

Chapter 6 **Foundations for Sound Decisions**

Organizational life involves a constant round of decisions about what to do and what to refrain from doing. All administrators must therefore be able to identify issues that affect them and make decisions that will enable them to take appropriate actions. Many of these decisions are quite routine, involving day-to-day operations, and many have minor consequences, such as the purchase of office supplies. Others, such as the development of major new policies or coping with important events in areas of concern to agencies, are likely to have significant consequences. Irrespective of their significance, all decisions involve gathering information and evaluating it to choose courses of action. Figure 6–1 identifies the multitude of interacting information streams that impinge on decision making.[1]

Managing Information Flows

Sound decision making requires a wide variety of information. That includes general facts like economic conditions affecting the agency and social and cultural values impinging on it. In the agency's more immediate environment it includes information about professional standards, budget controls, interest-group pressures, and the like. Finally, the agency needs operational information, including data concerning various staff and line functions such as planning and research, human-resource management, and financial operations. Figure 6–1 highlights the great dependence on a diverse array of external and internal data that require elaborate structures for producing and gathering this information. As problems become more complex, ambiguous, and unstable, more information will be needed to resolve uncertainties.

Because information is costly to produce, store, disseminate, and use, organizations need to determine how many resources should be allocated to producing and distributing knowledge. They must also consider that the marginal utility of new information often decreases progressively, especially when situations are highly uncertain. Thus, it is unwise to extend information gathering beyond the point where the costs of gathering and processing more information exceed its value for decision making.[2]

Initial information about problems requiring governmental action is normally easy to obtain so that expenses for each additional unit of information tend to be low initially. For example, it was easy to establish in 1996 that a TWA airliner had exploded in midair killing all aboard. Information-gathering costs rose as it became increasingly difficult to locate additional data to establish the cause of the disaster. Cost-effectiveness considerations usually make it

157

Figure 6-1 Information Needs of Public Sector Organizations

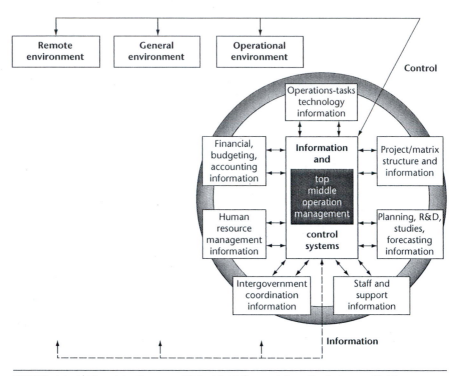

SOURCE: Adapted from John Stevens and Robert P. McGowan, *Information Systems and Public Management* (New York: Praeger, 1985), 25.

prudent to terminate the information search long before all potentially relevant data have been gathered. However, there is considerable risk in terminating information searches before all available information has been gathered because one can never be certain that the most important piece of evidence has surfaced.

Administrators are likely to make the greatest effort to gather all available information when decisions are very important, when they are irreversible, and when time and money resources are ample. Greater vigor in the information search is also common when the administrator who makes the decision is personally accountable. Absent such motivations, administrators prefer to "muddle through," as economist Charles Lindblom called it. They economize on information searches because resources are usually scarce and there are many hotly fought competing demands for them.[3]

Although there is a presumption that information is always good and that more information is better, this is not always true. When information lacks relevance, when it contributes little that is new, or when it is misleading or erroneous, it becomes undesirable noise that can become a hindrance to decision makers. Likewise, not all decisions require information streams from multiple sources.[4] In many circumstances, only a limited number of interests and their spokespersons need to be heard so that it becomes counterproductive to widen the circle of informants.

The structures created to control information flows for decision making, the political and philosophical orientations of decision makers, and the procedures used in processing information strongly affect the pool of information brought to bear on particular decisions. They determine who will be asked to participate in decision making, what information will be considered, and which options will become viable. For instance members of Congress, who make many important decisions, allow themselves little time to weigh all the information because they choose to serve on multiple committees that enhance their power base. "They take pride in their ability to 'read people' rather than read reports."[5] Therefore they gather information primarily through oral communication, such as meetings with constituents and interest groups, public hearings, and talks with their staffs and fellow members. Furthermore, "analysis is alien to the traditional style of the Congress' collection and processing of information."[6] Members filter information intuitively to reach judgments, buttressed by their past experience. They want scientific analysis largely to support the judgments they have already reached.[7]

The public sector faces especially serious problems in making structural and functional provisions for gathering and analyzing various strands of information and combining them to produce the best possible solutions because goals are often controversial, and political concerns receive priority. An example comes from the Carter administration's Youth Employment Initiative that was designed to prepare young Americans for employment by teaching them basic job skills. The president wanted new funding for the project, but faced a lot of opposition on that score, including a lengthy report by his own Office of Management and Budget. Nonetheless, Carter decided to go ahead, based on the advice of Vice President Walter Mondale, who noted,

> I think it would be of greater benefit politically to forgo increases elsewhere in the budget than to send the signal that our youth strategy is a go slow, highly cautious approach. . . . For $2 billion in new authority, *we can get exactly the right reaction and make this a genuine highlight of your 1980 legislative program.* Interestingly, this program has appeal for many conservatives. . . .[8]

The discussion that follows deals primarily with information needs for major decisions. This means that they affect large numbers of people in profound ways. Many involve high economic or political stakes for the public, politicians, or influential elites.[9] Compared with the millions of less significant decisions made daily throughout all levels of public bureaucracies, the number of major decisions that occur in government are infinitesimal. Therefore we will also pay brief attention to the major characteristics and problems involved in making routine decisions.

The Four Phases of Decision Making

To illustrate the decision-making process in public agencies more concretely, we shall use the Environmental Protection Agency's (EPA) decisions about the steps required to clean up an oil spill along the California coast as a hypothetical example.[10] Decision making entails four major information management phases, each requiring gathering and processing different strands of information. During the first phase the problem is analyzed. During the second phase various options to cope with the problem are explored. The third phase involves the selection of a particular option and its implementation. The fourth phase entails monitoring the consequences of the decision and feedback to the agency about changes that might be needed. My analysis focuses on the factors that influence the choice of information at these various stages, rather than on the substance of decisions or the intellectual processes by which they are reached.

Problem Analysis

First of all, EPA officials must have sufficient information about the oil spill to provide a basis for determining what options seem reasonable. The precise definition of the problem from the perspective of EPA's mission may not be easy. Should the chief objective of the investigation be on ways to reverse environmental damage, on preventive measures to forestall future oil spills, or on developing alternative fuel sources? Should the incident be treated as an act of negligence leading to civil or criminal liability or as an unavoidable accident? Should the costs of the investigation and the clean up be borne locally or from national resources?

Depending on the definition of the problem, information requirements will vary. This does not mean that everything about the situation can or must be known. The concept of "satisficing" as contrasted with "optimizing" is useful. Because the complexity of situations and time pressures usually make it too costly or even impossible to assemble all of the facts, satisficing allows fact-finding to stop when a reasonably satisfactory solution has come into view. Accumulating all of the available facts and options and weighing them against one another before deciding would constitute optimizing.[11]

Frequently, the facts of a particular situation are unclear. Administrators then may delay appraisals until more information becomes available, or they may decide to take no action at all. Alternatively, they may draw on organizational memories for analogous events in the past—such as previous oil spills—and the insights gained in coping with them. Past appraisals by staff members steeped in the organization's history form part of the organizational culture that strongly influences subsequent appraisals. Such insights can be valuable for dealing with current problems, but relying on them also poses dangers. It is easy to overlook contextual changes that invalidate analogies with the past. It may be risky to put too much faith in lessons from events that occurred only once or twice before and that may be unique. Depending on the extent of new elements in the situation, relevant information and suggestions must be sought from as broad a spectrum of informants as time and resources will permit.

Input can be solicited formally or informally from sources outside the agency, or it can be generated internally during brainstorming sessions where knowledgeable insiders pool their wisdom and, in the process, create new knowledge.[12] Many public agencies are constrained by their legal mandate, by internal inflexibility, or by political considerations from freely choosing informants, analysts, and policy options. Bureaucrats often feel compelled to tap only sources that are likely to support the goals of the agency's leadership and that are acceptable to the external organizations on which the agency depends.[13] Such constraints may pose serious problems because they may prevent a full and accurate appraisal of the situation. At best, such strictures are apt to severely curtail innovative approaches to various situations.

Problem definition does not always begin with the identification of an existing pressing problem. Proposals for action may come first. Congressional bills for expensive projects in politically important districts are often introduced for political reasons. Construction of a sports facility or a small airport are examples. Appropriate problems must then be invented to justify passing the bill. Obviously, the pork was on the congressional griddle before deciding what public purpose warrants the feast.

Option Exploration

Once the dimensions of the problem have been defined, the range of feasible policy options must be explored. To assess feasibility, EPA decision makers must have enough information about the agency's capacities and resources to be able to judge the kinds of decisions it can implement. They must consider the powers legally available to the EPA and its budget and personnel authorizations. If, for example, the agency is already overextended or lacks personnel knowledgeable about oil spills, the range of options warranting consideration narrows. If top decision makers are averse to using chemicals to control spills, that option becomes foreclosed. The EPA would also need relevant information about the external environment in which the situation is developing. The activities of other public and private actors must be considered. It might make a significant difference, for example, if state-level authorities were already taking measures to cope with the problem. Coordination of the activities of all involved parties would then become a major task.

Political culture traits must also be considered. Americans usually favor retaining the status quo to launching some unfamiliar situation with which they have not yet learned to cope. If changes seem imperative, they prefer incremental alterations to major or radical changes of direction. Small changes are also attractive because they are less likely to arouse opposition by those who dislike the direction in which the agency is moving. In most situations, it may be a waste of time to consider drastic options.

In the public sector, major decisions are open to public scrutiny. Proposed rules for regulatory agencies must be published in the *Federal Register* at least thirty days before adoption to solicit public reactions. In addition, many agencies publish an "Advance Notice of Proposed Rulemaking" to invite comments. Various interest groups then comment on the proposed rules. Although these comments rarely include major substantive suggestions, they do indicate the climate of opinion in which the proposed rules will have to operate. The need to consider the preferences of various segments of the public may severely limit the available decision options. However, it is a potent check on the danger that unpopular ideas will dominate decision making. To gain support for policy choices, agencies often justify them in terms of vague, nonoperational prized goals, claiming that the policy serves the "national interest," the "public interest," or "the general welfare."

Exploring an adequate range of options is the chief challenge during the option-exploration phase. Computers have made it easier to discover viable options and to compare their costs and benefits. But machines are only as smart as their users. Human savvy guides computer searches and human ingenuity must determine what combination of factors ought to be programmed into computers and what uncertainties will affect the ensuing calculations. Assessing the merits of alternative choices requires intelligence not yet fully mastered by computers such as knowledge about causes and effects so that the consequences of each option can be projected with reasonable accuracy. Finally, computer calculations based on economic factors must be assessed in political terms. A policy that maximizes economic utilities may be politically disastrous if it offends powerful constituencies.

Choosing Models for Deciding

Numerous typologies describe the various approaches through which public officials manage information searches at the third stage when decisions must be made to adopt particular options. Each of these approaches represents a different slicing of the same cake. Yet, as Graham Allison and Philip Zelikow point out, "Each conceptual framework consists of a cluster of assumptions and categories that influence what the analyst finds puzzling, how he formulates the question, where he looks for evidence, and what he produces as an answer."[14] We shall discuss a fairly simple set of four decision-making models identified by public administration experts. Each targets different types of information. Depending on the circumstances, the models are used singly or in combination.[15] Which approach is chosen and which yields the best results hinges on the nature of the situation, the available resources, and the preferences and skills of the decision makers.

The Rational-Choice Model. According to the rational-choice model decision makers must meticulously explore information about all options that have surfaced and compare their cost-benefit ratios. The model is based on the belief that decisions should be grounded in scientific principles of management. Figure 6–2 depicts a rational-choice approach for all phases of decision making. It postulates sequences of decisions that begin with delineating the various dimensions of the problem. Next alternative solutions are developed, based on a comprehensive search of all available information. This is followed by evaluations of the options and making final choices, based on cost-benefit considerations. Decision makers use sophisticated methods to make sure that they have carefully analyzed all relevant information. Pertinent information does include facts and appraisals about what needs to be done to win adoption of the decision that political rationality dictates.

This ideal model of decision making is often mandated by law. Regulatory agencies, for example, may be required by statute or directive to use cost-benefit analysis techniques to identify, quantify, and compare policy effects in the hope of encouraging rational decision making. For instance, the Consumer Products Safety Act stipulates that decisions about safety rules must consider the risks of injury; the number of products subject to the safety rules; the public's need for the products involved; the probable effect of the rule on the utility, cost, and availability of the regulated products; and the possibilities for minimizing adverse effects on competition and manufacturing.[16]

Despite much acclaim for rational-choice approaches, studies of actual decision making indicate that they rarely are an exclusive guide to policy decisions.[17] The reasons lie in the complexity of the political environment, which denies a dominant role to findings based solely on logically derived cost-benefit considerations. At best, the process is not as straightforward and orderly as the model suggests.[18] Information searches are never exhaustive, and the full range of options rarely surfaces, even in the age of sophisticated computer technology. Much information is withheld or never searched for technical and political reasons. Complete exploration of all facts and options may be so expensive and time-consuming that the potential gains are not commensurate with the costs. Public bodies are usually inundated with information, much of it contradictory, making it extremely difficult to digest and reconcile everything. In determining which information to examine and which to ignore, it is difficult to establish choice criteria and priorities free from politically relevant biases.

Final decisions generally result from the interaction of a series of previous decisions based on information provided by various stakeholders whose roles and perspectives may have colored their reporting. The National Labor Relations Board (NLRB) is a good example. It is a comparatively small and

Figure 6-2 Main Steps in Rational Choice Approaches to Decision Making

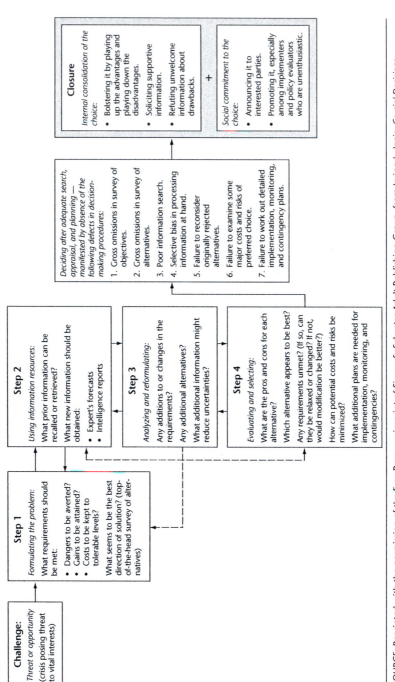

SOURCE: Reprinted with the permission of the Free Press, an imprint of Simon & Schuster Adult Publishing Group, from Irving L. Janis, *Crucial Decisions: Leadership in Policymaking and Crisis Management*, p. 91, © 1989 by The Free Press.

functionally simple body. Still, it makes decisions based on information provided by the White House, by presidential appointees to the board, by congressional committee members, and by estimates of the outcome of potential court decisions. Other decisions that may influence the thrust of the information on which the NLRB's decisions rely include internal agency procedures and goals and the nature of complaints brought to it by business and labor.[19] Even when a broad range of options surfaces, earlier events, predispositions, and decisions may have made them moot.

Rational-choice approaches are also hampered because costs and benefits, which include economic, social, and psychological elements, cannot be gauged accurately. Known "facts" become questionable decision criteria when situations change in unpredictable ways. The price of oil may triple, for example, if major oil wells are destroyed by an earthquake. It is difficult to compare alternatives because value considerations enter into determining which alternatives satisfy the multiplicity of goals of most public policies. Which interests should prevail when the timber industry and environmentalists clash over forest resources? Political considerations are likely to prevail even when they run counter to technical considerations. But political considerations are also subject to controversy because decision makers disagree about the merits of various options.

The Incremental Bargaining Model. If economic rationality does not prevail, or prevails only in part, what other guiding rules shape the choice of information when decisions are at stake? The *incremental bargaining model* is based on the assumption that policy choices in a democracy should emerge from negotiations among representatives of conflicting interests. Decision makers' information searches must therefore focus on ascertaining the preferences of all interested groups and calculating how various alternatives will benefit or harm them. The final choice of options represents a balancing of diverse political interests. It generally involves only small deviations from existing policies, obviating the need to gather extensive information about each of the alternatives that have emerged. A decision is "good" if all groups involved, including public officials, are willing to agree to it. That is more likely to happen when changes are small. Nonetheless, a series of small changes may ultimately amount to a major change without arousing the opposition that could be anticipated from moving quickly. But incremental approaches are slow. They also do not lend themselves to long-range planning and they discourage innovation. Still, they may be the ideal approach when policies are controversial and stakeholders are averse to compromises.

The style of communication that characterizes incremental decision making is far different from communication in rational-choice approaches.[20] The emphasis is on persuasion, debate, and bargaining, not on objective, dispassionate cost-benefit analysis. Proposals are framed with an eye to achieving consensus. The fact that there are usually many interested parties means that ample diverse options are considered, even though the choice and analyses of options are not systematic, as happens in rational-choice deliberations.

When the conflicting interests introduced into the decision process reflect primarily the diverse views of bureaucrats, the incremental-bargaining model may be labeled the governmental or bureaucratic politics model. Bureaucrats often control most of the salient information and are well-situated to present their evidence to decision-making executives in ways that make outcomes favoring their points of view highly likely. When the ultimate goals are fuzzy or change repeatedly as bargaining proceeds, severe misunderstandings may develop among the participants in a negotiated decision. At times, attempts to reach mutually acceptable decisions may also go astray when stakeholders submit false data or cover up information. The initial deception may have been intended as a beneficial "white lie," designed to ease negotiations. But lies debilitate decision making, especially when they generate a string of subsequent deceptions to conceal the initial falsehood.

The Aggregative Model. The bargaining maneuvers that determine the ultimate decision in the incremental bargaining model may leave the outcome vulnerable to mindless log rolling. The *aggregative model* constitutes a modification designed to lessen that chance while still allowing various interests to shape the outcome collectively. Proponents of the aggregative approach believe that a wide array of diverse interest groups should be consulted about their policy preferences but that their proposals should be considered on intrinsic merits rather than being chosen through bargaining among self-interested parties. Advisers, including expert consultants, may be assembled for brainstorming sessions at which various options are debated. The participants then vote for the option they prefer. The final choice represents an aggregation of individual preferences rather than a negotiated decision, as in incremental decision making.

The *aggregative model* has the advantage of introducing a wide array of options and reducing the political tensions that inevitably creep into negotiated settlements. However, the large volume of ideas that are brought to the table tends to discourage in-depth discussion of various options. Also, the model may be unrealistic because it ignores political interests and power relationships among the participants. In the end, political considerations will have to be factored into public agency decisions.

The Garbage Can Model. As public administration experts James March and Johan Olsen describe this model, it involves drifting into decisions more or less aimlessly.[21] Deliberative decision-making models are unrealistic in March and Olsen's view. In most decisions, problems are not fully understood, goals are not clear, and interpersonal relationships are unpredictable. Debates about various options reflect personal and social needs of the participants as much as an attempt to solve problems rationally. Solutions are generated haphazardly and final decisions emerge from the interplay of this "garbage can" collection of disparate ideas, decisions, and nondecisions. Retrospectively, the decision may then be attributed to goals that were never considered initially. Viewed in this way, attempts to gather relevant information to bring to bear on the decision would be mostly window dressing. If sincere, they would be futile.[22]

Decision making at the NLRB illustrates the garbage-can model. The NLRB begins its deliberations by deciding whether claims filed with it justify investigation of a particular situation. A negative decision usually means that the case will not proceed further. Even before this initial decision, earlier decisions by potential parties to a case on whether or not to file a complaint constrain the decisions that the board can make. Regardless of the importance of an issue and the board's eagerness to handle it, it cannot act until a claim has been filed. Its decisions are also influenced by its previous decisions, which potential complainants weigh when they assess their chances of making a successful appeal. As political scientist Terry Moe notes, "[T]he implication is one of reciprocal causality: constituent filing behavior is a basic determinant of staff and Board decision outcomes, but these outcomes have feedback effects that shape subsequent constituent decisions to file charges."[23] Moreover, the various staff members of the board are guided in their initial decisions by a knowledge of its past policies and goals. Relying on precedent therefore develops its own logic of consistency. But it is an unpredictable logic, because even precedents vary. Which information streams will be reflected in the NLRB's decisions hinges on an intricate interdependent web of decisions made by different players in the process rather than on deliberate, rational choices based on the most relevant current information.

Even seemingly orderly, rational procedures can still lead to making garbage-can style decisions. Lawrence Pinfield's experience as a participant–observer in a senior Canadian government task force is illustrative. The task force was charged with developing personnel policies for recruiting senior government executives. The decision process began with four background papers prepared by the task force that described various existing practices. These papers inspired various options included in the task force's prepolicy proposal. The prepolicy proposal was then circulated to interested parties for their suggestions. Just as the composition and attendance patterns of the task force had an impact on its work, so the list of critics and their attention to the project, in the face of many competing demands on their time, had an unpredictable, nonrational impact on the pool of ideas on which the final decision was based.[24]

Nonrational decision making was encouraged because there was no agreement among the participants about appropriate goals and technologies. Moreover, the political context for the decision changed over the two-year period of its gestation, as did the identity of the participants in the deliberations. All these circumstances fostered a garbage-can approach to decision making. Pinfield concluded—and I concur—that making decisions involves a mixture of rational and anarchic processes. Whenever goals and procedures are clear and uncontested, decision making moves in rational steps from problem recognition to resolution. When these conditions are not met, the process is anarchic. The critical factor in determining which process will prevail thus is the clarity and acceptability of goals and the steps to reach them.[25]

Monitoring Feedback

The fourth and final decision-making phase—monitoring the consequences of decisions so that corrections can be made—has become common practice in public agencies. In fact, because accountability is a political and legal necessity in public organizations, internal feedback systems tend to be more complex than in the private sector.[26] Positive feedback tells agency personnel that current policies are working; negative feedback indicates the need for corrections. There is also "feed forward," which means that information or guesses about the future state of the organization are used to anticipate situational changes.[27] An ideal cybernetic system would automatically correct itself in line with the feedback; but self-correcting systems have remained a dream. Automatic adjustments are nearly impossible to devise because there are too many chances for error in interpreting feedback information. The built-in rigidities of public agencies also deter corrections. Thus the mass of feedback data collected by many organizations is largely wasted.

In addition to internal feedback monitoring, public agencies are subject to external monitoring of their decisions, operations, and feedback. This includes both legally mandated and politically inspired feedback, as well as monitoring by government agencies and private institutions, including the news media. Lobby groups may insist on being privy to the feedback. Environmental lobbies, for instance, want to make sure that decisions about pollution standards and other regulations are carried out to the full extent required by law. Antinuclear groups closely follow nuclear licensing decisions and implementation of safety rules.

External monitoring by congressional committees—the congressional oversight function—may be particularly strict during tense political periods or during elections. Agencies must anticipate the political fallout of the type of feedback information that they are accumulating. Therefore, they collect data likely to be advantageous and shun data likely to be embarrassing. Unemployment agencies, for example, are much more likely to amass data indicating that their decisions have been procedurally fair than data about how well they have served the unemployed. They fear lawsuits about procedural fairness, which have been common in the past, rather than the far less-common suits about effectiveness of performance.[28]

Many types of management information systems (MIS) have been developed to provide upper-level administrators with quantitative and qualitative data about performance, either out of genuine concern about feedback or as window dressing. Usually MIS's rely more heavily on formal than on informal lines of communication to collect information and channel it to the proper people.

Monitoring performance by drawing inferences from feedback is especially difficult in the public sector because the value of the services provided by government is hard to measure. The goals of many public policies are expressed as broad concepts without explaining what terms such as *national interest, better economic security,* or *preservation of family values* mean in relation to specific policies. It is difficult to judge from feedback data whether these diffuse goals have been achieved, especially when people disagree about what should be considered good or bad results. When a governmental agency cuts back on its activities, wild applause may be mixed with loud shouts of disapproval and dismay. Response to feedback is extraordinarily difficult when clashing goals have to be accommodated and when national, state, and local laws conflict so that compliance with the laws of one governmental level means violation of the laws of another. On top of that, officials' professional aspirations may be an important deterrent to creating and using valid feedback because criticism is often unwelcome.[29]

Common Decision-Making Errors

Students of decision making in the public sector have identified many factors that lead to faulty use of information. Political scientist Alexander George, for example, in a book dealing with the effective use of information and advice, identified individual, group, and organizational psychological predispositions and pressures that hamper sound decision making.[30]

Problems at the Individual Level

To cope with the vast amounts of information they receive, people ignore most of it and abstract the rest. These mental abstracts—often called schemas—which are then stored in memory, become the basic framework into which subsequent information is integrated. Once established, this basic framework guides acquiring and processing of information so that a person's reasoning and actions become quite predictable. This mode of thinking is especially tempting for bureaucrats because following precedents carries the fewest risks of censure and saves time and effort. On the negative side, avoiding change and sticking with precedent stifles innovations and can lead to stereotyped reasoning that may be dysfunctional.[31] It was just this sort of reasoning that led NASA personnel to ignore danger signals when authorizing the launching of the ill-fated *Challenger* spacecraft in 1986.[32]

The quality of decisions is also impaired when they are routinely based on an existing consensus rather than on the objective criteria that ought to be considered. Established beliefs about correct strategies and tactics may be applied without retesting whether these operational codes fit the new situation. Traditional theories rather than data may drive information processing.

Avoiding making decisions, or delaying them unduly or making them hastily while ignoring relevant information sources, are all common human failings. Dodging tough decisions is particularly tempting in the public sector because nondecisions, despite their frequently serious consequences, are less likely to draw fire than decisions. Accordingly, public officials may ignore problems for long periods of time, failing to accumulate needed information. If information has been gathered, they may procrastinate in putting it to use. If a decision is unavoidable, they may decide in favor of small incremental changes even when their information indicates that bold new policy directions are required. Problems of indecision are also common in the private sector, but they are more pronounced in the public sector because of the career-damaging criticism that officials are more apt to encounter from the press or from hostile colleagues if decisions have unwelcome consequences.

When every choice has serious drawbacks, bureaucrats may end information searches prematurely to stop the stress. Practicing what has been called defensive avoidance, they may ignore or insufficiently explore important evidence, including reasonable options, and fail to examine thoroughly data about costs and risks. Once a decision has been reached, countervailing information may be ignored. During the invasion of Grenada in 1983, for example, President Ronald Reagan and his advisers were convinced that the Soviet Union and Cuba intended to use a new airport under construction in Grenada for military purposes. Contrary information available from the American ambassador to Grenada and the Grenada government was ignored.[33]

When choices are difficult, decision makers may engage in "bolstering," which entails exaggerating the attractiveness of one option and deflating the rest so that choice becomes easier. Analogies may be used inappropriately to rationalize replicating past decisions. The motives and action styles of other people may be misconstrued deliberately or otherwise manipulated to justify what the decision maker wishes to do. When individuals encounter information that challenges their established beliefs and modes of behavior, they feel uncomfortable. As a result, they are prone to misconstrue facts to reconcile them with previous beliefs. Another psychological weakness that impairs decision making is the desire to curry favor with powerful individuals. Decision makers may pander to the preferences of influential people within the organization and ignore or condemn unpopular options. Information searches and the ensuing decisions may also be warped by undue reliance on partisanship, ideology, or general principles to guide actions.

To ease and speed decision making, bureaucrats often use flawed common sense heuristics like drawing on readily available examples even when these constitute purely anecdotal evidence that is statistically unsound.[34] When situations are uncertain, they are more likely to assume favorable rather than unfavorable outcomes without exploring the real odds. When gains seem likely, they tend to be risk-averse; when faced with losses, they tend to choose high-risk strategies.[35] Such psychologically conditioned flaws have long plagued decision making. Historian Barbara Tuchman's book, *The March of Folly*, documents how decision makers throughout history have persisted in foolish courses of action contrary to canons of rationality.[36] A better understanding of these pathologies and ways to overcome them could lead to better use of decision-making information.

Problems at the Group Level

Most decisions in public organizations are made by small groups. Group contributions to decisions broaden the information base and often ease the implementation of decisions. Individuals who have participated in making a decision are usually more competent and more inclined to carry it out. The fact that a group participated in reaching the decision enhances its legitimacy. If it misfires, the burden of blame rests on multiple shoulders.

But the group process creates hazards for formulating sound decisions. Members develop personal friendships that they are loath to strain by expressing unpopular views. Group members settle comfortably into small communication ghettos where, secure in their shared knowledge, they resist unsettling information. Regular communication among group members increases consensus. It also blurs individual differences of interpretation and opinion that would enrich the group's thinking.[37] Many group reports lack incisiveness because conflicting views have been unduly blended.[38] The public sector is particularly prone to these pathologies because protected tenure of civil service employees allows groups to work together over long periods of time.

An experiment conducted with small decision-making groups illustrates the point. Sociologist Ralph Katz investigated the performance of fifty small research and development project groups in a large American corporation. He discovered that the groups whose membership did not change became increasingly isolated from key internal and external information sources. "With increasing group longevity, the effects of behavioral stability, selective exposure, and group homogeneity combine to reduce the group's willingness to search out and actively internalize new or conflicting knowledge and developments."[39] Isolation from communication channels, which did not necessarily mean a drop in overall communication, was accompanied by a plunge in quality of work performance. Whether or not groups need outside input and how much they need depends, of course, on the projects in which they are involved.

Group size and composition are important factors in decision-making effectiveness. Ideally, all interested parties should be involved in complex governmental decisions, but that is often impossible. Including all groups may be too unwieldy for conducting group business effectively. When group size is limited accordingly, important options and concerns may fail to be considered because they lack advocates or because they have so few that they may hesitate to speak up.[40] When groups include only top-level officials, as is often the case, they may lack crucial information that is available solely at lower levels. But when subordinates are included, they often pass on only pleasing interpretations and data to make superiors happy and earn praise for their good tidings. Top-level officials may be unable to detect whether lower level bureaucrats have engaged in "uncertainty absorption"—screening out information that casts doubts on prevailing assessments of a particular situation or is otherwise disturbing.

Another very dangerous pathology of group decision making is the phenomenon of "groupthink." It plagues highly cohesive groups, especially in times of crisis when the perception of external dangers heightens feelings of solidarity. Members of the group who have reservations about its decisions keep silent, lest they destroy the treasured image of consensus. The chief symptoms of groupthink are feelings of euphoria and overconfidence because group members believe that their shared opinions must be correct because no serious objections have been aired. Overconfidence may then lead to undue risk taking and even aggressive behavior. For example, sociologist Irving Janis claims that crisis decision making by the Kennedy and Johnson administrations was plagued by groupthink.[41] During the planning of the disastrous Bay of Pigs invasion of Cuba, the small decision-making group seemed to feel invincible and on morally unassailable ground. All twinges of doubt were suppressed in the wake of feelings that the group was in total agreement about the steps to be taken and that conformity was essential. Criticism and questions by outsiders were given short shrift.

Political scientist Lloyd Etheredge questions the groupthink diagnosis. He claims that group cohesiveness was ensured when Kennedy, like other chief executives, appointed like-minded people to his cabinet. In Etheredge's view, overconfidence is the hallmark of every new administration rather than a unique groupthink phenomenon.[42]

Problems at the Organization Level

Organizational dynamics can also lead to difficulties in reaching sound decisions. The hallmarks of bureaucracy—hierarchy, specialization, and centralization—cause major information-flow problems during decision making, such as message overload and message distortion. These problems have been discussed extensively in Chapter 3.

Error Avoidance Strategies

When there are so many possibilities for disastrous errors in decision making, it is prudent to search for safeguards. In the public sector, this quest has moved primarily in three directions: broadening the flow of information to increase the odds of discovering the best option, making sure that all parties to the decision coordinate their work, and using advance planning to reduce pressure levels that mar decision making during crises.

Enhancing the Information Supply

To make sure that disfavored options are explored rather than automatically rejected, devil's advocate tactics may be useful. A group member, who is chosen to play the role, acquaints the group with dissenting views. The tactic allows the group to develop formal rebuttal arguments that may be useful if the decision is later challenged. However, the process suffers from being artificial. In many instances, the devil's advocate may emphasize features that differ markedly from the positions that a real dissident would choose. Viewpoints favored by real dissidents thus may never receive exposure.[43]

The problem of considering too few options may also be alleviated by a *formal options* system. This involves creating interdepartmental committees composed of individuals drawn from various departments within an agency. To provide central direction and coordination, the top executive's chief of staff generally chairs these committees, which prepare options to be considered by various departments. The approach combines lateral coordination among departments with hierarchical direction. The system can also be used when several agencies are involved in a decision.[44]

The major drawbacks of this approach are that new structures have to be created and that options development and adoption occur at different levels. Departments may reject the options if they do not reflect departmental concerns adequately or simply because they resent suggestions by outsiders. If options are rejected, a second round of research and options development may be needed. Overall, the process tends to be slow and is therefore not particularly useful during crises.

Alexander George favored a *multiple-advocacy* strategy. Advocates of various points of view, he contends, cannot make an effective case if they lack adequate resources or if political concerns color their advocacy. To ensure that all viable options have an equal chance during deliberations and to expose distortions, the resources of various advocates must be equalized. Disadvantaged groups must receive support for gathering and analyzing information and for selecting skilled advocates whose status and power match that of resource-rich groups involved in the decision. Inter-department or interagency task forces may be appointed when necessary to counteract parochialism. Schedules must allow sufficient time for adequate presentation of information, appraisals, debate, and dispassionate analysis of pending decisions. The drawback of the multiple-advocacy strategy lies in the comprehensiveness of the process, which is costly and time-consuming. Because of the slow pace, it is unsuitable when rapid decisions are required.

Some of the barriers to expressing ideas that arise in group settings can be overcome through brainstorming techniques. Typically, brainstorming has three main features to spur spontaneous creation of ideas.[45] First, participants are asked to generate ideas without concern about their quality or practicality. Anything goes. Second, evaluation occurs only after all ideas have been presented. With no hints about the group's preferences, participants will feel freer to express their thoughts. Third, members are encouraged to elaborate on the ideas of others as well as their own. This allows for refinements that the originator of the idea may not have envisaged.

To aid decision making and problem solving, two other techniques have also been used. In *nominal group* techniques (NGT), selected persons who are assembled as a group are asked individually to generate ideas in writing about a task or problem. All of the ideas are then discussed for clarification and evaluation. Then the group casts secret votes ranking the acceptability of the ideas.

The *delphi technique* works similarly, often without actually assembling a group. Advisers are polled separately about their ideas and recommendations. The results are then circulated to the actual decision-making group, which clarifies and judges them. After repeated rounds of discussions and revisions, the advisory delphi group votes on the acceptability of final options. A prime advantage of NGT and delphi techniques is that they encourage participation by all group members without the intimidation often faced in ordinary groups where some individuals tend to dominate.

Quality circles (QC) is the term for another problem-solving and decision-making technique designed to broaden the flow of information. It has been used by many federal agencies such as NASA and the U.S. Customs Service. Groups of employees meet regularly for several hours per month on company time to talk about solving job-related problems. Viewpoints from the perspectives of people at the bottom of the hierarchy are thus tapped. The groups consist of five to ten volunteers who have been trained in group processes and problem solving. The effectiveness of such groups initially and over time has varied, as has the thrust of the quality management (QM) movement.[46] But many of its iterations have included techniques for generating ideas to promote excellence in performance.

For technical problems that might benefit from computer technology and other aids, *automated decision conferencing* (ADC) has been a useful technique. It involves executive teams assisted by staff members trained in decision sciences and computer techniques who test divergent views with data during two- or three-day sessions. The objective is to reach solutions that have been scientifically tested and found workable and advantageous.

Fostering Policy Coherence

The multiplicity of voices that must be heard because of their legitimate interest in particular public policy decisions makes it tough to develop coherent policies. For example, economic policy decisions generally cut across the interests of several departments and involve both macro- and microeconomic concerns that are difficult to integrate. A number of structural arrangements have been proposed to cope with the problem at the presidential level, where it is especially acute. The principles involved in these recommendations are applicable for executives at all levels of government.

Structural Solutions. To consolidate domestic security functions housed in 22 federal entities, President Bush proposed a structural solution in 2002. Security functions would be combined in a new Department of Homeland Security. Pundits and politicians applauded the consolidation concept but, as is typical, found it difficult to agree about which units should be included, which should remain in place, and which should be transferred elsewhere. Experience with existing superdepartments that integrate multiple services, such as the Department of Defense or the Department of Health and Human Services (DHHS), does not indicate that this is a particularly effective solution. Communication difficulties between the Centers for Medicare and Medicaid Services and the Social Security Administration were as troublesome when both agencies were in DHHS as when the Social Security Administration left the Department of Housing and Urban Development and became independent. Instead of creating unwieldy superdepartments, arrangements can be made for regular information exchange by departments. For example, various congressional research agencies have coordinated their work through an interagency research notification system and a directory of congressional research activity. Still, interagency coordination is inherently difficult and will remain so.

A National Economic Council resembling the National Security Council has been proposed as another coordination option at the federal level. It might consist of forty to fifty professionals appointed to manage the flow of communications between the president and the departments dealing with economic policies. Council members would be under the president's control and presumably in touch and in tune with the chief executive's preferences. They would therefore offset departmental parochialism and inertia. The council would coordinate the diverse departmental policy strands and make policy recommendations. On the positive side, the council setup would encourage careful, systematic examination of economic policy questions from a national perspective. On the negative side, the council might cling too closely to presidential preferences, thereby undermining morale in cabinet departments that administer economic policies.

Alexander George recommended creation of a cabinet-level council designed as a forum for multiple advocacy. It would bring the administration's leading economic policy officials together on a regular basis to advise the president on these issues. The council would provide a broader setting for appraising departmental concerns and developing coordinated economic policies. Designing such a council to overcome typical group-interaction problems would be difficult. The more talented advisers are likely to dominate the dialogue, even when their claims do not have the greatest merit. Group norms may stifle creativity. Such deficiencies could be minimized if the president insisted on genuine collegiality or if a manager for the council served as an honest broker to make sure that all viewpoints emerge.

Cross-Level Coordination. The coordination of policy decisions across various governmental levels ranging from the local to the international is also difficult. Political scientist William Gormley surveyed 780 federal environmental regulators from the EPA's midwestern offices and their state-level counterparts in Ohio and Wisconsin. He found that state regulators in Ohio sharply disagreed with federal regulators about pollution policies, and Wisconsin regulators disagreed with federal regulators over waste-management policies. Ohio officials, for instance, were willing to sacrifice clean air to foster employment and economic development, whereas federal officials gave far greater weight to environmental safety.[47] Such fundamental differences do not bode well for carrying out unified policies. Because the major decisions implementing environmental policy are made at the state level, producing consensus between state and federal regulators is especially crucial.

Gormley suggests four strategies that might ease these difficulties and achieve greater policy coherence. The federal government could encourage more citizen participation in environmental hearings so that citizens' views would be a counterweight to the strongly protective views voiced by special-interest groups. A related tactic designed to give greater exposure to environmentalist viewpoints is the establishment of a public intervenor office. Such a state official would represent the general public when environmental issues are discussed in various public offices and would also serve as a rallying point for environmental groups. In Wisconsin, a public intervenor's office has helped to build and sustain public support for environmental protection.[48] A third tactic, designed to mobilize the public to voice its support for stricter environmental rules, is the creation and airing of public service announcements on radio and television. Finally, there could be greater exchange of consensus-building information between regulators at various governmental levels. Programs such as the 1970 Intergovernmental Personnel Act are useful. The act permits officials in federal regulatory agencies to spend several years in state agencies and vice versa.

The success of cross-level policy-coordination efforts also hinges on the personalities of the individuals involved in decision making and on the organizational culture. Successful coordination requires parties who are willing to share information and fairly discuss all reasonable options brought to their attention.[49] They must also be willing to admit errors and to accept conclusions that run counter to their set preferences. Such flexibility is the exception rather than the rule. For example, during the investigation of the possible causes of the 1997 crash of TWA Flight 800, the Federal Aviation Administration (FAA) leaned toward a mechanical failure explanation, whereas the Federal Bureau of Investigation (FBI) thought that a terrorist attack was more probable. To make it more likely that its interpretation would prevail, the FBI then took steps to stop dissemination of a technical report by the Bureau of Alcohol, Tobacco and Firearms that also hinted at a fatal mechanical failure. Had the report been distributed, the mechanical weaknesses in the plane that made it prone to disaster might have been corrected earlier.[50]

Organizational cultures that encourage collaboration often select members who share values and socialize them to reinforce common attitudes.[51] The term "clan" has been used to characterize such organizations, which are usually small and meet frequently in person. That may produce exceptionally free information flows and lead to decisions encompassing the views of all participants.[52] When the group shares values and goals and disagrees only about how to proceed, decision making is generally collegial. Innovations are accepted and implemented fairly readily. By contrast, when values are in conflict and goals are uncertain, coordination of views is difficult. Decision-making systems then resemble markets where competing visions are thrashed out by the participants or arbitrated or adjudicated by the leadership.

Coping with Crises

Malfunctions are particularly common during crises because quick decisions must be made under extraordinary emotional and physical stress and communication overloads. This may lead to insufficient attention to information and flawed perceptions. Because of the time pressures and anxieties, decision makers may be unusually rigid in their thinking, unwilling to consider information that contradicts existing beliefs. They may have less tolerance for ambiguity. As stereotypical thinking increases, deliberations may be impaired and decisions made more hastily. Past experiences may dominate because there is little time to consider new alternatives. There may be less attention to long-range consequences and less contemplation of the side effects of various options. Perspectives thus become shortened and narrowed. If decision makers are aware of these pitfalls, they can guard against their consequences or take preventive steps.[53]

For example, President Dwight D. Eisenhower, among others, directed his staff to engage in continuous planning so that crisis decision making could benefit from broad-based, long-range studies.[54] During a crisis he could then draw on a small number of staffers for advice without sacrificing expertise and breadth of perspective. Eisenhower, whose managerial skills had been honed in military service as supreme commander of forces in Europe, also made it a point during crises to listen to dissenters and explore the reasons for their dissent. He kept his own public statements about policies deliberately ambiguous to allow himself greater flexibility to change his position.

Public agencies are expected to avert major crises like nuclear power plant meltdowns, catastrophic environmental pollution, or distribution of mail carrying deadly anthrax spores. Studies of decision making to limit these risks indicate that it is well-nigh impossible to use purely rational-choice decision-making approaches in such situations because they are rife with major uncertainties and value conflicts. Decision makers therefore continue to rely on various trial-and-error strategies designed to forestall the worst calamities. They then use feedback to correct mistakes.[55]

For example, the probability of nuclear-reactor failures cannot be estimated at present. No one even knows the scope of the consequences of a reactor-core meltdown. To protect the public from a worst-case scenario, the Nuclear Regulatory Commission has opted for increasing safety installations at nuclear-reactor sites. Beyond this initial decision, it has generated numerous proposals to cope with meltdown risks and has revised them as more technical and political information becomes available. Some of the cost-benefit issues that enter decision making about ill-defined, grave risks seem almost beyond resolution. Because the zero-risk option is unavailable, how safe is safe enough? What price is American society willing to pay to save a relatively small number of lives? What does "relatively small" mean? These are political and ethical issues that administrative agencies, in their search for viable decisions, find difficult to raise and research, let alone resolve.[56]

Designing Structures for Decision Making

Structural arrangements in organizations impinge on the issues discussed thus far. Structures determine the information flow patterns, which, in turn, affect decision agendas and outcomes. The direction of the flow of messages through the hierarchy determines which options surface first and may thereby influence which are accepted or rejected. The direction of information flow also determines which individuals make the preliminary decisions that so strongly affect final outcomes.

For example, when information and advice originate at the bottom and flow upward, top-level decision makers may make their choices from the predigested, truncated options brought to their attention.[57] Superiors do not ordinarily reexamine information that has been screened out at lower levels. Structural arrangements can also be used to determine who may participate in the initial problem analysis and option exploration and who may become involved only at the option-selection stage. Top-level executives may even leave final option selection to a group of trusted advisers, reserving the right to approve or reverse the adviser's choices. When agencies are structured so that important decisions are made at the bottom, these decisions may never come to the attention of upper-level officials. Therefore they tend to reflect the preferences of individuals in low-level positions. By and large, decisions are relegated to the bottom level when they are of minor importance, when they require expertise that abounds at that level, when speed is essential, when lower level officials are trusted by their superiors, and when upper levels are already clogged with decision-making activities.[58] Effective control from the top is unlikely when a large number of decisions are made at the bottom of the hierarchy.

Top-Level Structures

Alexander George described three basic models used by modern presidents to gather and process decision-making information: the formalistic arrangements used by Presidents Harry S. Truman, Eisenhower, and Richard M. Nixon (Figure 6–3); the competitive model used by President Franklin D. Roosevelt (Figure 6–4); and the collegial model used by President John F. Kennedy (Figure 6–5).[59] All of these models are also suitable for decision making at state and local levels.

The Formalistic Model. The formalistic model represents the typical hierarchy in which information travels upward from lower level to upper level agencies and personnel. Truman, Eisenhower, and Nixon, as well as other executives who used this very common model, created structures of varying complexity, but the basic principle of clear division of labor and hierarchical flow of information was the same. Lower level units screen and preprocess incoming data and then select the information that will be reported to mid-level decision makers. They, in turn, further screen and condense the flow to be passed on, eliminating options that they consider undesirable.

The formalistic model represents an orderly policymaking structure in which each unit performs well-specified tasks. Turf battles and intergroup bargaining among lower level units about the substance and framing of upward messages are kept to a minimum. Because final decision making is concentrated at the upper levels of the organization and problematic options are screened out along the way, the choice of final options is relatively easy.[60] When reports from lower level units to their chief executive pass through a chief of staff, the executive has the benefit—or disadvantage—of exposure to an even more tightly prescreened information flow, stripped of most data that subordinates deem extraneous. Even after the transmission channels through the many-layered hierarchy have screened out important data, informal grapevine communications can still cut across structural barriers and supplement the formal information flows.

The Competitive Model. In this model, favored by Franklin Roosevelt, lines of communication crisscross because lower-level agencies report upward to more than one department head. With jurisdiction over policy areas overlapping, policies are scrutinized from different perspectives and benefit from diverse information inputs. Presumably this cross-fertilization of ideas leads to

Figure 6-3 Formalistic Models of Decision Making Used by Presidents Truman, Eisenhower, and Nixon

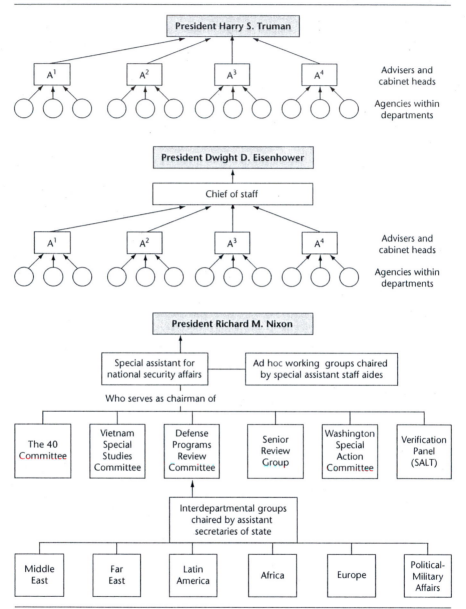

SOURCE: Alexander L. George, *Presidential Decisionmaking in Foreign Policy: The Effective Use of Information and Advice* (Boulder: Westview, 1980), 152, 154, 156. Reprinted with permission.

Figure 6-4 Competitive Model of Decision Making Used by President Franklin D. Roosevelt

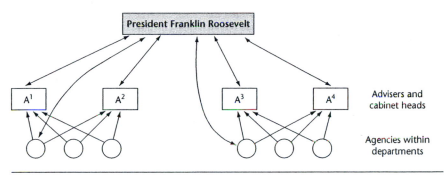

SOURCE: Alexander L. George, *Presidential Decisionmaking in Foreign Policy: The Effective Use of Information and Advice* (Boulder: Westview, 1980), 150. Reprinted with permission.

more broadly informed decisions. The price paid for this wealth of information sources and analytical perspectives may be tensions among competing departments, minimal cooperation, and often serious infighting. The many stakeholders involved in making recommendations may make it difficult to agree on a final decision.

Roosevelt thought that infighting spawned by the competitive approach would unearth deficiencies in policies that might otherwise remain hidden. He was willing to pay a high price for this benefit. He also kept in intermittent contact with units at the bottom level as a corrective to distortions of information that inevitably result when it travels through hierarchical layers. On the negative side, these additional contacts strained the energies of an already overburdened chief executive.

The Collegial Model. Favored by President Kennedy, the collegial model has interconnected units so that information flows freely back and forth through the system horizontally as well as vertically. Competition and infighting are reduced, new and diverse information becomes readily available, and units can solve problems jointly. Kennedy liked to create special task forces drawn from various units to deal with particular problems. Because these groups were task-oriented, members presumably could ignore loyalties to their respective units. The informal procedures made possible through the task force approach blurred status and power differences. Task force members were encouraged to act as generalists so that they would consider problems as a whole rather than focusing on their area of expertise, as specialists are wont to do.

The tone and quality of information flows and decision making in collegial groups hinge on several factors. The most important is the choice of the individual group members. Each brings a distinct fund and style of information and each contributes to the interpersonal chemistry of the group.

Figure 6-5 Collegial Model of Decision Making Used by President John F. Kennedy

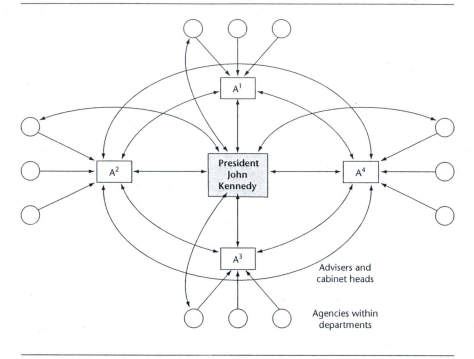

SOURCE: Alexander L. George, *Presidential Decisionmaking in Foreign Policy: The Effective Use of Information and Advice* (Boulder: Westview, 1980), 158. Reprinted with permission.

Group dynamics may produce constraints on expressing disagreements. The methods used by the group to collect, synthesize, and analyze information and to achieve consensus are important, as are the methods for identifying, discussing, and evaluating policy alternatives.

Wellsprings of Influence. Irrespective of the model used to structure information flows, the extent to which the executive dominates the decision-making process is vital. Even when the collegiate model blurs status and power differences, subordinates nonetheless tend to follow the chief executive's lead. This is especially true when major decisions are at stake and in times of crisis. Whether or not other high positions will translate into great influence on decisions hinges on the chief executive's views of the office, policy goals, management style, willingness to listen, and the openness of the decision-making system and on the type of policy at stake.

Four resources appear to be essential for influencing decisions: possession of relevant information, persuasion skills, internal capital, and a top executive open to persuasion. Possessing information is particularly important when others are unprepared or underprepared, as happened for Presidents Carter and Clinton, who were initially unfamiliar with the Washington scene. Willingness to use persuasive skills and opportunities for access to the chief executive are also important. Internal capital involves respect and support from the chief executive's staff. Clinton's communications director, David Gergen—a Republican—was hampered in influencing White House decisions because the White House staff never trusted him and therefore often withheld important information from him.[61] Advisers to chief executives are most likely to be influential if they carefully plan their strategies and build policy coalitions among the people likely to be involved in decision making.[62] Influence is also closely connected to the electoral cycle. When elections are imminent, executives often become more willing to listen and to heed new voices. Alternatively, election campaigns may take the president and some of his advisers out of the decision-making cycle while they are away on campaign errands.

External Advisers

Experts. For decisions that require a high level of professional expertise, advisory boards may be created, staffed by wizards in the particular field. The Council of Economic Advisers is an example. The council provides economic information and advice to presidents.[63] It forecasts future patterns of overall economic activity, provides presidents with economic analyses of various issues, and prepares an annual report to Congress. The council is not responsible for operations, making it more likely that its advice to the president will be guided by broad policy considerations.

The creation of advisory bodies also serves political and symbolic purposes. In addition to demonstrating the chief executive's concern about particular issues, they may assuage the bruised feelings of particular constituencies who have felt left out of the decision-making circuit.[64] Bruised feelings tend to become widespread when staffs from leading institutions are routinely consulted, allowing them to shape decisions and perpetuate their already great influence while other groups remain excluded.[65] A 1998 review of the information search tactics of the National Institutes of Health (NIH) found that doctors, lawyers, and professors from Ivy League universities filled most of the seats reserved for citizen input on the agency's advisory panels. Representatives of ordinary patients and groups with special health needs, like the elderly or blacks and Hispanics, were largely excluded from decisions on health issues meriting NIH research attention.[66]

Some government bodies specialize in brokering information, collecting, analyzing, using, and dispensing it.[67] The Office of Management and Budget performs such services for the federal executive branch; its counterpart in the legislature is the Congressional Budget Office. Advisory bodies are structured quite differently from the more traditional bureaus responsible for running the government's business or providing specific services to various segments of the public. In addition to professional staffs, there may be advisory councils that combine ex officio politicians with consultants drawn from industry, universities, private research organizations, and public interest groups. The advisory teams may also include representatives from groups likely to be affected by the issues at hand. It is important to include input from interested parties for substantive as well as political reasons. Substantively, all available expertise ought to be tapped regardless of where it exists. Politically, people are more likely to accept and cooperate with decisions in which they have had a hand.

Lay People. Many administrative decisions, particularly when they involve innovations, now require open hearings or other forms of public consultation preceding adoption of new policies. Since the mid-1960s, special efforts have been made to solicit opinions from groups who have lagged in political influence in the past, such as ethnic populations, the elderly, and women. Courts have encouraged broadening the circle of citizen advisers by allowing a steadily wider group of clients to ask for review of administrative decisions.[68] In fact, the *process* of decision making often may be more important in the public sector than the nature of the decision. This explains why the substance of citizens' advice is often ignored by public agencies while their requests about decision-making procedures and issues to be discussed by policymakers are heeded. Though such responsiveness may be largely symbolic, it is important nonetheless.

Citizen advisory boards have been used at all levels of government since the 1960s, but particularly at the local level. Public input into decisions by regulatory agencies has become especially common. Representatives of citizen groups regularly air their views at public utility commission hearings, during environmental-protection proceedings, on occupational licensing boards, and in hearings pertaining to nursing home regulations.[69] Cable television programs featuring government agencies have made the deliberations of various public bodies more readily available; this openness has further facilitated and encouraged lay input.

Agencies frequently create a special office to deal with citizen advisory boards to ensure that their input will be transmitted to the appropriate officials within the agency. Lay advisory boards can be quite influential because, unlike review boards, they become involved at the earliest stages of the decision-making process.[70] Their influence appears to be inverse to the power of the agencies they advise. To maintain full control over decisions, strong agencies avoid catering to advisory boards. Weak agencies, on the other hand, view these boards as constituencies that can lend them prestige and support.[71]

The use of lay advisory boards, which has faced a few setbacks in recent years, amounts to institutionalizing pluralism in the administrative process. Its main drawbacks are dilution of responsibility for decision making and undue slowing, or even paralysis, of the decision process. Public input may also be problematic when it comes from groups and individuals whose views are not broadly representative of their communities.

In his 1995 book *Public Participation in Public Decisions,* political scientist John Clayton Thomas cautioned public sector executives about indiscriminate use of lay advisers. When policies require adherence to professional standards or legislative mandates or budget or other constraints, lay advisers can be a major hindrance. Conversely, they may be essential when public acceptance of the policy and compliance with its terms are key to its success.[72] For example, it made little sense for the EPA to form citizen advisory committees to participate in decisions about water quality when the technical requirements and economic guidelines left little room for discretion. By contrast, it was essential to include potential users of a ferry terminal in decisions about the best location for the new transportation facility.[73]

Critics claim that openness requirements have prevented agencies from developing or pursuing coherent policy agendas.[74] They point out that agencies such as the Consumer Product Safety Commission spend a major part of their time analyzing and responding to outside grievances and proposed standards. Decisions may be delayed for years to allow various parties to present their carefully prepared arguments and counterarguments. When pluralism becomes excessive, it defeats the purposes of rationality and responsiveness in the decision process.

Table 6–1 compares various forms of public representation on decision-making bodies in terms of resources they bring to bear, the strategies used to achieve goals, and their effectiveness. The types of agencies most likely to use a particular form of representation are noted. In the cases on which the table is based, ombudsmen were most likely to be effective in reaching their goals; lay members of otherwise expert boards enjoyed the least influence.[75]

Making Routine Decisions

Most studies of decision making have focused on crucial policy decisions at the top, ignoring the decisions required at lower levels of the hierarchy to implement these policies.[76] The rationale has been that lower level decisions are less important and usually routine.[77] This is not necessarily the case. Many lower level decisions are very important and involve a great deal of discretion. This certainly holds true for decisions by street-level bureaucrats like police or public health physicians whose work cannot be totally or even largely routinized.[78] Their actions may be quite contrary to what top-level decision makers intended. Decisions at lower levels that allow bureaucrats wide discretion rarely receive the scholarly attention that they deserve.

Conversely, major top-level decisions that recur regularly may not deserve continuous scrutiny because they often become routine. For example, annual budget decisions commonly use existing budgets as baselines for requesting relatively small raises. Little new information is sought or needed. In one

Table 6-1 A Comparison of Public Representation Options

Form of public representation	Policy arena	Resources	Strategies	Goals	Effectiveness
Public hearing	Environmental regulation	Community support, strong statutes	Political pressure	Policy responsiveness (environmental protection)	Low to high
Ombudsman	Nursing-home regulation	Technical expertise	Jawboning	Service responsiveness (eldercare)	High
Proxy advocacy	Utility regulation	Technical and legal expertise	Formal intervention	Policy responsiveness (consumer protection)	Moderate to high
Public membership	Occupational licensing	Decision-making authority	Discussion	Policy responsiveness (consumer protection)	Low

SOURCE: William T. Gormley Jr., "The Representation Revolution: Reforming State Regulations Through Public Representation," *Administration and Society* 18 (August 1986): 191. Reprinted with permission of Sage Publications, Inc.

study of federal agencies, better than 90 percent of decisions about budget requests apparently resulted from such routine formulations.[79] The pattern was the same for budgetary decisions in Detroit, Cleveland, and Pittsburgh.[80]

Routine decisions constitute the bulk of decision making at the lower levels of the hierarchy. For example, when a mother applies for welfare support payments for her child, the criteria for granting such aid are well-established and usually enshrined in formal rules. The sole discretionary task left for officials is to establish whether mother and child meet the eligibility criteria. The overall goal of routine decision making is standardization so that decisions involve a minimum of personal discretion. The agency's performance can then be evaluated by assessing the rationality of its standard operating procedures, the consistency with which they are applied, and the conformance of the results to the agency's policy goals.[81]

Although bureaucracies, by definition, are routinized information-processing systems, bureaucrats as well as the public often resent the degree of depersonalization that this approach implies. However, studies indicate that routinized procedures, particularly when they are standardized via computerization, are fairer than discretionary tactics used by officials who are regularly subjected to personal and political pressures. If steps to a decision are properly programmed into a computer, the end result normally differs little from fair decisions made in less structured ways. As political scientist Michael Inbar points out, "Relying more heavily (or exclusively) on either man or machine for decision making merely represents a different choice of trade-offs, and a different partition of possible pay-offs; in either case a continuous process of review and monitoring is an unavoidable necessity."[82] However, because of the difficulty of fitting every decision into the same information norms, agencies frequently choose to forego standardization even when there are ample models for routinized decision making.[83]

It should be clear from the discussion in this chapter that decision making is an eclectic mixture of searching for policy-relevant information and shaping it into policy proposals that are politically viable. The outcomes are rarely perfect or lasting. Constantly changing political developments require new information searches and fresh decisions.

That same dynamic operates when public officials need to transmit their messages to communicate with various publics. Nothing ever remains settled for very long so that information management is a continual challenge. How do public officials communicate effectively with various publics for a multitude of purposes and what major problems do they face? Chapter 7 probes those issues.

NOTES

1. John M. Stevens and Robert P. McGowan, *Information Systems and Public Management* (New York: Praeger, 1985), 25.
2. E. Frank Harrison, *The Managerial Decision-Making Process* (Boston: Houghton Mifflin, 1975), 30; Terence R. Mitchell and James R. Larson, Jr., *People in Organizations: An Introduction to Organizational Behavior*, 3d ed. (New York: McGraw-Hill, 1987), 336.
3. Charles E. Lindblom, "The Science of 'Muddling Through,'" *Public Administration Review* 19 (1959/1): 79–99; also see Richard P. Nathan, *So You Want to Be in Government?* (New York: Rockefeller Institute Press, 2000).
4. Charles Walcott and Karen M. Hult, "Organizing the White House: Structure, Environment, and Organizational Governance," *American Journal of Political Science* 31 (February 1987): 117–119. Also see Arie W. Kruglanski, "On Methods of Good Judgment and Good Methods of Judgment: Political Decisions and the Art of the Possible," *Political Psychology* 13 (1992/1993): 455–475.
5. Richard F. Fenno, *Homestyle: House Members in Their Districts* (Boston: Little, Brown, 1978).
6. Carol Weiss, "Congressional Committee Staffs as Problematic Users of Analysis," 1984 American Political Science Association paper. Also see David Whiteman's description of congressional decision making. In *Communication in Congress: Members, Staff, and the Search for Information* (Lawrence: University Press of Kansas, 1995); and Keith Krehbiel's discussion of the motifs of Congress members in decision making in chap. 3 of his *Information and Legislative Organization* (Ann Arbor: University of Michigan Press, 1991).
7. G. R. Boynton, "When Senators and Publics Meet at the Environmental Protection Subcommittee," *Discourse and Society* 2 (April 1991): 131–155.
8. Quoted in Daniel E. Ponder, *Good Advice: Information and Policy Making in the White House* (College Station: Texas A&M University Press, 2000), 96.
9. Herbert Kaufman, *The Administrative Behavior of Federal Bureau Chiefs* (Washington, D.C.: Brookings Institution, 1981), 19–24.
10. For some actual EPA examples, consult Marc K. Landy, Marc J. Roberts, and Stephen R. Thomas, *The Environmental Protection Agency: Asking the Wrong Questions* (New York: Oxford University Press, 1990).
11. James March and Herbert Simon are credited with initiating the "satisficing" concept as part of the notion of "bounded rationality." They pointed out that limits to human attention and finite resources set bounds to the amounts of information that can be processed. James G. March and Herbert A. Simon, *Organizations* (New York: Wiley, 1958), 141. Also see Harold F. Gortner, Julianne Mahler, and Jeanne Bell Nicholson, *Organizational Theory: A Public Perspective* (Chicago: Dorsey, 1987), 258.
12. Scott D. N. Cook and John Seely Brown, "Bridging Epistemologies: The Generative Dance between Organizational Knowledge and Organizational Knowing," *Organization Science* 10 (July/August 1999): 381–401.
13. Martha S. Feldman, *Order without Design: Information Production and Policy Making* (Stanford: Stanford University Press, 1989), 24.
14. Graham Allison and Philip Zelikow, *Essence of Decision: Explaining the Cuban Missile Crisis* (New York: Longman, 1999), 379.

15. The various approaches are outlined in Gortner et al., *Organizational Theory,* 247–274; also see Irving L. Janis, *Crucial Decisions: Leadership in Policymaking and Crisis Management* (New York: Free Press, 1989), 114.

16. The act was adopted in 1972 and amended in 1995 as Pub. L. No. 101-608. William F. West, "Structuring Administrative Discretion: The Pursuit of Rationality and Responsiveness," *American Journal of Political Science* 28 (May 1984): 343, 350.

17. David Whiteman, "The Fate of Policy Analysis in Congressional Decision Making: Three Types of Use in Committees," *Western Political Quarterly* 38 (June 1985): 307–308. Whiteman, *Communication in Congress,* chap. 4.

18. Janis, *Crucial Decisions,* 125–129; Lawrence T. Pinfield, "A Field Evaluation of Perspectives on Organizational Decision Making," *Administrative Science Quarterly* 31 (1986): 365–388, and sources cited therein; Lucien S. Vandenbrouke, "Anatomy of a Failure: The Decision to Land at the Bay of Pigs," *Political Science Quarterly* 99 (fall 1984): 471–491, and sources cited therein.

19. Terry M. Moe, "Control and Feedback in Economic Regulation: The Case of the NLRB," *American Journal of Political Science* 79 (December 1985): 1095. For a comparable discussion of decision making at the state level, see Jeffrey L. Brudney and F. Ted Hebert, "State Agencies and Their Environments: Examining the Influence of Important External Actors," *Journal of Politics* 49 (February 1987): 186–206.

20. Gortner et al., *Organizational Theory,* 254.

21. James G. March and Johan P. Olsen, eds., *Ambiguity and Choice in Organizations,* 2d ed. (Bergen, Norway: Universitetsforlaget, 1979), 26.

22. March and Olsen, in ibid., present case studies to support their views. For an excellent comparison of decision making in structured and unstructured situations, see Pinfield, "A Field Evaluation of Perspectives on Organizational Decision Making," 365–388.

23. Moe, "Control and Feedback in Economic Regulation," 1098.

24. Pinfield, "A Field Evaluation of Perspectives on Organizational Decision Making," 365–388.

25. Ibid., 382.

26. Gortner et al., *Organizational Theory,* 204. For a full discussion of evaluation research, see pts. III and IV of Richard P. Nathan, *Social Science in Government: The Role of Policy Researchers* (New York: Rockefeller University Press, 2000).

27. Gortner et al., *Organizational Theory,* 207.

28. Ibid., 208.

29. Lloyd Etheredge, *Can Governments Learn? American Foreign Policy and Central American Revolutions* (New York: Pergamon, 1985), 95–107.

30. Alexander L. George, *Presidential Decisionmaking in Foreign Policy: The Effective Use of Information and Advice* (Boulder: Westview, 1980), chaps. 2–5. Also see Etheredge, *Can Governments Learn?;* Janis, *Crucial Decisions;* Philip E. Tetlock, "Policy-Makers' Images of International Conflict," *Journal of Social Issues* 39 (1983): 67–86. Also see Barbara Farnham, "Political Cognition and Decision-Making," *Political Psychology* 11 (1990): 83–111; and Allison and Zelikow, *Essence of Decision,* 1999.

31. Doris A. Graber, *Processing the News: How People Tame the Information Tide,* 2d ed. (Lanham, Md.: University Press of America, 1993), chaps 8–9.

32. Diane Vaughan, *The Challenger Launch Decision: Risky Technology, Culture, and Deviance at NASA* (Chicago: University of Chicago Press, 1996).

33. Frontline #602 Broadcast, "Operation Urgent Fury" (Boston: WGBH Educational Foundation, 1988), 6.

34. Richard E. Nisbett and Lee Ross, *Human Inference: Strategies and Shortcomings of Social Judgment* (Englewood Cliffs, N.J.: Prentice-Hall, 1980).

35. Terence R. Mitchell and James R. Larson, Jr., *People in Organizations: An Introduction to Organizational Behavior*, 3d ed. (New York: McGraw-Hill, 1987), 358.

36. Barbara Tuchman, *The March of Folly: From Troy to Vietnam* (New York: Knopf, 1984).

37. Ralph Katz, "The Effects of Group Longevity on Project Communication and Performance," *Administrative Science Quarterly* 27 (1982): 101.

38. Feldman, *Order without Design*, 2.

39. Katz, "The Effects of Group Longevity," 85.

40. For a discussion of ways to assess how group members are interacting, see Doris A. Graber, *Verbal Behavior and Politics* (Urbana: University of Illinois Press, 1976), 226–229, 261–265; also see George, *Presidential Decisionmaking*, 109–119. Common analysis methods include Bales's interaction analysis, sign process analyses, sociometric techniques, and psychiatric gaming.

41. Janis, *Crucial Decisions*, 56–60. For a more general discussion see Paul't Hart, *GroupThink in Government: A Study of Small Groups and Policy Failure* (Baltimore: Johns Hopkins University Press, 1994), esp. pt. II.

42. Etheredge, *Can Governments Learn?* 112–116.

43. George, *Presidential Decisionmaking in Foreign Policy*, 124–126, 169–174.

44. Ibid., 126–127, 242–244.

45. Mitchell and Larson, *People in Organizations*, 382.

46. Ibid., 586. The impact of participatory decision making on labor–management relations is discussed in Richard C. Kearney and Steven W. Hays, "Labor-Management Relations and Participatory Decision Making: Toward a New Paradigm," *Public Administration Review* 54 (1994): 44–51.

47. William T. Gormley, Jr., "Intergovernmental Conflict on Environmental Policy: The Attitudinal Connection," *Western Political Quarterly* 40 (June 1987): 291.

48. Ibid., 300.

49. John P. Burke, "Responsibilities of Presidents and Advisers: A Theory and a Case Study of Vietnam Decision Making," *Journal of Politics* 46 (August 1984): 827.

50. Ibid., 838–842; Robert D. McFadden, "F.B.I. Blocked Flight 800 Report, Investigators Say," *New York Times*, May 10, 1999.

51. Walcott and Hult, "Organizing the White House, 117–119."

52. Terrance L. Albrecht and Vickie A. Ropp, "Communicating about Innovation in Networks of Three U.S. Organizations," *Journal of Communication* 34 (summer 1984): 80.

53. Karl E. Weick, "The Collapse of Sensemaking in Organizations: The Mann Gulch Disaster," *Administrative Science Quarterly* 38 (1993): 628–652.

54. Richard M. Saunders, "Military Force in the Foreign Policy of the Eisenhower Presidency," *Political Science Quarterly* 100 (spring 1985): 111–112.

55. Joseph G. Morone and Edward J. Woodhouse, *Averting Catastrophe: Strategies for Regulating Risky Technologies* (Berkeley: University of California Press, 1986),

138–161. Larry C. F. Heimann, "Understanding the Challenger Disaster: Organizational Structure and the Design of Reliable Systems," *American Political Science Review* 87 (1993): 421–435.

56. Scott Sagan, *The Limits of Safety: Organizations, Accidents, and Nuclear Weapons* (Princeton: Princeton University Press, 1993).

57. Thomas Hammond, "Agenda Control, Organizational Structure, and Bureaucratic Politics," *American Journal of Political Science* 30 (May 1986): 384.

58. Kaufman, *The Administrative Behavior of Federal Bureau Chiefs*, 21–22.

59. George, *Presidential Decisionmaking in Foreign Policy*, 150–158. For a brief update of these models to include the Carter, Reagan, Bush, and Clinton administrations, see chap. 6 in Alexander George and Juliette George, eds., *Presidential Personality and Performance* (Boulder: Westview, 1998).

60. Gortner et al., *Organizational Theory*, 268.

61. Paul Light, "Vice-Presidential Influence under Rockefeller and Mondale," *Political Science Quarterly* 98 (winter 1983–1984): 629–632. Also see Daniel E. Ponder: *Good Advice: Information and Policy Making in the White House* (College Station: Texas A&M University Press, 2000).

62. Ibid., 636–639.

63. Roger B. Porter, "Economic Advice to the President: From Eisenhower to Reagan," *Political Science Quarterly* 98 (fall 1983): 404–406.

64. Ibid., 413.

65. Gregory A. Caldeira, "The Transmission of Legal Precedent: A Study of State Supreme Courts," *American Political Science Review* 79 (1985): 191.

66. Robert Pear, "Health Agency Urged to Review Spending," *New York Times*, July 9, 1998.

67. Gortner et al., *Organizational Theory*, 413.

68. West, "Structuring Administrative Discretion," 346. Diversity in the government's workforce also diversifies the viewpoints introduced into decision making. Sally Coleman Selden, Jeffrey L. Brudney, and J. Edward Kellough, "Bureaucracy as a Representative Institution: Toward a Reconciliation of Bureaucratic Government and Democratic Theory," *American Journal of Political Science* 42 (1998): 717–744.

69. William Gormley, John Hoadley, and Charles Williams, "Potential Responsiveness in the Bureaucracy: Views of Public Utility Regulation," *American Political Science Review* 77 (September 1983): 704–717.

70. William T. Gormley, Jr., "The Representation Revolution: Reforming State Regulation through Public Representation," *Administration and Society* 18 (August 1986): 179–196.

71. For evidence that citizen input is influential, see Paul A. Sabatier and Neil Pelkey, "Incorporating Multiple Actors and Guidance Instruments into Models of Regulatory Policymaking," *Administration and Society* 19 (August 1987): 236–263.

72. John Clayton Thomas, *Public Participation in Public Decisions* (San Francisco: Jossey-Bass, 1995), 36.

73. Ibid., 51, 60.

74. West, "Structuring Administrative Discretion," 356; Feldman, *Order without Design*, 2.

75. Gormley, "The Representation Revolution," 190–195.

76. Michael Inbar, *Routine Decision-Making: The Future of Bureaucracy* (Beverly Hills: Sage, 1979), 15–16.

77. E. Frank Harrison, *The Managerial Decision-Making Process* (Boston: Houghton Mifflin, 1975), 15–17.

78. Michael Lipsky, in *Street-Level Bureaucracy: Dilemmas of the Individual in Public Services* (New York: Russell Sage Foundation, 1980), makes the point throughout.

79. Inbar, *Routine Decision-Making,* 152.

80. Ibid., 158.

81. Walcott and Hult, "Organizing the White House," 220.

82. Inbar, *Routine Decision-Making,* 136.

83. Walcott and Hult, "Organizing the White House," 222.

Chapter 7 Refocusing on Serving the Public

Contacts between citizens and public agencies have been called "the human side of public administration."[1] The essence of this human side of interaction between bureaucrats and citizens "is the reciprocal and open exchange of information about right conduct. . . ."[2] In short, a well-functioning modern democracy requires that bureaucrats listen sympathetically and respectfully to citizens and vice versa.

Contacts between citizens and public agencies are the most frequent form of citizen participation at all levels of American government.[3] A single large agency like the Social Security Administration is in touch with more than 47 million Americans every year. It receives 60 million telephone calls annually on its toll-free lines and operates 1,300 field offices.[4]

These contacts provide essential feedback to government officials about the impact of policies on individual citizens, inequities in service, and the adequacy of bureaucratic routines. Citizens benefit from the opportunity to learn about government services, to question officials, and to form impressions about how well their government functions. Perhaps most significant for democratic politics, these encounters are a way to keep bureaucrats, who are appointed rather than elected, moderately accountable and responsive to the publics that they serve.[5]

Citizens' Contacts with Government

Citizens' contacts with government bureaucracies range from fleeting encounters on trivial matters, such as paying for a dog license at city hall, to life-and-death issues, such as public assistance to pay for life-saving medical treatments. They encompass services such as Medicare, welfare, retirement benefits, workers' compensation, unemployment insurance, and contacts with tax-collecting agencies, postal workers, and police officers. The numbers and percentages of citizens whose lives are strongly affected by the quality of such government services have continued to rise steadily.

Despite their importance and pervasiveness, interactions between the public and bureaucrats have not been studied extensively except for professionally specialized situations, such as relations between nurses and patients, police officers and offenders, and teachers and students.[6] A few studies have focused more generally on encounters between street-level bureaucrats, like police and social workers, and citizens who are seeking various public services.[7] From the client's perspective, street-level bureaucrats are often the most significant officials because they are the first point of contact between clients and public agencies. These bureaucrats usually make the initial determination about eligibility for particular public services. As political scientist Jeffrey Prottas points out, the gatekeeping powers of street-level bureaucrats shape the work of their agencies.

> In general, the street-level bureaucrat's autonomy is a result of his control of the flow of information between the organization and its clients. The bureaucrat is the client's major source of information about the rules and procedures of the agency. At the same time he is the agency's major source of information about the circumstances of individual clients.[8]

Encounter Types

Encounters between citizens and officials come in many types and shapes, and their particular characteristics affect the substance and manner of the communication and its effects.

General Issues. Important variables include the general sociocultural environment in which the encounter takes place, the characteristics of the agency, its officials and clients, and the nature and size of the client pool. If the prevailing cultural norms endorse open, uninhibited communication, and if clients and officials have no trouble communicating and cooperating with each other, problems are minimal. It also helps if their goals are shared and if officials find it easy to accommodate the client within the goals and resources of the agency.

The characteristics of the institutional climate in which the encounter takes place are particularly important. For instance, large social service agencies dominated by a single profession tend to be more impervious to external controls, more authoritarian in their proceedings, and less disposed to accommodate clients' wishes than most other types of agencies.[9] "As soon as an issue is institutionally defined as requiring scientific advice and expertise, the scope of legitimate participants is drastically reduced."[10] Clients in turn become more submissive. Jeffrey Prottas, who investigated bureaucratic encounters in veterans hospitals, found that

> medical situations tend to make people unusually passive and malleable. People will generally accept what is told them in a hospital or clinic and do what they are told even when they don't understand it. This minimizes what might otherwise be a check on the system, especially when combined with the fact that the clientele of the VA hospital is generally not skilled at dealing with large and impersonal bureaucracies. . . . This sort of client is unusually lacking in aggression and information, the qualities that provide clients of large bureaucracies with leverage. For these reasons, clients of the VA hospital play an unusually small role in checking the behavior of those they deal with. All the factors work against them.[11]

Organizational settings may range from total involvement to occasional contact. People in prisons, for example, are forced into constant contact with public officials. Because the prisoners' involvement is total and involuntary and therefore often resented, relationships with public officials are much more likely to be hostile than when contacts are brief and casual, like those with postal employees or public transportation personnel. Between these two extremes are intermediate institutional relationships, such as encounters in public schools or veterans' hospitals or Social Security offices that involve only limited compulsion and compliance with organizational rules.

Public encounters also vary in terms of who starts them. Citizens usually initiate contacts with social service agencies, whereas government initiates the contact when regulating harmful behavior or maintaining public order, such as arresting traffic-law violators. From the citizens' perspective, contacts initiated by government, especially when they are involuntary—like dealing with tax collectors—often generate resentment that deters open communication. This is why governments routinely make disclosure of information to such agencies compulsory and inflict penalties for withholding it.

Encounter Goals and Settings. The major purposes of public encounters are diverse as well. The goal may be primarily instrumental, to exchange information, as happens when citizens supply information to the Census Bureau, which subsequently is available to them in the form of census reports. Or the goal may be to obtain services for citizens, such as medical care, or to obtain resources from the citizen, such as tax money or military service. Alternatively, the purpose of the encounter may be purely expressive, allowing citizens and officials to signal their reactions to each other and to a particular situation. A letter to the Internal Revenue Service (IRS) complaining about high tax rates, without expectations that it will produce any changes, is an example. With little at stake, the sender may indulge in strong language that might be deemed counterproductive in other situations. The objective may be a combination of instrumental and expressive purposes, as happens when people complain vociferously about a government service like garbage collection but also include a request for specific improvements.

The physical locus and medium of communication may vary as well. For example, communication may take place on the street, as it does when citizens encounter police or sanitary workers, or in offices, where settings range from pleasant to daunting or depressing, or in the citizen's home. As discussed in Chapter 3, the messages conveyed through the physical appearance and maintenance of an office are important factors in communication flows. When clients queue up in front of an open counter, with long lines of people waiting, in a dingy, hot, and windowless room, the prospects for a satisfying exchange of information are diminished. The setting also speaks volumes about the low priority that the government has assigned to this particular service.

The characteristics of each medium of communication strongly affect the nature of the encounter. The impact of a recruiting poster in a military installation will differ from the same message delivered by a drill sergeant. Encounters may be conducted face to face, via telephone conversations, or through written, printed, or broadcast messages made available through direct contacts between clients and agencies or through mass media channels or, more recently, through computerized messages. Max Weber considered written communications best, claiming that they would insulate officials from improper interpersonal influences that might make it difficult to treat clients neutrally. Current American practices, contrary to Weber's recommendations, appear to favor personal or telephone encounters between citizens and bureaucrats, judging from interviews conducted with officials at the Social Security Administration, the Consumer Products Safety Commission, and Marine Corps recruitment offices. Citizens may conduct their own encounters or act through a chosen legal or political advocate.

Outreach Efforts

Although there are millions of public encounters, millions never take place because potential clients are uninformed or misinformed about a service from which they ought to benefit. Usually this indicates the government's lack of effective outreach efforts.[12] Twenty percent of American infants born in 2000 were unprotected against childhood diseases because the health system has not been able to contact their parents to urge vaccination during the most vulnerable years.[13] Only 43 percent of children had been vaccinated against chickenpox, despite recommendations by the federal Centers for Disease Control and Prevention. Only one-quarter of adults susceptible to influenza and only 13 percent of lung disease patients had been persuaded to get the vaccinations they need.

Missed contacts with public agencies are especially damaging for people at lower socioeconomic levels, who may fail to obtain health care services, food supplements, or housing subsidies. Political scientist Bryan Jones and his associates developed a mathematical model to indicate the quantitative relationship between socioeconomic well-being and the propensity to contact government agencies to secure city services.[14] The model suggests that increased socioeconomic status leads to more requests for services because people at higher levels know better which government services are available and how to obtain them. The request curve dips only when socioeconomic well-being is great enough to obviate the need for many services.

Congressional Budget Office data substantiate that programs designed for the poor are underused. For example, 12 million households eligible for food stamps in 2000, roughly 41 percent of the eligible population, did not receive them.[15] The low rate was blamed on a combination of communication and other factors, including the failure to inform people about the program and about the required procedures for participation. The procedures were formidable, ranging from thirty-six-page eligibility applications in Minnesota, along with warnings that misleading answers are punishable by stiff fines and up to twenty years in prison, to multiple required office visits and electronic finger-printing. In return for surmounting such bureaucratic hassles and enduring the stigma often associated with receiving public assistance, food stamp applicants could expect monthly benefits ranging from $10 to $73 per person. No wonder that applications were low and declining.

The record has been equally dismal for the Supplemental Security Income Program created to help elderly poor people achieve a minimum income of 75 percent of the officially designated poverty level.[16] Congress, which often authorizes programs without making sure that resources are adequate to implement them, had failed to fund $10 million requested for outreach programs to inform the elderly poor.[17] When a nationwide sample of eligible nonparticipants was interviewed in the fall of 1987, 55 percent said they had never heard of the program, and 62 percent said that they did not know where to apply or could not get there. Others objected to taking government aid or considered the benefits too paltry to apply. Obviously, extensive outreach activities were required to let people know that the programs existed and inform them about application rules and benefits. Streamlining application procedures is equally important.

The problem of underuse of public services is pervasive and long standing. In general, lower class and socially deprived people, especially women, are more apt to be uninformed about benefits available to them and less adept in getting them even when they are aware. Bureaucrats, who are likely to be drawn from the middle class, empathize more readily with middle-class clients.[18]

Accountability and Responsiveness

In a democratic society, accountability and responsiveness are the most important reasons for communication between public officials and citizens. In Chapter 8, we will discuss the relationship under the heading of "public information," focusing on communications designed to inform the general public and to influence public policy. The focus in this chapter is on interactions between citizens who must deal with government to solve individual problems. Although individual clients are the center of attention, broad issues are involved because public bureaucracies have an obligation to serve millions of individual citizens in a manner that conforms to democratic principles of respect for every individual.[19] Responsiveness is generally poorer in the public than in the private sector because public agencies are commonly flooded with more demands than they are equipped to handle. That leads to shocking situations, like those reported in a *New York Times* series of articles on "two-tier justice." These articles told the story of a public defender in New York City who was then responsible for the defense of 1,600 indigent criminal defendants. His clients complained that "he never returned phone calls or that he runs away when they try to speak to him."[20] The hapless overburdened lawyer had no filing systems and routinely missed crucial deadlines.

For average citizens, the crucial questions are whether their encounters with bureaucrats will elicit any response at all and whether the response meets their needs. For instance, many citizens are dissatisfied with police enforcement of "Megan's law," which was enacted in response to public demand. The law was designed to alert citizens when convicted sex offenders move into their neighborhood so that children can be protected.[21] In most states, police send flyers or registered letters to warn prospective neighbors of sex offenders in line with what citizens had demanded. But in fifteen states, citizens have to ask the local police for the information instead of being told. Then they may be handed folders in which the offenders are listed in alphabetical order, rather than by addresses, making it cumbersome to check any particular neighborhood. Moreover, address files of sexual predators are rarely kept current leaving potential victims vulnerable to predators who have recently moved into their neighborhood.

Some agencies ignore messages from citizens entirely or delay responses excessively, especially when the messages are unsolicited. Some treat citizens with condescension or rudeness, secure in the knowledge that retribution is unlikely. In fact, as Table 7–1 shows, bureaucrats have little faith in the capacity of the public to voice sound opinions or even care about participating in governmental business. Their views might change if they took a closer look at the quality of many of the messages dispatched by citizens to various government offices.[22]

Some critics of public bureaucracies claim that citizens with powerful sponsors receive preferential treatment. A study of responsiveness in Chicago and Houston, for example, showed that treatment of requests depended on the nature of available programs rather than on the political clout of the official whom the citizen had asked to intercede on his or her behalf. The process was more political in Chicago than in Houston, but outcomes, in terms of services rendered to citizens, were similar.[23] As exchange theories predict, agencies that rely on citizen input and are structured accordingly are generally most responsive. Examples are rabies control departments that depend on citizens for information about stray animals, water departments that are eager to be notified about broken water mains, and police departments responsible for controlling neighborhood crime.

Aside from concerns about responsiveness, client communication is also a practical matter because government agencies need massive amounts of information from citizens to perform the ever-increasing array of services rendered to individuals. If public employment agencies fail to get adequate data from job seekers about their qualifications and expectations, placement efforts are likely to go for naught. If people fail to file tax returns because they are baffled by IRS instructions, or if their returns abound in errors because of communication difficulties, government resources are diminished and citizens are put at risk.

Many agencies depend on citizens as their eyes and ears. Detroit's Depart-

Table 7-1 Bureaucrats' Images of the Public Compared with Those Members of Congress and Presidential Appointees (in percent)

Questions	Members of Congress	Political appointees	Bureaucrats
Americans don't know enough about issues to form wise opinions about what should be done.	47%	77%	81%
Average Americans don't want an activist government (Public's score = 41%)	58	63	69
The public distrusts government because that is a popular campaign theme.	37	59	55
The public distrusts government because government is not responsive enough.	49	56	55
The public distrusts government because politicians promise too much.	22	31	43
Trust in government could be improved by better communication/dialogue.	36	66	74
Trust in government could be improved by better performance and procedures.	36	48	43
Trust in government could be improved by political reforms.	24	13	11

SOURCE: Adapted from a 1998 survey by the PEW Research Center for the People and the Press in association with *National Journal*. PEW Research Center for the People and the Press: "Washington Leaders Wary of Public Opinion," 1998, www.people-press/org/leadrpt.htm. Reprinted with permission.

NOTE: Data are based on personal interviews with 81 members of Congress, 98 presidential appointees, and 151 members of the senior executive service. Questions have been paraphrased and condensed. Numbers represent affirmative answers.

ment of Building and Safety Engineering provides an example. Ninety-three percent of the actions of the Housing Improvement Bureau, 72 percent of the actions of the Electrical Inspection Bureau, and 65 percent of the activities of the Bureau of Buildings were initiated as the result of information volunteered by individual citizens.[24] Citizens also perform a service by reporting crimes, safety hazards, and other conditions requiring attention from government officials.[25] If citizens do not know the appropriate channels and formats for conveying these messages, the quality of public services suffers. Outreach programs by police departments that encourage citizens to call a toll-free number and often guarantee anonymity are among examples of ways to overcome communication problems.

The Wellsprings of Unresponsiveness

There are inherent tensions between bureaucratic categorization and democratic individualism. It is part of America's democratic credo that every individual is unique and deserves to be treated accordingly. Americans do not want to be mere numbers or impersonal "cases." However, standardization

SOURCE: Reprinted by permission of *Chicago Tribune.*

is the essence of bureaucracy. Clients are categorized so that all members of a group who share certain relevant characteristics will be treated equally even when they differ in many important respects. As Max Weber recommended, interchanges between officials and the public should be universalistic, task-oriented, and emotionally neutral. Just as clients should not seek individualized treatment or personal favors, officials should resist bestowing them. Although impersonal treatment does enhance efficiency from a variety of perspectives, including protecting public agencies from charges of unfairness and favoritism, it often creates an undesirable communication environment. Clients, especially when they are poorly educated, may feel demeaned and depersonalized, even to the point of shunning the services to which they are entitled.[26]

Treating Citizens as Unequals

Another major problem plaguing relationships between public officials and citizens springs from their unequal power resources. Contrary to democratic tenets that designate citizens as masters and public officials as their servants, bureaucrats are the de facto masters. Citizens neither elect them, control their stay in office, nor determine their mode of operation.[27] Bureaucrats' might stems from their official position that authorizes them to exercise the legal powers pertaining to their office. The precise interpretation of these powers may ultimately rest with courts of law, but bureaucrats' initial determinations usually go unchallenged. In general, agency goals and officeholder priorities, rather than the clients' wishes, guide these determinations even though clients have much greater stakes in the outcome than bureaucrats.[28]

Bureaucrats at the lowest level of the hierarchy, such as police officers on the beat or welfare caseworkers, commonly determine what actions will be taken and choose among multiple legitimate objectives and specific tasks authorized by their jobs, thereby giving operational meaning to broader public policies.[29] It is difficult for clients to challenge street-level rule interpretation because it develops case by case and because bureaucrats control the information needed to challenge the rules. Besides, the rules are usually couched in bureaucratic language that is difficult for the uninitiated to understand.[30] With citizens thrust into positions of inferiority and often treated condescendingly, the public encounter generally amounts to a duel of unequals. In an effort to even the score, some public institutions, such as hospitals and nursing homes, employ ombudsmen to act as advocates for the clients.[31]

Gaps in social and cultural status between many citizens and officials create additional problems. For example, clients' cultural backgrounds may make them submissive to public officials so that they may fail to correct the official's obvious misstatement of facts. Offers of gifts to officials, which are customary in many cultures, may be regarded as bribes in the American context.[32] Prevailing social stereotypes are another barrier to good communication. Many Americans blame the poor for their plight, characterizing them as lazy and lacking in self-respect and motivation. People who suffer from sexually transmitted diseases or those with prison records or records as substance abusers are scorned for their alleged failings.[33] Officials who disdain their clients are not likely to interact well with them and establish open lines of communication. The fact that many bureaucrats in the United States now come from groups that have experienced major social ills is lessening this problem somewhat.[34]

Disdain and the hostility that often accompanies it cut both ways, of course. For example, in many poor neighborhoods citizens dislike the police as much as or more than the police dislike suspects and convicted offenders. When police–community relations deteriorate, citizens may fail to supply information that is essential for law enforcement. That makes it more difficult, for example, to enforce drug laws or check on truants or errant fathers.

Citizen control is further weakened by the monopoly status and financial security of many public service providers. The private sector, where market conditions prevail, usually offers choices among service providers. To survive financially, these providers must compete for the favor of prospective clients. By contrast, service providers in the public sector are publicly funded and face little or no competition. That leaves them free from economic incentives to serve their clients well. There is only one Social

Security Administration, one Occupational Health and Safety Administration, one Immigration and Naturalization Service where people can take their business. Although people in large cities may have the option of dealing with various offices of these agencies, even that option is unavailable in most locations. Consumers needing services, or compelled by law to use these services, must deal with these monopolies according to the agency's interpretation of bureaucratic rules.

Most agencies have more clients than they can handle comfortably and inadequate resources to meet their needs. This imbalance affects the criteria by which performance is judged. Bureaucrats receive credit for doing their job well if they follow all rules and handle cases. Spending beyond budgeted resources to serve clients better may earn reprimands. The official's personal goal to win praise from superiors and the agency's goal to conserve scarce resources thus may conflict with the goals of the clientele being served. These tensions diminish the quality of treatment accorded to clients, including the quality of communication.[35]

Consumer Power Issues

In the past, bureaucratic structures usually made it tempting to be unresponsive to clients. This is why the National Partnership for Reinventing Government put heavy emphasis on client services. One entire chapter in the original report by Vice President Al Gore was devoted to "Putting Customers First."[36] The report urges structural changes in major agencies to facilitate cordial interactions. Unfortunately, in a huge, widely dispersed administrative establishment that is set in its ways, major changes will inevitably be slow and spotty. It is therefore not surprising that Charles Rossoti, the Commissioner of Internal Revenue, estimated that reforms to enhance responsiveness to client complaints would take nine years to complete. A twenty-four-hour hotline for clients and simplified language in IRS forms were among the first reforms that were actually implemented.[37]

The unresponsiveness problem takes many forms in addition to rudeness and superciliousness.[38] One of the most common forms is delay.[39] This may mean keeping people waiting in offices, failing to respond to inquiries in a timely fashion, or failing to communicate decisions for weeks or months. Many agencies are notorious for keeping clients waiting. Courts and agencies like the Immigration and Naturalization Service are among the worst because of their vast case loads.[40] By contrast, agencies such as the National Park Service and the Public Health Service consider it a matter of pride that their waiting periods are comparatively brief. These agencies will respond to inquiries within three weeks.[41] The explanation may be that the Park Service needs clients to justify its activities and the Public Health Service cannot risk major health disasters that might have been prevented by quick action. Most other public agencies, with less to gain from promptness, take longer. However, spurred by the Reinventing Government movement, many agencies are now promising shorter response times. The IRS has pledged refunds within forty days for "snail mail" returns. The Postal Service has vowed to deliver first-class mail within the U.S. within three days and serve customers at counters within five minutes.[42] Keeping clients waiting is usually due to understaffing, but it may also be a deliberate attempt to discourage clients from coming so that the agency's workload will decrease.

Exchange theory explains why elective officials are more likely than bureaucrats to respond promptly to client contacts. In exchange for help, the client can give the elective official her or his vote. In most situations, the client has little to offer the bureaucrat in exchange for the requested services. Burdensome rules and procedures and the inadequacy of many public services tend to fray everyone's temper. Resentful citizens may then vent their wrath on the bureaucrats they encounter, further straining the relationship. In turn, bureaucrats feel maligned when they have little control over the matters that have aroused the client's ire.[43]

Of course, citizens often play more influential roles than indicated thus far. Political scientist Kathy Ferguson, for example, identifies three different roles that citizens can assume in their interactions with bureaucrats. Citizens may be clients, constituents, or consumers. "Clients are those who must interact actively with bureaucracies upon which they are dependent but over which they exercise little or no control; for example, the relationship between the poor and state welfare bureaucracies is a client relationship."[44]

By contrast, constituents enjoy more power because they deal with bureaucracies through organized bodies. "Constituents are organized groups who are interdependent with a bureaucracy and who are able to exercise significant control over it; for example, the relationship between the Farm Bureau and the Department of Agriculture is a constituent relationship."[45] Farmers who push their demands through their representatives in the Farm Bureau are quite likely to have a major impact on agricultural policies and the actions of farm agencies. In public utility commission proceedings, citizen groups have been moderately influential, whereas demands by individual citizens have been ignored.[46]

Ferguson identifies consumers as people "who purchase goods and services through the market. Because consumers pay in money rather than in some less tangible form such as time, dignity, or autonomy, their dependency on the organization supplying the good or service is less acute."[47] Many adult education programs, which depend partly on fees paid by students and partly on public subsidies, represent consumer relationships. In many instances, consumers are under no obligation to buy the services. When constituent and consumer relationships exist between citizens and government agencies, communication problems, though similar to those faced in client relationships, are usually far less serious. Because the discussion in this chapter emphasizes client relationships, it deals with problems at their severest level.

Information Transmission Difficulties

Aside from the communication problems arising from the tensions inherent in bureaucratic settings, more routine problems occur as well. They happen because it is always technically and intellectually difficult to connect, especially when large numbers of diverse people are involved. Besides, the subject matter of communication is often highly complex. Language barriers and translation problems increase these problems.

Message Channels and Formats

At the most basic level, communication depends on the existence of adequate channels through which government can contact citizens reliably and vice versa. The mass media, of course, serve as major channels, although they are geared primarily to distributing very general, often sketchy messages, and their performance is erratic. When laws are passed to guide the behavior of citizens, such as those concerning professional or business standards or regulating the operation of motor vehicles or the sale of property, mass media channels are often silent or omit crucial details. Direct channels of transmission to the public that automatically reach most members of the relevant client groups are usually nonexistent. Unofficial sources, such as trade or lobby-group publications, have filled that gap only partially in the past, but the effective use of Web sites is easing the problem substantially.

When channels are available, including Web sites, they usually do not carry all of the information that citizens need, and they often are not user friendly enough for many potential clients. Moreover, staffs who deal with the public are often poorly trained. For example, during the 1987 tax season, the IRS acknowledged that only 61 percent of clients who requested help got complete and accurate information. The General Accounting Office (GAO) pegged the figure at 57 percent.[48] By 1993 that figure had risen to 88 percent, according to the GAO, proof that substantial improvement is possible.[49]

Government attempts to standardize information flows between citizens and particular agencies by mandating the formats have also been flawed. Complaints, compiled by the Commission on Federal Paperwork, pointed out that forms and reports required from the public are too complex and need to be simplified and staggered because too many of them need attention at the same time. People also complained about excessive numbers of required copies and unnecessary duplication of reports because there were no central data files shared by national, state, and local agencies. The complainants also thought that information was frequently misused and that confidential information was not properly safeguarded.[50] The Reinventing Government program has targeted many of these problems as action items in ongoing reforms of federal bureaucracies.[51]

To ease the citizen's task in communicating needed information in the appropriate form to public agencies, some agencies and institutions have created the position of ombudsman. Others have established advocacy offices mainly to represent consumer interests in public utility commission proceedings. They focus primarily on policy issues, such as the level of utility rates, and have often won victories for consumers. But they do not generally address problems of individual citizens.[52] That is done by ombudsmen who are experts on bureaucratic procedures within particular agencies. Ombudsmen serve as agents for individual citizens, helping them to collect needed information and transmitting their messages to appropriate officials. Ombudsmen focus primarily on solving individual problems when requested, rather than on initiating broad procedural or policy reforms.[53] Many requests for help come from traditionally underrepresented segments of society, such as women, the elderly, and racial minorities. Ombudsmen thus serve as important communication links between the bureaucracy and otherwise mute clienteles.[54]

Legislators serve as informal ombudsmen when they engage in casework. They are among the most powerful practitioners of the art. Their influence on bureaucrats is enhanced if they serve on committees that control the resources and powers of the bureaucrat's agency.[55] Similarly, local city council representatives often consider their ombudsman role paramount.[56] The unwritten expectation is that representatives who procure services for constituents will be compensated by receiving their vote.

Coping with Gobbledygook Problems

Jargon. Expressing complex rules and procedures in simple language that average people can understand is among the most intractable communication problems faced by public agencies. IRS codes and instructions and consumer credit regulations provide many examples of what has been called gobbledygook, federalese, or doublespeak. President Bill Clinton issued an executive order in 1998 that required all federal agencies to write new regulations in plain English, beginning in 1999. In turn, federal agencies like the Securities and Exchange Commission are demanding that private corporations couch their reports to consumers in plain English as well.[57]

Even though experts have been put in charge of drafting texts in plain English, doing so is difficult. For example, a new consumer guide on the Medicare program was abruptly withdrawn from general circulation because Medicare authorities feared that elderly citizens would be confused by the description of new healthcare options, such as health maintenance organizations (HMOs) and medical savings accounts. Based on focus groups and surveys, the recall seemed necessary, even though Congress had appropriated $95 million to educate beneficiaries with another $150 million projected for the following fiscal year.[58]

Complicating the gobbledygook problem is the vagueness of laws and regulations, which is often intentional when lawmakers cannot agree on certain provisions or want to ensure flexibility in interpretation. Administrators welcome flexibility because it gives them greater control over programs.[59] But it also means that laws and regulations defining the nature of programs and implementation methods often receive conflicting or wrong interpretations. For example, in 1989 when the Social Security Administration investigated a sharp rise in the number of homeless, aged, and mentally and physically impaired people suspended from its disability-pension rolls, it discovered that staff members had misinterpreted the vaguely stated rules.[60] Three quarters of 1,500 suspensions that were investigated turned out to be inappropriate.[61]

Communications directed toward clients vary widely in clarity and attractiveness. To assess the quality of bureaucratic communications, a group of social scientists examined 157 documents dealing with wildlife, public parks, tax, and welfare regulations in the fifty states and the District of Columbia.[62] The documents were judged on how well they conveyed their messages to average citizens and on their tone, which might affect citizens' reactions to them. To assess readability, the researchers used an index that gauges sentence length and polysyllabic words to determine the required grade level of reading competence. Judging clarity involved rating features such as logic of presentation, use of technical terms, typography, and layout. Tone was appraised by whether the message suggested respect for the audience or whether it sounded patronizing and whether there was an emphasis on penalties or rewards.[63]

Overall, the research team found substantial variations in these communications. The readability index showed that wildlife and park regulations were written at a twelfth-grade reading level, indicating that comprehension requires a high school education. State income-tax regulations were at a level two years beyond high school, and welfare documents were at a reading level five years beyond high school. Obviously, all of these levels are beyond the competence of most of the potential clientele for these services.[64] Scores on communication effectiveness, judged by whether a document is readable, clear, and usable, showed that welfare documents were the least effective. Difficult words such as *vendor, incapacitate,* and *encumbrance* were common. Documents concerning wildlife protection had the highest effectiveness scores; welfare and tax documents were most negative in tone.

Exchange theory may explain these rankings. Citizens have no burning need for state services involving hunting, fishing, and visiting public parks. With respect to these services, they are consumers rather than clients. To entice them to use these services, state officials therefore try to be pleasant and informative. The reverse is true for paying taxes and trying to obtain welfare support. Because citizens are compelled to use these services, officials need not cater to them. The intimidating language used in tax and welfare documents may be deliberately designed to discourage clients from cheating or even from applying for costly welfare services. It may bully them into paying

the full amount of their taxes or possibly more. It thus carries political benefits for the agency.[65]

Despite manifold problems, the researchers concluded from their analysis
that it is possible to frame rules clearly and concisely judging from the many
examples of good communication. Overall, the quality of documents was better than generally believed. Bad practices were unfortunately most common
in areas where clarity and an encouraging tone were most needed.[66]

To follow up on research into the clarity of messages disseminated to the
public by government agencies, my research assistants and I analyzed the content of randomly selected, widely circulated brochures produced by three federal agencies: the Consumer Product Safety Commission, the U.S. Army, and
the IRS.[67] We applied a widely used test—the Flesch index of readability—
to these documents. The index gauges readability, based on such measures as
sentence length and complexity, word difficulty, and logic of presentation.
The analysis revealed that one third of the documents were easy, fairly easy, or
average in readability. Most Americans would be able to use them successfully. But two thirds of the documents were difficult or fairly difficult, placing
them beyond the comprehension capabilities of average people. *All* forms obtained from the IRS were difficult; there was a mixture of levels of difficulty
for the other agencies. Box 7–1 shows the instruction page attached to Form
1040EZ, which is the simplest form that IRS has been able to devise for taxpayers with low incomes and uncomplicated returns. Still, it ranks slightly
above the tenth-grade reading level on the Flesch scale, and 16 percent of the
vocabulary consists of "big words." That means that they are likely to be unfamiliar to the average reader.

The Tower of Babel. Problems of message transmission are bad enough when
all parties speak the same language. They become well-nigh insurmountable
in a multilingual society such as the contemporary United States, which has
become like a tower of Babel because many recent immigrants fail to master
English. When the Immigration and Naturalization Service changed registration rules in 1997, for example, thousands of immigrants in cities
throughout the United States who had registered under the old rules spent
several days and nights waiting in long lines to register anew when that was
not required. They had misunderstood the new regulations that had seemed
quite clear and simple to English speakers.[68] In the Los Angeles area, where
large numbers of immigrants are concentrated, the court system alone em-
ploys more than 400 interpreters to handle some eighty languages and di-
alects, ranging from Albanian to Yoruba. It is not uncommon for plaintiffs,
defendants, and witnesses to speak different languages, requiring the pres-
ence of several interpreters.

Besides the danger of serious errors, translations strip messages of paralin-
guistic cues to emotions, hesitancy, or credibility. Much crucial information
is thereby lost. Most agencies can cope only with relatively common languages

---

Box 7-1 **Form 1040 EZ Excerpts: 2001**

Form 1040EZ (2001)   Page **2**

Use this form if
- Your filing status is single or married filing jointly.
- You (and your spouse if married) were under 65 on January 1, 2002, and not blind at the end of 2001.
- You do not claim any dependents.
- Your taxable income (line 6) is less than $50,000.
- You do not claim a student loan interest deduction (see page 8) or an education credit.
- You had **only** wages, salaries, tips, taxable scholarship or fellowship grants, unemployment compensation, qualified state tuition program earnings, or Alaska Permanent Fund dividends, and your taxable interest was not over $400. **But** if you earned tips, including allocated tips, that are not included in box 5 and box 7 of your W-2, you may not be able to use Form 1040EZ. See page 13. If you are planning to use Form 1040EZ for a child who received Alaska Permanent Fund dividends, see page 14.
- You did not receive any advance earned income credit payments.

If you are not sure about your filing status, see page 11. If you have questions about dependents, use TeleTax topic 354 (see page 6). If you **cannot use this form**, use TeleTax topic 352 (see page 6).

Filling in your return

For tips on how to avoid common mistakes, see page 30.

If you received a scholarship or fellowship grant or tax-exempt interest income, such as on municipal bonds, see the booklet before filling in the form. Also, see the booklet if you received a Form 1099-INT showing Federal income tax withheld or if Federal income tax was withheld from your unemployment compensation or Alaska Permanent Fund dividends. **Remember,** you must report all wages, salaries, and tips even if you do not get a W-2 form from your employer. You must also report all your taxable interest, including interest from banks, savings and loans, credit unions, etc., even if you do not get a Form 1099-INT.

Worksheet for dependents who checked "Yes" on line 5

(keep a copy for your records)

Use this worksheet to figure the amount to enter on line 5 if someone can claim you (or your spouse if married) as a dependent, even if that person chooses not to do so. To find out if someone can claim you as a dependent, use TeleTax topic 354 (see page 6).

A. Amount, if any, from line 1 on front . . . . + ____250.00 Enter total ▶ A._____

B. Minimum standard deduction . . . . B.____750.00

C. Enter the **larger** of line A or line B here . . . . C._____

D. Maximum standard deduction. If **single,** enter 4,550.00; if **married,** enter 7,600.00 . . . . D._____

E. Enter the **smaller** of line C or line D here. This is your standard deduction . . . . E._____

F. Exemption amount.
- If single, enter 0.
- If married and—
  —both you and your spouse can be claimed as dependents, enter 0.
  —only one of you can be claimed as a dependent, enter 2,900.00.
} F. _____

G. Add lines E and F. Enter the total here and on line 5 on the front . . . . G._____

If you checked "No" on line 5 because no one can claim you (or your spouse if married) as a dependent, enter on line 5 the amount shown below that applies to you.
- Single, enter 7,450.00. This is the total of your standard deduction (4,550.00) and your exemption (2,900.00).
- Married, enter 13,400.00. This is the total of your standard deduction (7,600.00), your exemption (2,900.00), and your spouse's exemption (2,900.00).

Mailing return

Mail your return by **April 15, 2002.** Use the envelope that came with your booklet. If you do not have that envelope, see the back cover for the address to use.

⊕   Form **1040EZ** (2001) such as Spanish, Polish, or Japanese. When agencies, such as the IRS and the Social Security Administration operate bilingually, Spanish is the most common second language. Speakers of other languages have trouble contacting such agencies by telephone or even in person. The mere identification of the language or dialect in which the speaker is trying to communicate can be a major puzzle. Those who do not understand English are often unable to complete forms, cannot read insurance or job contracts, and cannot follow a doctor's instructions. When speed is of the essence, as in hospital emergency rooms or police stations when a crime in progress is reported, language barriers have led to disasters.

Language Skill Deficiencies. Comprehension problems are made worse because many American adults are functionally illiterate, unable to read simple instructions let alone the complex directions on income tax forms or welfare applications. The ranks of the poorly educated are swelled by large numbers of senior citizens whose declining vision, hearing, and mental faculties impair their ability to cope with complex rules and regulations.[69] The lack of intellectual skills that commonly plagues economically and socially disadvantaged groups in American society is a self-perpetuating problem. It deprives these groups of political influence and access to social and economic resources.[70] Poorly informed people, regardless of the extent of their exposure to information, lack the incentive and predisposition to learn much new information, whereas the already well-informed absorb it with ease because it fits readily into their established knowledge base. Over a lifetime, information-rich people get richer in knowledge and other resources, while most of the information-poor remain poor. Thus, the knowledge gap between the privileged and underprivileged widens.[71]

Encounter Games

Clients' Strategies. Encounters may become ritual battles between knowledgeable clients who try to gain maximum benefits and officials who seek to husband their agency's resources. Bureaucrats usually hold a huge advantage because of their legal status, ready access to information, control of the resources wanted by the client, and lack of competition from alternative service providers.

Attempts to bargain with officials for better treatment are most common in three types of situations.[72] One of these occurs when benefits or services are not automatic so that the client must request services, including submitting evidence that they are needed. For example, clients requesting an interest-free loan after a hurricane must provide evidence of serious damage to their belongings that is satisfactory to the official handling the case. Appeals for better treatment are also common when the official has discretion to grant or refuse certain benefits. Admissions to job training programs or public works programs are examples. Finally, clients try to bargain with officials to reverse an adverse decision. In addition, clients occasionally make personal appeals for services when they are unaware that such appeals are not needed or when they are trying to pull strings—to gain special favors by extra effort.

What sorts of manipulative communication strategies should bureaucrats expect from citizens? To find out, a research team looked at letters written to Israeli customs officials by Israeli citizens pleading for lowered duties on goods sent to them from abroad.[73] The researchers discovered that appeals were both positive and negative and differed among sociocultural groups. For favorable actions, clients promised rewards like money or invocation of divine blessings. For refusals, they threatened penalties like physical harm to authorities or notification to superiors about the official's allegedly inappropriate behavior. There were references to the self-interest of the official or the public that would be served by granting the request. There were also appeals to the altruism or empathy of the official and to legal or moral norms, such as claims that the client had a legal right to import the goods free of charge or at a lower rate. Some clients appealed to the official's sense of pity for their presumably unusual plight, either with or without offering a material or symbolic reward. The researchers did not report which strategy worked well and which did not.

Bureaucrats' Strategies. The bureaucrats' arsenal of communication resources to cope with clients' ploys is heavily stocked, outweighing by far the clients' resources.[74] Client demands can be reduced, delayed, or rejected in a number of ways. If the official responds with jargon, clients may be unable to assess the situation and contest it if necessary. For example, when officials use technical medical terms to describe conditions excluded from Medicare coverage, few applicants can decipher the message. Standardized rejection letter formats often make it difficult or impossible to figure out Medicare payment criteria and to detect errors. The client's efforts to get services may also be short-circuited by conveying the impression that application procedures are arduous and humiliating and that a favorable outcome is unlikely. This type of advice is usually informal and remains unrecorded so that it escapes a superior's scrutiny and control. Such tactics enable officials to use encounters to unobtrusively weed out clients whom they do not wish to serve for legitimate or illegitimate reasons.[75]

Another tactic for discouraging client requests consists of evading decisions and dispatching clients to various offices within the agency where help is unlikely or sending them to other agencies in the hope that frustration will end their efforts. This is known colloquially as giving them the run-around. The tactic has been so common that it was tagged for reform by the Reinventing Government program. To abort runarounds and make it simpler for citizens to obtain services, the report recommended creating one-stop service centers or kiosks that could cut across organizational boundary lines.[76]

When errors occur and clients complain, agencies may take a long time to make corrections. For example, it has taken years to correct the duplication of a Social Security number issued to two different individuals or to remove a name from voter registration lists when the voter has moved to another state. A claim of error suggests that some bureaucrat deserves blame for incorrect discretionary judgments or for misapplying official rules or handling tasks carelessly. Like most people, bureaucrats are loath to correct errors that amount to a tacit admission that they failed to perform their duties properly.

Officials can also discourage clients by withholding information and evading questions. For instance, nurses in a public health clinic may claim to be too busy to answer questions or pass them off as requiring answers by a physician. The range of topics covered in conversations between officials and clients can be controlled by eliciting information only through highly structured interviews and allowing no side comments. Office hours may be scheduled at inconvenient times, and forms may be made deliberately complex with little assistance provided for completing them or even securing them. The rules for obtaining food stamps, for example, have required applicants to submit dozens of documents about household size, income, living expenses, and assets like automobiles or grave sites within thirty days of filing their application, with a thirty-day extension possible in only a few states.[77] Such requirements present major hurdles to socially disadvantaged applicants.

Officials can also discourage clients by making them feel uncomfortable. Clients may feel degraded when addressed by their first names by officials whom they must address more formally or when they are forced to discuss intimate details of their lives in a setting where others can listen. Bureaucrats can use their power to categorize clients to manipulate their eligibility for services and benefits. When a health professional classifies a simple stomachache as major abdominal pain, a patient may be allowed to see a physician at a veterans' hospital rather than a nurse practitioner with less medical training. Conversely, by categorizing major abdominal pain as a simple stomachache, a patient who ought to see a physician may be passed off to a nurse practitioner. Labels like "mentally disturbed" or "troublemakers" may be used to determine the disposition of clients. Although such classifications may be based on bona fide appraisals, they often spring from misunderstanding the client's culture. They can also be used to punish disagreeable clients and reduce their effectiveness in coping with bureaucracies.[78]

Likable clients who are cooperative and deferential may receive extra advice and encouragement. For example, they may be told that they are eligible for a little-known supplemental medical-aid program that may add as much as 15 percent to their welfare payment. Officials may even steer favored applicants to a particular doctor who is known to be very generous in certifying the client's eligibility for this program.[79] Favored clients may be told about exceptions to the rules and how to make themselves eligible for them. They may not be questioned about income from occasional jobs that might reduce their benefits. They may be beckoned to move to the head of a waiting line, as happens routinely when lawyers go to traffic court with their clients.

One may ask how it is possible for either clients or officials to modify procedures when bureaucratic rules prescribe what is to be done.[80] The answer is that rules are nearly always imprecise enough so that transactions can be shaped by the way questions are structured and information about opportunities is provided. Flexibilities in categorization schemes, special procedures for emergencies, and outright bending of rules allow officials to give preferential treatment to selected clients. The beneficiaries may be favored because their background is similar to that of the official, because they dress and act in approved ways, because they are emotionally appealing, or because they have powerful sponsors. Conversely, difficult cases involving troublesome clients may be steered away from the agency lest they blemish its record of accomplishments. Overall, states James Q. Wilson, "the imperatives of the situation more than the attitudes of the worker shape the way tasks are performed in welfare offices. The key imperative is to reconcile the wants of a variegated and somewhat suspect group of petitioners with the organizational need for achieving equity and managing the large case load."[81]

The Evaluation Puzzle

Appraisal Criteria

How can one measure the quality of communications between government agencies and their clients? This question has been tackled from several perspectives by government agencies and private researchers. Investigators have asked whether encounters are effective in conveying understandable, compelling messages to target groups. Thus far there appear to be many problems on that score. Messages may also be judged by the relation between input and output costs. Telephoning all licensed drivers to inform them about a change in the speed limit on national highways might be a highly effective method of message transmission, but it would not be an efficient use of resources. Many outreach programs have turned out to be excessively costly because few people responded.

Encounters have also been judged by the equity of the interchange. Does it present special advantages or disadvantages to particular clients and are the questions and responses fair and appropriate? As noted, encounters pose grave problems of equity when socioeconomically disadvantaged groups face bureaucracies. In the eyes of critical theorists, such encounters are prime examples of exploitative relationships.[82] Although many complexities could be simplified, the system, by its very nature, will remain forbidding for these clients and therefore inherently inequitable.

The area of evaluation that has received comparatively little attention is the clients' satisfaction with their contacts with bureaucrats. In a democratic society, bureaucrats ideally should be eager to discover how satisfied citizens are with their encounters with public servants. In reality, when provisions for feedback have been made, they usually have been limited to factual questions about existing services and the need for new or altered services. For example, before setting up a solid waste recycling program in Tennessee in 1989, the state surveyed residents to find out which options would be most acceptable to them. Considering that recycling success hinges on cooperation by users of the service, the survey was a good investment to ensure the program's success.[83] Similarly, the Environmental Protection Agency and Colorado state officials sponsored statewide surveys in 1989 to assess residents' policy priorities in environmental protection and their willingness to pay higher taxes and accept increased regulation to cope with problems that they deemed crucial. Although such surveys shed light on the kinds of policies and procedures likely to produce a satisfied public, they do not directly measure satisfaction.[84]

Most of the information about citizens' appraisals of public services and encounters is transmitted to officials through relatively informal, unsystematic personal contacts or through written or telephoned complaints and comments.[85] Public officials often prefer that to more formal evaluations. For example, when 279 Florida city managers and mayors were interviewed in 1985, 88 percent said that informal contacts with the public provided them with a good deal of information about citizen wants and needs. Most (80 percent) also deemed letters or telephone calls quite helpful. By contrast, only 48 percent found systematic program evaluations helpful in disclosing the public's needs.[86]

Some of the resistance to formal surveys springs from widespread reluctance to be evaluated, fear that a negative appraisal will hurt job prospects, and fear of adverse consequences if an agency's image is damaged by the evaluation. To forestall unfavorable survey responses, many agencies engage in "creaming" of client pools. They take care of large numbers of easy cases and ignore difficult ones. This gives the impression that they serve a maximum number of clients with relatively few difficulties and failures. Employment agencies, for example, routinely concentrate on the most readily employable people, leaving the hard-core unemployed behind. Welfare agencies concentrate on simple cases, preferably working with people who pose no communication or missing documentation problems.[87]

Client Satisfaction Scores

Overall Scores. Given the fact that client satisfaction has been a low priority for most bureaucrats in the past for a variety of reasons, and given the harsh criticism of welfare bureaucracies in the media and in much of the social science literature, one would expect client evaluations of their personal experiences with encounters and services to be unfavorable. That is not the case. Although public opinion polls show that people generally hold bureaucracies in low

Table 7-2 Satisfaction with Government Services

Service type	Customer types surveyed	Score
Services through state and local governments: Health and Human Services, Agriculture, Housing and Urban Development	Parents of Head Start students; food and nutrition aid recipients; community development grantees	80
Earned benefits programs: Social Security, Veterans' Health, Office of Personnel Management	Recent retirement beneficiaries; outpatients at veterans' hospitals; federal retirees and annuitants	77
Public information services: Education Publications, National Aeronautics and Space Administration, General Services Administration, Census Bureau, Environmental Protection Agency	Educators; National Aeronautics and Space Administration program clients; General Services Administration consumer information center clients; census data distributors; librarians	75
Use of recreational land: National Park Service (Interior Dept.), Forest Service (Agriculture Dept.), Bureau of Land Management	Recreational visitors to all three facilities	72
Grants and services: U.S. Mint (Treasury); Federal Emergency Management Agency; Student Aid (Education Dept.); National Science Foundation; Patents and Trademarks (Commerce Dept.)	Coin buyers; disaster aid recipients; electronic applicants for student aid; National Science Foundation grant seekers; patent and trademark seekers	71
International travel services: Consular Affairs (State Dept.); Immigration and Naturalization (Justice Dept.); Customs Service (Treasury)	Passport and renewal applicants; international travelers; international air travelers	68
Household consumer services: Food and Drug Administration (Health and Human Services); Food Safety and Inspection Service (Agriculture Dept.)	Principal grocery shoppers and food preparers dealing with these agencies	63
Tax filing: Internal Revenue Service	All tax filers; electronic filers	57
Regulatory services: Federal Aviation Administration (Transportation Dept.); Occupational Safety and Health (Labor Dept.)	Commercial pilots; health and safety professionals subject to regulation. Services exceed client expectations	51
Aggregated federal government score		68.6

SOURCE: U.S. Government Customer Satisfaction Initiative, 1999, www.customersurvey.gov

NOTE: Aggregated by service-type segments on a 1 to 100 scale.

regard and think that the negative treatment of these agencies by news media is warranted, they give high marks to specific agencies and bureaucrats.[88]

Table 7–2, based on a 1999 survey of 7,700 citizens who were asked to evaluate twenty-nine federal agencies, illustrates the point. These agencies included most of the high-impact agencies that handle 90 percent of the government's contacts with citizens. Each agency surveyed one major customer segment central to its mission, except for the IRS, which interviewed two segments—snail-mail filers and electronic filers. Questions probed satisfaction levels with program-specific activities, customer expectations, perceived quality, and complaint behavior.[89] The satisfaction levels turned out to be only slightly below those registered on similar surveys of prominent private organizations, such as Procter and Gamble, Maytag, or Hershey Foods.

As is generally the case, different types of clients judge agencies differently. For example, in another 1999 poll, 80 percent of Social Security recipients rated the agency favorably. That figure dropped to 57 percent for employers who had to deal with employee payrolls. Scores varied even more when respondents appraised specific features of agencies, like the complexity of rules, the courtesy of government employees, and the overall fairness of client treatment.[90]

After a critical review of a variety of polls in which people assessed their encounters with public social service agencies, Charles Goodsell concluded that "in light of attacks on bureaucracy's treatment of clients, the consistency with which citizens evaluate their personal experiences with public agencies in a positive light is remarkable."[91] Favorable response rates on questions concerning bureaucratic performance are usually above 70 percent and not infrequently in the 80 and 90 percent ranges. "In most instances bureaucratic personnel are described as helpful, efficient, fair, considerate, and courteous. They are, furthermore, usually perceived as trying to assist, ready to listen, and even willing to adapt the rules and look out for client interests . . . an almost complete contradiction of the hate image depicted in popular media and academic writing."[92]

The explanation for this puzzle of bad general evaluations and good specific ones seems to lie in stereotyped thinking. Average Americans are familiar with media accounts of bureaucratic incompetence and callousness and mention this stereotype when asked, but they judge particular services on the basis of their own experiences.[93] When it comes to services for the unemployed, the retired, the sick, the disabled, and the poor, apparently these experiences are usually quite positive for most clients.[94] Given the negative expectations produced by negative stereotypes, the positive appraisals may reflect the fact that the actual service is usually better than expected and is therefore positively evaluated. Besides, people are prone to evaluate events in their lives positively because that is psychologically comfortable even when there are signs to the contrary. For instance, they may express satisfaction with their job but still exhibit high rates of absenteeism and job turnover.[95]

Communication Scores. The vast majority of surveys have focused on evaluating satisfaction with the final disposition of the case. Questions about the quality of the encounter—the personal interactions between bureaucrats and clients during their encounter and the adequacy of the information given—have been asked only occasionally. Goodsell, for example, interviewed a random sample of 240 welfare clients in San Francisco, St. Louis, Duluth, and Evansville, Indiana, immediately after they had completed a visit to the main Social Security office, the Unemployment Compensation office, or the Public

Assistance office for Aid to Families with Dependent Children. Goodsell reported that 66 percent of the people he interviewed as they left Social Security offices said that their caseworkers had been very courteous. Sixty-eight percent were satisfied with the official's willingness to listen to them. Usual waiting time was thirty minutes or less. Only 5 percent of the clients waited for more than one hour to be served.[96]

To focus more directly on communication aspects of public encounters, my research assistants and I ran a pilot study patterned on Goodsell's approach. We conducted exit interviews at thirty-minute intervals with randomly selected clients at two Social Security offices in Chicago in low-income neighborhoods. When clients emerged from the office, we asked open-ended questions about the quality and tone of communication between them and public officials and their feelings about the encounter. In line with Goodsell's findings, most (88 percent) reported that they were treated cordially and courteously and that Social Security officials paid attention to what they had to say. In fact, more than half (55 percent) said that the workers in the Social Security office were friendlier than the employees in their local grocery store. When asked whether the officials explained what they were doing, 86 percent said they did and nearly everyone claimed to understand the explanation without much trouble. In terms of the substance of the transaction, only 64 percent of the respondents thought they had accomplished as much as they had hoped during this visit. Among those who felt the encounter had not met their expectations, nearly half (46 percent) blamed the official, and the remainder felt that circumstances beyond the control of the official had caused the problem.

The appraisals recorded in a 1999 survey that covered five federal agencies corroborate these findings. Occupationally diverse groups of respondents were asked how easy it is to contact the IRS, the Social Security Administration, the Environmental Protection Agency, the Food and Drug Administration, and the Federal Aviation Administration. The survey also inquired how well these agencies do when they try to inform the public and educate it about specific policies and how courteously employees treated clients. Roughly two thirds of the respondents gave the agencies favorable ratings. However, two thirds of the respondents thought that government forms were unnecessarily complex; that figure rose to three quarters for the IRS. Only half of the respondents thought that these agencies were easy to reach.[97]

Seeking Citizen Advice

In recent years, attention to public satisfaction with bureaucracies has increased, partly because of the work of organizations dealing with welfare rights and civil rights. Client demands for participation in public agency decision making have become more strident, and political forces supporting these demands have become better organized. New political norms have emerged that emphasize the public's right to receive more respectful treatment, to be consulted about services, and to be kept informed about agency performance. The numbers of citizens who contact government agencies on their own initiative is growing, as is the diversity of their concerns and motivations that range from crass self-interest to altruism.[98]

The Gunnar Clinic Case

The Gunnar Clinic project in Chicago is a classic case of major problems when concern with client views and sociocultural characteristics is slighted because of inadequate client communication.[99] Two white physicians opened the clinic in 1995 in a predominantly black neighborhood on Chicago's West Side that desperately needed a community health service. Nonetheless, hardly any patients came for treatment for the first two years. To solve the mystery, women from the community were hired in 1997 to investigate why residents sought health care at a considerable distance in preference to the community-based clinic. The reasons turned out to be surprisingly uncomplicated.

Unlike other clinics, the sign identifying the new facility said "Adult Medicine" rather than using familiar terms like "clinic" or "family" or "community." That led to the perception that the clinic was a drug abuse or sexual dysfunction center or a place to treat obscure medical problems rather than a place to go for care for common medical problems. The clinic's physical layout was a problem as well. Unlike familiar facilities, the new clinic had clear front windows and new furniture, and the receptionist's station was not walled off by the traditional thick-glass partitions. Neighborhood people thought the facility looked upscale and was therefore beyond their means.

The community survey, which included various local health care facilities, discovered other problems that had been ignored by West Side health care providers, even though the problems troubled the patients and could be easily corrected. For example, the uniforms worn by most clinic staffers did not distinguish between medical personnel and support personnel. Resentment arose when patients wondered why some uniformed people, who looked like medical practitioners, were idle while patients had to wait for care. Patients who wanted answers to questions could not tell which staff members they should approach. In several clinics, medical staffers had been puzzled when patients who received postcards telling them that their lab tests were positive never called back for more information, as requested by the card. It turned out that most of these patients never read the cards, tossing them away because they thought that written messages heralded bad news. Armed with that knowledge, clinics stopped sending messages and simply requested patients to inquire about the test results so that staffs could explain the findings directly to patients.

The Gunnar Clinic case is just one of thousands of instances where community input is essential to rendering good service. But input is not always beneficial. In fact, it can actually do harm. That raises the difficult question of developing criteria by which public officials can tell whether or not citizens' input is likely to be beneficial, neutral, or harmful.

The Limits of Pluralist Control

In *Public Participation in Public Decisions* (1995), political scientist John Clayton Thomas lays out a scheme for deciding whether a policy decision would benefit from citizen input or whether it would be harmed and which segments of the citizenry should be consulted in particular cases. Such decisions are particularly difficult when controversial public services are concerned, like busing to provide school integration, health services for mental patients or AIDS victims, or when communities are unwilling to host disagreeable or dangerous services such as prisons, nuclear-waste sites, or garbage dumps.[100]

Thomas's scheme begins with four questions and their answers (see Figure 7–1). The first question relates to "quality requirements." It refers to the fact that some decisions hinge on legal or budgetary or feasibility constraints or are quite technical so that the answers are beyond the ken of ordinary people. For example, scientists, rather than ordinary folks, should decide what percentage of fluoride makes drinking water safe and protects against tooth decay without making it toxic. Asking for public views on the issue is pointless and could lead to controversies about matters that require professional knowledge.

The second question relates to the information base on which the official's decision about public involvement is made. If the official lacks adequate information—for instance if she does not know whether fluoride decisions are controversial among respected scientists—then the decision should be postponed pending further inquiries and efforts to frame the issues appropriately—an exercise that may include consultation with local citizens. If the official has sufficient political, economic, and technical information and the answer to the third query indicates that the problem is "structured"—meaning that the opposing options are clearly defined—she must decide whether public approval is essential for the decision. In the Gunnar Clinic case, for example, community acceptance was essential for the clinic's success. Absent community approval, the project was doomed. When community acceptance is vital, soliciting community input is the only option. If the project can be carried out without community approval, asking for community input may still be wise but dispensable.

Community involvement may be disadvantageous when catering to the interests of vocal citizens harms the interests of the larger society. Many contacts between citizens and bureaucracies, whether initiated by citizens or by officials, relate to the narrowly private concerns of small community segments or even individual citizens. Groups claiming to represent the community rarely are fully representative. A cross-national analysis of citizen input into public policies revealed that yielding to such demands can produce profound policy consequences. According to political scientists Alan Zukerman and

Figure 7-1 Determining If Public Involvement Is Advisable: A Decision Model

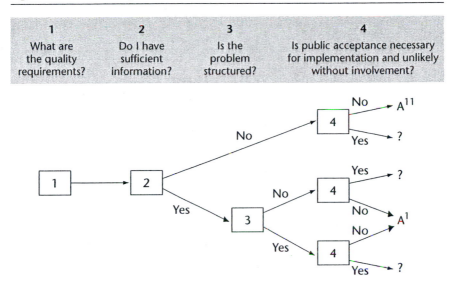

1	2	3	4
What are the quality requirements?	Do I have sufficient information?	Is the problem structured?	Is public acceptance necessary for implementation and unlikely without involvement?

SOURCE: John Clayton Thomas, *Public Participation in Public Decisions* (San Francisco: Jossey-Bass, 1995), 50.

A^1 Official decides without requesting community input.

A^{11} Official decides after consulting segments of the community.

Darrell West, "The more widespread contacting is within a country, the more time government officials spend responding to narrow demands. The more successful contacting is, the more government policies center around the production of private goods and public goods with very limited sets of beneficiaries."[101] As has been amply demonstrated in Congress, when casework takes up much of a member's time, important activities of concern to more broadly based constituencies suffer. Impartiality and fairness are at risk as well when resources go to interest groups rather than the general public.[102]

In weighing the pros and cons of citizen input, one must remember that agencies receive advice from many quarters. In the case of public utility regulation, for example, citizens' advice is balanced by that of industry representatives and regulatory commission members and their staffs. The advice of the more technically experienced people is likely to prevail in many instances over the opposition of citizen boards.[103] The same holds true for occupational licensing boards, where members representing the general public have little influence because they lack expertise.[104]

Some scholars have tried to identify the factors important in predicting which citizens are likely to seek out government officials and hence garner a disproportionately large share of benefits. The assumption has been that well-educated and well-organized clients fare best. The research findings are not clear-cut on that score, although outreach efforts, as we have seen, show that the most needy are often least aware of available public assistance and least likely to be organized to pursue their interests. Factors such as need for a particular service, awareness of its existence, and political sophistication are important predictors, but their impact varies so that disadvantaged groups do not necessarily lose out.[105] For example, when it is easy to reach government officials, even disadvantaged citizens who might ordinarily be averse to contacting officials are likely to do so. In Houston and Dallas, the existence of a central office for lodging citizen complaints increased input and requests by the lowest socioeconomic sector.

Nonetheless, the danger remains that encounters empower the haves more than the have-nots. When encounters become ongoing relationships, such as the relationship between lobbyists and bureaucrats, the danger of government dominated by vocal minorities is real.[106] The winners in this political sport of hunting for specialized advantages are usually the well to do, the educationally advantaged, and political activists from all socioeconomic levels.[107] It is the squeaky wheel that gets the grease that may be needed elsewhere to prevent major breakdowns.

Major government agencies obviously face staggering tasks in interacting with their publics, even without considering the difficulties inherent in all bureaucratic situations. Nonetheless, there has been immense progress in client communication in recent decades. Millions of people are benefiting from improved performance. If responsiveness is poor at times, if many serious errors continue, it may be quite unfair to ask why performance cannot be better. Instead, the appropriate question may be, "Why isn't it worse?"

American bureaucracies are wrestling with many pressing communication challenges in addition to those involving client relations and responsiveness. Among them, public information and public relations activities are high priorities. Unlike service-related interactions with individual clients, these efforts to create favorable images for mass consumption have received a lot of attention from scholars and practitioners. Chapter 8 explores the main normative and practical issues.

NOTES

1. Louis C. Gawthrop, "The Human Side of Public Administration," *P.S.: Political Science and Politics* 31 (1998): 763.
2. Ibid., 769.

3. For a discussion of the differences between contacts by citizens and other forms of citizen participation, see Alan S. Zukerman and Darrell M. West, "The Political Bases of Citizen Contacting: A Cross-National Analysis," *American Political Science Review* 79 (1985): 117.

4. Al Gore, *From Red Tape to Results: Creating a Government that Works Better and Costs Less. Report of the National Performance Review* (Washington, D.C.: U.S. Government Printing Office, 1993),46.

5. There are other accountability checks, of course, such as the Office of Management and Budget and the General Accounting Office, which allow Congress to ride herd on administrative agencies. For a fuller description, see chap. 6 in B. Dan Wood and Richard W. Waterman, *Bureaucratic Dynamics: The Role of Bureaucracy in a Democracy* (Boulder: Westview Press, 1994).

6. For a discussion of public encounters in various disciplines and bibliographic information, see Charles T. Goodsell, ed. *The Public Encounter* (Bloomington: Indiana University Press, 1981), 7–13, and sources cited therein; and Elihu Katz and Brenda Danet, "Communication between Bureaucracy and the Public," in *Handbook of Communication,* ed. Ithiel de Sola Pool and Wilbur Schramm (Chicago: Rand-McNally, 1973).

7. Relevant studies are Michael Lipsky's *Street-Level Bureaucracy: Dilemmas of the Individual in Public Services* (New York: Russell Sage Foundation, 1980), and Jeffrey Prottas, *People Processing: The Street-Level Bureaucrat in Public Service Bureaucracies* (Lexington, Mass.: D. C. Heath, 1979), as well as an earlier study by Elihu Katz and Brenda Danet, *Bureaucracy and the Public* (New York: Basic Books, 1973). See also Janet C. Vinzant and Lane Crothers, *Street-Level Leadership: Discretion and Legitimacy in Front-Line Public Service* (Washington, D.C.: Georgetown University Press, 1998). Bryan Jones, with Saadia Greenberg and Joseph Drew, in *Service Delivery in the City: Citizen Demand and Bureaucratic Rules* (New York: Longman, 1980), focused more generally on citizen interactions with urban public service bureaucracies.

8. Prottas, *People Processing,* 46.

9. Paul A. Sabatier and Neil Pelkey, "Incorporating Multiple Actors and Guidance Instruments into Models of Regulatory Policymaking," *Administration and Society* 19 (August 1987): 238.

10. Evelyn Z. Brodkin, "Policy Politics: If We Can't Govern, Can We Manage?" *Political Science Quarterly* 102 (1987): 579. The quote is from a 1979 convention paper by Claus Offe.

11. Prottas, *People Processing,* 65.

12. The federal KidCare program that subsidizes health insurance for children and pregnant women is an example of tripling enrollments through successful outreach programs. Crissa Shoemaker, "Enrollment in KidCare on the Rise, Official Says," *Chicago Tribune,* June 22, 2000.

13. Associated Press, "Vaccination System Needs Boost to Protect U.S. Health, Report Says," *Chicago Tribune,* June 16, 2000.

14. Jones, *Service Delivery in the City,* 50–52.

15. Nina Bernstein, "Bingo, Blood and Burial Plots in the Quest for Food Stamps," *New York Times,* Aug. 12, 2000.

16. Martin Tolchin, "Federal Aid for Destitute Reaching Just Half of Those Eligible," *New York Times,* May 10, 1988.

17. For a full discussion of this situation, see Martha Derthick, *Agency under Stress: The Social Security Administration in American Government* (Washington, D.C.: Brookings Institution, 1990).

18. Daniel Katz, Barbara A. Gutek, Robert L. Kahn, and E. Barton, *Bureaucratic Encounters* (Ann Arbor, Mich.: Institute for Social Research, 1975), 54.

19. Arnold Vedlitz, James A. Dyer, and Roger Durand, "Citizen Contacts with Local Governments: A Comparative View," *American Journal of Political Science* 24 (February 1980): 50.

20. Jane Fritsch and David Rohde, "For the Poor, a Lawyer with 1,600 Clients," *New York Times,* Apr. 9, 2001.

21. Mike Allen, "Girl's Slaying Exposes Limits of Connecticut 'Megan's Law,'" *New York Times,* Aug. 29, 1998.

22. Sidney Verba, "The Voice of the People," *PS: Political Science* 26 (1993): 684–685.

23. Kenneth R. Mladenka, "Citizen Demands and Urban Services: The Distribution of Bureaucratic Response in Chicago and Houston," *American Journal of Political Science* 25 (November 1981): 693.

24. Jones, *Service Delivery in the City,* 142–144.

25. Ibid., 86–87.

26. Michael T. Harmon and Richard T. Mayer, *Organizational Theory for Public Administration* (Boston: Little, Brown, 1986), 326–331.

27. Citizens' interactions with bureaucrats reflect their lack of power and control. See Jones, *Service Delivery in the City,* 7.

28. John L. Crompton and Charles W. Lamb, Jr., *Marketing Government and Social Services* (New York: Wiley, 1986), 9.

29. Lipsky, *Street-Level Bureaucracy,* 84–86.

30. Kathy E. Ferguson, *The Feminist Case against Bureaucracy* (Philadelphia: Temple University Press, 1984), 123.

31. William T. Gormley, Jr., "The Representation Revolution: Reforming State Regulation through Public Representation," *Administration and Society* 18 (August 1986): 179–196.

32. For examples of cultural differences among Western and non-Western populations, see Elihu Katz, Michael Gurevitch, Brenda Danet, and Tsiyona Peled, "Petitions and Prayers: A Method for the Content Analysis of Persuasive Appeals," *Social Forces* 47 (1969): 447–463.

33. For additional examples, see Clarence N. Stone, "Attitudinal Tendencies among Officials," in *The Public Encounter,* ed. Charles T. Goodsell (Bloomington: Indiana University Press, 1981), 54–59.

34. Barbara Nelson, "Client Evaluations of Social Programs," in *The Public Encounter,* ed. Charles T. Goodsell (Bloomington: Indiana University Press, 1981), 27–29.

35. Larry B. Hill, "Bureaucratic Monitoring Mechanisms," in *The Public Encounter,* ed. Charles T. Goodsell (Bloomington: Indiana University Press, 1981), 165.

36. Gore, *From Red Tape to Results,* 44–64.

37. David Cay Johnston, "Showing Good Form at I.R.S.," *New York Times,* Apr. 14, 1999.

38. Harvey A. Abrams and Peter Bidney, "When Clients Complain: Bureaucratic Responsiveness in Large Federal Agencies," *Journal of Sociology and Social Welfare* 6 (June 1979): 558.

39. Barry Schwartz, in *Queuing and Waiting: Studies in the Social Organization of Access and Delay* (Chicago: University of Chicago Press, 1975), discusses the power plays involved in delays.

40. Ibid., 26; Eric Zorn, "INS Visit a Breeze—If You Have Seven Hours to Kill," *Chicago Tribune*, Sept. 12, 2000.

41. Abrams and Bidney, "When Clients Complain," 559.

42. Gore, *From Red Tape to Results*, 46–47.

43. Yeheskel Hasenfeld and Daniel Steinmetz, "Client-Official Encounters in Social Service Agencies," in *The Public Encounter*, ed. Charles T. Goodsell (Bloomington: Indiana University Press, 1981), 84. Measures of unresponsiveness are discussed in Abrams and Bidney, "When Clients Complain," 558–561.

44. Ferguson, *The Feminist Case against Bureaucracy*, 123.

45. Ibid., 123–124.

46. Gormley, "The Representation Revolution," 184.

47. Ferguson, *The Feminist Case against Bureaucracy*, 124.

48. Joan Beck, "What If Taxpayers Can't Cope with New Forms and Give Up?" *Chicago Tribune*, May 25, 1987.

49. Gore, *From Red Tape to Results*, 45.

50. John M. Stevens and Robert P. McGowan, *Information Systems and Public Management* (New York: Praeger, 1985), 27. Gormley, "The Representation Revolution," 179–196.

51. Gore, *From Red Tape to Results*, 134–168.

52. Gormley, "The Representation Revolution," 188–189.

53. Ibid., 187–188.

54. Larry B. Hill, "The Citizen Participation-Representation Roles of American Ombudsmen," *Administration and Society* 13 (February 1982): 428.

55. Abrams and Bidney, "When Clients Complain," 562–574.

56. Mladenka, "Citizen Demands and Urban Services," 697.

57. Robert L. Kaiser, "Plain English Is Toppling Bureaucrats' Tower of Babble," *Chicago Tribune*, Nov. 9, 1998.

58. Robert Pear, "Medicare Officials to Limit Distribution of New Guide," *New York Times*, June 20, 1998.

59. Brodkin, "Policy Politics," 375–382.

60. The Social Security Disability program, though small by comparison with other Social Security programs, still involved roughly 4.5 million people at the time of the investigation. For more details, see Derthick, *Agency under Stress*.

61. Martin Tolchin, "Staff Is Cut, Many Lose Social Security," *New York Times*, Dec. 8, 1989.

62. Charles T. Goodsell, Raymond E. Austin, Karen L. Hedblom, and Clarence C. Rose, "Bureaucracy Expresses Itself: How State Documents Address the Public," *Social Science Quarterly* 62 (1981): 576–591.

63. Ibid., 579–581.

64. Ibid., 584.

65. Brodkin, "Policy Politics," 585–587.

66. Goodsell et al., "Bureaucracy Expresses Itself," 590–591.

67. Author's unpublished research.

68. Celia W. Dugger, "Fearful Immigrants Trying to Beat a Misunderstood Legal Deadline," *New York Times*, Mar. 21, 1997.

69. Robin Toner, "Extensive Effort Seeks to Clarify Medicare Maze," *New York Times,* Sept. 27, 1999.

70. Jones, *Service Delivery in the City,* 49.

71. Cecilie Gaziano, "The Knowledge Gap: An Analytical Review of Media Effects," *Communication Research* 10 (October 1983): 447–486, and sources cited therein.

72. Katz and Danet, *Bureaucracy and the Public,* 175.

73. Katz et al., "Petitions and Prayers," 447. For a similar analysis of Soviet citizens, see Wayne DiFranceisco and Zvi Gitelman, "Soviet Political Culture and 'Covert Participation' in Policy Implementation," *American Political Science Review* 78 (September 1984): 603–621.

74. Hasenfeld and Steinmetz, "Client-Official Encounters in Social Service Agencies," 89; Prottas, *People Processing,* chap. 1.

75. Prottas, *People Processing,* 130.

76. Gore, *From Red Tape to Results,* 48–49.

77. Tolchin, "Federal Aid for Destitute Reaching Just Half of Those Eligible." Excessive documentation requirements, designed to discourage welfare applicants, are discussed in Brodkin, "Policy Politics," 583–584.

78. For additional discussion of the importance of categorization, see Prottas, *People Processing,* 5–6.

79. Ibid., 32–33.

80. Of course some exceptions are actually built into the rules. For example, veterans receive preferential treatment in grading of civil service examinations.

81. James Q. Wilson, *Bureaucracy: What Government Agencies Do and Why They Do It* (New York: Basic Books, 1989), 53.

82. Goodsell, *The Public Encounter,* 9–10.

83. John Clayton Thomas, *Public Participation in Public Decisions* (San Francisco: Jossey-Bass, 1995), 106–107.

84. The research for Colorado agencies was done by Ciruli Associates of Denver.

85. Carol Ann Traut and Hal G. Rainey, "The Information Gathering Practices of City Officials," 1989 American Political Science Association paper.

86. Ibid.

87. Prottas, *People Processing,* 37.

88. Bob Dart, "Audiences Agree with Negative TV Portrayals of Bureaucrats," *Chicago Tribune,* May 8, 1999.

89. U.S. Government Customer Satisfaction Initiative, 1999 (June 1), http://www.customersurvey.gov/ federal.htm

90. The Pew Research Center for the People and the Press, "Performance and Purpose Report: April 2000" (June 1), http://www.people-press.org/npr00mor.htm

91. Charles T. Goodsell, *The Case for Bureaucracy: A Public Administration Polemic* (Chatham, N.J.: Chatham House, 1985), 21.

92. Ibid., 21, 29. For a critique of such analyses of evaluations on theoretical and methodological grounds, see Yeheskel Hasenfeld, "Citizens' Encounters with Welfare State Bureaucracies," *Social Service Review* 59 (December 1985): 622–635.

93. Katz et al., *Bureaucratic Encounters,* and Lloyd A. Free and Hadley Cantril, *The Political Beliefs of Americans: A Study of Public Opinion* (New York: Simon and

Schuster, 1968), report similar discrepancies between overall evaluations and specific judgments.

94. Hasenfeld, "Citizens' Encounters with Welfare State Bureaucracies," 629.

95. Nelson, "Client Evaluations of Social Programs," 34.

96. Goodsell, *The Case for Bureaucracy*, 31; the study is reported in full in Charles T. Goodsell, "Conflicting Perceptions of Welfare Bureaucracy," *Social Casework: The Journal of Contemporary Social Work* 61 (June 1980): 354–360.

97. The Pew Research Center for the People and the Press, "Performance and Purpose Report: April 2000" (June 1), http://www.people-press.org/npr00mor. htm

98. Verba, "The Voice of the People," *PS: Political Science* 26 (1993): 681–683.

99. Jon Anderson, "Clinics Learn from their Neighbors," *Chicago Tribune,* Apr. 30, 1997.

100. See Robert D. Miewald and John C. Comer, "Complaining as Participation," *Administration and Society* 17 (1986): 481–499, for a discussion of the pros and cons of citizen participation in the administrative process.

101. Zukerman and West, "The Political Bases of Citizen Contacting," 118. Also see Sidney Tarrow, *Between Center and Periphery: Grassroots Politicians in Italy and France* (New Haven: Yale University Press, 1977).

102. Harold F. Gortner, Julianne Mahler, and Jeanne Bell Nicholson, *Organizational Theory: A Public Perspective* (Chicago: Dorsey, 1987), 277–289, illustrates this point with a case of parental intervention in school policy.

103. William Gormley, John Hoadley, and Charles Williams, "Potential Responsiveness in the Bureaucracy: Views of Public Utility Regulation," *American Political Science Review* 77 (September 1983): 704–715.

104. Gormley, "The Representation Revolution," 185.

105. See, for example, Vedlitz et al., "Citizen Contacts with Local Governments."

106. Zukerman and West, "The Political Bases of Citizen Contacting," 118.

107. Ibid., 119, examined contacting in Austria, India, Japan, the Netherlands, Yugoslavia, and the United States.

Chapter 8

Public Relations and Public Information Campaigns

The Jekyll and Hyde Faces of External Communication

In their book *Leadership and Innovation: A Biographical Perspective on Entrepreneurs in Government,* political scientists Jameson Doig and Erwin Hargrove analyzed the careers of thirteen successful top-level administrative officials. One characteristic was crucial to success in all cases: the ability to generate support from key external constituencies such as Congress, the president, interest groups, and the general public.[1] As James Webb, administrator of the National Aeronautics and Space Administration, put it:

> The environment is not something apart from the endeavor; it is not just something in which the endeavor operates and to which it needs to adjust; it is an integral part of the endeavor itself. . . . The total (executive) job encompasses external as well as internal elements, and success is as dependent on effectiveness in the one as in the other.[2]

The Beneficent Face

These analyses point to the significance of external communications for the welfare of public agencies. This "beneficent face" reaches far beyond the power games played by public officials to support their agencies' and their own personal goals. As discussed in Chapter 4, transmitting information across organizational boundaries is crucial. The nation's social, political, and economic health hinges on the accurate and timely transmission by public agencies of vital information such as census data, economic indexes and forecasts, health and disease statistics, and crime information. Similarly, boundary-spanning communication among government agencies performing related tasks is essential to avoid undue overlap and policy incoherence. The public must be informed about available services and about the financial and service contributions expected from citizens.

In a democracy where the norms call for transparency in the conduct of the public's business, the public is entitled to receive performance reports from officials. "Meaningful communication between government and the people is not merely a management practicality. It is a political, albeit moral, obligation that originates from the basic covenant that exists between the government and the people."[3] Aside from the normative considerations, reporting eases the watchdog function of the press and public and may help agencies to perform their work. The Internal Revenue Service (IRS) commissioner, for example, has testified before Congress that the public's perception of the efficiency of the IRS is a crucial element in maintaining voluntary compliance.[4]

Among the most difficult tasks facing public relations staffs is the necessity to explain oversights, misdeeds, and other untoward events without destroying confidence in the agency. It is tough to explain to an impatient public why the Immigration and Naturalization Service is running more than a year behind in considering naturalization papers or why the FBI failed to discover a double agent in its midst for more than a decade and ignored messages that might have averted the 2001 terrorist attacks on the United States. How could the Justice Department save face when the attorney general has to acknowledge publicly that she was kept in the dark about the activities of FBI agents during a tragic siege in 1993 that cost the lives of fifty adults and twenty-five children who had refused to surrender to authorities?

The dividing line is fuzzy between public information activities, discussed as boundary-spanning communication in Chapter 4, and public relations activities, which are the focus of this chapter. Both involve dispensing information. Usually the distinction is based on the fact that public relations places primary emphasis on creating a favorable image for an agency so that its personnel and activities may be viewed positively by constituencies that are deemed important to the agency. Nonetheless, because image-building concerns play some part in most communications, it is often difficult to differentiate between primarily informative messages and those that are mostly image-oriented and therefore deemed public information's threatening face.

The Threatening Face

In the United States, concerns about the ethics of image-building information—often called propaganda—are deeply ingrained because propaganda connotes slanted information.

> All too often professional government communicators have been placed in the roles of "spin doctor," "department mouthpiece," or "damage controller." These roles tend to engender suspicion and loss of credibility on the part of citizens, elected officials and other stakeholders.[5]

Allowing public officials to disseminate image-building information seems contrary to the ethical requirement that public officials owe the truth, the whole truth, and nothing but the truth to the American people. Citizens in a democracy, it is argued, must be well informed, but the information should be value-neutral so that it does not prejudice their judgments. Despite these rampant fears about distortions, most information dispensed by public agencies is reasonably accurate. It may not be the whole truth, but it is unlikely to be deliberately false.

Disdain for image-building messages also ignores the widely acknowledged political requirement that leaders in a democratic society must communicate persuasively with citizens whom they are expected to lead. Nonetheless, citizens' concerns about government manipulation of public opinions have led to numerous restraints on government public relations activities. These do not generally take the form of legal restraints because that might violate the free speech clauses of the Constitution.[6] Among the few legal barriers are the prohibitions barring the U.S. Information Agency from distributing its propaganda materials inside the United States and some restrictions on government purchasing of advertisements.[7] Title 18, Section 1913, of the United States Code makes lobbying by government officials a crime.[8] However, this antilobbying act has been loosely construed. It does not apply to information disseminated by government agencies in the routine performance of their activities. Such messages are presumably impartial and geared to inform rather than persuade. The act does prevent officials from contributing money to political campaigns.

The main constraint on public relations activities arise from decentralized organization and haphazard performance because of the reluctance to acknowledge that these activities are essential and legitimate. Unlike many democratic as well as authoritarian countries, the United States has no major centralized departments of information or communication at either the federal or state levels. Efforts within various agencies to centralize control over external information flows by requiring officials to clear their speeches through agency heads, or even through the White House, have also floundered because of the ingrained reluctance to restrain free speech. Similarly, pressures exerted on agency heads by various administrations to tout the president's programs have met with meager success.

The lack of centralized control over external communications explains why public officials in the United States often do not speak with one voice about major issues. When authoritative pronouncements are contradictory, people become confused, annoyed, and often cynical. For example, it is embarrassing when the State Department announces that the United States will not exchange a Soviet spy suspect for an American spy suspect, while the White House press office announces that "all options are open."[9] It is equally embarrassing when the short-lived Office of Strategic Influence within the Defense Department claimed in the spring of 2002 that it had been authorized to use disinformation in the war on terrorism while the secretary of defense pleaded that he knew nothing about such plans.[10]

Public Relations Strategies

Wielding Political Rhetoric

Creating favorable political images is often more a matter of rhetoric—the art of speaking convincingly—than presenting substantively sound proposals. For example, "by transforming the 'estate tax,' which screamed wealth and privilege, to the 'death tax,' which tied together two of life's inevitable, un-pleasant rites," Republicans "helped the prospects of a tax cut that at first ap-peared to be an easy target for Democrats."[11] Calling a program for the men-tally retarded a school for "exceptional children" or a birth-control clinic a "family-planning center" creates a positive image for activities that might otherwise arouse negative reactions. Because message framing can shape opinions and guide actions, public officials must use it shrewdly to support their objectives.[12] As political scientist Murray Edelman sees it, "The strate-gic need is to immobilize opposition and mobilize support. . . . The key tac-tic must always be the evocation of interpretations that legitimize favored courses of action and threaten or reassure people so as to encourage them to be supportive or to remain quiescent."[13]

The power to verbally define issues usually rests with the established elites who can select appropriate frames from manifold, often antithetical icons available in American culture. The ultimate task of political language and symbolic activity "is to rationalize and justify decisions that are largely the re-sult of power and influence. . . . without this legitimation and rationalization, the exercise of power is hindered."[14] In line with this rationale, Environmen-tal Protection Agency (EPA) administrator William Ruckelshaus defined the agency's mission as "risk reduction" to trump the emphasis on costs that the Office of Management and Budget (OMB) had stressed to curb the EPA's programs.[15] Similarly, the Occupational Safety and Health Administration (OSHA) softened its harsh antibusiness rhetoric to preserve its budget after Republicans seized control over Congress from Democrats.[16] Many scholars of political rhetoric contend that conflicts over the meaning of political mes-sages are the essence of politics because meanings are always sufficiently un-clear to leave room for diverse interpretations.[17] One community's freedom fighter can be another community's terrorist.

Despite strong temptations to bend the truth, most agencies stress the im-portance of honesty and the avoidance of outright lies, which are deemed un-ethical, unprofessional, and often counterproductive because they may lead to a loss of credibility. The excerpts from the State Department memorandum to its public affairs officers, reproduced in Box 8–1, illustrate this emphasis. The memorandum was issued to clarify the ground rules for conversations with the press as well as communications between public affairs officials and their internal information sources.[18] Interviews with public affairs officers show strong support for obeying these rules, along with realization that cir-cumstances may compel officials to skirt the truth at times or even tell an out-right lie when the truth would harm important public interests.[19]

While outright lying is shunned most of the time, overemphasizing desir-able news or slighting undesirable matters are acceptable practices. Good news is shouted, and bad news is whispered. Announcements of new pro-grams rarely stress their cost or the fact that the public will have to pay for them. Unless required by laws or regulations, hospitals often shy away from

Box 8-1 **Rules for Press Relations at the State Department**

Some Do's and Don'ts. . . . The first and most important is to be *honest,* we don't have to divulge everything we know, but what we do say must be accurate. And where we have to hold some facts back, the sum of what we say should not give a misleading impression.

If an officer doesn't know the facts, he shouldn't talk about the problem. The most difficult stories to clean up afterward are those which result from uninformed guesswork. . . . If an officer doesn't want to admit he doesn't know the facts, he can always say he's "not in a position to talk about it."

Don't talk about somebody else's problem. Let the person in charge handle it his way. . . . Always take or return reporters' telephone calls, even when you know you won't be able to satisfy their questions. It's a small courtesy, but courtesy oils this relationship as much as others. And you may be able to spike a story that is just plain wrong—they can be damaging too.

What the Press Needs

—We need *the facts* without varnish, even when (or particularly when!) they add up to a skeleton in the closet. . . .

—We need *your guidance,* formal and informal. In tricky or sensitive situations, it's almost always better to sit down and talk the matter through, since the average written guidance is generally pretty well exhausted after the third question at the noon briefing.

—We need *absolute honesty.* The department's credibility is a matter of proud record over a long period of time, but it is tested anew every day of the year. As tempting as it may be in any given situation to shave the facts a bit, there is always another office which benefits on the same day in an equally tricky situation from the fact that the newsmen believe the department's spokesman.

—Finally, we need *ideas.* There are a lot of things going on which not only can—but ought to be talked about if the department is to have the kind of informed support it needs from public opinion. Your offices are closer to these "discussable issues" and we would welcome your suggestions. . . .

SOURCE: Extracted from a State Department memorandum to all public affairs officers found in Stephen Hess, *The Government/Press Connection* (Washington, D.C.: Brookings Institution, 1984), 120–121. Reprinted with permission.

publishing morbidity and mortality figures, and employment agencies focus attention on successful placements rather than the hard-core unemployed. The Corps of Engineers may call attention to its most successful construction projects while keeping silent about its failures.

To avoid unfavorable publicity, organizations may also prohibit informal communication between their employees and the media on selected topics.

They may designate special spokespersons to make it more likely that the organization will speak with one voice and that no harmful information will be leaked. Given the media's penchant for trying to ferret out negative stories, avoidance of negative publicity may be a primary concern of public relations efforts.

As Martha Derthick concluded after studying the Social Security Administration:

> Organizational leaders in any milieu, public or private, tend to emphasize the strengths and obfuscate the weaknesses of their organizations in order to sustain morale internally and elicit confidence externally. Candor is not intrinsic to the role; a certain amount of calculated delusion is. In a political setting, which is to say in a public agency, incentives to present the *appearance* of success are especially powerful, because such organizations are so heavily dependent on others' confidence. Agency leaders therefore do not ordinarily testify to Congress or to presidential officials that things are going badly in their agencies unless events have given them no choice.[20]

External Message Paths

External communication is a two-way street to and from agencies. Messages may travel horizontally or vertically. Horizontal messages are intended for agencies at similar levels of the administrative hierarchy. Generally speaking, horizontal messages are usually irregular and comparatively sparse because there are few formal channels for them. Vertical communications are more abundant. Examples are messages sent upward by administrative agencies to their legislatures or downward to their clients and suppliers.

At the federal level, upward messages are particularly significant. Administrative agencies need to keep in constant touch with Congress, which exercises important controls over them. Consequently, all federal departments now have their own congressional liaisons.[21] Federal departments usually bear the brunt of the burden for promoting the concerns of agencies under their jurisdiction. They receive only occasional help from the White House. At the state and local levels, various organized political bodies represent the collective interests of state and local agencies. Examples are the National Conference of State Legislatures, the National Governors' Association, the National Association of Counties, and the U.S. Conference of Mayors.[22] Lobbying the federal government for a share of its largesse is one of their primary functions.

Having personal connections to congressional offices is invaluable for successful external communication. It is especially valuable to have connections to units directly involved in funding decisions. During his many trips to Washington to solicit funds for Chicago, Richard Daley, the city's mayor, was fortunate to have Rep. Dan Rostenkowski, a fellow Democrat and Illinois citizen, in control of congressional purse strings as chair of the House Ways and Means Committee. The most frequent links between federal agencies and

Congress are congressional committees and subcommittees involved with the agency and congressional staffs that gather most of the information. The secretary of defense, for instance, is apt to court the leaders of the Armed Services committees in both houses; the treasury secretary will woo the Ways and Means Committee chair, and the secretary of agriculture will consult with the appropriate agriculture committees.

Because many different committees and subcommittees in both the Senate and the House are usually involved with the work of major agencies, maintaining adequate contacts with all of them on a regular basis can be quite arduous. In fact, government executives devote much more time than their private-sector counterparts to wooing external constituencies. Typically, business executives of large companies meet with their board of directors fewer than ten times a year. Government executives with a comparable scope of responsibilities meet with congressional committees—counterparts of a board of directors—more than twice as often. Moreover, although board of director meetings are generally harmonious, meetings with congressional committees are often acrimonious, with the executives' requests frequently denied.

The costs of these often wasted efforts to win favor with Congress are high because they drain valuable time from other agency activities. As James Q. Wilson has noted, "Government executives must spend so much time coping with their agencies' external environment that they have relatively little time to shape its internal life."[23] Expert staffs usually brief top administrators for encounters with external constituencies. These staffs may be trained in public relations principles and techniques and devote all their time to communication tasks, or they may also have other responsibilities and lack public relations credentials.[24] Briefings are particularly thorough for prospective encounters with appropriations and oversight committees. When committees ask questions for which top administrators are not prepared, the missing information may have to be gathered for subsequent insertion into the official records.

Report writing has become a finely honed art because agencies that are able to produce and transmit ample and convincing evidence about their achievements and needs are more likely to survive and flourish. Expertise in creating persuasive messages is particularly important for organizations that cannot appeal to large constituencies for grassroots support. Preparing reports requires excellent writing skills and familiarity with the technical and political aspects of the issues under discussion. It also involves knowing the mind-set and idiosyncrasies of those receiving the reports as well as the current political setting in both the receiver's and the sender's agency.[25]

Government reports have been dubbed "bureaucratic propaganda" by scholars who point out their image-building objectives. Official reports accomplish this mission by painting a glowing best-case scenario of an agency's prospects and achievements.[26] The goals are "to obtain further funding, promote organizational careers, assign responsibility for a particular act to an 'enemy,' and in general 'cover your ass' from revelation before a sanctioning body."[27]

Federal agencies must also keep in touch with other parts of the executive branch. Contact with the president and the presidential staff is made largely through the heads of the respective departments. For bureau chiefs and other officials below the top administrative levels, contact is rarely direct. Herbert Kaufman found that federal bureau chiefs mostly contacted the executive branch through OMB, which exercises budgetary controls. Otherwise, their external messages went largely to other offices in the department in which the bureau was located. Many of these contacts occurred during staff meetings. Other contacts were lateral, directed to other federal agencies outside the department whose work intertwined with their bureau's activities. Kaufman estimates that "taking stock of both lateral and hierarchical links, the chiefs probably spent as much time with elements of the executive branch as they did with components of the legislative branch."[28]

External communications also address a variety of nongovernmental publics. The federal bureau chiefs studied by Kaufman "probably averaged about as much time with a host of nongovernmental interests as with either branch of government." Most of these contacts were with various types of organized interest groups. To keep these lobbies favorable or at least neutral, all bureaus "had programs to explain their policies to the outside world, to discover the views and concerns of external groups and the media," and to enlist the support of favorable groups, especially when unfavorable ones were on the prowl.[29]

Public relations activities may also be essential to appease disaffected external publics. It may be necessary to mobilize agency supporters or counter-constituencies or solicit mass media backing. Maintaining support in the face of opposition may require regular contacts in meetings, speeches to professional groups, responses to requests, and the like. Advisory commissions may have to be set up. Major changes in services or eligibility rules need to be carefully explained and justified to publics who may feel that they are adversely affected.

To make transmission of difficult messages easier, they are often directed to opinion leaders or grassroots organizations from which others in the community seek information and advice. This two-step flow approach happens because advice from known and trusted sources is more persuasive than advice from strangers. Besides, opinion leaders usually know how to tailor messages to the needs of particular audiences. For example, local public health physicians or a local health department may find it easier to transmit information about childhood immunization to neighborhoods whose families they know than would the U.S. surgeon general appearing on television from Washington. The trick, of course, is to identify appropriate opinion leaders for various types of messages. Who, for instance, could effectively carry the antialcoholism message of the National Institute on Alcohol Abuse and Alcoholism to preteens and their parents and teachers? When that question arose, the Children's Television Workshop, producers of the alcoholism prevention campaign, recommended a music video that featured the Jets, a performing group who were popular with preteens.[30] It is doubtful that the Jets were equally popular with parents and teachers.

Structuring Public Relations Agencies

There is little agreement about how agencies should be structured to carry out public relations activities.[31] Preferences depend on the goals to be maximized. For example, to prevent the Federal Energy Administration (FEA) from casting itself in an unduly rosy light, Congress decreed that public information and relations functions should be kept separate from other operations. Accordingly, an Office of Energy Information and Analysis was set up within the FEA that was explicitly separated from other parts of the agency in hopes that data dispensed by the agency would then be free from any taint of advocacy.[32] In most other agencies, public affairs offices are more closely integrated to ensure coordination of efforts with the agency that they serve.

Jurisdictional Issues

Internal and external public relations efforts are distinct enterprises, pursuing different strategies. Therefore, they are often, but by no means always, assigned to different offices within the agency. Some officials are in charge of the Intranet; others handle external activities via the Internet. There has also been debate about appropriate structures to facilitate coordination of public relations activities when agencies have many local branches. What is the most desirable degree of centralization? If public relations activities are handled locally, they can be geared to local concerns, but this may lead to fragmentation and inconsistencies among local branches that could be avoided through more central control.

How is the typical public affairs office organized? Again, there is a great deal of variety, much of it dictated by the wide diversity of tasks performed by public agencies. Moreover, beyond the top levels in the executive and legislative branches, information about the organization of public affairs offices is scarce. All that can be said about the following description of the Agriculture Department's Office of Public Affairs, depicted in Figure 8–1, is that the configurations are not untypical for a large agency directly involved with multiple publics.[33] The agency has used several substantially different patterns, often switching back and forth, which illustrates the old adage that there is always more than one way to skin the proverbial cat. Irrespective of the public affairs structure, it was the very typical task of the Agriculture Department's public affairs staff to maintain liaison with other governmental units, the mass media, and the public at large. They also coordinated and provided support for communication services rendered by other units within the Agri-

Figure 8-1 Organizational Chart of the Office of Public Affairs in the Agriculture Department, 1990

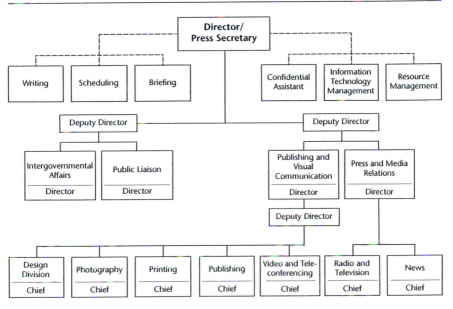

SOURCE: Department of Agriculture, Office of Public Affairs. http://www.usda.gov/agencies/ocpage.htm

culture Department. A staff exceeding 1,200 information specialists throughout the country handled these tasks.

Figure 8–1 shows two deputy directors in Agriculture's Office of Public Affairs. One combines intergovernmental affairs and public liaison; the other is in charge of media relations and various publishing and visual communication functions. Because the director doubles as press secretary, staff agencies include such functions as writing, scheduling, briefing, as well as resource management, information technology management, and one assistant charged with confidential matters. Work is divided according to the nature of the media and the various technical functions involved in publishing information in different media. Besides preparing news releases and briefings as well as coordinating releases and briefings from other units, the Office of Public Affairs prepares and coordinates speeches, feature articles, congressional testimony, and broadcasts, including many tailored for special audiences such as women, blacks, or Hispanics. The department also publishes books, magazines, brochures, technical reports, and newsletters that must be edited and coordinated. It has film, radio, and television units that produce training films, videotapes, and radio and television spots.

A major reorganization in 1980 was guided by two widely prevalent concerns. One was the realization that public affairs considerations must be part of all major decisions and that public affairs personnel must therefore be centrally located and given sufficient prestige and authority to be consulted in decision making at the highest levels. The director of public information should not, as often happens, be the odd person out. For this reason, the Office of Public Affairs was made part of the office of the secretary of the Department of Agriculture. The second concern relates to the common difficulty of coordinating an agency's diverse and far-flung activities. Many issues relating to external liaison and information activities originate at local levels and can best be resolved there, but local solutions must also be coordinated with the efforts of the agency as a whole and with the work of related agencies at local, state, and federal levels. The Agriculture Department's structures attempted to provide this coordination without impeding diversity.[34]

Tools for Image Construction

Officials have four basic strategies for using information to enhance an agency's image (see Figure 8–2). When policy considerations seem to require it, they can *withhold* information. This may be done by deliberately failing to gather information, by ignoring information that is tendered to the agency, or by keeping it secret and discussing it off the record. However, there must be legal justification for refusing to disclose information, such as claiming that secrecy is essential to protect national security or privacy rights, or that withholding is permitted under certain exceptions granted by the Freedom of Information Act—for instance, to protect trade secrets or the confidentiality of licensing examinations.[35]

Withholding, or even denying the existence of information, may be important when secrecy is essential. Concealing a planned raid on an illegal establishment, such as a crack house or a studio where child pornography is being created, are examples. During an economic crisis it may be wise to withhold bad economic news to forestall panic selling on the stock exchange. Whether such tactics are ethical, even when they are legal, is controversial. It is also questionable whether withholding information is ultimately counterproductive because credibility is undermined if concealment is discovered.

A second strategy involves the formal release of information, either through direct communication with other agencies and clients or through press releases or media briefings or the agency's own media. *Releasing information* through the press gives it greater credibility because the media, rather than an agency suspected of being self-serving, are viewed as the source. Besides, this strategy is apt to reach a much larger audience than direct contact by the agency. The disadvantage of working through the mass media is the loss of control over crucial decisions, such as framing the information to cast the agency in a favorable light, timing its release to the most opportune moment, and featuring it prominently. When agencies compose and release their own messages, they have full control over these matters. Agency-controlled

Figure 8-2 Model of the Government Communication Process

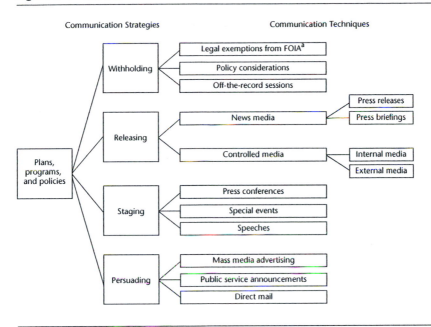

SOURCE: Ray Eldon Hiebert, "A Model of the Government Communication Process," in *Informing the People*, ed. Lewis M. Helm, Ray Eldon Hiebert, Michael R. Naver, and Kenneth Rabin (New York: Longman, 1981), 9. Reprinted with permission.

[a] Freedom of Information Act.

media include newsletters, information booklets, and reports mailed out directly to interested parties or featured on the agency's Web page.

A third strategy commonly used by public agencies to reach targeted audiences involves staging special events. These may range from declaring an Earth Day or Recycling Month to specially called press conferences, public addresses, and celebrations inaugurating a service or commemorating a historical event. Public hearings can occasionally be turned into grandstand performances that provide an opportunity for agency heads to make a reputation for themselves as well as for their agencies. In addition to the people who actually attend such events, there are potentially vast external audiences if the event attracts ample media coverage. The potential for reaching a mass media audience may indeed be the primary reason for staging the event.

Finally, various marketing techniques are used to disseminate persuasive messages. They are discussed more fully in the next section.

Although favorable publicity can be highly beneficial in promoting an agency's goals, it may also be harmful. When agencies emphasize the positive and shroud the negative aspects of programs and situations, public relations efforts lull observers into believing that all is well when it is not. For example, when concerned people are falsely reassured that aircraft safety regulations meet minimum standards or that water supplies are adequate in case of fire, they may relax the watchfulness that is needed to maintain appropriate standards.[36] The National Aeronautics and Space Administration apparently ignored warnings about problems with the *Challenger* spacecraft in its eagerness to launch the ill-fated mission in 1986 and win worldwide plaudits.[37] Similarly, it has been alleged that "the minutes of the Nuclear Regulatory Commission show that when the reactor was about to melt down at Three Mile Island, the commissioners were worried less about what to do to fix the reactor than they were about what they were going to say to the press."[38]

Public relations efforts may divert an agency's energies from important substantive tasks. When agencies call attention to themselves through public relations activities, their visibility may make them the target of more messages than they are prepared to handle. Communication channels may become clogged. Overwhelmed receivers may then ignore essential messages along with the nonessential ones. This problem has become increasingly serious for agencies that make themselves accessible via e-mail. Citizens become disillusioned with the agency when their e-mail messages receive a much delayed response or none at all.

Public Relations Staffs at Work

Message Channels. Modern public relations agents use a vast array of techniques to disseminate messages, ranging from personal contacts and mass media channels to videocassettes, direct mail, conferences, and computer services, including Internet advertising and Web sites. They also testify at congressional hearings, appear at public exhibits, and speak before key organizations. They may persuade supportive legislators to speak on behalf of their agency and insert the speech into the *Congressional Record*. When agencies do not wish to be tied directly to particular messages, they may release them surreptitiously as leaks planted by their own staffs or cooperating individuals.

Table 8–1 indicates the variety of advertising media available for government messages and lists some typical advantages and disadvantages. Dissemination venues vary in such factors as cost effectiveness, update flexibility, and the ability to individualize messages. Videotapes that explain a program, for example, are relatively inexpensive to create and keep current. The Social Security Administration uses them extensively, although they lack the personal touch that might come from direct telephone contact with a Social Security client. Recorded telephone messages not only have the advantages of low cost and round-the-clock access but also can be offered in multilingual versions. However, they also lack the personal contact that may be essential. Other tactics are weekly news bulletins or in-house magazines and newsletters that keep staffs informed of the agency's goals. When issues are very complex,

Table 8-1 Advantages and Disadvantages of Advertising Media

Media	Advantages	Disadvantages
Wire services	Wide circulation among all mass media; story release dates spread over several days	Multiple versions of story; no control over multiple editing processes; hard to gain access
Newspapers	Wide circulation among demographically diverse audiences; frequent publication; home deliveries; relatively attentive audiences; valued because it costs money	Short shelf life; competition among many advertisements; not selectively targeted
Magazines	Selective targeting; long shelf life; relatively attentive audiences; excellent reproduction capabilities	Focus on unduly narrow audience; high costs; long lead time; cannot deal with rapidly moving events
Radio	Large audiences with some selectivity; message can be easily changed; relatively low cost; free time for PSAs[a]	Unsuitable for complex messages; difficult to memorize; brief life span; competition from other media
Television	Extremely wide audience; low cost per client; joint audio and visual effects; free time for PSAs	Unsuitable for complex messages; brief life span; competition from other media; high costs; hard to create
Web sites	Potentially wide audience; inexpensive; easily changed content that is under advertisers full control; audiovisual and print formats	Misses most low socio-economic audiences; continuous upkeep requirements
Direct mail and videotapes	Highly selective circulation to targets chosen by advertiser; personalized approach creates goodwill; easy to measure success	Rejected as junk mail; expensive to create mailing lists and circulate; content not readily changed
Billboards and posters	Repeated exposure to targeted audiences; size may permit more graphic detail; cannot be discarded by audience	Message must be brief and simple; high cost of renting advertising space; low prestige of channel

SOURCE: Author.

[a]Public Service Announcement.

news briefings may be given to explain the story to reporters. Nonetheless time and space constraints in the mass media may make it impossible to supply audiences with needed details.

Agencies such as the Treasury Department, the Postal Service, and the military often use paid mass media advertisements. For instance, in 2000 the U.S. Army, which had been using New York–based Young and Rubicam Advertising for thirteen years to attract recruits, switched to Chicago-based Leo Burnett USA. As part of the change, the two-decades-old "Be All You Can Be" slogan that had pictured the army as a place to conquer tough challenges was to be replaced by a new marketing strategy directed primarily at African Americans and Latino Americans. Henceforth the army would be a haven for young Americans who want to prepare themselves for a good education and guaranteed good jobs in the future. The estimated annual price tag for the campaign was around $100 million.[39]

The military and other agencies also tell their stories through media-donated advertising, known as public service advertisements, or PSAs. National and local radio and television air thousands of PSAs each year. Among them are appeals by the EPA for automobile pollution inspection, pleas by the IRS to file returns early, the Forest Service's Smokey Bear campaign urging caution to prevent forest fires, and the Postal Service's eagle promising to deliver packages more swiftly and cheaply than competing private carriers.

With the country depending on volunteers for its branches of the military or for social services like the Peace Corps or Volunteers in Service to America (VISTA), it is cheaper to reach potential candidates through advertising than through other recruiting devices. Similarly, advertising is essential to compete with other agencies and government entities for a share of tourist, convention, and trade money. Many states and cities now have convention and visitors' bureaus with multimillion-dollar budgets. Audience surveys suggest that the public does pay attention to government advertisements, particularly when they relate to health and safety matters.[40] Judged by the volume of its messages, the national government ranks among the top twenty-five advertisers in the nation.[41]

Targeting Audiences. Social science research tools such as surveys, focus groups, interviews, and ethnographic observations are used to discover the best ways to appeal to the specific audiences to whom the advertising is targeted. Based on this research, various public relations strategies are developed for diverse target groups such as young people, medical experts, tobacco growers, or congressional representatives. Military recruitment appeals, for example, are often broadcast on sports programs, such as major football or basketball competitions. Good public relations also requires evaluation of the results.[42]

The sketch of interests of major stakeholders of a high school illustrates what might be involved in handling the public relations activities of a public high school (see Box 8–2). For example, parents might be inclined to support the school primarily because they have learned about its excellent curriculum, whereas the general public would be more responsive to appeals indicating that the school's excellence raises local property values. This box highlights the fact that successful marketing is grounded in thorough knowledge of prospective clients rather than in a probably futile effort to sell a service on terms that are most convenient for the agency.

Public relations activities are often condemned as blue smoke and mirrors. But at its professional best such image building becomes an exercise in responsiveness rather than manipulation. Public relations professionals should be chiefly concerned about keeping the public properly informed. Their agencies should strive to earn a good image for serving the public effectively, efficiently, and responsively. Unfortunately, this ideal is not practiced often enough. Citizens then become wary of government messages that smack of spin and hype and cover-ups.[43]

Box 8-2 **Diverse Interests of Major Stakeholders of a Public High School**

Primary stakeholders

Consumers (students and parents): Benefit directly. Potential benefits:
• Educational and vocational skills
• Development of self-confidence, self-esteem, communications skills

Supporters (school boards, foundations, civic groups, alumni): Provide funds for the school. Potential benefits:
• Knowledge that resources are used effectively
• Increase in personal stature and reputation in the community

General publics: Provide tax support. Potential benefits:
• Satisfaction of contributing to appropriate education of young people
• Increase in property values because of excellent school system

Employees (teachers, administrators, janitors): Work for the school. Potential benefits:
• Recognition of their contributions
• Opportunities for personal growth
• Pleasant working environment
• Good remuneration and security

Secondary stakeholders

Government (legislatures, accreditation agencies). They want:
• Evidence of a superior system and staff
• Efficient use of resources
• Noncontroversial programs that are unlikely to arouse public criticism

Competitors (alternative private schools in the area). They want:
• Compatibility of the services offered with their own operations

Suppliers (publishers, equipment and furnishing suppliers). They want:
• Opportunities to sell their products and services

Tertiary stakeholders

Media (broadcast and print journalists). They want:
• News items of interest to their publics; feature and human interest stories

Labor unions (professional and janitorial staff). They want:
• Improved working conditions for their members
• A voice in administering the school

Advocacy and special interest groups (advocates for the handicapped, athletic boosters, advocates for gifted students). Benefits they seek will vary. For example:
• Physical design features that accommodate the handicapped

Business community (employers of students). They want:
• Students with the basic skills to function effectively in the workforce

SOURCE: Adapted from John L. Compton and Charles W. Lamb Jr., *Marketing Government and Social Services* (New York: Wiley, 1986) , 35–36.

Media Relations

A Rocky Marriage

The dearth of readily available official channels for external communication forces government agencies to rely on the mass media. The government–media relationship is uneasy because their goals frequently conflict. The primary goal of most media is to produce interesting, dramatic stories, with only minor concern about their positive or negative consequences for the institutions and people featured in the story. In fact, there are strong incentives to produce negative coverage because American media see themselves as watchdogs over government, charged with publicizing misbehavior in the public sector. Besides, audiences love the drama of David and Goliath stories—the poor, harassed, underdog citizen bullied and hounded and even severely damaged by an arrogant, uncaring government.

Government agencies, by contrast, are very much concerned about the political consequences of media coverage. Officials therefore try to entice the media to cover stories they wish to publicize and to do so from perspectives that favor the government's positions. Agencies also seek to prevent the media from prying into matters that they want to keep out of the limelight. To succeed in media relations requires government agencies to employ professionals who understand the media's needs and can frame suitable messages. But even with professional help, bureaucrats find it far more difficult than elected officials to attract media attention.[44] There are exceptions of course, such as ample coverage of EPA policies and enforcement activities by the *Washington Post* and *New York Times*.[45]

Agencies' chances for attracting media coverage increase whenever the media lack enough government stories to fill their pages and air time. Government officials, especially elective office holders, are the media's main fountain of news. One-fifth to one-third of the content of American newspapers comes from government sources.[46] Washington reporters contact government press officers for almost half of their stories.[47] Given the limited resources of the news media, it would be impossible for reporters to gather this information on their own. When stories about government policies and activities are expertly prepared by public relations staffs to fit the needs of the particular medium for which they are intended, they can be godsends. As Pulitzer Prize–winning editor Harry S. Ashmore acknowledges, "The media as presently constituted could not function without the array of skills and resources provided them without cost in the name of public relations; and this consideration is compounded by their further reliance on advertising or political favors derived from the same sources."[48] Nonetheless, although newspeople eagerly use public relations output, they condemn public relations.[49]

Just as the media need government agencies, these agencies need the media to reach their various external audiences, including millions of low-level bureaucrats who cannot be contacted easily. Public relations staffs rely on the media to carry messages that will help their agencies gain the political supporters and widespread approval that are essential to carry out policies in the face of political obstacles. The mass media are particularly useful for publicizing government news because they reach sizable audiences and because they lend a cloak of credibility to political messages that self-promotions lack. Moreover, unlike advertisements, the direct costs of gaining access to mass media audiences are comparatively small.

Interaction Modes

Press releases are the most common method for submitting information to the media in hopes of enticing them to publish it. Nearly all government offices prepare press releases and shorter *press advisories* routinely, and media institutions, particularly those in Washington, D.C., receive them by the ton. Journalists discard most of them, often with only minimal attention to their content, but the occasional acceptances encourage agencies to maintain the barrage. Several factors increase the chances for publication of press releases, including the expertise with which the release is prepared, its newsworthiness, competition from other news stories clamoring simultaneously for scarce time and space, and the salience of the story for the particular media market. Stories of local concern are more likely to be selected, particularly in areas outside the major media markets.

Many of the larger agencies also routinely conduct press briefings, often on a daily basis, to give information and answer questions about agency business. When the media invest the time of their reporters to attend the briefing, it is more likely to pay off in publicity. Skilled public affairs officials can often anticipate correctly what questions particular reporters will ask and prepare detailed answers. When agencies have major news, they may call a *press conference* in which a high-level official announces and describes the happening and fields questions about it.

Agencies occasionally impose restrictions on publishing the news released at briefings, which are then termed *backgrounders*. Agencies may stipulate that the name of the official who disclosed the information should not be released, although the story may be published in full. It is then usually attributed vaguely to an "official source," a "high government official," or an "undisclosed source." At other times, agencies may prohibit direct quotation of the briefing official and any mention of sources. Journalists may also be told that the information is confidential and provided solely to enhance their understanding of unfolding events. The memo reproduced in Box 8–3 presents the definitions used by the Department of State for various types of media relations. In recent years several media institutions and individual reporters have refused to attend backgrounders or to follow the guidelines because they believe that government officials use the technique to escape responsibility for the accuracy of the released information.

Box 8-3 **Release Rules for State Department Information**

"On the record" means that you can be quoted by name and title. As a general proposition, and with the exception of the department spokesman, officers are on the record only in speeches, congressional testimony, or in formal press conferences.

"Background" . . . the rule was developed to permit officials to describe facts and policy more fully in a more informal way than they can on the record. . . . quotes are not to be used from a background discussion . . . the results of the conversation must be attributed to "state department officials," or "U.S. officials," or "administrative sources," or "diplomatic sources," . . .

The burden is on the officer to establish *at the onset* the fact that the conversation is on background and the nature of the attribution he desires.

"Deep Background" . . . means that the newsman cannot give any specific attribution to what he writes, but must couch his story in terms of "it is understood that . . ." or "it has been learned that . . .".

Obviously this ground rule . . . asks the newsman to assume a greater personal burden of responsibility for what he writes since there is no visible source for the facts. In turn, the officer assumes an even greater burden or moral responsibility not to mislead or misinform the reporter.

"Off the record" . . . means that the newsman can't use what he is told, except for such things as planning purposes . . .

SOURCE: Excerpted and adapted from Stephen Hess, *The Government/Press Connection* (Washington, D.C.: Brookings Institution, 1984), 118–119. Reprinted with permission.

Informal relations with the press are likely to involve high-level bureaucrats who are responsible for major policy decisions.[50] The content of informal transmissions, which often entail *leaks*, ranges from insignificant gossip to important policy-driving messages. For example, during the investigation of major chemical pollution at Love Canal in New York State, high-level bureaucrats leaked a Justice Department study about the hazards. The leak was designed to spur a reluctant EPA to relocate residents, contrary to its own judgment. It worked; the press served as a willing and effective tool for EPA's critics.[51]

During crises, such as airplane crashes or reports of poisoned food supplies or an impending military deployment, there is a massive speedup of all of the functions performed by public affairs officers of the agencies involved in the event. Special information offices may be set up at disaster sites. The principal challenge facing public affairs officials during crises is to obtain and release accurate information without causing unwarranted panic or complicating recovery efforts. Explaining often highly technical information under these circumstances can be exceedingly difficult.

Impact on Public Policies

Martin Linsky concluded his analysis of press impact on federal policymaking by pointing out that "policymakers will be more successful at doing their jobs if they do better in their relations with the press. . . . Having more policymakers who are skilled at managing the media will make for better government."[52] A poll that he and his associates conducted among upper-level officials who served in administrative agencies during the Johnson, Carter, Nixon, Ford, and Reagan administrations shows that these officials considered skillful handling of their media relations crucial.[53]

Ninety-seven percent agreed that the press has an impact on federal policy, with the majority stating that the impact is significant.[54] Three out of four of these officials reported that they had tried to get media coverage for their agency and its activities. Nearly all had used the media to obtain information about their policy area. Close to half of the officials had spent five hours or more weekly dealing with press matters, and one-quarter had spent between five and ten.[55] However, they usually denied that their own decisions had been affected by media coverage, probably because this would be an admission of lack of steadfastness in the face of pressure.[56]

Linsky's analysis sheds light on the areas in which press impact on the work of federal agencies appears to be most significant. Table 8–2 presents some of the evidence. The greatest impact apparently comes early in the policymaking process when media coverage may determine which issues will receive public attention, possibly moving them to the policy agenda and when media framing determines the images by which these issues will be appraised. This is the point at which public affairs professionals can have their greatest influence if they are able to seize the initiative from the media and define the issues to be addressed and the facets to be explored. Experienced government officials believe that officials succeed far too rarely. Senior federal officials, Linsky believes, "wait too long before involving their public affairs people in the policymaking process. As a result, policymaking is done without adequate attention to the way the policy will be received and the way it ought to be presented."[57]

One reason for keeping public relations experts out of the policymaking loop is that high-level officials distrust public affairs staffs and think they cater too much to media whims. Furthermore, these officials often believe—unfortunately erroneously—that a meritorious policy will sell itself and does not require publicity or mass media advocacy. Even when public affairs officials are excluded from early policy considerations, they are expected to rescue the policy from public disdain if it has failed. By that time, the agency's image may be damaged beyond repair. Nonetheless, the public affairs staff takes the brunt of the blame because of its generally poor image that, strangely, it has not been

Table 8-2 Press Impact on Policymaking (in percentages)

Question: When an issue in your office or agency received what you saw as positive or negative coverage in the mass media, did that coverage:	Positive coverage	Negative coverage
■ Increase your chances for successfully attaining your policy goals regarding the issue	78.5	6.4
■ Decrease your chances for successfully attaining your policy goals regarding the issue	4.8	71.4
■ Increase the speed with which the issue is considered and acted upon	38.8	36.0
■ Decrease the speed with which the issue is considered and acted upon	9.9	36.2
■ Make action on the issue easier	63.1	9.6
■ Make action on the issue more difficult	5.7	67.9
■ Increase the number of policy options considered	18.3	27.8
■ Decrease the number of policy options considered	15.8	27.5
■ Reshape the policy options considered	10.3	39.9
■ Cause you to reassess your policy position on the issue	7.6	49.0
■ Galvanize outside support	50.1	18.6
■ Undermine outside support	5.7	65.7
■ Move responsibility for the issue to a more senior official or officials	9.7	43.0
■ Increase the importance of the issue within the bureaucracy	26.2	49.0
■ Cause the public and/or other officials to assume the information contained in the coverage is accurate	31.7	33.8
■ Have long-term effects on your career	23.2	22.1
■ Affect your credibility on other issues	22.3	32.6
■ Have no effect	16.8	9.0

SOURCE: Reprinted from *Impact: How the Press Affects Federal Policymaking* by Martin Linsky, by permission of W. W. Norton & Company, Inc. Copyright © 1986 by the Institute of Politics at Harvard University, 236. Reprinted with permission.

NOTE: Respondents were asked to check the statements that occurred most frequently in each category of coverage.

able to overcome despite its image-shaping expertise. The ingrained distaste for propaganda that is so common among Americans is hard to overcome.

When the news media pay massive attention to an issue, decision making tends to accelerate. Public officials, eager to appear efficient or to move the issue out of the limelight, try to resolve it with exceptional haste, often bypassing normal procedures. When media coverage is extraordinarily intense or negative, decision making is frequently moved to officials who are up the ladder in the bureaucratic hierarchy. That endows the decision with more prestige and authority than if it were made at lower levels.[58]

Although media coverage can be an important asset, it can also be a liability. As Table 8–2 suggests, when coverage is negative, as happens frequently, the agency's work may be hurt seriously. The agency may be forced to react to the story, rather than carry out other plans. For example, plans to revamp Chicago's public housing in the 1990s had to be delayed because the Chicago Housing Authority had to respond to news stories about mismanagement. Likewise, the IRS had to shift its attention to damage control when stories surfaced about mistreatment of taxpayers. The agency head took personal control of efforts to restore the tarnished image to placate an irate public and concerned Congress. The tongue lashings that hapless agency heads receive is often brutal. FBI head Louis Freeh, for instance, was told by Sen. Charles Grassley, R-Iowa, during a Senate Judiciary Committee hearing that his agency represents "an ugly culture of arrogance that uses intimidation, disinformation, empire-building to get what it wants" and "puts too much focus on its image and budget and not enough on product."[59]

Similarly, when media framing puts a policy into an unfavorable light, it may fail. This happened when the Social Security Administration devised a new system to catch cheaters. The agency hoped that the media would focus on the savings to taxpayers and win their approval. Instead, the media pointed out that the new system might create hardships for deserving people, turning potential victims against the policy.[60]

To get and retain coverage, agencies have to adapt their information strategies to satisfy the media's need for exciting stories. The consequences can be unfortunate. If important stories that the agencies wish to publicize lack drama, agency personnel may withhold them, depriving the public of essential knowledge. Alternatively, officials may feel forced to dramatize stories excessively or to emphasize the wrong facets of the story. Officials may even create dramatic events solely for publicity purposes.

To keep stories attractive for mass media audiences, they must be told simply. Technical points and language must be omitted. To save television time or print media space, much of the context of stories must be excluded. The positions taken by the agency must be simplified so that they appear to be unambiguous. Given the complexity of many of the issues about which media audiences must be informed, such as environmental pollution or foreign policies, it is difficult to avoid creating overly simplistic images. Moreover, when agencies take clear stands, they may reduce the flexibility that is essential for political compromises. As has been said about members of Congress, the roles of publicity-seeking media "show horses" are rarely compatible with the roles of congressional "work horses."

Public Information Campaigns

General Features

Despite a political culture that disdains spin, hype, and outright propaganda, communication campaigns run by governmental agencies to shape public attitudes about various issues have been legion. Some campaigns advocate stands on controversial issues such as affirmative action, abortion rights, and foreign aid. Others support conservation issues, including forest fire prevention and recycling of waste. Still others promote healthful behaviors such as securing prenatal care and preventing AIDS.[61] The term "social marketing" is often used for campaigns designed primarily to foster the public's welfare. Some social marketing campaigns are one-shot affairs, but most deal with persistent problems that require recurrent campaigns.

Modern public information campaigns are run much more effectively than in the past because much more is known about the psychology of persuasion and more sophisticated technologies are available to carry messages and personalize them. Known as "segmentation" in marketing circles, personalization is considered an essential element in designing persuasive messages. The Achilles' heel of most public communication campaigns is the inability to relate them well enough to the lives of target audiences motivating them to change socially harmful but personally satisfying behaviors. Ultimate success often hinges on personal contacts with audience members that are normally too difficult and too costly to organize. Modern technologies range from satellite relays that can transmit messages to isolated areas, to mobile phones and beepers that now are constant companions for millions of people, to airplanes and helicopters that can carry visitors to remote areas to deliver messages by word of mouth and to give on-site demonstrations of new techniques.

Even though the elements of persuasion are better understood and message delivery is more efficient, success rates remain limited because efforts to change people's attitudes and behaviors face multiple obstacles.[62] They range from the inability to attract the attention of target audiences and frame comprehensible, culturally appropriate messages to the inability to produce or maintain the desired changes in attitudes and behaviors. Psychologist William McGuire developed a matrix of factors that are important to the success of public information campaigns. Figure 8–3 lists the twelve phases of output — the responses that campaigns seek — along with the five main inputs — communication variables that must be designed so that they jointly produce the desired results.[63] The input variables include the goal of the campaign, the source of the communication, the message, the channel, and the receiver. The twelve outputs sought from the persuasive inputs range from securing initial exposure to the communication to designing messages that consolidate the changed behavior.

The variables that form part of the matrix suggest that the impact of persuasive communications hinges on such factors as the credibility of the source, the type of information presented in the message, the modality of the channel in which it is carried, such as television versus radio, the personality of the message receiver, and the type of behavior required for compliance, such as stopping an existing behavior or preventing it before it has started.

For example, in the well-known Smokey Bear campaign to prevent forest fires, the source of the communication is a cartoon bear dressed like a forest ranger.[64] The message is "Remember, Only You Can Prevent Forest Fires." It has been publicized through repeated million-dollar campaigns featured on radio, television, and billboards as well as in newspapers and magazines. Smokey also participates in the annual Rose Bowl Parade and in Macy's Thanksgiving Day Parade, both nationally televised events. Children are offered membership in a Smokey Bear junior forest ranger program that distributes an official fire-prevention kit to them.

Figure 8-3 Communication/Persuasion Input-Output Matrix

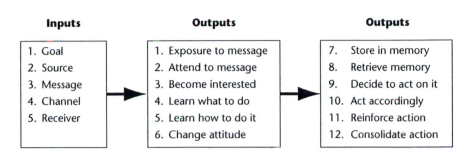

Inputs	Outputs	Outputs
1. Goal	1. Exposure to message	7. Store in memory
2. Source	2. Attend to message	8. Retrieve memory
3. Message	3. Become interested	9. Decide to act on it
4. Channel	4. Learn what to do	10. Act accordingly
5. Receiver	5. Learn how to do it	11. Reinforce action
	6. Change attitude	12. Consolidate action

SOURCE: Adapted from William J. McGuire, "Theoretical Foundations of Campaigns," *Public Communication Campaigns*, 2d ed., eds. Ronald Rice and Charles K. Atkin (Newbury Park, Calif.: Sage, 1989).

Planning with all twelve output steps in mind helps avoid tactics that may be beneficial in generating success at early campaign stages but are counterproductive for the crucial final steps. How does the Smokey Bear campaign measure up on these elements? No comprehensive evaluation of its success has been made. But given the fact that the forest-ranger bear is as familiar to Americans of all ages as most Walt Disney characters, the campaign seems to have achieved the first four output objectives shown in Figure 8–3. Ninety-eight percent of the public were able to identify Smokey in a 1976 poll.[65] The next eight steps shown in Figure 8–3 seem to have been achieved as well. Acreage lost through wildfires dropped from thirty million per year in 1942 to fewer than five million thirty years later. And the campaign objectives have been reinforced through continuous campaigns year after year.

Major Campaign Phases

The organization of modern public information campaigns involves the four main phases outlined in Figure 8–4. Initially, the problem requiring action needs to be carefully analyzed so that goals for the campaign can be set. This phase may require collecting extensive amounts of data about the social, political, and economic environment in which the problem is occurring. Surveys of the target population and community leaders and organizations are common, as are analyses of past campaigns and community resources to sustain them.

The second phase involves choosing strategies to achieve these goals. It may be advisable to run a series of pretests to determine how well various types of messages fit the information-processing styles of the target audiences. For example, to induce selected audiences to enroll in payroll savings plans at their workplaces, the Treasury Department produced television sketches that mimicked popular television comedies. The characters in the sketches extolled the

Figure 8-4 Social Marketing Campaign Phases

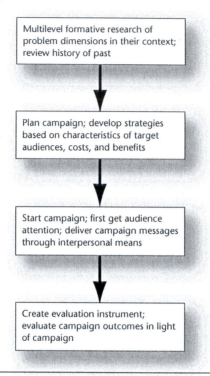

SOURCE: Author.

virtues of saving through U.S. government savings bonds. Test runs show that audiences become more receptive to messages that use formats and actors with whom the audiences can readily identify.[66]

Selection of specific persuasion strategies poses touchy ethical issues. How much advocacy is appropriate in campaigns conducted by public officials who seek to foster important policy goals such as the sale of government securities, military recruitment, protection of the health of various population groups, or protection of the environment? If it is ethical for government to market public causes, must it follow stricter criteria of taste and decorum than private marketing? For instance, are suggestive sexual themes permissible? Must special efforts be made to keep marketing messages acceptable to racial and ethnic minorities? For example, was the mayor of Atlanta correct when he fired an aide for using the word *niggardly* in a speech because some people misinterpreted it as a racial slur? How much humor is appropriate? Must there be rigid standards to avoid promising too much too soon? The answers are difficult.

Allegations of ethical violations have been common. For example, the Federal Trade Commission has received complaints alleging that military recruitment messages raise undue expectations that enlistees will travel widely throughout the world, receive training that will lead to profitable civilian jobs, and have interesting and fulfilling military duties. Similarly, advertisements for long-term government bonds have been criticized for failure to explain that the face value of the bond does not reflect the likelihood that its buying power will be sharply diminished at the time of redemption.[67]

When strategies have been chosen and appropriate message transmission channels secured, the third phase—the actual campaign—can begin. It usually starts with messages designed to alert target publics about the issues involved in the campaign. Given the large number of messages with which people are now bombarded, gaining attention is no easy feat. Once the target public has been alerted, the issue needs to be framed in ways that make the message relevant, understandable, and logical to lay people. Thus Smokey Bear tells people how they personally can prevent forest fires. Messages must motivate the audience to heed the advice. The Smokey Bear campaign emphasized the value of public parks to average Americans and the high costs of wildfires. It gives them the essential implementing information to carry out the recommendations of the campaign. Because the behavior must be sustained over prolonged periods of time, the campaign reminds them periodically about safe behaviors.

Knowledge is not enough unless it generates motivation. People whose unhealthful behaviors are ingrained must be motivated to change, even though this may be physically and psychologically taxing. Motivating them by promising a future benefit such as better health or longer life is often unsuccessful. Even appeals to change for the sake of protecting their loving families may fail. It may also be exceedingly difficult to explain ramifications of medical problems to at-risk lay publics and to provide them with "implementing information" that teaches them how to lower their risks. The fight against the spread of AIDS is a graphic example.[68] Finally, most difficult of all, people must be taught to continue desirable behaviors indefinitely. Because the new behavior usually involves loss of gratifications, backsliding is the rule rather than the exception. Again, the AIDS campaign is a case in point. Just as soon as medical advances slowed the ravages of the disease, risky sexual behaviors escalated again.[69]

At the end of each campaign, in the fourth phase, instruments to evaluate its success must be designed and applied. This is particularly important for public information campaigns that require frequent repetition and therefore need new funding periodically. Careful evaluation should indicate which features of the campaign should be retained and which should be dropped or altered.[70]

Playing the Lobbying Game

Going on the Offensive. Government agencies frequently engage in lobbying—public information and public relations activities that are highly structured and directed toward achieving specified responses and actions. The term was originally limited to describing organized efforts to influence legislation. Advocates of special interests would gather in the lobbies of legislative assemblies to plead their causes whenever the members emerged from the chambers. Nowadays the term is used more broadly to apply to well-organized pleadings designed to influence all phases of making and enforcing public policies. This more comprehensive use of the term obscures the boundary between lobbying and other public relations activities.[71]

Although lobbying is a hallowed tactic in American politics, protected by First Amendment free speech guarantees, it is prone to major abuses. Therefore, steps have been taken to forestall misconduct by lobbyists, including compulsory registration requirements. The Administrative Procedure Act of 1946 and subsequent court decisions impose legal restrictions designed to limit the power of lobbies to influence the operations of administrative agencies. Still, the persuasive power of lobbies remains vast, especially when they are well connected and well financed.

Washington, D.C., the center of American government, is the primary site for lobbying of public agencies and lobbying by them. Just like private-sector organizations, many federal agencies maintain lobbying staffs in the nation's capital. In addition, state governments, and most major cities, such as Chicago and Detroit, as well as other governmental units, have their own Washington lobbyists. Among them are organizations such as the U.S. Conference of Mayors, the National Association of Counties, and the National Conference of State Legislatures.[72] A survey in 1996 and 1997 of nearly 800 interest groups with Washington offices showed that government lobbies rank considerably above average in size and in lobbying activities.[73]

Many causes for which public agencies lobby also concern lobbyists for private and semipublic groups such as trade and professional associations. This has led to numerous coalitions between public- and private-sector lobbyists. Before joining a coalition, public administrators need to assess the costs and benefits of pursuing the coalition's strategies. Such assessments involve gathering information about many technical, practical, and political factors. What sorts of coalitions exist in the issue area in question? Who are the dominant players and how much political clout do they have? What are the soundest policies from the agency's perspectives? How many resources should it devote to this policy? Will policymakers lose touch with the general public if they work closely with interest-group representatives? Will they lose credibility?

Ethical questions arise as well, especially when public agencies combine forces with private-sector lobbies on behalf of controversial issues. Is it democratic to align with one policy faction and give it access to policymakers when denying similar access to the opposition? For example, was it fair for the Justice Department and police forces throughout the country to lobby for passage of President Clinton's controversial Violent Crime Control and Law Enforcement Act (HR-3555) in 1993 and 1994?[74] Would it have been more democratic to create opportunities for multiple advocacies, with special efforts to elicit minority viewpoints? Do people most likely to be affected by the policy deserve special consideration? Or should one give preference to the solution that an agency's leadership deems best for the country in general?

Defending Agency Turf. In addition to their own lobbying activities, public agencies are heavily involved in coping with lobby efforts directed at them. Corresponding to the expanded scope of activities of governments, the scope of interests for which various nongovernmental publics are likely to lobby public agencies has grown. It is difficult to keep track of all these cross-cutting lobbying ventures and determine who wields power at a particular time and who has influenced a particular decision.[75] As discussed in Chapter 4, Hugh Heclo claims that these amorphous webs of communication and influence, which he calls "issue networks," determine public policies on many issues. Case studies of particular lobbying campaigns largely support this conclusion.[76]

Participants in such networks range from the powerful to the powerless and from those pleading for widely shared public interests to those mainly focused on their own, narrow concerns. According to Heclo, all share a "detailed understanding of specialized issues that comes from sustained attention to a given policy debate."[77] It is their knowledge of particular issues and political processes that gives them influence and convinces the targets of their pleadings. For example, labor unions have been very influential in getting OSHA to enforce occupational health regulations by publicly calling attention to lagging performance. After analyzing annual enforcement data from 1976 through 1983 for all fifty states, investigators concluded that "direct labor interaction through the filing of complaints had the most consistent effect on all enforcement output."[78]

As discussed in Chapter 2, many private-sector lobby groups are expert in researching data relevant to the performance of public-sector organizations. Moreover, these data are often packaged in ways that make it very tempting for public agencies to use them without much additional scrutiny, especially when they lack the resources to do their own research. For example, public officials have been unable to generate their own reliable data to assess the oil reserves controlled by major American oil companies. They need these data to plan defense and regulatory policies. When lobbyists for the oil companies approach federal agencies with information concerning these reserves, or when these data are available only from associations like the American Petroleum Institute, the temptation to base policy on industry-controlled information is almost irresistible. The costs of verifying industry-supplied information are often staggering. It may indeed be impossible to verify data when resources are privately controlled. Public-sector agencies may then be forced to rely on the inferences drawn by industries from their own files. Hence the government's claim that oil supplies are scarce may have to be made without an opportunity to inspect the actual data.

Because Congress can control the activities of most federal agencies, it has become a magnet that attracts lobby groups. The advice to lobby groups is "get a horse." That means that they should latch on to a member of Congress to carry their message to the legislature. That body will then take steps that will ultimately influence policy at the agency level in tune with the lobby's requests.[79] There are even congressional organizations who sponsor specific issues that are dear to lobbyists. The bipartisan congressional Environmental and Energy Study Conference, for instance, distributes information on environmental issues to Congress. The conference also holds meetings, briefings, and workshops on environmental issues, to which it invites members of the executive branch.[80]

At times, the two-step lobby approach, in which lobbyists try to contact administrative agencies via the congressional route, escalates to three or more steps. Lobbies, including several organized by incumbent members of Congress, may attempt to mobilize various general publics, urging them to pressure Congress to adopt desired policies and implement them through administrative agencies. For example, the Congressional Space Caucus has contacted scientists throughout the nation, urging them to lobby Congress on behalf of various space issues. The caucus sponsors briefings and speeches by public officials, in addition to producing reports, information kits, and brochures. Similarly, the Congressional Black Caucus has created an "action alert communication network" to mobilize members of more than 150 black grassroots organizations. These organizations inform fellow citizens about issues of concern to the caucus, besides lobbying Congress directly. The influence exercised in Congress by the Congressional Black Caucus has been enhanced by its ability to demonstrate that it represents the views of a large segment of the African American community.[81]

Case Study: Passing the North American Free Trade Agreement

The passage of the North American Free Trade Agreement (NAFTA) in 1992 illustrates the array of lobbying activities required to promote an issue successfully. It also demonstates how government agencies collaborate formally and informally with private-sector interest groups. The participation of such groups may lend the operation an aura of being legitimated by public opinion.[82]

When Mexico, Canada, and the United States signed NAFTA on December 17, 1992, it looked as if the pact would have smooth sailing through Congress. By spring 1993 the prospective treaty, designed to eliminate all trade barriers among the three countries, was reeling from attacks by labor and environmental lobbies. In fact, these private-sector interest groups bore a large part of the lobbying burden, as frequently happens. They mobilized their members, their lobbyists in Washington, and their close allies among other interest groups. An anti-NAFTA caucus in Congress, and a well-orchestrated campaign by presidential contender Ross Perot, joined the attack in hopes of blocking the agreement.

Meanwhile, pro-NAFTA forces, composed of officials from state and local governments and private businesses, united under the banner of the U.S. Alliance for NAFTA to promote a "yes" vote in Congress.

The president, the vice president, and other members of the executive office became public lobbyists for the treaty as well. They called on former presidents Gerald Ford, Jimmy Carter, Ronald Reagan, and George Bush to voice their support for the treaty. Chicago's William Daley, a future Clinton cabinet member and confidant, was named NAFTA czar. Daley immediately dispatched cabinet secretaries to key districts throughout the country to beat the drums for NAFTA passage.

Members of Congress and congressional committees were key targets for both pro- and anti-NAFTA forces. During the final stages of legislative activities concerned with the bill, the president and vice president personally contacted legislators via telephone or in their offices to drum up support and make sure that no legislative vote would be lost through absenteeism. Aides prepared target lists of key legislators to be visited by lobby groups. Both pro- and anti-NAFTA forces used news stories, paid advertisements, infomercials, and public speeches in an effort to mobilize public support. This is a perfect example of issue-network coalition building and the battles that can develop among competing networks. In the end, the Clinton network forces prevailed. Congress approved the treaty, albeit narrowly. Passage was a victory for the private–public coalition of lobby groups supporting the president's views.

The major message of this chapter is that public information and public relations activities are essential to the successful conduct of American government. To get funding and supportive legislation, public agencies must woo Congress and the executive branch and also gain the support of the courts and the public. Public agencies work in a contentious environment. They must compete for resources in a melee of clashing interests and power plays that forces them to minimize their weaknesses and exaggerate their strengths.

The necessity for gilding their image springs from American political culture. When mass media publicize problems, undue cynicism and condemnation abound because most Americans equate failures with avoidable shortcomings or misdeeds of people and institutions. If blame automatically attaches to failures, it becomes necessary to deflect attention from them and carve positive images into the public's consciousness to sustain the support that is essential for public agencies. The disdain of public relations activities thus promotes hypocrisy and subterfuges when essential public relations activities are undertaken. The time is therefore ripe to mount concerted efforts to put public relations activities into proper perspective.

How likely is it that these and other reforms will be undertaken? If they are enacted, will they succeed? Chapter 9 sketches out possible scenarios in light of past and present trends.

NOTES

1. Jameson W. Doig and Erwin C. Hargrove, *Leadership and Innovation: A Biographical Perspective on Entrepreneurs in Government* (Baltimore: Johns Hopkins University Press, 1987), 14–17.
2. Ibid., 183.
3. Joseph P. Viteritti, "The Environmental Context of Communication: Public Sector Organizations," in *Handbook of Administrative Communication*, eds. James L. Garnett and Alexander Kouzmin (New York: Marcel Dekker, 1997), 82.
4. Herbert Kaufman, *The Administrative Behavior of Federal Bureau Chiefs* (Washington, D.C.: Brookings Institution, 1981), 76.
5. James L. Garnett, "Administrative Communication: Domain, Threats, and Legitimacy," in *Handbook of Administrative Communication*, eds. James L. Garnett and Alexander Kouzmin (New York: Marcel Dekker, 1997), 1–20.
6. *The Washington Lobby*, 5th ed. (Washington, D.C.: Congressional Quarterly, 1987), 33–41. Various limitations on private sector lobbying are discussed. The major law, the 1946 Federal Regulation of Lobbying Act, was so vague that its provisions concerning registration and spending limits were almost unenforceable. It was replaced in 1995 by the Lobbying Disclosure Act, but controlling lobbying remains difficult.
7. John L. Crompton and Charles W. Lamb Jr., *Marketing Government and Social Services* (New York: Wiley, 1986), 394–395.
8. Lewis M. Helm, Ray Eldon Hiebert, Michael R. Naver, and Kenneth Rabin, eds., *Informing the People* (New York: Longman, 1981), 169.
9. Leslie H. Gelb, "Speakes Defines His Role in Shaping Events," *New York Times*, Oct. 10, 1986.
10. James Dao and Eric Schmitt, "Pentagon's Foreign Media Plan Includes False Reports," *Chicago Tribune*, Feb. 19, 2002.
11. Lizette Alvarez, "In Two Parties' War of Words, Shibboleths Emerge as Clear Winner," *New York Times*, Apr. 27, 2001.
12. Joel J. Davis, "The Effects of Message Framing on Response to Environmental Communications," *Journalism and Mass Communications Quarterly* 72 (1995): 285–299; for a full-length treatment of defensive rhetoric, see Lee Clarke, *Mission Improbable: Using Fantasy Documents to Tame Disaster* (Chicago: University of Chicago Press, 1999), esp. chap. 6.
13. Murray Edelman, *Constructing the Political Spectacle* (Chicago: University of Chicago Press, 1988), 104. See also Kathleen M. McGraw, "Managing Blame: An Experimental Test of the Effects of Political Accounts," *American Political Science Review* 85 (1991): 1133–1157.

14. Jeffrey Pfeffer, *Power in Organizations* (Marshfield, Mass.: Pitman Publishers, 1981), 184; see also Cheryl Zollars and Theda Skocpol, "Cultural Mythmaking as a Policy Tool: The Social Security Board and the Construction of a Social Citizenship of Self Interest,"in *Research on Democracy and Society,* vol. 2, ed. Frederick D. Weil and Mary Gautier (Stamford, Conn.: JAI Press, 1994), 381–408.

15. J. Patrick Dobel, "Managerial Leadership in Divided Times," *Administration and Society* 26 (1995): 500–503.

16. Stephen Franklin and Michael Arndt, "OSHA Changing Longtime Image of Business as Foe," *Chicago Tribune,* Jan. 27, 1997.

17. For example, see Edelman, *Constructing the Political Spectacle,* 104.

18. Stephen Hess, *The Government/Press Connection* (Washington, D.C.: Brookings Institution, 1984), 118–121.

19. Ibid., 24–26. For a companion study, see Zollars and Skocpol, "Cultural Mythmaking as a Policy Tool."

20. Martha Derthick, *Agency under Stress: The Social Security Administration and American Government* (Washington, D.C.: Brookings Institution, 1990), 183.

21. *The Washington Lobby,* 14. For examples, see David Whiteman, *Communication in Congress* (Lawrence: University of Kansas Press, 1995), 50–68.

22. Charles H. Levine and James A. Thurber, "Reagan and the Intergovernmental Lobby: Iron Triangles, Cozy Subsystems, and Political Conflict," in *Interest Group Politics,* 2d ed., ed. Allan J. Cigler and Burdett A. Loomis (Washington, D.C.: CQ Press, 1986), 202–220.

23. James Q. Wilson, *Bureaucracy: What Government Agencies Do and Why They Do It* (New York: Basic Books, 1989), 27.

24. John Anthony Maltese, *Spin Control: The White House Office of Communication and the Management of Presidential News,* 2d ed. (Chapel Hill: University of North Carolina Press, 1994), discusses how professionals handle White House communications.

25. See Martha S. Feldman, *Order without Design: Information Production and Policy Making* (Stanford: Stanford University Press, 1989). The major considerations that go into report writing are discussed on pages 61–69.

26. David L. Altheide and John M. Johnson, *Bureaucratic Propaganda* (Boston: Allyn and Bacon, 1980), 4–17.

27. Ibid., 19.

28. Kaufman, *The Administrative Behavior of Federal Bureau Chiefs,* 65–66.

29. Ibid.

30. Ronald E. Rice and Charles K. Atkin, eds., *Public Communication Campaigns,* 2d ed. (Newbury Park, Calif.: Sage, 1989), 224–225.

31. Maltese, *Spin Control,* 11.

32. "About the Energy Information Administration" (2000), http://www.eia.doe.gov; also see Edward Cowan, "Problems with Government Advocacy: A Journalist's View," in *Informing the People,* ed. Lewis M. Helm et al. (New York: Longman, 1981), 48.

33. All data about the department come from Edie Fraser and Wes Pedersen, "Department of Agriculture: A Structural Model," in *Informing the People,* ed. Lewis M. Helm et al. (New York: Longman, 1981), 283–286. The 1990 chart was supplied by the staff of the Office of Public Affairs.

34. Hess, *The Government/Press Connection,* 13–14.

35. Andrew C. Gordon and John P. Heinz, eds., *Public Access to Information* (New Brunswick, N.J.: Transaction, 1979), 189–222, 280–308. For a wide-ranging discussion of issues of government control over information, see Shannon E. Martin, *Bits, Bytes, and Big Brother: Federal Information Control in the Technological Age* (Westport, Conn.: Praeger, 1995).

36. Martin Linsky, *Impact: How the Press Affects Federal Policymaking* (New York: Norton, 1986), 81–82.

37. Charles Peters, "From Ouagadougou to Cape Canaveral: Why the Bad News Doesn't Travel Up," *Washington Monthly*, Apr. 1986, 29.

38. Ibid., 28.

39. Michael Kilian, "Feeling It Can Be Something More, Army Taps New Ad Agency," *Chicago Tribune*, June 28, 2000.

40. Rice and Atkin, *Public Communication Campaigns*, chaps. 5, 7, 10, 12, 13. Also see Ronald E. Rice and Charles K. Atkin, eds., *Public Communication Campaigns*, 3d ed. (Thousand Oaks, Calif.: Sage, 2001), parts III and IV.

41. Crompton and Lamb, *Marketing Government and Social Services*, 380.

42. Rice and Atkin, *Public Communication Campaigns*, 3d ed., 151–195.

43. Garnett, "Administrative Communication: Domain, Threats, and Legitimacy," in *Handbook of Administrative Communication*, 8–10.

44. Mordecai Lee, "Reporters and Bureaucrats: Public Relations Counter-Strategies by Public Administrators in an Era of Media Disinterest in Government," *Public Relations Review* 25 (1999): 451–463.

45. Cary Coglianese and Margaret Howard, "Getting the Message Out: Regulatory Policy and the Press," *The Harvard International Journal of Press/Politics* 3 (1998) 39–55.

46. Scott M. Cutlip, "Government and the Public Information System," in *Informing the People*, ed. Lewis M. Helm et al. (New York: Longman, 1981), 32.

47. Stephen Hess, *The Washington Reporters* (Washington, D.C.: Brookings Institution, 1981), 18.

48. Quoted in Cutlip, "Government and the Public Information System," 23.

49. Ibid., 30.

50. Hess, *The Government/Press Connection*, 75.

51. Linsky, *Impact*, 73–75.

52. Ibid., 203.

53. The final sample size was 483. However, 10 percent of the sample population lacked administrative experience in the executive branch.

54. Linsky, *Impact*, 84.

55. Ibid., 81–82.

56. Ibid., 87.

57. Ibid., 125.

58. Ibid., 87.

59. Naftali Bendavid, "Weathering the Storms within FBI," *Chicago Tribune*, July 28, 1997. Examples of the image problems of the IRS are presented by John M. Broder, "Demonizing the IRS," *New York Times*, Sept. 20, 1997.

60. Linsky, *Impact*, 52–60.

61. For a history of public communication campaigns, see William Paisley, "Public Communication Campaigns: The American Experience," in Rice and Atkin, *Public Communication Campaigns*, 3d ed. 15–38. For an excellent analysis of all

aspects of public communication campaigns, see Philip Kotler and Eduardo L. Roberto, *Social Marketing: Strategies for Changing Public Behavior* (New York: Free Press, 1989).

62. Rajiv N. Rimal, June A. Flora, and Caroline Schooler, "Achieving Improvements in Overall Health Orientation: Effects of Campaign Exposure, Information Seeking, and Health Media Use," *Communication Research* 26 (1999): 322–348; Richard A. Winett and Kathryn D. Kramer, "A Behavioral Framework for Information Design and Behavior Change," in *Media Use in the Information Age: Emerging Patterns of Adoption and Consumer Use,* ed. Jerry L. Salvaggio and Jennings Bryant (Hillsdale, N.J.: Erlbaum, 1989), 237–257.

63. Rice and Atkin, *Public Communication Campaigns,* 3d ed., 151–195.

64. Ibid., 215–217.

65. Ibid., 216.

66. Richard Marin, "Selling Uncle Sam for a Laugh," *Insight,* Feb. 29, 1988, 46.

67. Cowan, "Problems with Government Advocacy," 39–40.

68. Tim L. Tinker, "Recommendations to Improve Health Risk Communication: Lessons Learned from the U.S. Public Health Service," *Journal of Health Communication* 1 (1996): 197–217.

69. Caroline Schooler, S. Shyam Sundar, and June A. Flora, "Effects of the Stanford Five City Project Media Advocacy Program," *Health Education Quarterly* 23 (1996): 346–364.

70. Rice and Atkin, *Public Communication Campaigns,* 3d ed., chaps. 6, 7, 8; also see Ronald E. Rice and Charles K. Atkin, "Principles of Successful Public Communication Campaigns," in *Media Effects: Advances in Theory and Research,* ed. Jennings Bryant and Dolf Zillman (Hillsdale, N.J.: Erlbaum, 1994), 365–387; Schooler, Sundar, and Flora, "Effects of the Stanford Five City Project Media Advocacy Program," 346–364; Thomas W. Valente, Patricia Paredes, and Patricia R. Poppe, "Matching the Message to the Process: The Relative Ordering of Knowledge, Attitudes, and Practices in Behavior Change Research," *Human Communication Research* 24: 366–385.

71. For the argument that public relations and lobbying are part of a seamless web, see Randall Rothenberg, "P.R. Firms Head for Capitol Hill," *New York Times,* Jan. 4, 1991.

72. Hugh Heclo, "Issue Networks and the Executive Establishment," in *The New American Political System,* ed. Anthony King (Washington, D.C.: American Enterprise Institute, 1978), 95.

73. Beth L. Leech and Frank R. Baumgartner, "Lobbying Friends and Foes in Washington," in *Interest Group Politics,* 5th ed., ed. Allan J. Cigler and Burdett A. Loomis (Washington, D.C.: CQ Press, 1998), 222–225.

74. Ronald G. Shaiko, "Reverse Lobbying: Interest Group Mobilization from the White House and the Hill," in *Interest Group Politics,* 5th ed., 260–263.

75. John T. Scholz and Feng Heng Wei, "Regulatory Enforcement in a Federalist System," *American Political Science Review* 80 (December 1986): 1262.

76. Heclo, "Issue Networks and the Executive Establishment," 102.

77. Jeffrey M. Berry, *The Interest Group Society,* 2d ed. (Chicago: Scott, Foresman, 1989), 177–179.

78. Heclo, "Issue Networks and the Executive Establishment," 99.

79. Leech and Baumgartner, "Lobbying Friends and Foes in Washington," 220–221.

80. Susan Webb Hammond, Daniel P. Mulhollan, and Arthur G. Stevens Jr., "Informal Congressional Caucuses and Agenda Setting," *Western Political Quarterly* 38 (December 1985): 592.
81. Ibid., 693–695.
82. Darrell M. West and Burdett A. Loomis, *The Sound of Money: How Political Interests Get What They Want* (New York: W. W. Norton, 1999), 1–7.

Chapter 9 **Vistas of a Likely Future**

The Information Marketplace will transform our society over the next century as significantly as the two industrial revolutions, establishing itself solidly and rightfully as the Third Revolution in modern human history. It is big, exciting, and awesome."[1] So predicted Michael Dertouzos, director of the MIT Laboratory for Computer Science and a highly respected and successful forecaster of trends in technological advances. James Cortada, an IBM executive consultant, projected what these changes might mean for the public sector, using the U.S. Postal Service as an example. That giant information-moving agency might be transformed into a national e-mail service, centralizing electronic voting and allowing the government to be in constant two-way touch with the citizenry.[2] While I share the optimism of these two computer scientists about the advances heralded by technology, I also share the reluctance of social scientists to proclaim a revolution when the concept of evolution seems a more appropriate metaphor for changes in human societies.

Although vast technological changes have transformed information-gathering and transmission methods, the major features of information management in the public sphere are likely to remain on a steadfast course. The reason is simple: The main communication challenges facing the public sector are bound to continue into the future. Human frailties, cultural barriers to communication, and the inherent weaknesses of all organizational designs will continue in the twenty-first century. In these final pages, I will try to sketch out how these information management challenges are likely to be met in the coming decades if past trends are harbingers of future developments.

Bridges from the Past

The Durability of Theories

Although information management in the public sphere will continue to benefit from rapid, technology-based advances made in some related fields, like cognitive science, it is unlikely that its own spectrum of theoretical approaches will expand in the near future. Rather, we seem to be in an era when scholars will concentrate on existing theories, developing them more fully and striving to integrate them with each other more successfully. The reasons for concentrating on consolidation are twofold. Information and communication theories, like those in other fields, tend to move from initial formulations to refinements that modify the earlier iterations. The refinements spring from knowledge gained from testing them under diverse conditions. Much testing of existing theories remains to be done. The second reason for foreseeing only evolutionary changes is that attempts to merge midlevel theories into grand, overarching theories have been only modestly successful in the social sciences. It will be very difficult to capture the richness and complexity of organizational communication phenomena in correspondingly rich and complex theoretical formulations.

Nonetheless, some important theory changes are in progress in the wake of shifting organizational goals. In the past, public agencies in the United States have been viewed largely as tools of the executive branch. Policy directives from top-level officials percolated through various levels of the organizational hierarchy to lower-level governmental structures where bureaucrats were expected to carry out chief executives' mandates. In recent years, public-sector agencies have been viewed increasingly from the perspectives of theories of pluralist democracy. This change suggests that public agencies should prioritize communication with their publics over intraorganizational communication issues. Obviously, no agency can be primarily both a tool of the executive branch and of the agency's clientele because the goals of these constituencies are often antagonistic. Creating an integrative model will require identifying the aspects of each agency's work that benefit most from close interaction with clients and those where openness and responsiveness are most likely to impair operational control and cost-effectiveness. Chapter 7 provides some guidelines. Developing sound theories to accommodate the new orientation involves quintessentially political issues such as defining the meaning of "public interest" and determining the appropriate role for public opinion.

Human Behavior Characteristics

Aside from theory, there are many contextual reasons for questioning the likelihood of developing distinctively new patterns of public-sector organizational communication. Primary among them is the fact that the characteristics of human behavior that shape organizational reality in the public sector are ingrained. They include a general reluctance to change, which has been discussed in previous chapters, and the various psychological barriers to altering established behaviors that hamper information use and produce poor decisions. Human frailties that lead to defective communication and cloud judgments by individuals and groups can be ameliorated but they can never be totally eliminated. Greater awareness of communication difficulties and more professional attention to identifying and discussing them have been helpful in controlling damaging effects. For example, many organizations now offer their personnel training in effective communication, including periodic intercultural sensitivity training.

Among the most persistent barriers to change is the pressure within large organizations to cling to standard operating procedures. Such procedures become ingrained because, as James Q. Wilson points out, they "represent an internally defined equilibrium that reconciles the situational imperatives, professional norms, bureaucratic ideologies, peer group expectations, and (if present) leadership demands unique to the agency."[3] Even when new technologies, like computers and electronic conferencing, make it feasible to streamline operations, many individuals within established organizations prefer to rely on established patterns of communication because they are familiar and because they have unique features, like offering body language cues. Accordingly, many agencies dealing with the public still require an applicant's personal appearance at a government office to complete forms when e-mails or fax transmissions or Web-based forms would be much faster, cheaper, and more convenient for everyone. When new operational modes do develop, they, too, become frozen very quickly, making further changes difficult. Like giant tortoises, giant government bureaucracies lumber along ever so slowly and cautiously.

Compared with major private-sector organizations, public-sector organizations generally offer fewer incentives for developing and applying new approaches. They provide little support if and when innovations fail, as is bound to happen from time to time. The unlucky agency and its leaders then may face a barrage of widely publicized condemnation. The lack of incentives and the prevalence of disincentives discourage public employees from experimenting with new strategies for interpreting their missions and carrying them out. Little change can be expected as long as failures are not accepted by bureaucracy watchers, including the public, as part of the cost of progress.

Previous chapters have described the many institutions and institutional processes that serve as anchors to the past and obstacles to change because they have become vested interests for various groups. These groups are likely to strongly defend the status quo, including familiar operating procedures. They are apt to disagree about the merits and drawbacks of proposed changes. Even when some groups welcome new approaches, the ripple effects of change in an interconnected organizational system will mobilize opposition from numerous groups that believe that the new system will affect them adversely.

Changes are most likely to happen when new claimants enter the fray, such as the many interest groups that have been able to make themselves heard more effectively than before thanks to the Internet. Competitive pressures are another spur for change. They come into play in areas where public and private services compete, like mail services and operating schools, hospitals, and correctional facilities.

Institutional Characteristics

The very nature of American political institutions also diffuses pressures for change. The principles on which these institutions are based—separation of powers, federalism, and a system of checks and balances—lead to fragmentation of governmental authority. Fragmentation forces organizations to spend considerable time and effort in communicating with diverse institutional levels and integrating conflicting policies and procedures, rather than carrying out activities at the heart of their mission. Successful coordination involves nurturing diverse constituency relationships by remaining in frequent touch with them. The inevitability of compromises and accommodations to the political environment makes it difficult to keep decisions rational and consistent. Little change can be expected in these constraints because the American pattern of divided government is here to stay.

Public-sector officials will continue to be torn between the claims of professionalism and the necessity for political adaptation. They will be forced to say things that they do not mean and disguise what they mean to pass political muster. They will continue to battle the problem of interpreting ambiguous, often conflicting goals that have been set for their agencies for political reasons. Their efforts to manage their agencies effectively will be further hampered by prescribed structures, limited control over personnel, incessant demands for public reports of their activities, and limited information about the resources that will be available for the long-range conduct of their work. Of course, similar problems exist in the private sector because politics and fragmentation of authority are ubiquitous. However, the magnitude of the problems, and hence their effect on organizational communications and operations, is considerably less in the private sector because fewer barriers to effective performance are a matter of law and because economic concerns more easily trump political concerns.

The large size of the American administrative sector, the vast array of its activities, and the intertwining of these activities and concerns make long-range planning along all fronts nearly impossible. Serious problems are likely to arise suddenly, totally altering the assumptions on which earlier decisions have been based. If one is to judge from past experience, this will not change. The unexpected will continue to happen without fail, either propelled by physical events or the currents of politics or as an unexpected policy consequence. Decision makers then must react to these problems without the careful research that ought to precede important determinations.

For example, in the wake of a massive overhaul of the nation's welfare programs in 1996, more than a million low-income parents unexpectedly lost Medicaid coverage.[4] Most of them became uninsured because laws providing for Medicaid extension did not work as planned and the low-wage jobs to which these parents were able to move either carried no health benefits or offered benefits at a cost that they could not afford. Initially, stories about the plight of these families were familiar only to individual case workers and did not reach decision-making levels. When the situation was finally brought to the attention of decision makers, it required quick fixes at state and national levels to restore the Medicaid lifeline and subsequent reforms of the underlying legislation. Such problems are unavoidable.

Cultural Legacies

Chapter 5 explains why and how organizations develop unique cultures that consist of written and unwritten, explicit and implicit rules of behavior as well as unique myths and symbols. Some of these become part of the organization's basic philosophy and values, so that the chances for changing such ingrained beliefs are small. The requirements for open communication that are widely observed by agencies, other than those dealing primarily with domestic and foreign security issues, are good examples of permanent cultural constraints that profoundly affect public policies. Similarly, it would be difficult to change the generally pragmatic orientation of American bureaucrats that allows them to bend principles slightly when this seems politically opportune.

As we have seen, the requirements for openness constitute a mixed bag of disadvantages and benefits. On the negative side, for example, the requirements create concerns about exposing important public-sector communications to hostile, prying eyes. Top agency personnel feel that they are living in fish bowls, constantly exposed to the public gaze. They may feel hounded by reporters. They may spend large amounts of time in symbolic activities to create good images for their agency and for themselves. Openness also tends to discourage innovation because administrators do not wish to be caught on the proverbial limb. They know that bold proposals are likely to encounter many nay-sayers eager to throttle changes.

Fear of subjecting themselves to criticism may restrain bureaucrats from acting in perfectly appropriate ways that do not comport with the image that they feel compelled to portray. For example, to maintain the image of the impartial official who works strictly by the rules, a welfare bureaucrat, against her better judgment, may deny the request of an elderly husband to receive payment for serving as his ailing wife's full-time nurse because payments to relatives are prohibited. This decision may force the couple to divorce, so that the husband becomes an unrelated caretaker, or it may lead to placing the wife in a public institution where nursing care is far more expensive. However, if the situation involves important public figures, political pragmatism may prevail so that the otherwise impossible action becomes possible. Although the openness of the public sector exacts a high price, it has a positive side as well. It can prevent misconduct by public officials by enhancing accountability. If mistakes have occurred, the media and the general public find it easier to discover them.

Despite strong support for a policy of candor, it has been imperfectly implemented, creating problems that are likely to continue. Many bureaucracies at the national, state, and local levels escape public scrutiny entirely or intermittently. Despite, or perhaps because of, the many requirements that public agencies submit reports to legislatures and other agencies, the monitoring processes rarely operate effectively. Reports are far more likely to gather dust than gain adequate attention. For the most part, the media, which serve as the informal monitor of governmental operations, pay little attention to the routine operations of most public-sector agencies. Usually, only extraordinary misbehavior captures media attention. The discovery of serious problems is generally a matter of happenstance rather than design.

The high respect for openness also influences the choices available to decision makers when new options for conducting the public's business arise. For example, many public administration experts have recommended transferring selected public-sector tasks to private-sector contractors who bid competitively for the work. Privatization can reduce waste and red tape so that the end result is greater efficiency and lower costs. However, political leaders have rejected many privatization proposals on the grounds that the activities in question would then be less open to public scrutiny. Private companies, the argument goes, are not subject to the Freedom of Information Act or other laws that make it possible to force public-sector officials to release information that they would prefer to hide. The flaw in this argument, of course, is the fact that private companies are subject to contractual obligations. Alert public officials, who are themselves subject to public scrutiny, are responsible for monitoring the performance of all work that is contracted out. If private companies fail to perform as stipulated, public officials can terminate their contracts. That remedy is not so readily available when public-sector personnel performs poorly.

Although privatization may be good for running a cafeteria for public employees or providing janitorial services, it may be inappropriate for running a prison, a hospital, or public schools where controversial policy decisions must be made about the kinds of services to be offered. In these situations, concerns about openness and accountability, rather than keeping costs of services low, may be more important.

Openness means not only that the business of public agencies is exposed to public scrutiny but also that agencies are accessible to communication from individual clients and from interest groups. The number and diversity of these groups and the intensity and sophistication of their operations have mounted steadily. When these groups voice conflicting claims, government agencies may face serious problems. Satisfying the demands of one group may be detrimental to the interests of other groups and to the agency's mission and resource allocations. There are no formulas for resolving such problems, and none seem on the horizon. Deciding on the right course in specific situations will remain a challenge for human wisdom at each particular time and place.

Bridges to the Future

Loosening Structural Rigidities

New information technologies are currently producing, and will continue to produce, substantial changes in communication-related structures and functions. These changes affect primarily problems posed for bureaucracies by hierarchy, centralization, and specialization. For example, task forces that cross jurisdictional boundaries to deal with issues involving multiple bureaucracies and bureaucratic levels can now operate efficiently thanks to the ease with which information can be channeled and widely distributed across such barriers.[5] But task force creation and operation, although resolving some problems, create others. It may be difficult, for instance, to determine who is responsible for task force supervision and for implementing its findings.

Flattening hierarchies has been another major consequence of the information technology revolution. Midlevel positions have been eliminated from bureaucracies. As a consequence, decision making has in many instances moved to lower levels while supervision of operational results has moved upward. Similarly, barriers arising from specialization have been surmounted by adding generalists to the information pipelines used for specialized decisions. Such changes often entail new job assignments and new training and promotion patterns even when the overall size of the bureaucracy is shrinking. They also require more advanced and more flexible technical and interpersonal communication skills.

Shrinking bureaucracies and flattening hierarchies raise questions about optimal sizes and configurations. When control over services becomes decentralized and hierarchies are flat, the benefits may be bought at the expense of reduced coordination and uniformity.

James Q. Wilson recommends placing the authority over public-sector services at the lowest level at which information essential for sound decisions is available.[6] Bureaucracies differ greatly in this respect. It is even controversial which level meets Wilson's criteria. When uniformity of treatment and precision are important, as in IRS matters or in prison administration, control should probably be centralized at the top. When many decisions are made at the street level, or when they are highly unpredictable, as happens in much police work, control should be at the street level. Even when control is dispersed, the new information technologies reduce the tension between centralization and decentralization because shared databases are available throughout the organization.

Problems posed by structural reorganization may be solved more readily than ever before through careful network analyses of communication flows. Evolving network analysis techniques hold promise for depicting human communication in more realistic ways than in earlier models. The computer difficulties that have plagued this type of analysis when it involves huge data sets seem to be yielding to new techniques. The ability to analyze larger networks should be beneficial in detecting and resolving boundary-spanning problems. In fact, it may be possible to move beyond the analysis of actual networks and project potential networks and test them through simulations. Such exercises may suggest how a particular organization can make the most fruitful connections with the fewest overload problems. Network simulations could also provide information about required changes to cope with novel communication situations.

Harnessing New Technologies

Computer capabilities and the Internet hold the potential for solving a number of major organizational communication problems. One of the most difficult and vexing of these problems concerns the spotting of crucial information that may have entered the system at lower levels. It may be useless if its importance to forestall or lessen the damage from impending disasters is not recognized until after the disaster has struck. Even if lower-level employees fail to recognize the significance of particular messages, computer databases available to executives offer another chance for detection. In fact, throughout the entire system, computers and the Internet are excellent devices for nearly automatic redundancy.

Aided by advanced computers, future communication analysts should also be able to devise more systematic ways to identify the characteristics of noise that should be discarded and the characteristics of important information that must be speeded along. Computers can quickly scan huge amounts of electronically submitted raw data and identify key words and concepts as well as patterns. Computers can also be used to simulate situations and detect various patterns better and faster than humans can, though they are less adept than humans to read between the lines and catch nuances of interpretation. Technical monitoring of the performance of complicated machinery and many simulations conducted by the Defense Department provide precedents for programming computers to detect problems, although much remains to be learned on that score.

Computer programs, and the Internet data treasure chest accessible via computers, may also make it possible to bring greater rationality to decision making during crises as well as in more ordinary times. There has been a tremendous increase in the capability of computer programs to handle large data sets and reduce them to key indicators that may be useful to decision makers. These enhanced capabilities may allow the inclusion of more political factors in decision-making models than has hitherto been possible. These factors are crucial in public-sector communication to cope with essential political concerns.

Faced with a growing universe of data from which they must select information to make decisions and to construct effective computer models, decision makers will have to pay more attention to clarifying and specifying their assumptions and perceptions of the basic facts of each situation. That requirement is bound to add rigor to decision making. All participants in the decision process are apt to develop a clearer understanding of the basic factors and stakes involved. The fact that decisions are apt to be more solidly grounded and that computerized results are seen as "scientific" and "objective" also may make them more widely acceptable to diverse stakeholders and less vulnerable to challenges.

Harnessing computer power to the fullest will require training top-level bureaucrats appropriately. Decision makers who were trained in the precomputer age may feel overwhelmed by the vast amounts of information now at their fingertips. They may find it difficult to determine at what point information searches should be concluded and decisions made. When decision-making models are tested under a variety of assumptions, so many possibilities may surface that even bureaucrats who are sophisticated computer users may find themselves riding off in too many different policy directions. It will be the task of the educational establishment to analyze such problems and devise ways of teaching future bureaucrats how to cope with them. It is not enough to teach the technical capabilities of advanced electronic tools. Training must also include instruction in the new ways in which computerization can help to conceptualize and solve problems. Information is of little value unless it is transformed into knowledge.

Climate and Culture Adaptations

Just as public-sector officials have tended to ignore structural factors that are important in human communication, so they have slighted factors of climate and culture. Many public-sector agencies are inefficient because they are far too large to attain and maintain a sound organizational climate in which individuals are happy and work well. Reorganization could reduce their size if more functions are transferred to the state and local levels and if—and it is a big if—the federal government also reassigns the necessary resources to perform these functions. However, one needs to keep in mind that decentralization has vastly escalated the demand for boundary-spanning communication.

Currently, organizational cultures, and often climates as well, seem to evolve more or less haphazardly. It should be possible to design some aspects of cultures and climates more deliberately because many of the new communication technologies have the potential to alter organizational cultures. Reallocating decision-making authority in the wake of network analyses and permitting people to work at dispersed locations, including their homes instead of in large offices, are examples. Thus far, this potential for changing cultures has been realized on a small scale only because of the tendency to use the new horses of computer technology to pull old wagons of organizational structures and functions. As one astute analyst of bureaucracy points out, changing a culture resembles moving a cemetery. "It is always difficult and some believe it is sacrilegious."[7] Nonetheless, adjustments are being made, particularly if they can be justified as enhancing efficiency in executing specific tasks rather than stressing that they are intended to reshape organizational cultures.

Among changes that can be justified on the grounds of efficiency are improvements in the physical settings in which public-sector organizational communication takes place. In the past, public-sector bureaucratic cultures have generally striven for an image of austerity in physical settings that would convey frugality and a concern for not spending taxpayers' money on "frills."

Little consideration was given to the part that well-planned physical settings can play in the success of organizational transactions. The impact of interpretive theorists, with their stress on human feelings and concerns, has made it easier to shift thinking toward constructing climates conducive to raising the comfort levels of the parties to various transactions. If such concerns become dominant, offices may be designed with an eye to making them attractive and convenient for office personnel as well as for clients.

In the past, cultural differences between bureaucrats and clients have often made the communication climate in public-sector agencies seem harsh and even hostile to the participants. Computers can help to ease several currently serious encounter problems. For instance, interactive videoconferencing can match clients who do not speak English with officials fluent in their native language. Computer capabilities for translating written and even spoken language are growing rapidly so that government forms and explanatory materials can be translated into many more languages. They can be distributed electronically at low cost. It has also become far easier to revise documents that do not conform to the cultural norms of the target clientele. For example, the imperious tone in many State Department documents directed to foreign consulates has been criticized as demeaning by various Asian clients who are used to more deferential language.

Computer capabilities can also create a better climate for outreach efforts. Messages can be customized to meet the needs of hard-to-reach populations and can be disseminated through a broader array of channels. If technical advances are accompanied by greater efforts to understand the many cultures represented in an increasingly diverse citizenry, and by attempts to respond sensitively to cultural differences, client communication will improve greatly. Current social pressures seem to augur well for major improvements along these lines, between officials and clients as well as among government personnel at all bureaucratic levels.

Efforts to improve client communication are particularly important because many features of bureaucracy militate against sensitive treatment of clients. As discussed in Chapter 7, when Max Weber stressed the importance of standardization and routinization, his main concern was operational efficiency. Pleasing clients was not considered important because they were deemed a captive breed, doomed to deal with bureaucracies on the bureaucrats' terms whenever they needed government services. By contrast, in the current cultural climate, serving clients on the clients' terms has become a much-touted goal. The private sector discovered long ago that organizations benefit from studying clients' preferences and catering to them as much as possible. For example, physicians have learned that good "bedside manners" make the patient more trusting and cooperative. This may speed recovery and deter costly malpractice suits against physicians whose treatments are unsuccessful. There is no reason why comparable benefits should not ensue if public officials were to have better "office manners." Many officials, cognizant of the importance of good client communication, already perform well on that score.

One way to hasten greater concern about creating an empathetic climate is to build scrutiny of climate factors into the many formal audits and analyses of organizational communication that have come into vogue, as well as into performance appraisals of public-sector personnel. If high quality in client interactions becomes a factor in these appraisals, and if public servants are rewarded for good performance, improved behavior is likely. In the past, the incentive structure in the public sector has been skewed toward administrative efficiency and cost control rather than client concerns. Fortunately, that seems to be changing.

Overcoming Negative Image Burdens

Whenever the work of public-sector agencies suffers because demonstrably false myths have gained currency, there is now more than a glimmer of hope that reasoned discourse will soften or even counteract the false myth. Public relations activities are a case in point. Public scorn has made it difficult to incorporate them smoothly into the activities of public agencies. Hiding such activities behind various euphemisms will not dispel existing negative attitudes; rather, the perception of public relations must be explicitly dissociated from the notion of intentionally deceptive persuasion. It must and can be shown that public relations messages, properly framed, do not involve deception. A more positive attitude toward public relations activities will mean that the subterfuges often used to conceal their nature can give way to openness. If that happens, public relations activities can be planned and carried out much more carefully.

As pointed out in Chapter 8, exaggerated public expectations about what is achievable in the public sector compel agencies to engage in more image building than would be required otherwise. Public agencies are supposed to perform their work flawlessly at the lowest costs, often with personnel paid at rates far below comparable work in the private sector. Astronauts have joked about the fact that the safety of their missions hinges on perfect performance by the hundreds of thousands of parts that make up their multimillion dollar equipment. Yet assurance of high quality of the equipment is not the top priority. It may rank behind the demand that contracts be given to the lowest cost bidders who meet the stipulated specifications, as well as a number of political considerations that have nothing to do with quality.

Public agencies inevitably fall far short of the idealized unattainable performance against which they are measured. The resulting image problem is made worse by the fact that "bureaucracy" has become a pejorative term, so that bureaucrats are presumed to be plodding, ineffective managers, enmeshed in red tape and swollen with their own importance. Viewed in the abstract, as a vocational category, they no longer enjoy the trust and public respect that they enjoyed in years past, even though most people compliment the services rendered to them by individual bureaucrats.

Suspicion and hostility have been fed by the greater intrusiveness of government into the lives of private citizens, by the failure to find satisfactory and widely acceptable solutions to pressing societal problems with which government has not dealt in the past, and by a series of widely publicized scandals involving high-level bureaucrats in agencies such as the Central Intelligence Agency, the Federal Bureau of Investigation, the Environmental Protection Agency, and the Department of Housing and Urban Development. Moreover, in recent election campaigns, including presidential elections, attacks on the bureaucracy have been prominent. Rather than pointing with pride to the many achievements of bureaucrats, most presidential candidates have disparaged their services.

To create a sound database for setting the record straight and placing it in proper perspective, a number of comparative studies might be undertaken; conditions under which U.S. public agencies work could be compared with similar agencies in other countries and also with comparable enterprises in the private sector. I believe that such studies would demonstrate that the public sector ordinarily works quite well when its accomplishments are judged in light of its resources and constraints. The achievements of the Forest Service and the Social Security Administration are prime examples that merit being brought to the public's attention. Studies would also show that the private sector does not work as smoothly and efficiently as idealized versions have suggested. Comparative evidence would enable American officials to learn from the experiences of other administrators in both the public and private domains.

In addition to clearing the atmosphere generally and improving the effectiveness of agencies in dealing with their many constituencies, a better image for the public service would enhance employee morale. As James Q. Wilson observes, "Most people do not like working in an environment in which every action is second-guessed, every initiative viewed with suspicion, and every controversial decision denounced as malfeasance."[8] If such a hostile climate can be improved, higher morale may also spell better performance and the ability to attract and retain better-qualified personnel.

Officials charged with conducting public information campaigns must learn more about various social marketing efforts. The somewhat disappointing results of campaigns to encourage safe sexual behavior, to forego illicit drugs, and to eat wisely and exercise to maintain health point to the vast stakes involved in effective social marketing in the health field. It is therefore likely that research to improve social marketing campaigns will accelerate, especially when it becomes evident that many campaigns do, indeed, succeed partially or fully.[9] Technical issues, such as market segmentation, timing, and choice of media, have been explored in the past, but much more work remains to be done to test strategies and tactics in diverse circumstances.

Ethical issues have received less attention. It is not clear what limitations, if any, should be imposed on public social marketing campaigns. For example, is the graphic depiction of condom use appropriate in a publicly financed brochure? Is it appropriate to require children to be exposed to such information at the grade-school level? At what age is such exposure appropriate? Given the importance of effective social marketing, such issues need to be resolved.

Establishing Goals and Priorities

One of the biggest obstacles to planning organizational communication development in the public sector is the lack of agreement on goals and priorities, beyond cost-effectiveness and rationality. Even when lawmakers have defined an agency's missions, the precise nature of these organizational goals and their order of priority require interpretation. Some agreement must also be reached about the best ways to reconcile conflicting goals. How can administrators be responsive to their superiors in the agency and to elected officials and, at the same time, be sensitive to diverse interest groups and to the public at large? If officials must treat all citizens impartially, how can they remain attuned to individual differences? How can they be loyal to the goals of the agency while safeguarding national interests? How can they maintain standards and obey the letter of the law, yet be willing to bargain and to compromise? Answers are difficult, but that is no excuse for dodging them while specific dilemmas cry out for solutions.

Agencies and their personnel must try to reach some kind of agreement internally about which norms should prevail or receive preferred status. Concern about societal needs in the twenty-first century should guide these choices but that requires determining which needs warrant priority treatment. However, it is unclear whether such decisions can and should be made categorically or whether they must remain forever flexible, depending on specific circumstances, the public's preferences, and the predilections of officials involved in a particular decision. The need to compromise may require expressing goals in vague, flexible terms that permit different claimants to see them in ways that suit each claimant's purposes. Still, it is essential to clarify goals, even for the short run.

In the past, the goal of public service has primarily been to accomplish the agency's mission with the support of dedicated public servants. Major criteria for effectiveness have been relatively low costs for accomplishing tasks, speed, accuracy, and the ability to serve all rightful claimants to the service. The authors of the *President's Private Sector Survey on Cost Control*—which came to be known as the Grace Commission Report—argued in 1984 that the government should be run according to private-sector business principles to avoid waste and inefficiency.[10] The 1993 Report of the National Performance Review implies the same message, as suggested by its lengthy title: *From Red Tape to Results: Creating a Government that Works Better and Costs Less.*

In the twenty-first century, in addition to stressing frugality, this means that the welfare of employees and the welfare of clients, which have been secondary in the past, have moved out of the shadows into the center of attention. The National Performance Review Report declares that "customers"— which means citizens who need specific services—deserve primary consideration.

> Effective, entrepreneurial governments insist on customer satisfaction. They listen carefully to customers—using surveys, focus groups, and the like. They restructure their basic operations to meet customers' needs. And they use market dynamics such as competition and customer choice to create incentives that drive their employees to put customers first.[11]

When it comes to employees, the report stipulates that

> [e]ffective, entrepreneurial governments transform their cultures by decentralizing authority. They empower those who work on the front lines to make more of their own decisions and solve more of their own problems. They embrace labor-management cooperation, provide training and other tools employees need to be effective, and humanize the workplace.[12]

The realization that catering to employees and to clients enhances bureaucratic performance is not new. Even by the end of the nineteenth century, social scientists had demonstrated that the average person does not measure the worth of life by monetary rewards alone. Human communication aspects of jobs are equally, and often more, important than material rewards. The same holds true for clients of public services, who would often gladly trade speedy services, and even low costs, for service that is sympathetic and respects the client's dignity. How people feel about the goals and quality of public-sector services is as important in a democratic society, or more important, than the objective achievements recorded in official reports.

The extent of changes that will be made in the culture and climate of public-sector organizations will, of course, depend heavily on the general political climate within the nation and on available economic resources. In prosperous times, the outlook is bright for improved communications with clients and with employees and for improved services. It seems less bright in good times and bad for shedding other troublesome characteristics of bureaucratic communication patterns and behaviors. Turf battles, red tape, and hyperbole in promoting agencies are prime examples.

Research Needs

If ours is, indeed, the age of communication, a time in which information is acknowledged as the predominant resource, then it seems clear that concern about communication and information management will remain high. In fact, concern will probably rise because it is the nature of information to increase in significance the more it is exchanged and shared. With the passing of time, ever larger numbers of organizations become drawn into communication networks, with all sharing information and contributing new data that must be integrated into the existing databases. Doing so efficiently and effectively will be a major task.

Given the importance of abundant good information, if organizations are to function well, whatever their goals might be, it is clear that more resources, in both time and money, will have to be devoted to communication tasks and to research. That involves more than extra appropriations for computers. It also means more time for gathering and analysis of information and for experimenting with new ways of networking and information distribution. It means more time to study information flows within organizations and between organizations and their environment and more time to coordinate efforts.

Specifically, to improve communication in the public sphere, a vast increase in the number of case studies focusing on communication within public agencies and in important policy domains is urgently needed. As part of the research for this book, I combed the literature dealing with specific public agencies for information about communication issues and problems. The yield was discouragingly low. Communication problems and patterns were mentioned occasionally but very rarely rated more than cursory discussion.[13] This is truly astounding in an era that has professionalized communication more than ever before and that bears the label "communication age."

External communications are a major concern for public-sector organizations because they are in touch with literally millions of people. They are accountable to the public and far more open to public scrutiny than private-sector organizations. Yet they are prevented from systematically tackling public relations issues because of the cultural reluctance to accept persuasive communication as essential and not inherently dishonest. Research in the areas of image formation and public relations might enable agencies to convey a more accurate image of their strengths and weaknesses, while retaining the loyalty and support of their employees and their clients.[14]

A number of endemic organizational communication problems also require more attention from researchers. These include network-related problems of message overload or underload for key individuals or groups, failure to make the most advantageous connections and avoid the disadvantageous ones, and finding the most efficient ways to route routine and nonroutine messages. Distortion problems that are fostered by the hierarchical structure of organizations, task specialization, and excessive centralization or decentralization also need to be addressed, as do problems of client communication during public information campaigns and during public service–related encounters between citizens and bureaucrats.

When communication failures lead to major difficulties, the analysis of reasons for failure has usually been quite primitive. One rarely sees theory-based analyses that take into consideration important contributing factors, such as the context, including the political and psychological elements in which communication occurred, the diversity of meanings inherent in messages, and the relationships between message senders and receivers. Important new research findings by cognitive psychologists and communication scholars need to be added to the tool kits of information managers. Specialists in organizational communication need to add to that literature from the perspective of public-sector information management to clarify what is happening and how failures might be prevented.

It is also important to analyze the impact of new communication technologies on various aspects of organizational communication more fully than has hitherto happened. For example, before-and-after studies are needed to determine the impact of computerization and the Internet on communication patterns and organizational power structures. The changes in information technologies in the public sector are raising important issues about the best way to use the new tools to improve performance, to plan for the future while engulfed in a sea of change, and to develop tools for evaluating the merits of goals and procedures.

Finally, it is important to carry out more comparative research to understand the impact of various cultural and subcultural elements on organizational communication. This includes comparing American organizations with those in other societies as well as comparing organizations at state and local levels in different parts of the United States. Because the nature of an organization may affect communication patterns, comparisons of large and small organizations or high- and low-technology organizations may be useful.

The goal for all these research endeavors, beyond their social-scientific contributions, should be improvement of communication in public agencies. Given the importance of these organizations to the nation's welfare, they deserve the very best efforts of the social science community. It is my hope that major studies and experiments in public-sector organizational communication will be among the research priorities of social scientists. If this book galvanizes the academic and professional research community into greater action in this exciting field, it will have fulfilled its purpose.

NOTES

1. Michael L. Dertouzos, *What Will Be: How the New World of Information Will Change Our Lives* (San Francisco, Calif.: HarperEdge, 1997), 306.
2. James W. Cortada, *Making the Information Society: Experience, Consequences, and Possibilities* (Upper Saddle River, N.J.: Prentice Hall, 2002).
3. James Q. Wilson, *Bureaucracy: What Government Agencies Do and Why They Do It* (New York: Basic Books, 1989), 375.
4. Robert Pear, "A Million Parents Lost Medicaid, Study Says," *New York Times*, June 20, 2000.
5. Jane F. Fountain, "The Virtual State? Toward a Theory of Federal Bureaucracy in the Twenty-First Century," in *democracy.com? Governance in a Networked World,*

eds. Elaine Ciulla Kamarck and Joseph S. Nye Jr. (Hollis, N.H.: Hollis, 1999), 133–155.

6. Wilson, *Bureaucracy,* 372.

7. Ibid., 368.

8. Ibid., 369.

9. Ronald Rice and Charles K. Atkin, eds. *Public Communication Campaigns,* 2d ed. (Newbury Park, Calif.: Sage, 1987).

10. *President's Private Sector Survey on Cost Control, A Report to the President,* 47 vols. (Washington, D.C.: U.S. Government Printing Office, 1984).

11. Al Gore, *From Red Tape to Results: Creating a Government that Works Better and Costs Less. Report of the National Performance Review* (Washington, D.C.: U.S. Government Printing Office, 1993), 6.

12. Ibid., 7.

13. For examples of what needs to be done, see Edward O. Lauman and David Knoke, *The Organizational State: Social Choice in National Policy Domains* (Madison: University of Wisconsin Press, 1987); Martha S. Feldman, *Order without Design: Information Production and Policy Making* (Stanford: Stanford University Press, 1989); and Nancy Wyatt and Gerald M. Phillips, *Studying Organizational Communication: A Case Study of the Farmers Home Administration* (Norwood, N.J.: Ablex, 1988).

14. The literature is reviewed in J. Michael Sproule, "Propaganda and American Ideological Critique," in *Communication Yearbook* 14 (Newbury Park, Calif.: Sage, 1991), 211–238.

Index